Perception and the Evolution of Style

Perception and the Evolution of Style
A new model of mind

Jane Gear

Routledge
London and New York

First published in 1989 by Routledge
11 New Fetter Lane, London EC4P 4EE
29 West 35th Street, New York, NY 10001

© 1989 Jane Gear

Typeset in Great Britain by Photoprint, Torquay

Printed and bound in Great Britain by
Biddles Ltd, Guildford and King's Lynn

British Library Cataloguing in Publication Data

Gear, Jane
  Perception and the evolution of style :
  a new model of mind.
  I. Title
  150

Library of Congress Cataloging in Publication Data

Gear, Jane
  Perception and the evolution of style.
  Revision of author's doctoral thesis.
  Bibliography: p.
  Includes index.
  1. Perception. 2. Individual differences. I. Title.
  BF311.G37 1989   150.19   88–32540

ISBN 0–415–02636–9

You had to be a crank to insist on being right. Being right was largely a matter of explanations. Intellectual man had become an explaining creature. Fathers to children, wives to husbands, lecturers to listeners, experts to laymen, colleagues to colleagues, doctors to patients, man to his own soul, explained. The roots of this, the causes of the other, the source of events, history, the structure, the reasons why. For the most part, in one ear out of the other. The soul wanted what it wanted. It had its own natural knowledge. It sat unhappily on superstructures of explanation, poor bird, not knowing which way to fly.

Saul Bellow, *Mr Sammler's Planet*

Contents

Figures

Foreword

The celebrated Cambridge psychologist, Sir Frederic Bartlett, who was my teacher, used to say that the trouble about psychology is that neat results (such as Ebbinghouse's learning curves with nonsense syllables) are generally trivial and tell us very little, while interesting data are too complicated and uncontrolled to understand. Bartlett pointed out that this happens especially when *meaning* is involved – and indeed he is remembered for his concept of the especially human 'Effort-After-Meaning' which characterizes and also distorts our perceptions and memories.

In these, or any other terms, this book by Jane Gear is a brave start from a conceptual model – APM-A theory – in which perception, memory, attention, arousal, and thinking are interactively related, to produce ideas that are applied to many aspects of life. These include art and education.

Of art, Jane Gear says: 'Involvement in the arts offers opportunities for what might be called *chained symbolizing and hypothesizing* and the pains and delights of continuous sensory and emotional involvement in problem solving.' Of education she says: 'As it is, education for the majority might more accurately be described as an experience of incremental deficit in self-esteem. . . . Children are tested, sorted, and graded regardless of differences in *individual style* and consequent potential levels and kinds of *orientation need*.' Art is suggested as a way of gaining orientation and self-knowledge to face the world and other people, to find success and enjoyment.

This is a hedonistically-based account, in which life and learning should be for pleasure – when pleasure includes complex mixes of psychological pleasure *and* pain, such as those involved in caring and creating – with art and science representing two aspects of the personality, both serving discovery.

This is certainly not Ebbinghouse-like neat and tidy psychology without human meaning. The APM-A theory has its basis in the physiology of the autonomic nervous system, and relates what are now seen as principal psychological concepts and variables. So it covers virtually everything. Whether this ambitious and intelligent Effort-After-Meaning has the explanatory power of a 'hard' scientific theory may well depend, as the theory suggests, on the 'adaptive style' of the reader.

Richard L. Gregory
February 1989

Acknowledgements

Perception and the Evolution of Style was originally the title of a doctoral thesis whose sub-title was 'a unified view of human modes of learning and expression'. It was the result of research into what were originally the insights of an artist and educationist immersed in the psychology of learning and individual differences in particular, rather than those of a neuropsychologist, psychiatrist, psychoanalyst, criminologist, art historian, or professional psychologist with a world-wide knowledge of the application of psychology in the arts and education. Consequently, considerable reliance has been placed on the availability for interrogation and/or critical consideration of different parts of what follows by a number of persons who are professionally involved in these fields. I am, therefore, greatly indebted to Professor Richard Gregory, Director of the Brain and Perception Laboratory at Bristol University, for helpfulness beyond his generosity in writing the Foreword to this book; Dr Benjamin Beit-Hallahmi of the Department of Psychology, University of Haifa, Israel; Dr Nathan Adler of the California School of Professional Psychology, USA; Professor J. E. Thomas, Director of the Department of Adult Education, University of Nottingham; Professor John Wilton-Ely, former Professor of Art History, University of Hull; and Dr Premysl Maydl, Director of the European Centre for Leisure and Education, Prague, respectively.

I am also especially grateful to both Dr Frances Clegg, a clinical psychologist at the Institute of Psychiatry, London, and her husband Dr Brent Elliott, a psychologist as well as historian, for their very generous expenditure of time and effort in making critical appraisals of the original thesis. Similarly, I am particularly indebted to both Professor Jay Appleton and Professor Bernard Jennings, who originally agreed jointly to supervise a difficult interdisciplinary field. It must also be added that had I not found myself 'supervising' the experimental paintings of the author of *The Experience of Landscape* (Appleton 1975), and therefore privy to Prospect-Refuge Theory long before most of the rest of the world, the synthesis between my own knowledge and experience in art, psychology, and education, which this book represents, would almost certainly not have taken place. In fact, the institution in which this initiation took place was itself one of the origins from which this work has sprung. It was one of a number of primary sources of awareness of some of the theoretical issues in question: specifically, consciousness of apparent stylistic differences in adult learning which appeared to relate to stylistic differences in creative output and other behaviours.

Neither would such a synthesis have taken place without the extremely stimulating material put before me by Dr Geoffrey Squires, who also supervised earlier research on which both the doctoral research and this book are based. More thanks of a special kind are appropriate to Margot Brown, who not only managed to remain apparently fascinated throughout the original research, but also identified numerous examples of literary evidence supporting the general theory. It is unfortunate that space has not permitted the exploration of the many learned suggestions which she made. I am also grateful to Dr Gwyn Harries-Jenkins for alerting me to Louis Zurcher's highly relevant notion of mutability of self-concept in *The Mutable Self* (1977).

Many other acknowledgements should be given of help given and gained in sometimes less formal, direct, or conscious ways. Of those to whom such thanks are due I can identify the direct, indirect, conscious, and not conscious help of a small, long-suffering, but extraordinarily tolerant family, and the help of several psychologists and one art historian in particular. These are Anne Barham, John Holt, Dr Geoffrey Lowe, Dr Alex McLaughlin, and Sarah Dodd, respectively. Having strayed so far from the mainstream, however, I must stress that the onus of responsibility for a text which deals with so many different levels and kinds of interaction as to make somewhat heavy demands on the reader is entirely my own.

Picture acknowledgements

The author and publisher would like to thank the following for permission to reproduce illustrations in this book: Academy Editions, London: Studio Competition, Book Covers 1898 from *Art Nouveau* by A. Melvin (60); Georg Baselitz: 'Adieu', Tate Gallery, London (57); Stephen Cox: 'Gethsemane', Tate Gallery, London (58); Design and Artists Copyright Society: Joseph Beuys, 'Fat Battery', Tate Gallery, London (50), Salvador Dali, 'Autumnal Cannibalism', Tate Gallery, London (37), Juan Gris, 'Violin and Fruit Dish', Tate Gallery, London (41), Georg Grosz, 'Funeral Procession', Staatsgalerie, Stuttgart (36), Piet Mondrian, 'Composition with Red, Yellow and Blue', Tate Gallery, London (48), Pablo Picasso, 'Seated Nude', Tate Gallery, London (40); Ferens Art Gallery, Hull City Museums and Art Galleries, UK: 'Ulysses and the Sirens' (59), Bridget Riley, 'Arround' (62); Barry Flanagan: 'A Aaing Guiaa', Tate Gallery, London (52); Richard Long: 'A Line in Bolivia, Kicked Stones' (2nd version) Tate Gallery, London (63); Robert Longo: 'Sword of the Pig', Tate Gallery, London (49); Manchester City Art Gallery: William Holman Hunt, 'The Hireling Shepherd' (34); Marlborough Fine Art Ltd.: R. B. Kitaj, 'The Rise of Fascism', Tate Gallery, London (51); Metropolitan Museum of Art, New York: Francisco Goya 'Disasters of War' (44); Musée Gustave Moreau, Paris: 'Salome Dancing' (39); Musée D'Orsay, Paris: Puvis de Chavannes 'Poor Fisherman' (38); Museum of Modern Art, New York: Claes Oldenburg, 'Soft Drainpipe, Blue (Cool) Version' (53); The Nolde Foundation: Emil Nolde 'Candle Dancers' (32); Omar S. Pound: Wyndham Lewis, 'Composition', Tate Gallery, London (46); The Royal Collection: Frank Holl, 'No Tidings from the Sea', reproduced by gracious permission of Her Majesty the Queen (35); Stedlijk Museum, Amsterdam: Kasimir Malevich, 'Suprematist Painting, Yellow Rectangle' (47); Tate Gallery, London: Christopher Nevinson, 'The Arrival' (45), A. R. Penck, 'West' (33), Jackson Pollock 'Number 23' (43), James Abbott McNeill Whistler, 'Nocturne in Blue and Gold' (42); Victoria and Albert Museum, London: Oliver Bernard, Entrance to the Grand Palace Hotel (61).

General introduction

What follows could be said to be about many different things, for the simple reason that one of its central notions, the suggestion that, as a species, our most fundamental needs include the achievement of a number of different kinds of orientation, is seen to touch on all the things we think and do and, most importantly, the *ways* in which we think and do them. It is most obviously about what is seen to be a crucial relationship between thinking and emotion, and about how this relationship is likely to be at the root of human variability as well as human adaptability.

The book offers definitions and an explanation of differences in 'styles' of experience and behaviour and a new evolutionary perspective called APM-A theory because it is rooted in a particular view of the interaction of attention (A), perception (P), memory (M), and arousal (-A). Instead of a linear sequence such as attention → perception → thought → feeling → memory, the relationship between attention, perception, memory, and arousal is deemed to be variable. Change in one is seen to affect the others so that an interactive model is seen to be more appropriate.

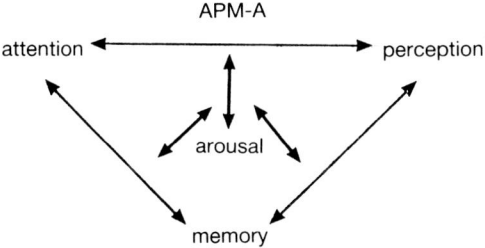

It might be simpler to say that the book is about the effects of emotion and arousal on thinking (and, essentially, the scanning and focusing functions of attention, perception, and memory), were it not for the fact that it is also about the effects of thinking on emotion. In the most general terms, however, it represents an attempt to show how an evolutionary explanation of the relationships within APM-A can provide a large enough

1

canvas to begin to relate to one another (albeit at the most fundamental level) phenomena of individual, social, cultural, and artistic kinds in terms of man–environment interaction. The explanation rests on a concept of the species, and individuals, being 'tuned' to different levels and kinds of change: as being susceptible (and vulnerable) to different and changing patternings of autonomic nervous system activity which, in turn, affect our APM-A – that is, the ways in which we attend, perceive, remember, and become aroused. Other variables are seen to be the extents to which these processes are experienced predominantly consciously or not consciously; and whether thought is experienced as predominantly sequential or as more diffuse (both of which are seen to hold benefits *and* drawbacks); and how different levels *and* kinds of arousal affect our psychological as well as physical needs. Some idea of these variables may be gained by reference to Figures 3, 4, 5, and 12–17.

The chief aim is to offer a *unified context* within which better sense can be made of the very large number of different and apparently contradictory theories which attach to most aspects of experience and behaviour. In order to do this and provide a theory consistent with so many possible ways of experiencing and responding to the same event, it has been necessary to take account of highly interactive processes at both micro and macro levels. These range from (1) the interactive nature of attention, perception, memory, and arousal labelled APM-A, which, in turn, requires acknowledgement of (2) the interaction of conscious and unconscious processing of information – at micro level – to (3), the interaction of the internal state of the organism with changing environmental conditions and (4), interaction between individual learning and what is called species learning (longer-term, species adaptation) at macro level.

In addition to the need frequently to make qualifying statements, and acknowledge complexity, a prerequisite for taking into account so many levels of interaction has been the identification of concepts and language with sufficiently wide applicability to be able to cross conventionally useful, but sometimes 'hardened' disciplinary boundaries. One incidental effect of this is the need occasionally to use what might be considered by some to be 'uncongenial language'. For instance, despite some effort to come up with a rather less sexually loaded phrase than the *'intercourse principle'* to describe interactions promoted by arousal between people and objects, people and places, people and ideas, and people and other people *not* of a sexual nature, as well as interactions which may be, I failed. The phrase 'interaction principle' did not seem to convey quite the same potential level of engagement, while the repetition of 'externalization of neuronal excitation resulting in a felt need to engage with a stimulus' was certainly worth avoiding.

A particular problem of crossing arts/science boundaries is that modes of expression of the people in different fields also differ. Therefore, depending on the cognitive style of the reader, the need in what follows sometimes to accept broader than usual applications of some terms and/ or temporarily forsake an acquired technical usage could be found difficult. It may help to regard the exercise being undertaken as rather like shaking a kaleidoscope. In order to discover a new pattern of relationships between the same component colours and shapes, some disorganization of the existing pattern has to be tolerated first. A difficulty experienced by scientists may be a need to tolerate a 'looser' and more general view of phenomena than they have been brought up to regard as valid; but the nature of the exercise is to define *general principles*. It is also to state a case for both an 'art', as it were, *and* a science of psychology, to make a move towards seeking the validity of what is called in Chapter 6 'bimodal knowledge', so that we do not rely on the results of empirical testing alone, but seek some consistency between scientific data and theory, and findings in other fields, and, above all, between psychological data and evolutionary possibilities.

It is argued that, in order to confirm the validity of any data, it is necessary to view them in relation to other data arising from research into whichever other aspects of experience and behaviour they most obviously interact with, and which must necessarily modify or enhance any interpretation. In fact, the exercise of attempting to relate to one another the many apparently conflicting theories which confront us has itself served to identify some possibly distorted and misleading conclusions. Such interpretations seem very often to arise from insufficient account being taken of polymorphism – that is, the existence of many forms of response to the same event, emanating from the fundamental evolutionary principles of adaptability and variability. In short, just as introspection was eschewed and revealed as an inadequate means of investigation by the behaviourist psychologists, so can our current dedication to experimental method, 'hard data', and the scientific mode, be regarded as inadequate, if we ignore the significance of general contexts.

The desire to begin to redress the balance towards what are defined as arts modes of perceiving and understanding, and emphasize the need for much greater complexity to be taken into account in the interpretation of data, are therefore important aims of this synthesis. But, above all, it is an attempt to offer a new way of looking at human nature – at 'who we are', 'where we have come from', and 'where we are going', and to define the implications of the new perspective for two of the most obvious ways in which we intervene in the development of mind;[1] by attempting to promote effective and rewarding physical and mental experiences in others – namely, education and psychotherapy. The point is stressed that we may create hypothetical constructs such as intelligence, personality, and motivation, or even madness, and test aspects of human functioning without reference to what or how else the organism thinks, feels, and does; but we must not then mistake the constructs for a reality *not* necessarily composed of isolable components. It has to be acknowledged that each aspect of mind is part of a more complex whole.

Implications of the new theory and its models[2] include the need to make radical changes in the education system, for it to take account of the critical role of *emotion* in learning, and for it to acknowledge fully the importance of the concept of *'lifelong learning'*. Emphasis is laid on the need for integration of the education system – particularly child/adult education – and a need for a shift from its dominance by the acquisition of facts in childhood to the acquisition of frameworks in which to stand them. A number of arguments are offered to support a plea for a shift to long periods of environmental *interaction* (with stress falling on both prefix and suffix of the word) for most pupils during primary *and* secondary education. Not only would the likelihood of alienation from the system during childhood be lessened, but also access to factual information, when it is most likely to be sought, during adulthood, would be likely to be enhanced. Because the APM-A framework includes definitions of variability in sensory, cognitive, social, and intellectual *needs for orientation*, and a resultant 'dynamic model of style', it also allows so-called 'normality' to be related to 'abnormality', and therefore psychotherapy and education *both* to be viewed as processes of orientation – that is, means for individuals to locate themselves successfully in their own physical, social, and cultural 'worlds' and find their own 'directions' and 'purposes'.

The aim is to provide a new perspective rather than new data. In fact, most of the material cited is readily available in existing textbooks and will be familiar to students of the relevant disciplines. The challenge has been to evaluate dominant and competing theories in the light of the new perspective, but not from the position of any particular application of evolutionary theory to date.[3] Key characteristics of the APM-A view are the recognition of the role that emotion plays in cognition from the very moment of perception, and what are regarded as the species' extremely complex and powerful, but often misunderstood and usually under-estimated, emotional needs.

The book arises, in part, from an appreciation of drawbacks as well as benefits, of the single discipline, and the necessity for some intellectual risk-taking in the face of lack of any theory of human nature which relates well to our experiences of the real world, or which applies in a very helpful way to our current extraordinarily rapid rate of social change. The biggest and the most obvious of the drawbacks is the sheer volume of material to be handled. Because of the amount of literature in each field, and since no material has been found which is inconsistent with, or cannot be reinterpreted and accommodated within, the new framework, reference has been made to a sample only, selected on the grounds of obvious relevance and usefulness for the purpose of illustrating particular points. However, care has been taken to consult with experts in the various fields in question, in order to check the current states of knowledge, as well as to help confirm the non-existence of evidence which might invalidate the APM-A framework. This exercise was in fact part of the original research involved in the Ph.D. thesis (Gear 1985) out of which this book has arisen.

What follows is in two parts and moves from micro process to macro process: from the APM-A model and an interactive view of affect and cognition (see postulates 1 and 3, Appendix 2) and how this dominates 'normal' and 'abnormal' styles defined in Part 1, to an explanation of how, at the most fundamental level, manifestations of the same process can be observed within artistic and cultural styles, in Part 2. Given so many different styles of perception, it may be helpful to the reader in his or her quest for orientation – which, after all, the book is about – to make occasional reference to the skeletal outline of the theory offered in Appendix 1 and to the postulates in Appendix 2. It must be stressed, though, that 'The APM-A framework' (Appendix 1) is intended to give some general bearings only. It is offered as an extremely small-scale map, as it were, of how the various models relate to one another.

Part 1

Homeostasis and individual differences: kinds of equilibrium

Introduction

As early as 1908 Titchener made the exciting but then largely ignored suggestion that attention was the 'nerve of the whole psychological system' (Titchener 1924:173). Such a claim was not only difficult to support at that time but was made with reference to a concept intimately related to difficult questions about consciousness, whose complexities most psychologists preferred to ignore – or deny completely.

Some support for the idea that this aspect of experience does occupy a key role in both conscious and unconscious thought processes has already been offered elsewhere (Gear 1987), but now this view is elaborated and extended to a position from which Titchener's claim should not appear at all exaggerated. It is shown how an interactive model of attention, perception, memory, and arousal can be used to relate and give insight into a wide range of psychological theory and findings, drawn from all of its major schools[1] and fields.[2]

Specific conclusions from earlier research which are developed here are (1) that a theory of attention can also embrace explanations of both conscious and unconscious aspects of perception and learning, and (2) that within such an explanation two kinds of processing,[3] related to behaviourist and Gestalt views of learning, take place simultaneously (postulate 6, Appendix 2). The framework is evolutionary and biological. This allows an ecological approach with the incidental advantage of relating very easily to other disciplines within the biological, behavioural, and social sciences and, as will be seen in Part 2, to art as well as science. It also lends itself very well to synthesis. Unfortunately, and contrary to popular belief, greater generality in the application of a principle does not necessarily imply greater simplicity of underlying theory. On the contrary, whereas attention, perception, memory, arousal, and motivation are usually discussed in unitary terms, by making use of the APM-A construct this view will be seen to be far too simplistic. In fact, in order to explore and clarify the connections made in the title of this book, between perception, evolution, and style, it becomes necessary for analysis to shift to the complexities of the very non-unitary nature of all of these aspects of human experience and behaviour.

The theoretical position arrived at, after sufficient evolutionary and physiological background has been given to allow its full definition, offers the possibility of accommodating previous ideas critically so that, although a previous theory may not be accepted in its entirety, its usefulness can be acknowledged, its limitations explored, and its underlying mode of thinking placed in context. At the nub of the theory is a relatively simple dynamic model of style outlined in Chapter 3 which embodies some equally simple principles based mainly on known effects on behaviour and experience of the hormones adrenalin and noradrenalin; but as a tool of analysis which offers a holistic view it necessarily also reveals some more or less complex relationships and concepts represented by other APM-A models. A skeletal outline of how these relate to one another is offered in Appendix 1 and, as was mentioned in the General introduction, occasional reference to this should help the reader to find his or her own way to the new position described in what follows. Numbered postulates appear in Appendix 2:1–7 arise directly from the original APM-A model defined in detail in *Attention, Affect and Learning* (Gear 1987), while the others surface mainly in Part 1.

Postulates 1–6 refer mainly to the interactive processes involved in attention, affect, and learning; 5–7 and 11 relate to interests and needs and offer various models arrived at by exploring the relationship between the characteristics of attention identified in the first postulate; 9 and 10 refer to processes which are seen to link together the fields of learning and aesthetics; while 12 and 13 relate to particular kinds of vulnerability unique to the species. Postulates 14 and 15, together with postulate 11 which refers directly to needs, can be seen to hold important implications for education and for clinical psychology in particular, and 16 emphasizes the necessity for psychological theory to acknowledge and accommodate human paradox: a subject explored in Chapter 1. Whereas the earlier postulates refer mainly to human adaptability, postulates 17–25 will be seen to concern human variability.

It should be noted that in postulate 4 the terms physical or mental 'comfort' or 'discomfort' are used in preference to 'pleasure' and 'pain' because it is to be argued that pleasure and pain are not mutually exclusive alternatives. Where the term 'optimal' is used, as in postulate 9, it does not refer to a static condition which represents a species-trait, but to a condition susceptible to individual differences and phenomenological change.

Chapter one

Maintaining the balance

Summary

The purpose of both Chapters 1 and 2 is to help move the reader to a new vantage point from which to view human adaptability and variability. For instance, one of the arguments of this chapter is that the human species is the most emotional *as well as* the most rational of species and that ultimately emotionality overrides rationality – but not simply in the Freudian sense. Neither is instinct seen to have been replaced by reason but, alongside cognitive ability, it is seen to have greatly increased in complexity. We are described as, above all, *responsive (tuned) to change* but, having different levels of need for perceiving and experiencing change, subject to variable *thresholds of risk tolerance.*

Just as interaction between our external and internal 'environments' and the reaction Pavlov labelled the 'orientation reflex' are crucial to physical survival behaviour, it is argued that similar responses of the autonomic nervous system to arousing stimuli in our physical, social, and cultural environments also underlie what are defined as predominantly psychological pleasures and pains. In fact, the highly focused attention we recognize as fascination, which is defined below as dependent on the perception of optimal (to the individual) mixes of perceived threat and promise, is seen to link the processes of learning, art, and science: a link more fully explored in the following chapters.

Some essential facts about the physiology of arousal and how it affects attention, perception, and memory (the APM-A process) are discussed with particular reference to *scanning and focusing functions of attention;* while perception – both in its technical and broader senses – is seen to be limited by our biochemical states as well as much more obvious cognitive, social, and cultural factors. Indeed, it is argued that not only are we composed of the very equal and opposite forces which have intrigued us for so long, but that the inherent paradox of the human condition can actually be related to biology.

A general principle emerges – the *intercourse principle* – which refers to how we interact with environmental stimuli, including objects, other people, and ideas, according to levels and kinds of limbic arousal.

1.1 Body and mind

Although the concept of psychological survival is not an unknown concept, the effects of this particularly human and most complex instinct on perception and behaviour have remained hitherto undefined. However, their definition is central to all that follows, and psychological survival needs will even be deemed to provide more powerful motivation than, and occasionally to override, our instinct for physical survival.

Similarly, the concept of homeostasis – the process of maintaining a state of equilibrium within the organism – is most frequently referred to within the context of physical survival, as a mechanism which triggers participation in one or other of what McLean (1958) referred to so graphically as 'the four F's': feeding, fighting, fleeing, and undertaking mating activity. The task now is to examine (1) how homeostasis may also function as a means of psychological survival and (2) its relevance to psychological adaptability and variability. In this book emphasis will be on questions concerning change and variety in the *ways* in which it is possible to *attend, perceive, remember, think,* or *act.* It is about *how* and *why* behaviour and experience differ within and between individuals and at different cultural stages, rather than *what* is most likely to be perceived, attended to, remembered, thought about, or acted on. Questions concerning the latter are not seen as entirely separate and will be touched on, but they have already been explored elsewhere (Gear 1987). It must also be stressed that the evolutionary and physiological explanations being offered are by no means to deny direct environmental influences on experience and behaviour, but these are seen to interact with human organisms who differ biochemically, as well as socially and culturally, from one another. Moreover, one of the key points being made is that longer-term environmental influences – on the species and its learning – must also be taken into account.

It is argued that not only are attention, perception, memory, and arousal (APM-A) wholly interactive but that a credible theory of human experience and behaviour can be arrived at only if the dynamics of mind, body, and environmental interaction are all acknowledged. Only in this way can we create a sufficiently large canvas to be able to relate such apparently different aspects of human functioning and individuality as intelligence, cognitive style, and creativity to personality and motivation; these in turn to notions or normality and abnormality; and ultimately, all of these aspects of consciousness (and unconsciousness) to one another in such a way that not only can some apparently conflicting psychological data be accommodated, but also greater insight gained, some degree of prediction allowed, and testable hypotheses formulated.

The adoption of an evolutionary perspective in order to make sense of observations or data about human beings is far from new, but its acceptance is by no means general or total (Spilsbury 1974), even though it is the biggest unifying theory in biology, and its influence in psychology is increasingly recognized. What is generally accepted, however, is that the greatest challenge for evolutionists is the need to offer a theory which can accommodate all of the apparent paradoxes of human nature: most obviously, our manifest capacities for altruism and creativity existing alongside often more obvious indulgences in competitiveness and destruction. It is suggested that, so far, plausibility is most often lacking for two main reasons. One of these is a tendency for explanations to be in terms of physical survival only, so that the significance of a need for psychological 'survival' as an identifiably different, though inextricably related, need from that of physical survival is either ignored or simply not recognized; and the other is that successive theorists have presupposed that rationality gradually and necessarily replaced instinct. The position here is quite different; not that instinct has been diminished, but that it has been added to, and that as we have evolved we have become more emotional, not less so. Instead of being seen to be mutually exclusive alternative behaviours, rationality and emotionality are seen to be wholly mutually *dependent*.

In addition to the functionalists,[1] whose approach was essentially a psychology of the adjustment of the organism to the environment, there have been three major applications of evolutionary theory in psychology: namely, behaviourism, psychoanalysis, and sociobiology.[2] As Gruber (1980) points out, however, all of these applications have tended to place overwhelming emphasis on the animalistic origins of humanity, and similar criticisms have been levelled at some of the more recent contributions to the psychology of motivation by ethologists such as Lorenz and Tinbergen (Hinde 1982).

By contrast, other recent theorizing and research has aimed to show how human capacities not actually shared with other species can still be seen to have evolved from primitive instinctive behaviours. Among the more prominent theories of this kind are those of Razran (1971), who provides a synthesis of behaviourism, Russian Pavlovianism, and western 'cognitivism' to explain the evolution of learned behaviour, higher nervous activity, and cognition; Alexander (1980), who uses evolution as an explanatory principle to help understand a wide range of human social activity including ethics, law, and justice; Crook (1980), who considers the evolution of human beings into essentially conscious beings from the standpoint of sociobiology; and Riedl (1984). Riedl's title, *Biology and*

Knowledge, also echoes Piaget's contribution to epistemology titled *Biology of Knowledge* (1971), and the difference between their aims is no less subtle. Piaget describes his aim as being 'to discuss problems of intelligence and of knowledge (in particular logico-mathematical knowledge), in the light of contemporary biology', while the stated aim of Riedl's book is to solve some 'basic epistemological questions precisely within the theory of evolution': to analyse the source ('the ancestral basis') of reason in relation to established biological principles.

Applications of evolutionary theory in attempts to explain more specific aspects of experience and behaviour have been made by Gooch (1973), of personality; and by Stenhouse (1974), Skemp (1979), and Davis (1981), of learning. Rather than attempting to offer an explanation of learning in general, Davis actually identifies a new kind of learning dependent on the greater power of anticipation of the human species. His thesis is that humans are the only animals to anticipate as a result of experience what will happen more than sixty seconds into the future, and that it is this capacity for 'separated learning' which actually differentiates us from other species.

The other major field whose applications are of relevance to the APM-A perspective is that of theories in which arousal plays a key role. Significantly, the earliest and one of the most recent contributions are both combined with evolutionary hypotheses, and both refer to individual differences. A key link between these two – namely, the work of Pavlov (1927), the father of the orientation reflex which assumes a crucial role within the new perspective, and Zuckerman (1979), whose research is referred to in Chapters 3 and 4 – is Eysenck's (1967) personality theory. This is discussed and criticized in the same two chapters, and Gray's modification of the theory (see Eysenck 1981: chap. 8) is also discussed and criticized in Chapter 4. The arousal theorists Hebb (1955) and Berlyne (1960) are referred to in Chapter 2, and Berlyne's theoretical stance on aesthetics in particular is discussed in Chapter 5.

A fairly recent arousal theory – Apter's reversal theory (1982) – also purports to be a unifying theory. However, although it is obviously accepted within the new perspective that *level* of arousal plays a crucial part in all experience and behaviour, it is also stressed that *kinds* of arousal, beyond Apter's 'pleasant' and 'unpleasant' kinds, must be taken into account. This omission is not the only problem with Apter's theory; it can be criticized on a number of grounds. An example at the most fundamental level is that one of the four states of arousal on which the theory rests, 'boredom', is assumed to be a state of 'unpleasant low arousal', while in APM-A terms boredom is regarded as a concomitant of a state of *high* arousal and a *high* level of need for change and expression, for which no means of satisfaction are immediately available. Boredom is seen to be a state of dissatisfaction, that is, a high need (and therefore high arousal) state rather than a low need/arousal state.

Just as Apter has recognized the crucial role of arousal in human experience and behaviour, Helson (1964) has recognized the potential, at least, for a unified view of experience and behaviour, in the concept of adaptation. However, among many points of difference between APM-A theory and adaptation-level theory is Helson's belief that 'Feeling states initiate, direct and terminate almost all types of behaviour'. The APM-A view is that affect initiates, directs, and terminates *all* types of behaviour *and* experience.

One of the earliest attempts to offer a unifying perspective by reference to biology was that of Adolf Meyer (see Lief 1948) at the turn of the century. He viewed psychiatry as distinct from psychoanalysis in that he believed that 'practically any function [not only sex] can take a lead in the personality', but he did not see the patient as a 'mere summing-up of cells and organs, but a human being in need of adjustment to the demands of life'.

Finally, there are two superficially quite different contributions to a biological view of human psychology which demand mention on the grounds that, in quite different ways, they relate very strongly to the APM-A position. They are by Menninger *et al.*, *The Vital Balance* (1963), and by Stephen and Rachel Kaplan, *Cognition and Environment* (1982).

The view of mental disorder put forward by Menninger *et al.*, based on principles of organization, interaction, homeostasis, heterostasis, steady-state maintenance, adaptation, modification, and regulation – with definitions in terms of different orders, or degrees, of 'dysfunction', 'dyscontrol', and 'dysequilibration' – relates quite strongly to the view put forward in Chapter 4. Their fundamental aim to relate normality and abnormality to each other and their concentration on process are essentially similar to some of the aims of this book. The major differences are (1) their model is essentially a medical model, and (2) the view they adopt is basically a unitary view of mental disorder, with the aim of reducing categories so as 'to have only one class – mental illness', which makes no attempt to define kinds of 'personality dysfunction' or 'living impairment', as opposed to the dynamic view of individual differences presented in Chapters 3 and 4.

By contrast, the integrated view offered by the Kaplans is concerned with the relationship between cognition and environmental perception and recognition that the understanding of the interplay between mind and environment is essential to an understanding of human behaviour in general.

It is perhaps not surprising that some of the most active and persistent theoretical applications of evolutionary theory are being expressed by researchers into environmental perception. That this is a key area is indicated by the fact that its literature is spawned variously by geographers, landscape architects, planners, zoologists, and anthropologists as well as psychologists; and together with that on aesthetic theories will be referred to again in Chapter 5.

However, no other attempt has been made so far (to this author's knowledge) to offer explanation by this means of *modes* of behaviour and experience – that is, of historical, or individual, differences in style – or to investigate perception within an evolutionary framework to provide a link between different schools of psychology, particular disciplines, and the different (and common) processes underlying art and science.

In fact, the attempt which follows also permits human behaviour and experience to be viewed in both phylogenetic and ontogenetic terms revealing patterns common to both[3] within a single, unified, homeostatic theory. The new evolutionary perspective also accommodates a whole spectrum of so-called 'normality' and 'abnormality' of function while emphasizing the need to acknowledge the importance of body–mind interaction.

Interaction of body and mind is clearly and increasingly recognized by a number of groups, including practitioners of the new cognitive behavioural therapies. On the other hand, some of those clinicians whose treatment rests on the practice of associating relaxed bodily states with known sources of fear and anxiety and gradual *familiarization* with a phobic object, as forms of behaviour therapy, continue to deny the involvement of mind in their treatment, only to remind us of some of the claims of the early learning theorists which have already been refuted elsewhere (Gear 1987: chap. 3).

Therefore, it is to be argued, the complexities of mind–body interaction must be incorporated into any theory of human nature in order to ensure the broadest possible application and explanatory power. Moreover, such an approach is necessary to establish a fundamentally important position: acknowledgement of an inherent, but grossly underestimated, greater potential for the influence of mind over body than body over mind (except, of course, in extreme cases of irreversible tissue damage). It also allows for the possible influence of one or more minds over the minds and actions of others.

To this end, the case will be put that the well-known stress reaction associated with activation of the fight/flight mechanism (Cannon 1929) requires that we engage in action, not only on those occasions when it is necessary to avoid physical danger but also in order to avoid psychological 'danger', for which, it will be maintained, some people have a considerably greater predisposition than others.

In order to define this homeostatic mechanism as having a critical role to play in serving psychological as well as mere physical needs and, incidentally, making a decisive contribution to our whole manner of functioning, it becomes necessary to explore some of its evolutionary background, and to offer a basic physiological explanation of the relationship between emotion and arousal: thereby introducing some of the concepts to be taken up in much more detail in Chapters 2, 3, and 4.

1.2 The attention mechanism defined

In his excellent summary of the literature and data so far accumulated from research into arousal, Claridge (1981) mentions two features considered to be of particular significance by Samuel (1959). The first of these is the existence of physiologically distinguishable brain stem and thalamic reticular systems which 'appeared to be responsible for, respectively, tonic or long lasting and phasic, or short duration, arousal responses', and the second:

> the demonstration of ascending and descending, both excitatory and
> inhibitory connections between the cortex and reticular system, a
> feedback arrangement which had the right kind of flexibility to
> account for the subtle variations and shifts in attention and arousal
> which psychology felt it needed to explain.
>
> (Claridge 1981:120)

The autonomic nervous system (literally translated 'self-governing' nervous system, that is, largely independent of conscious thought), of which the brain stem and excitatory and inhibitory connections between cortex and reticular system form part, has continued to excite a great deal of interest ever since. In particular, research into parts of the brain implicated in ANS (autonomic nervous system) functioning known as the hypothalamus and limbic system which, interestingly in this context, are both closely connected with the oldest and most primitive parts of the brain, has yielded much information about learning and memory. It has to be emphasized, of course, that it would be quite incorrect to say that any one part of the brain is responsible for any particular function of mind, as areas of the brain involved in autonomic functioning are intimately connected with, and interact exceedingly closely with, other parts of the central nervous system (brain and spinal cord) and peripheral nervous system.

The importance of the hypothalamus lies in the fact that it regulates the ANS by control over the pituitary gland (known as the 'master gland'),[4] thereby maintaining physical homeostasis. It has also been established that, in addition to electrical stimulation delivered to this part of the brain promoting engagement in survival activities such as eating (Hoebel and

Teitelbaum 1962), it also offers pleasurable sensations in response to electrical stimulation. This effect is sufficiently marked for Olds and Milner (1954) to have been able to show that pleasure gained by self-stimulation overrides the organism's response to fatigue.

Clearly, an established physiological basis of emotion (Leukel 1976:306–7, 371–2), and an established relationship between emotion and survival, have fairly strong implications for the existence of a relationship between the maintenance of physical equilibrium and a need for psychological 'comfort'. But early ideas of drive reduction as a motivating force, which such a relationship most obviously suggests, were presented in terms of satisfying tissue needs only.

Even Freud's almost universal application of the concept was nevertheless limited by its dependence on reference to the satisfaction of physical needs only, of which, of course, the sex drive and procreation were considered to be of most significance, and Hull (whose name is most frequently linked with the concept of drive reduction) could account for behaviour other than the direct satisfaction of bodily needs only by the introduction of the concept of 'secondary reinforcers', as an indirect means of satisfying physical demands: a strategy which was wholly consistent with behaviourism's denial of cognition. The limitations of behaviourism, with which drive reduction theories have been most strongly associated in the past, have already been discussed in detail (Gear 1987: chap. 2), but the concept of drive reduction itself will be seen to have much wider application, providing we consider other means and ends for the reduction of neuronal excitation.

But before ideas of a possibly more complex relationship between physical well-being and psychological well-being can be explained and elaborated, more consideration has to be given to the physiology of attention, affect, and learning, which will, incidentally, provide some further support for the necessity for such a highly interactive model as that being postulated.

Not only are some of the same areas of the brain known to be implicated in attention, memory, learning, and emotion, but more interestingly still, in the light of arguments yet to be put forward in this and following chapters, the same areas are also implicated in personality functions. The limbic system (with which the hypothalamus is also intimately involved) comprises such areas. In addition to its involvement in learning, memory, and emotion, its chief role is in monitoring stimuli from all of the sense organs, and providing an agency of control over what is to be attended to from moment to moment. It is also connected with the frontal lobes, which mediate complex personality functions, and with the POT areas (parietal, occipital, and temporal lobes) of the neocortex which are integrative areas of the brain, again involved in learning and memory.

The necessary feedback between the brain stem – the most primitive part of the brain, which exerts control over waking and sleeping and general arousal cycles by either excitation or inhibition of nerve-cell activity throughout the brain and body – and limbic system and cortex, is provided by the reticular activating system (RAS). This consists of fibres going up via the ascending reticular activating system (ARAS), through the thalamus, which acts as a kind of relay station, and back down via the descending reticular activating system (DRAS) to the brain stem, thereby passing sensory information from sense receptors to the cortex and other parts of the brain, and back from the cortex to motor effectors.

Vital 'decisions' therefore, about incoming sensory information, are taken at cortical, limbic-system, and hypothalamic levels, which may or may not activate ANS and pituitary gland – depending on the strength of stimulus and consequent rate of firing of neurons from sense receptors.

As the ANS divides into a sympathetic system (SNS) and a para-sympathetic system (PNS), excitatory and inhibitory systems respectively, which are in constantly changing balance, the kind of action, if any, which results from a stimulus, that is, which division of the ANS dominates, the response can be seen to depend at its most fundamental on whether the signal is interpreted as threat, promise, or neither; and on the basis of such processing, whether the 'decision' is essentially whether to stop, go, or continue as before.

Clearly, some decisions about whether or not action should be taken as a result of phenomenologically lower priority signals may take days, months, or even years to reach. And remembering that it is exceedingly rare for us to be able to make only simple decisions, without being aware of any possible incidental or 'knock-on' effects, and that human motivation is complex at the best of times, decisions likely to have medium- or long-term effects are likely to be undergoing processing continually, and in conjunction with one another, at conscious and unconscious levels – or both – in between the processing of more immediate demands on attention. Such is the degree of change to which we are subjected, that each and every patch of changing light we perceive demands comparisons to be made (with what is already known as a result of species[5] or individual learning and experience), and decisions to be made according to (1) the degree of arousal experienced and consequent consciously or unconsciously perceived need for action or not, and (2) the relevance of such changes to individual needs according to a very particular store of information encoded from *all* of the senses.

The constant interplay of excitation and inhibition which the SNS and PNS provide, is in fact vitally important to the organism, as in order to function adequately it is always necessary to inhibit some activities in order to carry out others, and to exercise priorities of interest. In gross terms, without the balancing inhibitory system, excitation could build up to a point at which there could be a massive discharge of neuronal energy, as in an epileptic fit, or conversely, inhibition of action could become so strong as for the organism to fail to be moved into action at all, as can happen in extreme cases of schizophrenia, for instance, when victims may eventually lapse into the extreme condition of a catatonic state.

Evidence will be offered to support the hypothesis that this complicated organization of inhibition and excitation and consequent continuous decision making is the accepted basis not only of all behaviour (Luria 1976:5), but of experience too. This is to say that all human experience, from the scanning and focusing functions of attention which occur in learning and memory (postulates 1–6, 13) to characteristically different modes of thinking (for example, sequential – so-called 'logical'–thinking, as opposed to more intuitive thought processes)[6], is seen to depend on the kind of balance and *differences in basal rates* and *patterns* of release of major neurotransmitters at synaptic junctions.[7]

The chemical transmitters of most significance in this context are those which are known to have a role to play in memory and learning and in expanding or limiting attentional capacity (by adjustment of scanning and focusing tendencies). The one extends our perceptions of possible alternative interpretations of situations and/or possible behaviours open to us and the other makes selective attention possible: adrenalin (McGaugh 1980:7, 132) and acetylcholine (Campbell and Singer 1979:50), respectively.

Acetylcholine is released as a result of activation of the cholinergic system (with which serotonin, necessary for normal sleep, is also associated) by the PNS, which is involved with the conservation of energy and effort and is most obviously dominant during relaxation. Adrenalin and noradrenalin, on the other hand, being neurotransmitters of the adrenergic system, and otherwise known as epinephrine and norepinephrine, are released as a result of SNS activity, dominant during emotional excitement. They are also intimately concerned with activating the body and, importantly – by increasing electro-chemical activity in the brain – the mind. They service physical homeostasis, and produce the well-known reaction of increased pulse rate and changes in both respiratory and digestive systems associated with need for action. It is also important to note that SNS activity characteristically produces diffuse responses and general arousal, which is of course consistent with scanning functions of attention, whereas PNS activity produces discrete, sequential, and more specific reactions (Leukel 1976:88–90, 101–2), suggestive of focus.

The SNS and PNS are most often described as working in antagonism to one another, but Michael Day (1979:24) makes a crucial point; that in fact they work in concert, closely together *and* with the somatic nervous system in producing complex adjustments of balance. Day is critical of the fact that Cannon's famous and vivid linking of ANS activity to fight/flight reactions dominates thinking about its functioning. He points out that it is not *always* like that (that is, *either* PNS *or* SNS activity), but very usefully and graphically uses the analogy of a man riding a bicycle, who must be constantly making fine adjustments, but may suddenly hit a patch of oil and skid.

The usefulness of such an analogy to the APM-A view lies in the possibilities it suggests for variability in degrees of control that the PNS might exert (in its balancing role) over SNS activity. The picture presented is one of extreme flexibility, and of possible variation ranging from finely adjusted and highly efficient conscious control, of the kind which might be required in response to the demands of riding through heavy traffic, say, to control of a highly flexible and hardly conscious kind, appropriate for meandering through country lanes. Day's analogy allows not only for the possibility of skidding, but also of freewheeling, and even of actually stopping and getting off for a while – intentionally or unintentionally.

Above all, it allows for the paradox that PNS and SNS divisions of the ANS work *both* in harmony, *and* in opposition to one another – contrapuntally, as it were. This happens to the extent that sympathetic activity beyond a certain point will produce a 'rebound' effect (Van Toller 1979), so that ultimately it is the amount and rate of adrenergic activity (as a result of internal or external stimulation) which determine to what extent SNS activity dominates a response, and for how long. Within such a system, should 'skidding' of a dangerously serious nature occur, stopping may well be equally sudden, as, for instance, in the case of emotional withdrawal after prolonged anxiety or bereavement; and, of course, a tacit assumption has to be made that even in apparently grossly underaroused individuals, such a condition is only relative to more excitable states. Logically, if SNS activity did not predominate to at least a marginal extent, *Homo sapiens* would not only be passive in the extreme, but *entirely* inactive, a totally dependent creature, to whom boredom would be a quite unknown phenomenon, whereas even those to whom such a description would *seem* to apply, will be known to participate in some kind of 'unnecessary' activity.

Such a system, then, provides for the greatest possible flexibility of response to a world of phenomenologically alternating threat and promise in which, frequently, signals present themselves as difficult to recognize as welcome or not. This results in a state of uncertainty which might be described as *fascination*, as the perceiver responds to alternating familiarity and novelty – both of which kinds of signal have already been identified (postulates 5, 9, Appendix 2, and Gear 1987) as being extremely effective in gaining attention.

1.3 The pleasure of paradox

That people are motivated by challenge is a statement which has so hardened into cliché that its potential for offering explanation of much of what is uniquely human about human behaviour is easily overlooked.

The position has been adopted (postulates 4, 9, 10, Appendix 2, and Gear 1987) and reinforced earlier in this chapter, that motivation is not just sometimes but always hedonistic. Later, this argument will be extended to show that it is not necessary to invoke the concept of kin selection (Trivers 1971), for instance – a concept which fits very well within the framework of physical survival, but still rather uneasily within the concept of individual survival or beside any notion of the individual as the unit of the evolution of the species – to explain altruistic behaviour, or activities not directly or obviously relevant to personal interests. Such behaviour can be shown to be an incidental effect of the satisfaction of individual needs. Acts of self-sacrifice even, and many other apparently maladaptive or 'unnecessary' actions, can be explained in quite different terms, providing we take into account the more recently evolved demands of the psyche.

A hedonistic rephrasing of the opening cliché tells us that human beings *take pleasure* in challenge, and leaving aside for now the idea that some enjoy challenge more than others, only a minor distortion (namely, that human beings *take pleasure in manageable threat*) offers an expression of what is at least intuitively accepted, and indeed much exploited in the arts, particularly in theatre and cinema production: that human beings enjoy being frightened – a little. And of course, we only have to think of such so-called leisure pursuits as rock climbing, wrestling or hang-gliding to note some fairly widespread support for the claim being made, to gain insight into some of the complications of the relationship between pleasure and pain,[8] and between threat and promise. Clearly, they are not entirely separable aspects of physical or psychological experience.

Pleasure, it is being argued, is so much derived from a *combination* of excitation and inhibition (the nature of which will be discussed in more detail later), weighted necessarily towards arousal (excitation), and *not* simply from excitation alone, as experience might lead us to believe, that its achievement can be seen to underlie all of our behaviour and experience. The widespread human practice of collecting provides one example of the satisfaction and pleasure to be gained from combinations of familiarity and novelty; a source of *fascination* which takes the form of acquiring *new* examples of some already *familiar* kind of object.

One of the most powerful examples, however, which by reference to a 'hierarchy of diminishing interest' (Figure 66, Appendix 2, and Gear 1987) might be expected, is the sexual one in which orgasm is achieved by the very means in question, which, as every school-child and most television viewers now know, involves a repetitious and extraordinarily pleasurable cycle of going and stopping (pausing), until ultimate satisfaction, in the form of a highly paradoxical state of 'unendurable pleasure', is achieved by at least one partner.

The point made about a necessarily greater proportion of going than stopping in pleasurable activity echoes what has already been said earlier in this chapter about man being essentially active, and will develop into something of a theme throughout this book, particularly in discussion of how intelligence and consciousness are most likely to have evolved. But the major point to be made here, despite the example just cited, is that human pleasure is not derived either directly or indirectly from the satisfaction of physical needs only, although it is acknowledged that the more complex and newer sources of pleasure have evolved from the satisfaction of more obvious and simpler physical drives; just as the sophisticated powers of reason and creative abilities of *Homo sapiens* have evolved from more primitive creatures and organisms with no capacity for consciousness at all.

It is accepted though, that pleasure *does* derive from the fact that human beings are composed of irritable (that is, sensitive) tissue, but are made more keenly aware of this on some occasions than others, and then only in terms of physical pleasure or pain. Patterns of excitation and inhibition taking place within the brain are also experienced as pleasurable or painful, but as they are manifested as emotions, feelings, intuitions, thoughts, or ideas, only the most extreme kind seem remarkable as sensations (are in fact 'sensational'), and of these, only the most intense, concentrated, or fascinating are likely to be acted on or remembered.

Thought of in these terms, it will be seen that our unique capacity for pleasure of an apparently purely abstract, rather than obviously physical, kind has evolved so as to be dependent, very often, on precisely *not* attaining the physical satisfaction of complete drive reduction (for example, of total removal from a threatening stimulus), or the immediate satisfaction of a desire stimulated by a promising one. The argument to be developed will be that being 'tuned to change' (see postulates 1, 2, Appendix 2, and Gear 1987), that is, being more aware of environmental change than of anything else because it is that element of experience which presents greatest potential threat, we will, whilst striving to impose order on our internal worlds by seeking the security of the known and the familiar, nevertheless *seek* a degree of change, as a source of reassurance and 'feedback', because of the most fundamental paradox of all: that it has always been consistent with our experience that a perceivable degree of change is a constant element of the environment.

Physically experienced pleasure and pain, it is suggested therefore, exist on continua of intensity of stimulation, so that, for example, the same physical gesture, such as simple hand-to-face contact with another made as an expression of care, at a different level of intensity could cause tissue damage and suffering. Further, thresholds of pleasure and pain, it will be argued, vary, not only from person to person, but in accordance with environmental conditions. How and why these variations manifest themselves is to be explored in the following chapters, but for now, a general principle emerges: in addition to what has been established earlier and by others, about pleasures to be derived from the reduction of drive (that is, by the satisfaction of visceral and other physical needs), it can be said that what we do not like in potentially disorientating or damaging intensity, we positively enjoy in a form we can cope with, and that *thresholds of risk tolerance*, and therefore following the earlier argument, individual need for risk within the social and physical environment are a human variable.[9]

Manifestly, at a cognitive level, extremely complex combinations of threat and promise, in the form of the known and the unknown, and the familiar and novel, become possible, but when a need arises for us to make adjustments in these elements of our security the potential for gross and emotionally painful rearrangements of neural firing patterns (Milner 1970:104), as a result of the 'unlearning'[10] involved in changing previously much rehearsed and reinforced processing of information, is high. Instances may include thwarted expectations, unavoidable acknowledgement of the reality of situations hitherto effectively refused, or other forms of breakdown of long-held beliefs. Conversely, the discovery of a high degree of match between hoped-for outcomes of events, in which there has been an equally high degree of emotional 'investment' (in the form of much rehearsed processing), can result in concomitantly profound experiences of pleasure.

Austen Clark (1980:1–38) has made a very useful distinction between the concepts of reductionism, with all of its emotive overtones, and *'explanatory* reductionism'. It is hoped that here, the employment of explanatory reductionism will not only lend insight into complex levels of mental functioning, but that by teasing out process from its possible variety of manifestations, it will also be possible to define more clearly some of the effects of the social and physical environment upon the organism; and that by the same means, it will be seen that biological determinism is not the only possible philosophical position to be arrived at within an evolutionary perspective, as is very often assumed. On the contrary, the view of *Homo sapiens* to be developed is one which will highlight evolved complexity and consequent need to choose between alternatives – to become a cultural being.

Cultural influences, as well as our own biology, obviously determine some of our potential, but of at least equal importance is the fact that we respond to these pressures in such a way as to change both.[11]

1.4 The source of paradox

The point has already been made that we are both the most rational *and* the most emotional of all the primates, and it can be added that besides human nature never being free from apparent contradictions, because of this highly developed capacity for rationality existing alongside emotional complexity, man's very evolution is paradoxical; *Homo sapiens* is quite literally composed of paradox.

Lorenz exposes some of the paradox of human nature this way: 'Mutation and selection, the great "constructors" which made genealogical trees grow upwards, have chosen, of all likely things, the rough and spiny shoot of intra-specific aggression to bear the blossoms of personal friendship and love' (Lorenz 1967:39).

Some of the contradictions of our evolution will be elaborated, but that the current stage (all too easily regarded as the end product) is full of paradox, requires only very little elaboration for the point to be made effectively. Just as it is accepted that our perception is constantly limited by what we are – as a species, and genetically as individuals – as well as what we have become as a result of physical, social, and cultural factors, it is also suggested that mind–body interaction is such an unavoidable aspect of the perceptual process that its dependence on inherent characteristics extends even to our physical makeup: that it extends beyond the fact that learning involves physiological changes.

Perception depends on continuous comparison making, comparing the novel with the familiar and identifying 'match' and 'mismatch', whether it is our beliefs with the beliefs of others or, in tangible terms, the sizes, shapes, and colours of objects with one another. Part of this comparison making clearly involves perceiving other people and things by assessing how similar or different they are from ourselves. It is possible that this means of perception, by association, extraction of common elements,[12] and comparisons made between our internal and external 'worlds', is not only the basis of our orientation and of our thinking, but is so fundamental as to extend to perceiving in terms of our own chemistry and biology (Reiser 1972). For the purpose of the present argument, however, it is sufficient to note that we are actually composed of the very kind of opposite and equal forces which have proved to be such a source of interest to us for so long.[13]

That we have identifiably different central and peripheral nervous systems, each dividing into two parts – brain and spinal cord, and PSNS and ANS, respectively – has already been noted, as has the most significant fact that the ANS divides into opposing yet harmonizing sympathetic and parasympathetic systems. These aspects of the functioning of the nervous system alone suggest some competition for resources, whether the energy in question is conceived of as finite and available only within the kind of closed energy system visualized by Freud, or as supplied by the sort of hydraulic model suggested by Lorenz. In addition, knowledge that human energy is not boundless is readily available from personal experience, as well as it being a universally accepted and observable phenomenon that on occasions it is necessary to 'stop to think', when the requirement for either thought or action is not in connection with some very predictable or routinized task or event. Obviously, both doing and thinking make demands on our limited capacity of attention (Miller 1956).

Also of profound significance to the current argument, as well as to what has already been described as simultaneous but different means of processing information, are the implications of new knowledge being gained about the ways in which the brain is organized into two hemispheres. We now know from recent advances in split brain surgery, for instance, that two quite different solutions can be produced by the same person – in effect simultaneously – to the same problem (Gazzaniga 1973). And as we also know that we are conscious of only a small proportion of the activity of the brain, it is hardly surprising that we are capable of such extremes of self-knowledge *and* self-deception.

Our need to impose order on our internal worlds, however, tends to make us intolerant of contradictory elements in our own thinking, so that of all the interpretations it is possible to make in any given situation, we are most prone to thinking in terms of bipolar continua or dichotomies, and all too easily see alternatives as mutually exclusive; so that whilst being dogged by needing to make decisions of an 'either/or' or 'right or wrong' nature – and with a seemingly inherent dislike of compromise – we best avoid mental discomfort by 'knowing one way or the other', unless the paradox in question can be viewed objectively as one which we perceive as being of no direct threat to our own belief systems or schemata, when it can be accommodated. Such non-threatening paradox may even be enjoyed, if conceived of within the context of art, perhaps as an oxymoron, to provide the kind of fascination so often produced by Evelyn Waugh, for instance, in phrases such as 'sensational ignorance'.

Most anthropologists, ethologists, and social biologists agree about the significance in the evolution of consciousness, intelligence, and creativity, of such changes in our behaviour as bipedalism and the subsequent freeing of hands which was necessary for tool using, and in turn, the development of practical skills which made demands for longer-term memory. There is also a measure of general agreement about the importance in the emergence of language and in the development of a capacity for mental mapping, of hunting activities, as obviously, incidental effects of hunting would have included the need to find the way home from longer distances (Lancaster 1975:79, 80; Crook 1980: 130, 148) and the need to establish other means of indicating phenomenologically changing motivational states than sign language, or other forms of non-verbal communication, when members of the group were dispersed.

Another important, and readily accepted, factor in effecting change in human behaviour is the role of crisis. Links between innovation, hardship, and crises are made by Crook (1980: 10) who cites René Thom's Catastrophe Theory as being relevant to evolutionary changes, whereas Denis Postle (1980) applies the same theory to explain sudden changes in individual behaviour. Parallels between phylogeny and ontogeny in theories seeking to explain changes in human behaviour have of course been drawn by many, and most notably by Piaget (1971). It is hoped, though, that by moving beyond correlations between changes in behaviour and changes in events, which may or may not be causal, to (1) exploring the general principle that rigid thinking and behaviour patterns can be considered to be maladaptive within changing environmental conditions – let alone crises – and (2) investigating what possible forms human biological responses can take, it will become possible to see that hypotheses which are made about inherent contradictions in our evolution can be expanded to offer insight into most aspects of why human beings think and behave in such an impressive variety of ways. Not for the first time paradox will be invoked to explain paradox.

That different theoretical positions most often viewed as mutually exclusive can be accommodated within an evolutionary perspective has already been shown with the juxtaposition of behaviourism and cognitive psychology (see postulate 6, Appendix 2, and Gear 1987), and later it will be shown how other conflicting theoretical positions can be related to one another by applying principles which emerge from particular psycho-physiological processes.

To offer the greatest possible explanatory power, theory has to avoid expression at too early a stage of an either/or mentality and the rejection of paradox. It is necessary, as it were, to avoid taking one path or another, only to find that there exists another alternative offering the scenic advantages of both. Just as it has already been pointed out that both of the chemical transmitters, acetylcholine *and* adrenalin, are crucial to the functioning of memory (p. 20), it is suggested that superior intelligence in men and women, along with all those other aspects of mind which we consider to be unique to ourselves, developed not simply as a result of crises, or as a result of the development of a 'P' factor (Stenhouse 1974), but as a result of hardship followed by relatively easier conditions; paradoxically, of responses necessarily speeded up *and* slowed down.

Mention has already been made of the fact that secretions of adrenalin actually precipitate a balancing release of acetylcholine, and it has already been argued that a fine interplay of excitation and inhibition produces what we call fascination and (quite literally) concentration. In fact, the oscillatory character of inhibitory and excitatory potentials as a feature of brain–behaviour mechanisms during learning, recognized by Hull (1943: 304–21), may well be manifestations of this process of arresting attention, which in Part 2 will be shown to be a vital link between learning and art.

Now it is being argued that in evolutionary terms, arousal, as stress in reaction to harsh and steadily worsening climatic conditions, is likely to have brought about a steady tuning of hominid functioning, as natural selection favoured those able to adapt most effectively to such drastically changing environmental conditions. Secretions of adrenalin and noradrenalin associated with stress, among other effects, simultaneously increase energy and – a factor less often taken into account – increase available neuronal firing in the brain (Van Toller 1979: 127), literally allowing 'more connections' to be made; so that whilst the body is made ready for action, mental activity also increases, offering more likelihood for physical energy to be directed in the most adaptive manner possible.

Of key interest is the fact that the SNS operates as a closed feedback loop (Abel 1974:45) so that its activation tends to be self-perpetuating, wearing off only slowly: a phenomenon manifested by the need, very often, to make a deliberate effort to 'wind down' after periods of excitement or stress. The idea of self-perpetuating activity, besides being reminiscent of Watsonian interpretations of learning (Watson 1919), is also consistent with our 'tuned to change–need for change' argument: that increased arousal has the effect of heightening basal security needs and activities. As thresholds of sensory awareness are lowered, one of the effects is a need for more feedback from the social and physical environment; and, incidentally, as awareness of such stimuli increases, response to them becomes more positive and active.

Increased responsiveness applies equally to those arousing stimuli which fall within the range with which we know we can cope, as to those which make us doubt our defences. Such signals include the wholly familiar, to which we may respond with loving, liking, or loathing; mixes of the novel and familiar, providing fascination and, necessarily, learning, as the novel is accommodated; or the entirely novel, with all of its inherent threat precluding learning by the need it presents for avoidance action, unless familiarization can be gradual.

Approach *and* avoidance actions are in this way *both* heightened. This is a physiological process.

Under usual day-to-day conditions, after a period of stress, the closed feedback loop of SNS activity slowly returns to a basal rate of functioning. Meanwhile, in the absence of developed 'purpose' (postulate 7, Appendix 2, and Gear 1987), and during respite from external demands on attention, we may utilize the extra energy and ideational capacity available to us in various kinds of intercourse with our environments in order to alleviate feelings of restlessness and boredom. This interaction between organism and environment can happen in intellectual, social, or purely physical terms.

Homo sapiens, it is being argued, is above all else a biological response to the environment: the most complex biological response of all. We are sufficiently complicated to attempt most often to devise ways of avoiding being controlled and, at our most creative, do not accept defeat easily; but any notion that there resides a 'ghost in the machine'[14] would perhaps be more accurately conceived of as a 'ghost *around* the 'machine'.

Once stimulated into action, our behaviour, being directed by attention, shares the characteristics of attention. This is a key point which will be elaborated in subsequent chapters, but for the sake of the current argument it is sufficient to confine our interest to the internal–external dimension of attention. In terms of behaviour, this takes the form of activity being directed towards ourselves or towards other people, things, or places, and apart from those activities which for the most part may be placed under the general heading of 'grooming', most of our activities take the form of having exchange of one kind or another with these other sources of satisfaction.

Such intercourse will again be promoted by phenomenological decisions based on degrees of perceived threat or promise in any given situation, and in fundamental terms, our actions will be to approach or to avoid, more or less energetically.

In threatening circumstances where avoidance or retreat is impossible and confrontation with the offending stimulus inevitable, the kind of intercourse promoted may be of such an intense, and possibly uncontrolled, nature, as a result of extreme general arousal, that it may result in violence. By the same token, if the stimulus is full of promise (of pleasurable experience), we may become so excited as to act upon it with equal intensity – but not usually with such vigour as actually to destroy, or rid our presence of it. Of course, such losses are known to occur as incidental effects of attentions delivered to favourite objects, as in the case of, say, overzealous polishing to the extent of removal of patina or essential fine detail, or when simple over-enthusiastic investigation results in disintegration. If it is not possible to have intercourse directly with the object of attention, then the energy and ideas generated by it, or being expanded upon it, may be expressed by doing something *about* it: such possibilities are so broad as to range from behaviour as simple as an expression of consciousness in terms of looks or gestures towards the object, to a communication with others at a variety of possible intellectual levels about the particular threat or promise in question. It may even demand more intense activity, promoting constructions of elaborate two-

or three-dimensional facsimiles, or expressing fantasy by means of music, literature, or drama.

The unnecessary embellishment of hand-axes thus turning them into objects of beauty, during the Acheulian culture (Ardrey 1977:134), could easily be interpreted in this way. At its height, half a million years ago, it coincided with relaxation of the climate after the climax of the Pleistocene, and was marked by 'unnecessarily beautiful symmetry and delicacy . . . far beyond functional demand'. Ardrey actually speculates (1977:129) that the Acheulian hand-axe was the 'beginning of what we regard as both technology *and* art' (my emphasis).

The hypothesis being put forward here could be classified as a displacement theory. Freudian displacement theory, however, would not tell us why, for instance, the ego should suddenly have needed to become so much more active 500,000 years ago, or conversely, why the id should have become so much more turbulent then. Even Lorenzian displacement theory would not explain *why* either more 'action specific energy' should suddenly 'spill over', or *why* further pressure from the 'downward pull' of innate releasing stimuli should create such a need for displacement.

A need to *externalize* neuronal excitation (and here we have been talking essentially about increases in mental and physical energy, as sources of ideas and action which, it has been argued, accompany arousal) also offers possible explanation of why novel, intense, or otherwise arousing environmental stimulation will promote *investigation,* with varying degrees of caution – that is, *varying patterns of inhibition and excitation,* depending on the perceived degree of threat.

When sufficiently aroused we act – preferably directly towards or upon, or directly away from the source of stimulation – but if opportunity for either action, as appropriate, is denied, externalization may take an indirect form. The relationship of this to the original stimulus may be so complex as to be manifested only in the form of anxieties, neuroses, phobias, compulsions, or other so-called 'pathological states'.

Throughout this chapter it has been stressed that instinct has not been replaced by reason, but that alongside evolved cognitive ability, instinct has also greatly increased in complexity. The view being developed actually requires that we stand back from accepted definitions of aspects of human behaviour and experience, and from accepted interpretations of data, in order to be able to gain a wide enough perspective to allow us to see possible new relationships between them, whilst nevertheless striving to keep as much of the view in focus as possible: indeed, to employ scanning *and* focusing techniques which, it is being stressed, are both necessary for successful adaptation – which is, of course, learning.

It is being advocated that we use a wider-angle lens, as it were, so that by moving to a particular strategic position, it may be possible to offer a view of a well-known place which captures more of its characteristics than was possible before, with a different lens, used from the hitherto accepted and more popular vantage point.

The 'wider angle' being adopted requires above all that we accept paradox. This way, it is suggested, philosophical questions of an either/or nature can be reconciled, to the end that by the time the picture is completed, it will be possible to see ourselves as neither entirely shaped by the environments – as B. F. Skinner, for instance, would have us believe[15] – nor entirely capable of becoming shapers of it.

The position from which the 'picture' must be taken is one which, for reasons explained below, admits of instinct as implying the motivation to survive *only*, but includes notions of physical *and* psychological survival, as interdependent although identifiably quite different aspects of surviving – or *not*. Certain specific behaviours, if admitted as innate – such as Piaget's 'genetic epistemology' or Lorenz's 'fixed action patterns' (FAPs) – may therefore be regarded as *species learning* (see note 5 and postulate 2, Appendix 2, and Gear 1987). This point of view holds at least two important implications. The first is that apparently rigid species traits may be 'unlearned' if no longer adaptive – remembering, of course, that Darwinism and natural selection are not just about survival, but necessarily, and equally importantly, about organisms *not* surviving. The second implication of the same point of view is that it allows for much greater variability and flexibility of behaviour, and has the added advantage of being much more consistent with what we all know happens in the 'real world'. Even in our most primitive acts we do not all satisfy physical survival needs by responding with the same rigid behaviour patterns. Certainly, if we take any notice at all of what Kinsey *et al.* (1948, 1953) or Masters and Johnson (1966) have revealed, FAPs are not to any great extent part of human sexuality and procreation, which at the best of times are already mostly incidental effects of the fulfilment of a complex of other needs, often far removed from maternal or paternal considerations.

Even 'exploratory behaviour' *per se*, which is confidently regarded as a prototype of instinct by many, can be seen to be contingent on the basic *intercourse principle* which has been described, and could conceivably be selected against, if conditions in which considerably more cautious and rigid behaviour became more adaptive, prevailed for long enough. For such selection to take place, however, not only would climatic conditions have to become extremely stable and predictable over millions of years, but also the human race itself would have to do a considerable amount of 'growing up'.

Quite simply, it would become necessary for us to learn to understand ourselves and each other sufficiently well to be able to reduce perceived novelty or 'strangeness' in our fellows (*and* in ourselves) to below the threshold at which we feel either self-threatening, or threatened by one another, and to a level at which fascination (and, it is suggested, concomitant learning) takes place instead. But for this to happen, the concept of growing up must not presuppose less playing. Lorenz (1974) has claimed that when being childlike includes 'playful and exploratory curiosity persisting into old age . . . to be childlike is one of the most important, indispensable, and in the best sense, human characteristics of man'.

Even a hardened cynic can view the possibility of human beings eventually growing in understanding and awareness, as being greater than that of total climatic stability. The result could be a combination of conditions offering potential for us to identify ourselves, at last, as essentially creative rather than destructive, and for the most obvious paradox of human behaviour and experience to shift to the *form* of aggression we exercise; for it to become creative aggression.[16]

Chapter two

Psychological survival

Summary

In essence this chapter is about the evolution of mind and psychological means of 'coping' and 'defending'. It is also about the relationship between *species and individual* needs. It defines largely *unconscious needs* in such a way that *individual differences in levels and kinds* can be accommodated. Species adaptation, individual adaptation, and the APM-A process are related to one another initially by placing a new interpretation on changes in behaviour and the apparent shift to 'higher-order needs' which happened about half a million years ago. Mind as a whole is actually viewed as a defence mechanism *par excellence,* but one which itself became vulnerable alongside the evolution of the means of constructing our own 'realities'.

The chapter begins, however, with APM-A interpretations of some well-known findings about *organization and disorganization of behaviour* in order (1) to define and relate to each other certain characteristics of the APM-A process and kinds (styles) of external expression; (2) to explore the relationship between physical and psychological survival; and (3) to include cultural phenomena within the new evolutionary hypothesis. Chapter 1 and this chapter (if not the entire book) are actually both about 'maintaining balance' *and* 'psychological survival'. This is because the achievement of psychological 'orientation' – knowing 'who we are', 'where we are', and 'where we are going' – is seen to be interactive with the physiology (SNS–PNS activity, in particular) of what Pavlov called the 'orientation reflex' described in Chapter 1.

The emphasis in this chapter is on needs labelled *orientation needs* because of their relationship to the ANS and what is seen to be better described as the *'need for* orientation response'. An important concept to the understanding of variability in these needs – *tension thresholds* – is identified as underlying differences in levels and kinds of needs. The *revised hierarchy of needs* offered at the end of the chapter therefore acknowledges Maslow's hierarchy, but moves beyond a unitary hierarchical concept to a dynamic one, which also takes account of the state of the organism and environmental interaction at sensory, cognitive, social, and cultural levels.

2.1 'Concentrating the mind wonderfully'

So far, manifestations of our sensitivity to change have been mentioned as occurring at three different levels of organization: (1) within the individual from moment to moment; (2) as between individuals whose variable sensitivity to change may be said to include different thresholds of risk tolerance (p. 20); and (3) at species level, as a characteristic shared at least to some extent by all other living organisms. In Chapter 3, the scope of human variability which, it will be argued, this process accounts for in large measure, will be discussed at length; the task now is to define its source and its potential.

The division of the ANS into SNS and PNS (p. 19) has already been indicated as underlying our recognition of any response to paradox (1.3), as well as providing for flexibility of response to change. Now, a closer definition of the significance of this process and its relevance to the notion of tuning, as it is used here, will be offered, in order to clarify the range of possible relationships between attention, perception, memory, and arousal (APM-A) – and, consequently, behaviour. Manifestations of the underlying process of SNS–PNS antagonism and co-operation will also be seen to be the basis of what we perceive as micro–macro parallelism of the kind intimated earlier, and to offer us a large repertoire of analogy, as well as the propensity for the use of paradox, which was discussed in the last chapter.

In Chapter 1 and elsewhere (Gear 1987), discussion has centred mainly on the effect on the organism of *kinds of stimuli*: on internal reactions to environmental and visceral *changes*, and some ways in which attention is gained and learning may take place have been postulated. This may happen either as a result of fairly dramatic events guaranteed to capture interest and promote action in the most phlegmatic, or, as the result of some degree of fascination, whose relationship to priority signals may be more obscure, but exists in the perception of a signal, or complex of signals, containing degrees of threat or promise, or – most pungently – both.

Now we are to move on to consider possible *kinds of action and reaction*, that is, to include behaviour and performance within the dynamics of the homeostatic process, and to consider some rudimentary matters of style. These will be described as being dependent on the very process in question: the process of 'tuning'.

In considering modes of behaviour, three key concepts introduced in the last chapter will assume crucial importance: namely, the idea that individuals have *thresholds of sensitivity to change,* which from now on will be referred to as *tension thresholds*; the idea that the organism seeks ways of *externalizing neuronal excitation* which exceeds threshold level; and the resultant *intercourse principle* (see pp. 28–31).

Differences in *reactions to change* are also to be identified as the major source of complexity in any analysis or definition of aspects of human nature. This claim is being made for two reasons, which refer to different characteristics of such reactions. The first reason concerns the sheer breadth of variability in human ways of perceiving and behaving, which, in this chapter, are referred to in simple, bipolar terms but in the next are more specifically defined within a dynamic model of style. The second reason is that variability in response to change itself affects both the kind of intercourse we undertake and our feelings as a result of whatever feedback we gain. Present behaviour *and* experience, therefore, not only affect future kinds of behaviour and experience but also alter our responses to and needs for change.

The process is at the same time highly dynamic, within certain parameters, and self-perpetuating; partly because of the closed feedback loop of the SNS (logically of most significance with reference to low tension thresholds) and, at the other extreme, partly because low sensitivity towards, and concomitant low requirement for, change promote only low activity. In the latter case this means less exposure to threatening stimuli liable to exceed what is already a high tension threshold. These factors are of critical importance to the understanding of the notions of *psychological survival* and *variability of psychological needs,* terms which are used here in connection with the experience of mental comfort or discomfort and the maintenance of psychological equilibrium, or disequilibrium and possible breakdown – or even death (Selye 1974:50): to survival or not.

Later, this process of *dynamic change in APM-A* will be defined as being a fundamental element in social, cultural, and artistic, as well as individual style. Through its interaction with existing schemata, gained as a result of already processed information, it can be seen to control the mental and, in part, physical position from which the most basic associations, comparisons, and decisions about match and mismatch take place. However, before this can be explained fully it is necessary to address certain remaining issues in the light of some highly relevant findings:

The issues are these:
a) how the relationship between attention, perception, memory, and action may have changed half a million years ago to produce the possible beginnings of art and technology;

b) the possible effects of social as well as environmental changes and demands on hominid functioning;

c) the relationship between physical and psychological survival;

d) how characteristics of attention relate to characteristics of behaviour; and

e) the relationship of the two processes corresponding to behaviourist and Gestalt views of learning identified in postulate 6 (Appendix 2) and Gear (1987), to other major concepts and principles which have been, and are being, introduced.

The findings in question are of four kinds, all highly relevant to arousal-behaviour interaction and the concept of tuning; that is, variability in sensitivity to change, and to psychological survival.

The first finding derives from data originally furnished by Yerkes and Dodson (1908), who drew attention to the interactive effects of task difficulty, arousal, and performance, and established the idea of *optimal levels of arousal*. Although the Yerkes–Dodson Law which they established has not so far been confirmed by other arousal theorists, it has been supported by Broadhurst (1957), who also showed that the optimal level of motivation is lower given a difficult task rather than an easy one.

Arousal theorists are responsible, however, for positing and researching the second important idea, that of *optimal levels of stimulation*. The fact that human beings suffer anxiety and even hallucinate when deprived of sensory stimulation is now well-established (Zubek 1969). Consistent with this is the suggestion by arousal theorists that we are *stimulus seekers* as well as being the *stimulus reducers*, which theorists such as Freud and Hull, in particular, are famous for postulating. But the view of the latter of the relationship between the level of tension experienced and consequent benefit, or not, to the organism, was entirely simple and linear: behaviour was always seen to be reducing drive to an optimal level – of zero.

It should be noted that Berlyne appears to have pinpointed the problem at the crux of the drive-reduction–stimulus-seeking controversy by acknowledging a somewhat higher degree of complexity in the relationship between internal and external events (see Weiner 1980:135). He suggests that, although it may appear that individuals are seeking stimulation in order to increase tension[1] (to an optimal level), in reality such behaviour represents an attempt to decrease arousal (to a minimal level) because too low a level of stimulation, as well as too high a level, creates tension.

Interestingly, too, Berlyne concludes that stimuli of intermediate complexity are most attractive – a point to be taken up later, but of course quite consistent with the arguments contained in the previous chapter (see also postulate 9, Appendix 2).

The third kind of finding has to do with *organization of behaviour* and arousal, which was empirically researched by Hebb (see Figure 1), who actually described behaviour as varying from 'alert and attentive' to 'disorganised and without appropriate control'.

Figure 1 Organization of behaviour related to degree of non-specific arousal, adapted from Hebb (1955) and reproduced from Weiner (1980:130)

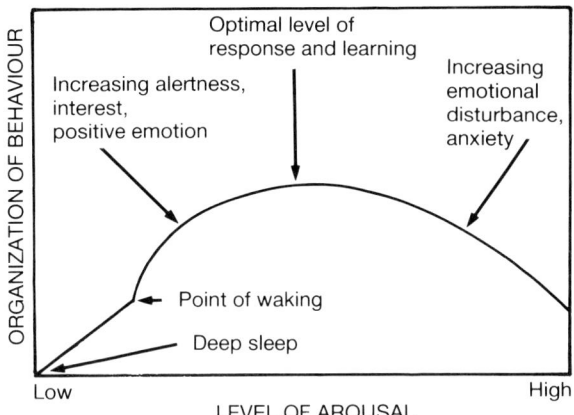

Apparently much less well-known, or used, is Luria's identification of the importance of this dimension as early as 1932. Devoting the first chapter of *The Nature of Human Conflicts* to 'The problems of disorganisation of behaviour', he points out that 'Organisation and disorganisation of human behaviour, conditions, laws and forms appear thus as the most important problems of psychobiology' (Luria 1976:8), and relates the dimension to 'affective processes' and 'levels of excitation' (ibid.:178, 179).

Malmo (see Figure 2) also relates arousal to performance, and the diagram reproduced below shows the well-known inverted U shape produced by their correlates.

Welford, on the other hand, relates demand and performance, but in a discussion of his findings along with the findings of others, Cox (1978: 15–17) emphasizes the relationship of demand to stress. He also emphasizes the fact that Welford's argument is that submaximal performance is indicative of stress, which can exist because of too high *or* too low a level of demand. Further, Cox goes on to discuss the negative effects of stress induced by excess or insufficient 'input of stimuli' on homeostasis.

Our fourth class of finding has to do with *externalization of neuronal excitation,* and again, research by the Soviet neurosurgeon Luria provided very early indirect evidence of this phenomenon, as a fundamental organic reaction to affect. His methodology in researching disorganization and

Figure 2 Arousal related to performance, adapted from Malmo (1966) by Weiner (1980:132)

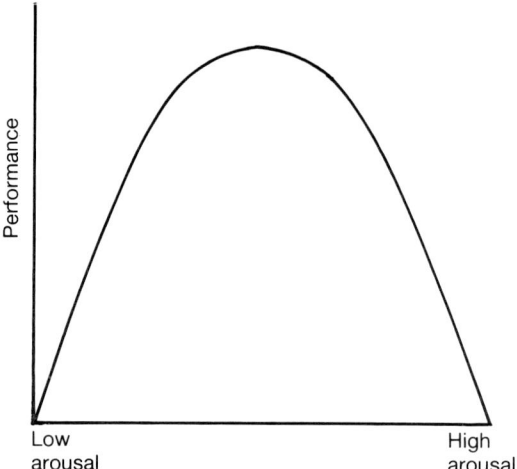

Low
arousal

High
arousal

control of human behaviour rested on his belief that 'every marked affective disorganised character of the central process does not remain without influence on the structure of the compounded motor reaction'; and that 'differences in the neurodynamic structure of the central process are reflected in the evident structure of the motor curve' (Luria 1976:24).

We can best begin to make use of these particular contributions of Yerkes and Dodson, Berlyne, Luria, Malmo, and Welford by first of all placing them together within a meaningful framework.

This can be done by offering an APM-A interpretation of the data, whilst bearing in mind the relevance of the two kinds of processing identified in postulate 6 (Appendix 2) and Gear 1987, as taking place simultaneously, together with the fact that in the last chapter these *scanning* and *focusing* functions were associated with SNS and PNS activity respectively (p. 20). We must also bear in mind the suggestion above that it is the interaction of SNS and PNS activity which provides for the most effective concentration of neurotransmitters, and subsequent neuronal firing necessary for the sustained processing of information to take place. Such activity, it has been postulated, is stimulated by consciously or unconsciously recognized *manageable* threat and/or overt or covert promise of identifiable reward. In either case *arousal becomes organized and specific,* rather than *disorganized and general,* and a high degree of focus is effected, whilst scanning activity is minimized.

If this position is adopted, the fact that optimal levels of arousal are lower, given a difficult task, and higher for an easier one, can now be interpreted as follows: obviously, the more difficult the test is perceived to be the more likely it becomes that concomitant anxiety will raise arousal beyond an optimal level, thereby activating the fight/flight (stress) response and shifting arousal to a level at which it can no longer remain specific and highly concentrated. This orientation response, or what might be more aptly called an *expression of a need for orientation,* produces heightened awareness, distractability, and at least some change in motor functions, the extent of which will depend on intensity of affect and consequent increases in energy resources.

In sum, a degree of flexibility and a state of preparedness become available to the organism to provide conditions which are obviously highly adaptive for escape from danger, or seizure of any other maintenance or propagation activity (all depend on similar resources: see p. 20), but the same state, according to Yerkes and Dodson, Berlyne, Luria, Malmo, and Welford, is not necessarily appropriate for the execution of specific skills which demand longer spells of concentration, and more careful and finer motor control.

To take the case of the easier task, for which Yerkes and Dodson and later Broadhurst indicated the need for a higher level of arousal; a possible explanation could be that the easier task actually demands a higher level of motivation in the subject for interest to be maintained because the task is intrinsically lacking in challenge, which within the terms of APM-A theory also makes it intrinsically less stimulating (arousing). The implication is that low arousal could allow a counter-productive over-focusing of attention. In this case action would be slowed down as a result of the individual not being stimulated to move on to successive stages of the task. Sluggishness may be displayed, as the subject is unable to sustain interest because attention becomes static and action rigid, rather than fluid. Disorganization of function and accompanying inefficiency can therefore be seen to be a possible outcome of under- *or* over-arousal.

A similar interpretation can be applied to the need for optimal levels of stimulation, but in this case stimulation of too high or too low a level are both likely to be experienced as threatening as 'expected' demands on attention are either not met, or represent a change beyond the range of the species norm. In either case (of too much or too little stimulation) some degree of disorientation is likely to lead to anxiety and general arousal, which, for all of the reasons already given, may render concentration on even routine tasks difficult to maintain.

The APM-A explanation offered for the Yerkes–Dodson Law also applies to Hebb's well-known arousal and performance curve, but care has to be taken here not to equate organization with focus, as is very often done. Concentrating the mind does not have precisely the same meaning as focusing attention. As has already been pointed out, concentration derives from an optimal dominance of focus over scanning, to the effect that disorganization (or need for orientation) could be a possible outcome of either over- *or* under-involvement of focusing *or* scanning activity. It could imply too much rigidity, rather than the more obvious and common interpretation of too much fluidity. Therefore, use of the term 'organization' has to acknowledge and imply (1) the need for an *optimal* relationship between focusing and scanning, and (2) the fact already emphasized: that maximum efficiency requires a capacity for *flexibility* of attention and behaviour, as well as *control*, in response to demand. Acceptance of (1) and (2) also offers an explanation of why different tasks are performed best at different levels of arousal. Clearly, the *nature of the task,* as well as its difficulty, places a demand for *more or less fluidity of attention.*

The relevance here of Luria's early position on the relationship between affective processes and motor reactions, and the possibility of extending the APM-A construct to include behaviour, is fairly obvious, but his linking of organization–disorganization with affect and with motor reactions will be seen to be particularly apt to the dynamic model to be developed in Chapters 3 and 4.

From everything that has been said up to this point it can be seen that the kinds of attention, perception, and memory (lasting or not) that we experience, and our behavioural responses, do all change as arousal levels change, and within a range which allows some degree of predictability; in addition, not only are there measurable differences between individuals (Luria 1976:44), but the hypothesis being developed is that such differences can be described as *differences in tension thresholds* and that these thresholds constitute the major identifiable sources of difference in efficiency of function, and in modes of function, within and between individuals; differences which conventionally go under headings such as IQ, cognitive style, or personality. It will also be argued that the thresholds in question are a major source of difference between social groups, communities, and cultures.

It is now possible to consider in a little more detail what is likely to have happened half a million years ago to change evolving man's perceptions of what consititued worthwhile activity, and how he came to apply his evolving mental powers to the production of the beauty and technology incorporated into the Acheulian axe. We can even hypothesize what these evolving powers were and try to offer some description of this capacity of mind; in fact, we can boldly attempt a description of what it was – and is.

The case to be put is that the greatest change in thinking was promoted by a shift to *higher-order needs.*[2] But such is the case with higher-order needs – and most other kinds of need, for that matter – that they are most easily identified when not being met, and that, even then, the danger always exists that if they are of an unconscious kind,[3] as orientational needs most often are, the need itself may never be accurately identified, as identification of a need very often remains incidental to its fulfilment.

The view being expressed here is that the manifestations of a psychological need – as mental discomfort – are most likely to be attributed to a source for which some prescriptive form of satisfaction already exists. As with everything else we don't profess to know anything about, we tend simply to know what we like. But the point must be made, and will be taken up again in Chapter 4, that saying that we do what pleases us is not of course the same as saying that what pleases us is necessarily in our own best interests – as we all find out to our cost at some time or other.

So it is likely to have been half a million years ago. At whatever stage higher-order needs did evolve, those who survived to procreate will have identified them unconsciously and in a manner incidental to the fulfilment of those needs. We can only surmise by the successful adaptation of those who did survive, and by reference to changes in their activity for which we have evidence, what those more complex needs are likely to have been. It may be noted in passing that the word 'mind' has connotations of both 'memory' and 'concern' (for example, for threats, hazards and so on), and it is being argued that millions of years of harsh conditions resulted in the development of the human mind to a stage of sensitivity at which it required its own means of defence.

Apparent contradictions are seen to have increased as the orientation response itself, the very *source* of defence, became so sensitive as to produce a new kind of vulnerability – as defence systems of any kind are apt to do. Eventually, resources of mental activity allowed the instrument of mind to become (partly) perceivable to itself; its manifestations became recognizable to the extent that it became possible consciously to mind, that is, to watch out for self, and eventually to reflect upon its own process. But as a mind with an acquired ability to perceive and define new kinds of match and mismatch in the form of changes and inconsistencies to do with self and others, it became a threat indeed.

Optimal levels of arousal, and consequently, resorting back to our earlier argument (p. 28), optimal levels of stimulation during the Pleistocene, would not, for all of the reasons put forward so far, have been optimal levels of arousal after the climax of the Ice Age; and as the closed feedback loop of SNS activity takes time to settle back to functioning at basal rate, even under phenomenologically changing conditions, it would not be unreasonable to believe that a steady increase in sensitivity and range of function over millions of years – constituting *species learning* – might take millions of years to (species) 'unlearn'.

During more stable times then, it can be assumed that as a species no longer optimally aroused, we would have suffered some decrement in efficiency of performance. In addition to this factor placing us at risk physically, as a species we would also have been subject to feelings of what could be called 'primeval boredom' and 'anxiety', as a result of finding ourselves tuned to more change and stimulation from the environment than was currently available. Certainly this hypothesis follows if we are to take heed of the findings of those such as Yerkes and Dodson, Hebb, Malmo, Welford, and Cox, mentioned above, to name but a few.

The full significance, indeed potential horror, of this situation may be appreciated by imagining a species-wide manifestation of what might today go under the label of the bored housewife syndrome (be the 'wife' female or male) or more topically, that attributed to unemployed youth, without there being possible resort to alcohol, Librium, voluntary work, or government training schemes. However, that is of course not to say that such tuning cannot emanate from a whole variety of sources, and even, as will become clearer in the next chapter, be congenital.

The postulated benefit to the 'at risk' SNS type becoming, say, a training scheme participant or a voluntary worker is that he or she is more likely to survive psychologically in modern western society by externalizing, or otherwise reducing, excessive neuronal excitation to manageable levels and, therefore, as will be explained, is also more likely to survive physically. It would not seem to be idle conjecture, or even an unreasonable leap into fantasy, to suggest that similarly, the hominid whose intercourse and consequent expenditure of ideas and energy was of a productive, purposeful, and socially acceptable kind, was the least likely to succumb to self-destruction either directly or indirectly. He would have been less likely to display sheer ineptitude, clumsiness, or pugnacity, *or* to risk the ire of kith and kin or fellow tribesmen by exercising his excess energies and new potential for low cunning, in order to indulge his own primitive appetites, whilst threatening the security of others.

It is suggested that the axe-maker – nay, master axe-maker and decorator – was amongst the best equipped for survival, in any sense, during the transition from a species of fully occupied physical survivors to the social and cultural beings we most like to think ourselves to be.

The associations being made between artist and social deviant, and between the Acheulian culture and so-called 'western civilization', and 'leisure problems' then and now, are entirely deliberate, and will be returned to. But it must not be thought that what is being said here is that Neanderthal man or Cro-Magnon man, or any other early representative of the history of man, instinctively created culture, as the earliest known form of escape attempt in the sense of Cohen and Taylor (1978).

What is being suggested is that an extremely complex development took place as an outcome of increased mental activity and realization of social dependence, and that cultural activity was an incidental effect of the intercourse principle at work amongst those having developed (or developing) purpose:[4] purpose as a result of intercourse using skills learnt by steady practice, with the familiar tools to hand, or, acquired by imitating significant others. By 40,000 years ago these skills could also have included story-telling as well as making and doing, and all would have had the effect of reducing otherwise potentially maladaptive levels of SNS activity by using concomitant resources of mental and physical energy.

Germaine Greer (1971:64) expresses some of our intuitive understanding of these processes, when she remarks that energy which is not used creatively has self-destructive potential; and although he doesn't attempt to define or analyse it, Anthony Storr (1970:12) also acknowledges a common root of aggression and creativity.

Obviously, there is no ultimate test of theory involving the evolution of mind. We have no access to earlier minds, and no chance of finding even fragments of early electro-chemical activity. A theory can stand or fall only by virtue of its explanatory power: first, in terms of its capacity to accommodate what evidence still exists of minds no longer existent, in the form of artefacts produced as behavioural responses to events, needs, or fears, or as responses to materials which could be worked to express ideas *per se*. Second, plausibility has to be judged in terms of how consistent such theory is with what we know, so far, about our present stage of evolution of mind. But theory which can unify past and present stages of evolution should also offer new insights into our understanding of the present, and afford some prediction of possible outcomes of present actions. Certainly, evaluation of the present and prediction of future events by reference to the past has been the way in which we have most successfully dealt with information, as a species, so far; and after all, the application of basic organic principles at micro and macro levels of organization is crucial to the subject matter of this book.

By the formulation of theory which concerns itself with what we have been – by tracing the lead back, as it were – it should be possible to judge our present view of ourselves as valid or not. And with yet another reference to micro–macro parallelism – this time in connection with ontogeny and phylogeny – it is argued that the need to achieve self-knowledge and a sense of identity as a species may be just as vital to our mental health, and ultimately to our survival, as the achievement of a sense of identity, independence, and self-confidence are to the individual:[5] another point to be amplified in later chapters.

Without a unifying theory of human nature, policies and programmes of action and, in particular and most vitally, those to do with education (which represents our most direct form of action on the species' mind) can be evaluated only rather primitively, on a trial and error basis; rather as a teenager in search of identity must experiment, often at high risk, until he or she finds out what kinds of action and experience best suit – that is, are most adaptive for him or her. The more sophisticated and technically able we become as a species, however, the more dangerously high is the possible price of error and the more crucially important it becomes to identify our positive potential, but, above all, we must recognize our extremely wide range of psychological variability in order for any very helpful view of ourselves to emerge.

Unfortunately, as will be explained, our orientation and our belongingness needs seem to be so high (Maslow 1970:43–5), and generalization such a robust phenomenon, that the acknowledgement of individual differences in function – outside academe, that is – appears to present one of our greatest perceptual difficulties.

The interpretation of data and events being offered reflects and reinforces the notion that positive *and* negative human potential have evolved in concert *and* in antagonism – when we are using the terms 'positive' and 'negative' to refer directly to SNS and PNS activity, rather than to the concepts of creativity and destruction; in which case it is also possible to add that they will have evolved in direct proportion to each other. Thus a *positive–negative* dimension may apply either to simple *activity–inactivity*, which correlates most closely with SNS–PNS interaction, or to *creativity–destruction*, in which instance both poles are being ascribed here to SNS dominance.

The relationship between the two dimensions just identified, and what we perceive as positivism or negativism, is complex, but can be defined by regarding the former as implying *action or no action*, and the latter as referring to *kinds of action*. Complications arise, it is suggested, because we can approach *or* avoid in at least two different ways. Approach has already been described as involving different possible kinds of physical, social, or intellectual intercourse, depending on the degree, if any, of perceived threat (pp. 29–30), whereas avoidance may mean no action *or* flight.

2.2 Pleasure and pain of another kind

If what has been said about speeding up of responses and a capacity for the restraint of impulse evolving together is correct, then the effect will have been to produce an increase in the entire range of autonomic activity. This will have occurred as a result of increased environmental demands for much greater flexibility of action, together with a demand for more sustained attention and vigilance, both of which must have accompanied the alternating glacial and inter-glacial phases of the fickle Pleistocene: the Ice Age which began three million years ago and climaxed a little over half a million years ago.

During this time, both hunting activity (p. 26) and the incidental effects of scarcity of food, such as the need for sharing, the need for a home base, and coincidental more complex social intercourse, will have afforded conditions for our very early ancestors to develop much richer conceptual possibilities. Affect and learning will have been extended to furnish a social memory, as well as a skill memory; but whereas it is commonly acknowledged that mental development took place during the Pleistocene, to the extent that man is said to have 'acquired' his brain during that period (having 'acquired' his body during the Pliocene), it took place relatively slowly, compared to what has been described as a comparative 'brain explosion' (Wilson 1980:19) during the last 500,000 years.

Growing social dependence, individual learning, and gradual freeing from stereotyped species-wide reactive responses will have served to increase complexity of attentional and behavioural activity, and to offer choice from alternative interpretations of given situations. But such phenomenological choice and decision making would not only have allowed greater variability of response *within* the individual, and more variability *between* individuals, with the acquisition of schemata (see Oatley 1978:166), it would also have produced *Homo sapiens*, the cultural being. Formerly selected *for* and relatively *passive*, he will have acquired the ability *to* select, and to make *active* decisions, in a limited sort of way, at first.

The earliest sign of cultural activity was the ubiquitous Acheulian axe, first evidenced 1,500,000 years ago, but whose zenith coincided with the relaxing of climatic conditions and, relevantly, other qualitative advances. These included inventing, designing, and experimenting, as well as indulgence in more wandering and exploratory behaviour (Ardrey 1977:144): all of which are entirely consistent with the kinds of human intercourse which, it has been suggested, high levels of SNS activity promote.

Increased mental activity, bequeathed by harsh times now relaxed, or more precisely, mental and physical resources in excess of current demands which could not simply be 'switched off', will have yielded all kinds of potential, some of which (as has already been intimated) will have been distinctly threatening. Alongside greater access to stored information, enabling easier recognition of situations met before, and the possibility of more effective use of such knowledge in order to *make sense* of physical and social changes – that is, to be able to *construct* reality and generally *create* a safer seeming world – as a result of access to more facile classification and organization other significant changes will have taken place. These will have included a greater capacity for prediction of (possibly frightening) alternative outcomes of own actions and the actions of others and an ominously wider scope for misinterpretation.

A capacity for constructing our own realities will clearly have opened up many possibilities of a not necessarily adaptive kind, as the families of the around 1 per cent of the general population who become schizophrenic, and therefore dwell in their own 'unreal' worlds, would doubtless testify

(Tsuang 1982:23). Opportunity for the exercise of choice by no means always makes life easier, at any level of organization.

The inverted U-shaped graph produced by correlates of arousal and performance – and all we know about arousal as a non-unitary concept – tell us that no simple or linear relationship exists between levels of arousal and levels of *consciousness* any more than simple and linear relationships exist between arousal and any other aspect of psychology; but nevertheless, a complex relationship does exist, and it can be hypothesized. Arousal and consciousness *do* correlate at their most primitive levels – at the point of waking and sleeping, that is – but increase in arousal level is not necessarily or simply accompanied by 'expansion' of consciousness or 'heightening' of *awareness* – or, in our terms, increased scanning activity. In fact, the changes which do occur will eventually be described as moving from focusing to scanning, and back to focusing.

In evolutionary terms, it is suggested that emergent *Homo sapiens* was no longer just sufficiently aroused to be aware, or conscious of external or internal changes promoting reactions to ensure physical survival; we became sufficiently active in comparison-making to be able to become conscious of self. Our limited capacity of attention was no longer limited to physical survival alone. Consciousness could now extend to our own activities and reactions, and to our social relationships; to provide awareness of their appropriateness or inappropriateness – *before* it was too late, that is. We became able to evaluate critically our own performance, and ultimately, to perfect physical and social skills until it was possible to select from a repertoire of possible behaviours. The effects of reduced external physical demands, whilst physical and mental resources for activity remained at the same level, made us the essentially active beings we are: decision-makers, doers, actors, choosers, and therefore (in making selections from alternatives), unavoidably, stylists.

The model of mind being developed is still an *attentional* model, and, except for the fact that it would lead to an unacceptable amount of repetition of the same word, all that has been said could be said without using the terms 'consciousness' or 'awareness' at all, if it were not of course that an attempt is being made to elucidate that very fact.

Mind, consciousness, and awareness are all viewed here as manifestations of arousal; all of which can be described in terms of how attention is given or gained. Later, the point will be made that those other concepts yet to be discussed – motivation, intelligence, personality, and cognitive style – can also be described within the same context (and with reference to tension thresholds: see postulate 14, Appendix 2, and p. 40). But for the sake of clarity a diagrammatic explanation of the relationship between the various concepts being used here could be helpful (see Figure 3).

Essentially, it is suggested that in evolutionary terms, the most

Figure 3 A unidimensional* representation of the relationship between key concepts of mind employed within the APM-A framework (see also Figures 66 and 68 (Appendix 2))

UNCONSCIOUS SCANNING & FOCUS		CONSCIOUS SCANNING & FOCUS
Increasing tendency towards highly individual interpretations of events and/or increase in physical activity (see Chaps. 3 & 4)		
Creativity – given 'purpose' (identified problem) & medium	—— IMAGINATION —— anticipation, flexibility of thought & action ⟁	creativity – given 'purpose' & medium
Increase in arousal & increase in orientation needs to include greater anticipation, more future planning (given 'purpose') & anxiety		
unconscious & sub-threshold selection from alternatives	—— AWARENESS —— use of expectancy and prediction ⟁	consciousness of choice & selection from alternatives
Increase in arousal & in sub-threshold *and* conscious scanning activity		
as species learning	—— REACTIVITY —— ⟁	as a result of individual learning (conditioning)
Increase in arousal & in resources for coping with *current* internal and external demands		

(left margin, bottom to top) UNCONSCIOUS ATTENTION/PERCEPTION/MEMORY

(right margin, bottom to top) CONSCIOUS ATTENTION/PERCEPTION/MEMORY

environmental change

⟁

LOW AROUSAL

LEVELS OF 'MINDING'
relevant to phylogenetic, ontogenetic, and
phenomenological changes in arousal

*Not, for instance, taking into account the inverted U shape created by correlates of efficiency and arousal, and not taking into account the different kinds of arousal identified in Chapter 3.

significant changes in consciousness concerned attention to others and attention to self, producing awareness of social and internal events in *addition* to attention already being given to, or gained by, the pleasures and pains to be derived from coping with the complexities of the physical world.

In the discussion of new sources of pleasures and pain which is to follow, a very important, but usually overlooked, distinction should become evident: the crucially important difference between *hedonistic motivation* and *hedonistic manifestations* of motivation.

Although usually taken to imply so, hedonistic motivation is not necessarily the same as gaining pleasure for self *only,* as has already been pointed out. The incidental effects of seeking psychological comfort may very often be apparent in the form of what we call altruistic behaviour, or even self-sacrifice. It should become clearer that such a view is not simply an expression of hardened cynicism. It can be substantiated.

Awareness of similarities and differences between self and others will not by any means always have made a positive contribution to early man's psychological comfort or development. Such knowledge as he acquired this way will have offered potential for self-growth *or* self-destruction; of a psychological and physiological, if not what we commonly refer to as a physical kind. These new and highly complex sources of pain as well as pleasure had to be both acknowledged and dealt with, so that homeostatic mechanisms had to include the maintenance of psychological as well as physical equilibrium.

2.3 Reassurance and justification

As climatic conditions changed and became relatively more stable, and mental activity moved beyond the requirements of species learning and reactivity, and beyond the requirements of individual learning for the satisfaction of physical needs only, minding (p. 41), it is being argued, became mind: an entity in itself. What is more, mind eventually became sufficiently active and complex to upset routine, to pose awkward questions, which at any level of information-processing, phenomenological or philosophical, or indeed, at any level of human organization, individual or societal, is sufficient to disorganize attention and behaviour to some extent, unless reorganization is quickly seen to be possible – that is, an alternative goal comes into view.

It has already been suggested that new sources of pleasure were invented, or rather recognized – by some, at least – as a result of various kinds of intercourse, and with the effect of externalizing what had become excessive SNS activity, 500,000 years ago and onwards. But certainly, by 35,000 years ago Cro-Magnon man would again have been facing new threats to be coped with.

Greater awareness (one of the terms we use for the kind of electro-chemical activity under discussion when it is apparently working efficiently on incoming information, or *imagination,* as we are apt to call it) will have been, and remains, an incidental but inherent threat to the integrity of concepts of self: the very self which the same activity in fact furnished.

Equally significantly, greater awareness will also have provided a more directly perceivable threat to survival; a threat experienced as a reflected view of self, as awareness of what others *might* be thinking. *Orientation needs* will therefore have increased to include many new kinds of feedback requirements and, consequently, awareness of, or attention to, new kinds of change concerning how the genus *Homo* felt about self: conclusions arrived at, for the most part, by sensing the reactions of others. Crucial sources of reassurance will have been his closest social bonds, threat to which, Jane Lancaster (1975:21) tells us, evokes similar reactions to those evoked by threats to life itself.

From what we know about how the mind functions today, it can be assumed with confidence that with growing dependence on the co-operation and, therefore, esteem of others, need for reassurance will have grown and extended far beyond the comparatively very simple kind of feedback which was already necessary from the physical environment. In short, as a result of increasing dependence on others, we will have needed to know that we were not on our own, and further, that those who were within striking distance felt friendly towards us. The absence of blunt instruments will no longer have been enough.

Just as we needed to communicate – and justify – our own changes in motivation, we needed to understand, or at least not to perceive threat where none existed, in the changing motivations of others. In addition, we needed tactile experience, or what anthropologists call rather charmingly 'contact comfort' with those closest of all. Nevertheless, evolving language must have added considerably to what must doubtless have been a huge repertoire of non-verbal communication, used to justify, reassure, and convey non-violent intent. A similar, but much more complex and covert, repertoire of communication for the purposes of reassurance and justification exists today, but it extends to very much more sophisticated social conventions than, for instance, Cro-Magnon man had to familiarize self with and choose from, and includes an almost incredible range of possible alternative 'uniforms'.

As Maslow obviously recognizes, but those Social Learning Theorists who believe that they have identified a form of learning which is not dependent on reward clearly do not, belongingness and acceptance are indeed rewards in themselves. Most of the time such needs remain fairly well-hidden at an unconscious level, certainly whilst being met, which is probably why they, and other needs being labelled here 'orientation needs', are grossly underestimated, and why Maslow (1970) places them in at least second position.

However, just as a whole field of psychology devoted to illusion offers indirect evidence for the need for a degree of consistency between our internal models and the external 'reality' of our physical surroundings, in order for us to be able to enjoy the security of some measure of predictability, a considerable weight of research offers indirect evidence of similar needs concerning our social and mental lives.

Milburn and Watman (1981), for instance, identify the enormous range of subtlety of threat we perceive in our relationships with others. Goffman too, on the presentation of self in everyday life (1971), describes in detail the kinds of 'performances' we put on, and the impression management we employ, which could be said to be orientational devices, to ensure our acceptability to others. Similarly, on the question of stigma (1968), he draws attention to the personal and social effects of disfiguration. The effects he describes are disorientational to the extent of creating mental and physical disequilibrium. What Goffman reports could be interpreted as meaning that the disfigured, and those in contact with them, react to a state not just perceived as identifiably different, but different (that is, unfamiliar) beyond the point of fascination (p. 28), to be perceived as unmanageable threat, with all of its potential for disrupting and disorganizing accepted patterns of behaviour.

On the potency of threats that we actually pose to ourselves, Sackeim and Gur (1978:139–97) have provided very striking evidence of the aversive nature of self-confrontation with their findings of increased arousal and disorientation as subjects perceived aspects of themselves they did not like. Further, they concluded that self-deception is an experimentally real phenomenon which they linked to hemisphericality.

The biggest single field of psychological research and theory which addresses questions of orientation, though, must be that devoted to cognitive consistency. The tendency for us to seek consistency is sufficiently robust for it to have become the subject of a number of theories, the best-known being Festinger's (1962); but it is posited here that a great deal of confusion arises amongst consistency theorists for the very reasons that earlier applications of evolutionary theory lacked plausibility (p. 13).

In addition, the concept of consistency is rarely analysed to the extent of teasing out dimensions such as conscious–unconscious, or other complexities to do with questions of dynamics or levels of organization (Gear 1985:104). It is also suggested that to differentiate between the concepts of consistency and other related concepts, such as expectation and predictability, would help considerably to alleviate some of the confusion in the field. The biggest error of all, though, viewed from the position being developed, is a tacit assumption that because we find inconsistency aversive, we necessarily seek *absolute* consistency: this is of course reminiscent of the similar mental trap identified – separately and inadvertently – by Freud and Hull, in believing that we are happiest when stimulation is at zero level.

To be able to make sense of theories of cognitive consistency, just as it has been shown to be with theories of attention and learning (Gear 1987), a much broader canvas is required in order to obtain the possibility of seeing specifics in relation to one another. Only then can analytic taxonomies be adequately constructed.

Abelson *et al.* tell us that 'as originally presented, the various consistency theory formulations included the implicit assumption of a basic tendency of the human organism to maintain a state of consistency or equilibrium within the cognitive system' (1968:301). Usefully, this quotation embodies an assumption which identifies the major difference between consistency theory and the homeostatic theory being developed. According to this homeostatic theory, the flaw in their original 'formulations', from what Abelson says, is that they appear to equate consistency and equilibrium, when consistency *may* or *may not* be the same thing as equilibrium, depending not only on individual differences (Luria 1976:71), but also on the significance to the individual of the source of the inconsistency. And obviously, just as there are *degrees* of inconsistency, there are also situations in which inconsistency is likely to contain more inherent threat than others.

A high degree of match or fit between the merely half-expected – or even the deliberately hoped-for or predicted – and the actual, can be a source of relief, or extreme joy even, as either literally or figuratively we achieve a goal as a result of having to overcome obstacles of varying levels of difficulty: alternatively, it might just constitute a totally unconscious source of mental comfort, as would be the case if the inconsistency in question were perceived as wholly devoid of personal threat. Obviously, inconsistency observed in the behaviour of a father, mother, husband, wife, or any other significant other, contains more potential threat than something perceived as a trifle odd, or unusual, in the relationship between a couple of strangers.

Of key importance, is that any inconsistency – or 'conflict', in Luria's language – which we do perceive can either be explained, or remains on an impersonal and therefore, usually, not critically threatening level. But in cases where we are likely to be personally affected to a high degree, the explanation has to be watertight if the problem is not to continue to be a source of mental discomfort.

A cognitive threat deriving from inconsistency becomes manageable immediately a non-threatening plausible explanation or rationalization can be furnished. Even some of the more subtle threats, of the kind identified by Milburn and Watman (1981), for instance, are likely to become at least more manageable (to the reasonably self-confident, at least) when they are understood. The *need to be able to explain* what is going on around us, physically and socially, and, most importantly, to be able to explain ourselves (our own behaviour and experience) to ourselves – for which most, alas, still resort to magico-religious beliefs, folklore, myth, or legend – is being regarded here as a basic orientational need: in fact, our prime orientation need.

Such an analysis is seen to offer far greater explanatory power than consistency theory, for instance, because the need for consistency, which has to be qualified anyway – to be described as 'a need for a sufficiently high degree of consistency to be able to make non-threatening sense of our perceptions' – is considered here to be only one of a range of orientation needs.

It may appear simplistic to say that the scale of this urge to be able to explain, arising from a need to understand – wanting to know and its accompanying need for expression, which have been described as being manifested as curiosity and exploration when external demands are low – depends on the mental and physical resources (energies) of the individual as well as, crucially, how wide a range of 'problems' a person is exposed to; but manifestly, the theory behind the statement is not simple.

At macro level, it has been hypothesized that the Acheulian culture, and in particular the Acheulian axe, marked a shift to higher-order needs. Interestingly, Cox (1978:v) posits the idea that civilized man has moved to higher-order needs than primitive societies, and this suggestion is certainly consistent with the, as yet, fairly oblique correlations which have been made between stress, levels of consciousness, and changing needs; and the fact that higher-order needs vary between individuals (see Chapter 3) as well as between cultures and societies is axiomatic to the entire APM-A thesis.

In rather more extreme terms, which Chapters 3 and 4 should serve to explain, it is also postulated that for some, orientation needs become priority needs, both at the phenomenological level – when it will be argued that they are priority needs for all of us anyway – and at more complex and more gross levels of experience which demand understanding and expression.

It also has to be added, that alongside the *need to know,* a development wholly consistent with human paradox took place: the evolution of a *need not to know*. Already we have noted that mental activity in excess of the requirements of external and internal demands allows a phenomenon usually only observable at levels of organization at which politics apply and, most obviously, acknowledged by governments world-wide: that thinking, with its well-known capacity for upsetting routine, is dangerous. It might be said that information management is not just something done by the PR man, governments, or the press, or even just something we do to each other. We do it to ourselves all of the time. Should potential threat be subconsciously perceived as *un*manageable in its present form, then it has to be managed in a different form.

Access to what cannot be understood – the inexplicable, the undefinable, or the indescribable – unless the superlative applies to 'wonder' or 'beauty' (as responses to intense versions of things not entirely unfamiliar or unpleasant) can upset individual psychological equilibrium, just as it can upset mass psychological equilibrium. Therefore the retention of a capacity for unconscious processing, for the repression of threatening information, will have been as adaptive as those other well-known manifestations of self-deceit, namely, rationalization, attribution, and projection: all aspects of intelligent defence rather obviously dependent on emotion.

The move from stereotyped, species-wide FAPs (see p. 31) and the achievement of greater flexibility of behaviour allowed sufficient disorganization of previously established behaviour patterns for adaptive reorganization to take place. Previously a species phenomenon, rather than one characteristic of individuals, variability became part of individual development and behaviour, to provide the means of individual selection described earlier.

At first, greater flexibility of behaviour will simply have allowed the learning of adaptive skills but, later, such a facility will have begun to pose threats. Certainly, by the time we were equipped with self-awareness and language, it will have become most adaptive for new possible explanations to be arrived at before old ones were broken down. It must have become vitally important, in fact, for us to *refuse* to know things, on those occasions when we could not classify or rationalize new information in terms of what we already knew: a principle which obviously applies, once more, at all levels of information processing, simple or complex; whether with reference to the smallest detail of our physical environment or to entire belief systems. We dissent at our peril, which might imply a risk of personal disequilibrium or persecution by others, depending on whether the doubts we acknowledge or express are about the evidence of our own senses, or about the accepted wisdom of our particular cultures. Clearly, Watson's frequency and recency principle (Watson 1919) *does* apply at cognitive levels, in that predominating conditions shape our perceptions, but that is of course only a very small part of the story.

The need for retention of cognitive organization, either as formulated aims or goals at micro level, or in the form of belief systems at macro level, in order to perform effectively, highlights a wealth of meaning hidden in the indispensable little phrase 'in order to'. No action is possible without its preceding organizational phase, even though we may not consciously experience that phase for what it is. We are putting things 'in order' 'to do' something or other, all of the time.

2.4 Mind over matter

As J. Z. Young points out (1978:10), it is the essence of all living things to maintain integrity, and here it is added that it is also an observable phenomenon at all levels of organization of natural life, and according to certain laws and rhythms including that which is known as the life-cycle, that there exists a tendency to self-destruct – mostly, and reassuringly, at certain predictable stages of change within the organism.

Our inclination, in the late twentieth century, to ignore death until actually confronted with it provides an example of our need for long (even lifelong) familiarization with concepts, as well as with objects embodying unmanageable threat, before we come to regard them as non-threatening. Even motivation theories to date, except Freud's, have consistently ignored it.

Self-destruction in the human being can obviously take many more forms than a variety of well-known suicide techniques, or even the less well-known prescriptions of the Voluntary Euthanasia Society, and, in common with every other aspect of mental activity discussed so far, it can be unconscious as well as conscious. It does, however, always result from loss of integrity of one kind or another, but in addition to the kind of 'mechanical' risks to which the entire species is prone, let alone the life-cycle, the most dangerous form of loss of integrity is the kind which has been recognized since time immemorial, and which is freely described as 'loss of will' or 'loss of faith' or 'hope'. But because such terms are surrounded by all sorts of mystique, they are not often regarded as particularly fruitful areas of research, and are certainly not yet regarded as very legitimate topics to include in any corpus of scientific knowledge, or healing practice. Hypnotism, for instance, still remains part of alternative medicine and is certainly regarded with at least some suspicion by most lay persons, as well as many professionals.

Hypnotism and concepts such as faith, will, and hope are all viewed here as referring to the achievement of sufficient organization of information to be able to act towards a desired end. They are seen to refer to potentially much longer-term mental organization than the use of the term 'focus' has implied so far, and to the necessity for a sequence of events to be worked out and priorities to be ordered, before anything purposeful can be done. Some priorities are so much part of our species learning (see postulate 5, Appendix 2, and Gear 1987), and these events and others have such easily predictable outcomes, that it is not surprising that all of the necessary processing can take place within micro-seconds; whereas other priorities and complexities of behaviour *can* take most of a lifetime to order sufficiently well for effective action. In addition to their connection with the ordering of priorities, these longer-term 'focus' concepts also relate to our need to believe that we can actually achieve something before we get involved. If there is any serious doubt, that is in itself threatening to our psychological integrity, and therefore our ability to perform. Anxiety, however slight, manifests itself as a need for orientation: an expression of lack of direction.

Psychology does have at least one concept besides hypnotism, which acknowledges the effects of mental organization over physical activity at micro level, and another which recognizes the power of expectancy, if not what we generally refer to as belief. The first is known as the 'ideomotor response' (Ousby 1967:chap. 2), and the second as 'set' (Uznadze 1966).

The ideomotor response refers to the effects of concentrating the mind on a particular activity without consciously signalling action. It is usually demonstrated by 'willing' a small weight suspended on a cord to rotate in a particular direction. Presumably, when rotation appears to occur on its own, it is because the physiological processes involved are unconsciously ordered and so minute that no hand movement can be perceived.

Set is a concept rooted in our extremely powerful tendency to make assessments of situations according to previous experience. It refers to the fact that alternatives sometimes cease to be acknowledged. Uznadze, who has done considerable research into the phenomenon, says that 'should the subject meet the same situation, with the same intentions again, then the previous set must return appreciably quicker than a new set would develop in a completely new situation' (1966:41).

At its most functional it obviously facilitates orientation by rapid ordering and classification of sensory information, at an unconscious level and within an existing framework of experience. Logically, it must also have an effect on decisions we take about the appropriateness of behaviour within given situations and what kind of new action might be necessary. Decision making is therefore facilitated by virtue of a particular expectation providing an interpretative mechanism – albeit with the likelihood of its producing a self-fulfilling prophecy – with the effect of minimizing threat and maintaining arousal at a level at which performance is likely to be effective, or, put differently, maintaining specifically focused arousal to the same effect.

Fairly recently, the world was able to witness a living example of the unconscious effects of specific arousal on a grand scale. The effect was dubbed the 'Falklands effect'. Rise in confidence (which tends to happen when specific arousal is coupled with the strong possibility of a successful outcome of action) and effective focusing of attention accompanied each other, as a result, it is suggested, of what was perceived to be manageable threat.

The same event also offered a wonderful example – at macro level – of the effects of optimal and specific arousal producing effective organization of behaviour composed of an optimal mix of rigidity and flexibility, as massive resources became mobilized and organized ready for action. And, always a characteristic of an effective show of military power, lines and patterns of resources in the form of machines and ranks of men (who are required to be almost just as reactive as the machines they use) were to be seen ready to be *re*ordered and directed, at the will of those above them in the hierarchy who are able to exercise more flexibility of control but who, in turn, are firmly controlled by the few high-ranking personnel with the most power, and choice, of all.

Presumably, the phenomenon of which the Falklands effect was reminiscent, and whose name it echoes, is the Hawthorne effect (Roethlisberger and Dickson 1939). This refers to a series of experiments carried out in the United States which aimed to increase productivity at the Hawthorne Electricity Company: the most surprising outcome of the research to the investigators was that it was not apparently specific technical changes which had beneficial effects, but incidental factors which made the workers feel more valued, and, therefore, we can argue, changed states of arousal to more productive kinds. A possible relationship between this effect and the psychology of the effect of the Falkland Islands conflict on the confidence of the nation, and on mass perceptions of its leader, becomes more obvious when we consider the relationship between levels of arousal and focusing and scanning functions of attention postulated above (section 2.1 and Figures 1–3) within the context of 'manageable threat' (p. 22), together with evidence that need for environmental feedback in the form of change is a crucial orientation need in itself. The deleterious effects of lack of change are legendary with reference to lack of time or opportunity for, say, a summer holiday but of course in reality, whether change provides welcome stimulation or a source of threat, for the cell, individual, or the group, obviously depends on kind and degree. But, apart from evidence about our need for sensory stimulation from the physical environment, the only testimony to a need for social feedback, from those others on whom we become either physically or emotionally dependent for fulfilment of our needs to belong, comes from known effects of its denial: from the well-known aversive effects of excommunication, or more tortuously, the effects of solitary confinement as a means of punishment in a variety of institutions.

The established psychological concepts just described, however (the ideomotor response, set, and the Hawthorne effect), all demonstrate psychological dominance of the physical organism, and all demonstrate the power of the unconscious mind over behaviour. And all three, incidentally but importantly, relate specific arousal to effects on organization of mental and physical activity. The Hawthorne effect also serves as a further demonstration of the deeply unconscious (most of the time), but powerful, influence of our orientation needs, if the interpretation offered is accepted.

The suggestion being made is that mental equilibrium is rather more finely balanced, more sensitive, than physical equilibrium, so that our tolerance of prolonged exposure to other than optimal levels of arousal and/or stimulation (that is, mental stress) is potentially more dangerous to the organism than similar periods of, say, an unbalanced diet, or pain, or other forms of physical stress, whose effects may well be damaging, but within a greater range of tolerance.

The logic of the situation is that the more sensitive or finely tuned the mechanism, the more crucial are its needs. It is being argued not only that temporary mental pain is therefore of more critical importance to the organism than temporary physical pain, but also (as will be explained later) that unconscious monitoring of external and internal events is more sensitive than conscious monitoring, so that unconscious needs actually predominate over conscious needs.

A great deal more evidence could be cited and interpreted, using the APM-A model in support of the notion that orientation needs exert control over action. Most powerful of all, perhaps, would be Milgram's findings on conformity and obedience (Milgram 1974); although research cited by Berkowitz, suggesting that dissonance effects can be so powerful as to override the physiological and behavioural signs of motivational states such as hunger, and even lessen the effects of electric shocks, makes a fairly dramatic point (Berkowitz 1968:309).

For two reasons, then, the maintenance of psychological integrity is seen to be a prerequisite for the maintenance of physical integrity: first, and most obviously, because it has been argued that psychological imbalance renders us less efficient, and therefore a greater potential (mechanical) danger to self, both directly and indirectly (as a result of posing greater threat to others); second, the implication of the APM-A thesis and its hypothesized evolution of mind is that physical defence and psychological defence share the same mechanism.

Quite simply, it is being said that mind is a highly complex development of the orientation response; that it does not just include defence mechanisms, but that it *is* a grand, highly sophisticated, and extraordinarily complex orientation response: a defence mechanism *par excellence*.

APM-A became APM-A→Verstand (see Figure 67, postulate 6, Appendix 2) it is suggested, as the organism moved from being merely reactive to becoming a decision-maker – a planner and active shaper of places, objects, and events, and a manipulator of ideas. This evolutionary leap is seen to have accompanied the development of increased awareness and skills in communication and, eventually, the capacity to be conscious not only of dependence on an immediate group, but also of inherent threats to self and own interests (including, of course, other people): a leap in awareness in response to threats described above (section 2.2) posed to the *species*.

An incidental effect of this grand version of the orientation response having developed sufficient capacity and complexity to be able to monitor itself, mostly unconsciously, is that self-destruction actually became adaptive. Just as it has been argued that given a need to know, it is adaptive also to have a need not to know, it is also argued that given a will to live, not only can that will break down, but the possibility arises of adopting – consciously or unconsciously – a will *not* to live. This is in fact to be analysed at much greater length in Chapter 4, but for the purpose of points already made about unconscious needs, unconscious actions, and the effects of unmet needs, discussion at this stage will remain with the most directly perceivable relationships between psychological defence and physical defence.

In essence, the argument is that physical defence comes into play only providing that psychological defence remains effective enough for psychological organization to remain intact. The consequence of breakdown of organization could, on the one hand, lead to deliberate but unconscious exposure to unnecessary risk, as tuning to change and thresholds of risk tolerance are modified as a result of stress; or, on the other hand, psychological disequilibrium could result in the body's defence (equilibrium) breaking down in response to excessive secretions of those hormones and transmitters associated with SNS activity.

Campbell and Singer make a similar suggestion: 'increase in stress hormone levels could be the link between psychological stress and the lowered immune response which makes a person more susceptible to disease' (1979:111). They also regard 'failure of psychological defences' as a particularly important factor in the onset of disease, through its effect on the immune system.

Part of their evidence comes from a study of 250 cancer patients, in which a high incidence of four psychologically crucial factors were associated with the disease. They were:

1 The patients' loss of an important relationship prior to the development of a tumour.
2 The patients' inability to express hostile feelings.
3 The patients' unresolved tension concerning a parental figure.
4 Sexual disturbances.

Campbell and Singer also note the similarity between these factors and those associated with other diseases where there is a disturbance of the immune system (ibid.:111).

The point being made is not, however, to deny two-way interaction of mind–body pathology, or the influence which physiological changes have on moods, feelings, and motives, although attempts to argue that certain complaints or problems are *always* attributable to *either* physiological *or* psychological factors are frequently made.[6] What is being said is that, once psychological disequilibrium is effected, it presents a major threat to physiological integrity.[7]

So far we have identified, as prime orientation needs, feedback from the physical and social environments in the form of optimal levels of stimulation which are provided by optimal levels of perceptible change;

but a full definition of these needs must include reference to the apparent and legendary destructive effects of what is usually referred to as loss of meaning or loss of purpose in life.

A need for meaning can be accommodated in what has already been said about needing to know; but it can also imply either a more global, or more long-term, concern. Whereas originally our only source of defence was the orientation response in its most primitive and reactive form – that is, triggered by fundamental internal or external changes which either threatened or frustrated *physical* survival needs – our evolution into social and cultural beings created circumstances in which an array of *new* needs, associated with awareness of and dependence on others, must, in turn, have placed a premium on a tendency to hypothesize.

Quite obviously, consideration of the possible outcomes of behaviour, *before* action takes place, is adaptive, but formerly we would have been capable of only a very limited degree of anticipation in the form of passive expectancy: just that endowed by species learning (commonly called 'instinct'). This may have included, say, a fear of heights (Gibson and Walk 1960), in addition to physiological responses based on expectancy, such as salivating at the sight or smell of food. In fact, only as we evolved a capacity for quite complex kinds of classification and association of information, and longer-term memory, will we have been able to recognize and use feedback from a much larger repertoire of situations met before. But not only did we get much better at it, we became *essentially* predictive; and, to evoke a by now familiar argument, having developed a capacity for assessing longer-term and more general meanings and implications in events, we now *seek* longer-term and more general meanings.

Davis (1981) has actually brought together evidence from several fields, to argue that the capacity to anticipate what will happen more than sixty seconds into the future constitutes the major difference between us and all other animals.

If it is accepted that being tuned to predict, we need to predict, it can also be argued that it is just as important for what we imagine is going to happen, or not happen, in the *long-term future* to hold an optimal balance of threat and promise (in order for optimal levels of stimulation and arousal, and therefore effective functioning, to be maintained), as it is for our perceptions of the present, that is, the *immediate future*, if such hypothesizing is not to threaten the integrity of the organism.

In the next chapter it is argued that, not only is this consciousness of possible future events and concomitant needs – in addition to other orientation needs which have been identified – more evident in some than in others, but that, the degree to which it is evident is a crucial factor in vulnerability to different kinds of so-called 'abnormal' experience and behaviour. Most obviously, the prediction of negative outcomes of action may lead to what is commonly referred to as 'loss of purpose'; or 'loss of meaning' may arise from the breakdown of an explanatory or belief system (so that disorientation may be the outcome of finding that newly acquired information cannot be classified or understood), or from perceiving actions as 'pointless', as holding no foreseeable benefits at all. Whether it is called loss of purpose, loss of meaning, or disorientation, in each case arousal is likely to be more general than specific, offering too little focus for effective action.[8]

In any case, stages of breakdown of psychological and, potentially, physical integrity are seen to be *disorientation*→[need for *orientation*] *response*→more *scanning*, as opposed to focusing of attention,→*disorganization* of mental activity, and at least some disorganization of motor reactions. If disorientation is prolonged or intense, the likelihood of its affecting the immune system is also increased.

Many of the needs which are being described here as being of crucial importance to the organism are freely recognized as being of prime importance for babies and children, but for a variety of possible reasons, they appear to be grossly underestimated in adults. First, and most obviously, such needs are largely unconscious. Second, because obvious and observable physical differences exist between babies, children, and adults, there seems to be a tendency to expect there to be just as easily definable, measurable, and sequentially ordered stages in psychological development. Even if this should be so,[9] it is argued that we don't just *develop* psychologically, we undergo *dynamic* changes in response to our surroundings, and, as has been indicated, mind and body are both so dependent on the balance of secreted hormones that physical changes and rhythms throughout life have to be taken into account. The behavioural effects of insecurities conventionally ascribed to early childhood can be, and are, also manifested as the insecurities of adolescence,[10] of middle age, and of old age – all of which can take place at a variety of chronological ages. Third, Victorian ethics, principally, have bequeathed us what are regarded here as skewed perceptions of what kind of behaviour and experience is appropriate to children and what kind to adults. But part of this confusion, if not gross and unjustifiable distinction between children and adults, arises from obsessions with norms, and once more, it is stressed, a failure to accommodate variability in needs as well as in development.

Weiner (1980) groups motivation theories under the headings of *drive reduction* theories, including of course those of Hull and Freud; *expectancy-value* theories, such as field, achievement, social learning, and attribution theories; and *mastery and growth* theories, a heading which includes the humanistic theories of Allport and Maslow.

If we replace the first two of Weiner's categories with the headings

Figure 4 A summary of orientation needs

Feedback from the physical environment

Sensory needs		Physical reassurance derived from both:
	(a)	*optimal levels* [1] *of sensory stimulation* (mainly tactile/visual/aural) [2]
	(b)	(implied) optimal levels of perceived environmental stability

---

Cognitive needs	1	Reassurance derived from optimal levels of *consistency and change,* with an obvious need for a very high degree of *predictability.*
	2	An *explanatory system,* including
	(a)	*a need to know* which may rest on (i) simplistic rationalization based on experience, (ii) folklore, myth, or legend, (iii) magico-religious beliefs, (iv) a corpus of knowledge; [3]
	(b)	*a need not to know* when existing belief systems, experience or knowledge prove inadequate to provide explanation.
	3	*'Purpose':* [4] in terms of engagement with identifiable problems – offering optimal levels of threat and promise and concomitant optimal balance of focusing and scanning functions of attention.
	4	*a medium of expression.* [5]

Feedback from social, cultural and intellectual environments

Sensory needs		Reassurance of social acceptability and personal identity derived from optimal levels of contact (mainly tactile/visual/aural) with intimate and familiar social bonds as well as with unfamiliar individuals and groups.

Cognitive needs	1	Reassurance derived from optimal levels of consistency and change in the perceived behaviour of self and others.
	2	An explanatory system including a need to know and a need not to know (as above).
	3	'Purpose'
	4	A medium of expression.
	5	*Shared communication.* [6]
	6	*Shared values.*

---

[1] Optimal levels dependent on species learning – of the species norm – but variable between and within individuals (species and individual adaptation levels).
[2] It is accepted that not only may there be individual differences in the dominance of any one of the senses, but that substitution and compensation also take place.
[3] Clearly, a corpus of knowledge is viewed as holding most potential as a reliable source of explanation.
[4], [5] 'Purpose', and a medium of expression, may be furnished by the physical, social, or intellectual environment, or all three.
(6) Implicit in any notion of shared communication is what Maslow would call 'belongingness', or what can be called 'enmeshment', but here it must be pointed out that in both cases the question of degree is important, i.e. that some freedom from the demands of other individuals and groups is also of key importance.

'physical' and 'orientational' respectively, it becomes possible to classify the needs which motivation theories identify, together with all of the usually unconscious needs under discussion, under the three headings *physical needs, orientation needs,* and *mastery and growth needs.*

Maslow's physiological and safety needs (see Figure 66, postulate 5, Appendix 2), for instance, could be classified together as physical needs; his belongingness, love, and esteem needs – which would be termed here 'reassurance needs' – would go under the general heading of 'orientation needs'; and his self-actualization needs under the heading 'mastery and growth'.

Because these mastery and growth needs are yet to be put within a framework which takes intensity of affect into account, they are to be reclassified, as *second-order orientation needs.*

But before constructing a rather different hierarchy from that conceived by Maslow, three important observations must be made. The first is to reinforce a point made earlier with the example of social learning theory that, however invisible or intangible rewards are, *the satisfaction of conscious or unconscious orientation needs is reward in itself* – that is, arousal is reduced to an optimal level. Obversely, the frustration of such needs and concomitant experience of disorientation is stressful. Second, just as this conscious–unconscious dimension has been neglected by recent theorists, so has another vitally important to the APM-A perspective; namely, *intensity of affect.*

Quite obviously, if it is accepted that intensity of affect is a crucial factor in attention and learning,[11] it is implicit that it must be a crucial element in wanting/needing/being 'moved' to learn. It has already been argued – and substantiated with Luria's research (see section 2.1) – that affect produces arousal which, in turn, produces movement. Patently, however, there are many things which may affect us, either directly or indirectly, which do not actually 'move us' into action; an individual threshold has to be crossed before intensity of affect is strong enough to motivate.

It has also been argued already that we are hedonistically motivated to satisfy needs in order to maintain physical and psychological defences, and by reference to the *intercourse principle* described above the conscious or unconscious effort to gain information from animate or inanimate sources, or to justify or reassure, or simply to eat, depends on the degree of threat inherent in not doing so.

This takes us to the third point, which has to do with the notion of *differences in tension thresholds,* which relate directly to intensity of affect experienced and which, as is to be explained in the next chapter, constitute a major difference between people. Therefore, for a hierarchy of needs to have as wide as possible application, it must take these differences into account.

Figure 5 A revised hierarchy of needs

Weiner's classification	Reclassification	Description of needs
(Mastery and growth)	*Second-order orientation needs*	Heightened orientation needs as a result of intensity of affect: need for more feedback/change; greater need to know, with reference to longer term, more complex and/or more abstract issues; increased communicative and expressive needs.
(Drive reduction)	*Physical survival needs*	Fulfilment of physiological demands: need for shelter, warmth, avoidance of danger, food, drink, sleep, sexual expression.
(Expectancy-value)	*First-order orientation needs*	See Fig. 4 for a summary of orientation needs.

Note: Second-order orientation needs are not species-wide, but vary between and within individuals, as do the relative dominance of physical survival needs and kinds of orientation needs. Attention signals (see Fig. 66), on the other hand, derive from species-wide and conscious physical survival needs.

Chapter three

Individual differences

Summary

The new explanation of the evolution of mind is extended here to account for the relationship between the *right and left hemispheres* of the brain and *conscious and unconscious mental processes*. Essentially, Chapter 3 is about biochemical bases of psychological variability and the evolution in the species of a considerably wider range of individual differences than existing models reveal.

The phenomenon of 'cognitive style' is related to hemisphericality, but the lateralization of brain function is not seen, as is conventional, to be causal of the development of contrasting ways of dealing with environmental information, but as an incidental effect of other, *biochemical,* factors. After differentiating the APM-A view from others with which it could be confused, a *dynamic model of style* is introduced. By reference to (1) differences in *urgency* of processing environmental information according to relative dominance of limbic over cortical arousal, and (2) a potentially infinite range of *patterning* of secretions of adrenalin, noradrenalin, and acetylcholine in particular, the model is shown to accommodate an extremely wide range of psychological variability and allow the concepts of cognitive style, personality, motivation, intelligence, and creativity to be related to one another within a holistic model of adaptive styles.

Although the underlying theory refers to the relationship between limbic and cortical arousal, the point of view is quite different from Eysenck's. Eysenck's theoretical stance is, in fact, criticized and turned on its head.

Intelligence is defined quite simply as 'the ability to cope effectively with new situations', and some other new definitions of over-used concepts are suggested with a view to avoiding some common misconceptions and confusions. Significance is also given to some hitherto unrecognized aspects of individual differences; for example, apparent variability in tendencies to anticipate future events, and hormonally based differences in degrees of maleness and femaleness beyond those attributable to levels of testosterone or oestrogen. However, the model is essentially an energy model, but not in the sense of either Freud's closed energy system or Lorenz's 'hydraulic' model.

3.1 Being in two minds

The increasingly harsh environmental conditions cited in the last chapter as having been responsible for providing much greater flexibility and variability of mental and physical responses within individual organisms will have also had the effect, it is argued, of generating a much richer source of human variability *per se*. An incidental effect of the dynamic changes in the perceptual process of the individual which have been hypothesized will have been significantly greater potential for differences *between individuals* in styles of perceiving and coping with environmental change, enhancement of potential for species survival, as well as for individual survival.

Whereas the last two chapters have been concerned with relating the phenomena of paradox and analogy respectively to human biology, and to the physiology of the perceptual process in particular, this chapter is concerned with the biological bases of polymorphism as they are manifested in what is being called *individual style*. Specifically, it is concerned with the fact that, because we remain for the most part unaware of other than our own characteristic and habitual ways of perceiving the world, we fail, mostly, to take account of how many of the terms we use to classify and describe ourselves and one another are open to a wide variety of interpretations, as will be shown.

Acknowledgements of some of the problems of polymorphism are frequently made, but our language and definitions remain limited for a number of possible reasons. There are, for instance, our extremely robust tendencies to generalize, simplify, and stereotype, but above all, it is suggested that the existence of different forms of (apparently) the same behaviours are not taken into account because they are not fully understood.

For instance, it becomes more and more widely accepted – in academe, that is, as well as in the 'world outside' where most people 'know' already but lack any convincing rationale – that terms such as 'intelligence' and 'creativity' are by no means unitary (see, for example, Gardner 1983) and that many kinds of behaviour may fall under each heading. However, our resort to blanket terminology, frequently rendered even more meaningless by the use of abbreviations such as 'ESN'[1] or 'MBD'[2] and, at least more promisingly, the current use of the broad classification of 'disaffected' (Humberside Education Committee 1982), suggests that we still consistently fail to note that there must also be many different ways of being *un*intelligent, *non*-creative, or stupid, in fact, let alone 'sensitive' or 'insensitive'. For example, by 'sensitivity' do we mean something which has to do with the dimension of stability–instability, and sensitivity (or indeed 'over-sensitivity') to needs of self? Or do we mean something which has more to do with degrees of kindness shown towards, and regard for the needs of others? Or both? They are by no means mutually inclusive.

Similarly, even the use of terms such as 'analytical', 'logical', and 'rational', all terms used to categorize mental activity and people, will be brought into question and eventually shown to represent rich sources of potential miscommunication and misunderstanding.

By viewing aspects of individuality and the processes underlying polymorphism from the position which has been set out in previous chapters, and by developing the alternative evolutionary hypothesis being offered, it will be seen to be possible to produce a unified theory of differences in perception, experience, and behaviour: a theory of differences within *and* between individuals. This will offer the means of explanation of, and the possibility of relating to one another, aspects of our variability and adaptability which we mostly label with terms, which instead of indicating the richness and variety of human perception and performance, have a tendency to become problematic. Such terms are sometimes rendered almost meaningless out of awareness of the very fact that they are polymorphic and imprecise. However, with no widely understood frame of reference to offer explanation of their complexities, so that an accepted range of possible interpretations can be seen to exist, the traditional solution to the problem is avoidance.

To be able to refer to particular *kinds* of intelligence or *kinds* of creativity, for example, or to use more accurately terms currently used in descriptions of persons and personality, it becomes necessary to develop theory which can make sense of and accommodate the many inherent paradoxes and complications which abound in these areas, so that meaning can be enhanced by context.

In this chapter it is hoped to be able to show how a multi-dimensional model of human nature, based on research into a number of different fields concerned with characteristic differences between individuals, can provide a holistic theoretical framework. This will be used first to relate and make sense of all the hypotheses and postulations about human adaptability and variability made in this book so far (and hopefully much more besides), and subsequently, to make a broad analysis of artistic and cultural styles in Part 2.

The proliferation of research into asymmetry of brain function which has taken place since the first commissurotomy ('split brain' operation) was performed in 1940, and the escalation of the clinical use of the operation in the 1960s, have served to confirm what Springer and Deutsch (1981:59) call 'the most salient and profound difference' between the right and left hemispheres of the brain, as well as furnishing what has become fairly common, but usually rather simplistically interpreted knowledge: that the left brain carries out functions concerned with the processing and use of verbal material and skills, whereas the right brain deals with the processing of visuo-spatial information. Largely on the strength of these findings, many have at least tentatively related lateralization of brain function to characteristic and apparently consistent differences between people, in how information is dealt with and the kinds of strategies which are adopted in problem-solving situations; the inference being that one hemisphere may be habitually 'taking control', or that it underlies preferences for a particular 'cognitive style' (see Messick 1976). To make such correlations is certainly tempting given that so many differences between people, in their consciously or unconsciously adopted strategies to classify experiences or perform tasks, seem to occupy bipolar continua.[3] However, those who infer this relationship also tend, intentionally or not, to imply causality: to suggest that individual differences actually derive from the effects of lateralization.

Although correlations which have been made by others will be referred to and for the most part accepted, the approach here will differ in two respects: first, some criticism will be made of analyses which suggest that particular characteristics and functions of mind belong exclusively to one half of the brain *or* the other – and are therefore particular to one mode of processing only; second, lateralization will be viewed here as an *incidental effect* of contrasting styles of handling information, *rather than their source.*

Eventually, individual differences in kinds of intelligence, cognitive styles, and motivation (with reference to first- and second-order needs – see Figure 5), and major differences in personality, will be attributed to differences in endocrinology[4] rather than to differences in hemispherical dominance.[5]

The evolution of hemisphericality – that is, changes in the organization and functioning of the human brain to the effect that the workings of the two hemispheres became mostly separate, allowing them to function independently and to deal with information (that is, to attend, perceive, and remember) in different ways, and therefore for each to deal with *different kinds of information* more effectively than the other – has been attributed to a variety of possible causes. These include the development of language (Lancaster 1975:69); the need for the left hemisphere to become more adept at generating rapidly changing motor patterns, as involved in fine motor movements of the hands as well as the vocal tract (Springer and Deutsch 1981:56–7); and the basic incompatibility between the mechanisms generating the different styles of processing (ibid.:57). Most tenuously perhaps, but probably on the grounds that the brain, as well as other organs, incorporates considerable redundancy, the suggestion has even been made that the possession of 'two brains', as it were, provides spare capacity should one hemisphere be subjected to tissue damage. Now another, more fundamental, explanation, which takes into account the likelihood of a number of related and coincident sources of selective pressure operating to reinforce one another, is to be offered.

If the hypothesis put forward in Chapter 2 is accepted – that greater sensitivity of both excitation *and* inhibition of physiological responses, and therefore, within the APM-A context, of psychological responses, evolved simultaneously – it must logically also be accepted that divergence between the characteristics of SNS and PNS functioning (see section 1.2) will have taken place at the same time. Taking this possibility together with the fact that (1) above all else the brain is an organizer of information, either perceiving or failing to perceive relationships between various items of information, and (2) that those perceived links may be either sequential or diffuse[6] (or indeed both), greatest efficiency in parallel but diverse processing of information would most likely derive from these processes remaining as separate from, and therefore as uncontaminated by, each other as possible, whilst remaining in communication.

It is suggested, therefore, that as the two different but simultaneous modes of processing (see postulate 6, Appendix 2) evolved to become as diverse as empirical evidence now suggests they are, and as information crucial to survival (that is, psychological as well as physical survival) assumed greater complexity (see sections 2.2, 2.3), it also became highly adaptive for the readily available, consciously organized, and most frequently and recently used information to become separated from the less immediately useful, less adaptive, or worse, currently maladaptive information.[7]

The belief being expressed here is that asymmetry of brain function, and in fact most other characteristics and complications of human nature, are a product of the kind of evolutionary changes in SNS and PNS functioning already hypothesized in Chapter 2 (2.1), whose wide-ranging incidental effects are yet to be described in more detail.

Within the sort of information-processing system suggested by all that has been said so far, greatest efficiency in life-threatening situations (or in those situations perceived to be potentially life-threatening) must rest on rapid exchange of information between right and left hemispheres. The exigencies of the current situation must be checked against what is already 'known', or even remotely relevant, from the recent and distant past, to furnish at least sufficient information to decide on appropriate action for defence. Ideally, and more rarely, some deeper perception may also be furnished by the same process: sufficient insight may be offered into the essentials of a situation to produce some brilliant strategy which may have longer-term application than the immediate relief of threat.

Clearly, maximum efficiency is likely to be coincident with simultaneous and different kinds of processing of the 'same' information, with the effect of providing two potentially quite different points of view: one an organized and/or verbalized, readily available solution based on past actions, successes, or failures – the ritual solution, say – and the other, much more existential in character, highly conscious of the moment and of possible alternative interpretations and behaviours, but drawing on a mass of more loosely associated sensory (already lived) experience triggered by the situation in hand.

A second likely source of selective pressure placed on the evolution of the separate location of these distinct means of processing is that, prior to this development focusing and scanning functions of attention (whose relationship to the phenomena of ritual and encounter[8] should emerge in this chapter) must have been carried out consecutively and alternately. The effect of this, it is suggested, would have been rather bird-like jerky movements of the head, as a result of action made up of short periods of concentrated performance – say, feeding – interrupted by the need to look about and to watch and wait, momentarily, for any hint of threat or (equally distracting) promise (1.3), before continuing with the task in hand.

The evolution of simultaneous processing, as divergence between scan and focus increased, and as their relationship with each other became more complex in response to the dramatic environmental changes which took place, would clearly have obviated the necessity for alternating attentional activities, and would therefore have proved to have been considerably more economical, as divided attention became possible.

Being able to continue practised, routinized (or ritualized) skills which required very little conscious attention, without the hazard of completely ignoring environmental change, would have meant that from that stage on only first-priority signals (see hierarchy of diminishing interest, Figure 66, Appendix 2) would have demanded full attention. Others would have been picked up by sub-threshold scanning (Figure 67, Appendix 2) and then either ignored, so as not to create any serious distraction from more urgent business on hand, or have been taken account of and made to await full attention until the first priority task was completed.

However, as well as offering greater efficiency for coping with internal and external physical demands by economizing on attentional capacity, the possession of two hemispheres, with different abilities and only limited communication between them, will also have considerably enhanced our defences against what were described earlier (sections 2.2, 2.3) as the relatively new threats emanating from the growth in sensitivity and enormous sophistication of the very means of orientation itself. Our evolution from an extremely primitive stage of being able to make only rigid, unconscious, and routinized responses to environmental change, and from awareness of threats to physical comfort *only* to awareness of different states and possibilities of 'being', will have created a demand for an ever more complicated relationship between consciousness and unconsciousness. Therefore, it would seem more than reasonable to suggest that a third source of reinforcement[9] of changes taking place in the organization of the brain into two hemispheres performing rather different tasks, would have taken effect in service of what was described in the last chapter as a 'need not to know', as a concomitant of 'the need to know'.

The already long history of the development of dynamic psychiatry (as compared to a mere century or so of psychology) including all of its metamorphoses from notions of 'lost souls', and absorption with visions which differ from conscious experience (concepts central to primitive healing), to magnetism and the newer dynamic schools, has always assumed a model of mind which incorporates concepts of conscious and not conscious. And of course the abundance of research into asymmetry of brain function, in addition to the kind of research undertaken by Sackeim and Gur (1978:139–97), has served to reinforce the need to take this aspect of mental organization (unconsciousness) into account, although it remains amazingly taken-for-granted, or just ignored, beyond the bounds of psychiatry.

Despite at least some support being offered to aspects of the psychoanalytic point of view, the position being adopted on the relationship between conscious and unconscious mental activity does not follow any particular earlier formulation, whether psychodynamic or not. Instead, just as Freudian concepts such as repression and rationalization will be seen to be relevant to the concerns of this and succeeding chapters, so will references to Gestalt psychology and behaviourism, as was the case in the development of the original APM-A model (Gear 1987). However, in this chapter, characteristics of attention are to be much more closely defined than previously, and their significance to many different kinds of experience and behaviour will be explored. But it must be stressed that consciousness is being viewed as a qualitative state of attention (or more accurately, of APM-A) to whose mechanisms the means of orientation of all kinds, immediate, long-term, physical, social, and intellectual, have been attributed.

So far, levels of consciousness have been discussed mainly with reference to species learning – conventionally but, it has been argued, confusingly referred to as instinct – and as complicating the psychology of attention, perception, memory, and motivation. However, in this chapter consciousness will be regarded as opposite and complementary[10] to unconsciousness while having a dynamic, changing, and at times blurred rather than distinct relationship with it. Questions of how each relates to the other will also be seen to be crucial to any discussion of individual differences.

Again, belief in any degree of unconscious influence over the contents of consciousness is obviously reminiscent of the Freudian position: concepts of id and ego. It is reminiscent of censorship by the ego of all of the turbulence of the socially unacceptable (id) desires and frustrations raging in the unconscious mind, so that thwarted emotion is safely transmuted by the ego into neutralized drive; this, in turn, provides us with the energy to do whatever we think (in other, more altruistic terms) we have to do, in order to survive as dynamic entities enmeshed within a dynamic environment. Here, certain modifications must be added. First, sources of arousal (and therefore energy) exist other than sexual arousal, and second, the degree and kind of altruism (self-denial) we believe it necessary to exercise will depend on at least two variables. The first is the intensity of orientation needs (including need for self-esteem) and whether needs are of first- or second-order (which is not to say that there exists any simple equation to be arrived at). The second variable is the source from which we have derived an acceptable self-image. This will also bring into question, for instance, which social group we most easily identify with, although, if sufficiently rebellious, original, or critical in our thinking, the influence of the prevailing culture will not be as strong as a relatively independent formulation of values.

This last point is about degrees of human suggestibility and condition-ability, which are not only being regarded as relevant to the well-known nature–nurture controversy[11] (as they are regarded to be to *any* attempt to define universals beyond those to do with process, within a dynamic system of human variability and adaptability) but are also highly relevant to the definition of individual differences which will emerge.

Later, the complexities of the relationship between degrees of aware-ness, unconscious motivations, and the crucial concept of suggestibility will be taken up in more detail. But for now, it can be said that although the Freudian view of the unconscious mind is not taken on *in toto*, it is by no means rejected. However, the view of the mechanisms involved, and the supporting rationale, are obviously somewhat differently construed, and total dominance of the organism by sexuality is not seen to be quite true of the entire species all of the time, as is stressed above and has also been made clear by our hierarchy of diminishing interest (postulate 5, Appendix 2).

Although the view of the power of the unconscious which is to be elaborated is markedly different from that of Freud, it nevertheless acknowledges similar potential. It is the manner in which control is exerted over consciousness that is viewed so differently; but the theoretical position being adopted does coincide with the view of those (for example,

Springer and Deutsch 1981:195–7) who believe that the functions of mind most closely resembling those to which Freud drew attention are usually (that is, where lateralization is 'normal', with the left side serving speech) served by the right hemisphere (see Figures 6 and 7).

However, this is not to suggest that either hemisphere has absolute control over consciousness. As may be anticipated by now, a much more interactive and more complex approach is about to be adopted. It conceives of overt *and* covert control – that is, conscious and/or

Figure 6   A list of labels used to describe the processes of the left brain and the right brain, reproduced from Springer and Deutsch (1981:185)*

Left hemisphere	Right hemisphere
Verbal	Nonverbal, visuo-spatial
Sequential, temporal, digital	Simultaneous, spatial, analogic
Logical, analytic	Gestalt, synthetic
Rational	Intuitive
Western thought	Eastern thought

* They say, 'The most widely cited characteristics may be divided into five main groups, which form a kind of hierarchy. Each designation usually includes and goes beyond the designation above it. The descriptions near the top of the list seem to be based on experimental evidence; the other designations appear more speculative.'

Figure 7   A summary of characteristics of the left and right hemispheres of the brain recorded by Springer and Deutsch (1981:1–4, 13, 14, 36, 37, 43, 46, 185, 202)

Left hemisphere	Right hemisphere
verbal skills;	damage to the right produces lasting effects on perception, attention, recognition, spatial orientation and matching;
sequential processing;	
analysis (particularly the production and understanding of language);	other abilities associated with the right include visuo-spatial abilities, perception of part– whole relationships, holistic processing, simultaneous pro-
control of 'purposeful' movements	cessing and musical abilities;
in sum: processes 'in terms of details and features'; 'something like a digital computer'.	speculation about the right: capacities for processing abstract-ions of vision, touch and movement, and for synthesis;
	in sum: perceptions of 'simult-aneous relationships and more global properties of patterns'; 'more like an analogue computer'.

Both reprinted with the permission of W. H. Freeman and Company.

72

unconscious control – depending on many variables. This position is actually already implicit in the identification of attention 'given' and 'gained' (postulate 1, Appendix 2), but for reasons yet to be amplified, the right is still being seen to play the role of ultimate censor over what is brought – or allowed – into consciousness.

The suggestion is that most of both, right *and* left hemispheres, hold information unconsciously, in addition to both hemispheres holding and using information at a conscious level: that information of different kinds (as well as of the same kind), processed and stored in different modes, is held unconsciously for different reasons.

As indicated above, the right is still seen to be the guardian of the kinds of unconsciousness identified by Jung, Janet, and Freud in particular, and to which others of the school of dynamic psychiatry make reference (see Ellenberger 1970), but here not *all* of the right is being viewed as unconscious, any more than the left can be viewed as *wholly* conscious. To hold otherwise is seen to represent gross over-simplification, which is easily attributable to another over-simplified concept: that which commonly equates verbal (only) with conscious.

Strangely, distinction between verbal and conscious, within the context of asymmetry of brain function, is very slow to become established, despite the accumulation of a great deal of evidence which indicates that the non-verbal certainly does present itself to consciousness (Kaufman 1979), and despite growing use of the newer dichotomy (that is, newer than verbal–non-verbal) of sequential–simultaneous. Consciousness of the non-verbal seems obvious enough every time we search for the 'right phrase', or otherwise struggle for the means of expression of concepts whose complexities seem to reveal themselves only when unravelled into sequences of words.

On the other hand, we clearly do not experience consciously *all* of the searching, making of associations and reshuffling of data which go on. Thinking would have to become a much slower business for that to be the case. Also, most of what *is* allowed into consciousness is not stored at a wholly conscious level, as is evidenced by our need, very often, to use 'cues' in one sensory mode or another (if not several) in order to 'retrieve' information. In fact, the conventional use of the term 'retrieval' with reference to recall from long-term memory of so-called 'consciously held' information, can itself be read as implying *lost* from consciousness, however temporarily. Such information might much more accurately be described as information which has *been* conscious, and which we 'know', or might be able to reconstruct (Herriot 1974:46), however inaccurately.

The APM-A position admits therefore of levels (that is, degrees) of availability to consciousness in *both* right and left hemispheres, but holds that different reasons may apply for the lack of immediate availability of most of the information subjected to the different modes of processing and storage[12] associated with each.

The position may be clarified by summarizing some possible reasons for failure to retrieve, or gain access to, information from each hemisphere. Logically, from the position which is being described, any of the following possibilities (which are not intended as a conclusive list) could apply to failure to retrieve information from its control[13] by the left hemisphere:

1 the information in question may no longer be sufficiently recently or frequently used for it to be readily available, in which case conscious strategy for retrieval may be adopted, but could result in inaccurate reconstruction rather than recall;

2 the particular item of information may originally have been only briefly scanned at an unorganized level (not consciously associated with other relevant information), rather than having been subjected to focused (more intense/deeper) processing (see postulate 6, Appendix 2) at the time of input;

3 the left hemisphere may have *had* conscious control over the information in question, but no longer has so. It may be repressed from consciousness, but still be taken into account so as to have indirect effect on the processing of new information and decision making. It may also be allowed gradual introduction to consciousness in symbolic or distorted form and, incidentally, affect creative output or dreaming.

Failure to retrieve information controlled by the right is seen here to be more *obviously* attributable to emotional factors, although the position being adopted is that *any* success or failure in registration, retention, or recall of information is attributable to degree of intensity of affect. What is being argued additionally in the case of the right hemisphere is that information may be withheld from consciousness as a result of the need 'not to know' (p. 52).

The right side is being viewed as being in possession of more of the 'whole picture', for a number of reasons: (1) it is regarded as having had prime access to information during what is being called sub-threshold scanning (see postulate 6 and Figure 67, Appendix 2); (2) even after conscious and/or verbal organization it is still seen as being in possession of other sensory representations of the same information; (3) more gross associations are likely to be made consciously and unconsciously by the right than by the left; and (4) the right is viewed here as the hemisphere most likely to be active in long-term unconscious problem-solving attempts. The right, then, is seen to be the 'more informed' decision-maker – if not the most obviously rational – in its mostly *covert control* of the means of physical and psychological survival.

The left hemisphere, by contrast, is seen as having *overt control* of information. It is viewed as a verbalizer/organizer, and as assisting in analytical and rationalization processes, as best it can, with the limited amount of information the right side allows it to have. Control of conscious attention is seen to be the outcome of negotiation between right and left hemispheres, but with the right acting as ultimate censor, regardless of any individually preferred mode of processing of information, or of the location of its eventual organized storage: the right is being defined as keeping pressure *from* the left, as it were, in order for its processing to *remain* sequential, as will be explained.

3.2 Two ways of perceiving the world

Clearly, the traditional view of the left as the dominant hemisphere is being challenged.[14] Neither right nor left is seen to be dominant *per se*; rather, it is argued that the two hemispheres exercise different *kinds* of control over consciousness and that the function and abilities of each are necessary to the most effective functioning of the other.[15] For example, the well-established verbal skills of the left are being viewed as dependent on the *perceptions of the right* for their most effective and appropriate use; for any degree of richness and variety; for the most original ideas that are voiced; and for any depth of emotion which may be expressed. Any dominance of the workings of the one hemisphere over the other is being seen, therefore, to be more to do with degrees of relative dominance of SNS or PNS activity, and individual differences in their patterns and rates of interaction, rather than with any species norm related to hemispheric asymmetry of function alone.

Extremely useful to the elaboration of this point of view, but not quoted as being written by one who would necessarily subscribe to it, is Bogen's discussion (1973:101–25) of the difficulties involved in characterizing the abilities of the right hemisphere. He also considers it to be extremely misleading to think of the right as being simply non-verbal, and quotes the very early view of Hughlings Jackson (ibid.:108) that, the distinguishing feature of what he still however refers to as the 'major hemisphere' (the left), is not its *possession* of words but its *use* of them. He stresses that there is a significant right hemisphere capacity for speech, but where more abstract terms may not be verbalized as a result of lesions to the left, descriptive phrases, similes, and metaphorical expressions are often used in an appropriate manner. He also points out that in right hemisphere lesions errors are made, but are *existential* rather than phonetic or semantic (ibid.:107).

Bogen also refers to Jackson's use of the term 'imperception', meaning an inability to recognize familiar persons, objects, and places, to describe a defect which he regarded as just as special as aphasia,[16] but one which results from right hemispheric damage rather than left. In addition, and in acknowledgement of the right being involved in other processes than just visuo-spatial ones, he gives evidence for its involvement in music, kinaesthetic functions, and artistic activity. Extremely usefully, he offers the term *'appositional'* for the more complex role and abilities of the right which 'apposes or collates data' in contrast to the left 'receiving the very same stimuli' but 'often aiming at very different results' being *'propositional'* (ibid.:109).

The qualifying statement has to be made, though, that right and left are not seen here as always or necessarily giving access to the 'very same stimuli'.[17] Neither are the phenomena described by Bogen as apposition and proposition viewed as necessarily exclusive to right and left respectively: the view here is that the right is more likely to be predominantly appositional and the left predominantly propositional.

Figures 8 and 9 are tables devised by Bogen, with and without reference to cerebral lateralization, which summarize the diversity of dichotomies suggested by various researchers to describe key characteristics of left and right hemispheres.

A confusing array of other dichotomies could be added, in an attempt to give as broad a view as possible of the two very different ways of processing information, but just two others beyond Ruddock's ritual and

Figure 8 Dichotomies with lateralization suggested

Suggested by	Left* hemisphere	Right hemisphere
Jackson (1864)	Expression	Perception
Jackson (1874)	Audito-articular	Retino-ocular
Jackson (1876)	Propositionizing	Visual imagery
Weisenberg and McBride (1935)	Linguistic	Visual or kinaesthetic
Anderson (1951)	Storage	Executive
Humphrey and Zangwill (1951)	Symbolic or propositional	Visual or imaginative
McFie and Piercy (1952)	Education of relations	Education of correlates
Milner (1958)	Verbal	Perceptual or non-verbal
Semmes, Weinstein, Ghent, Teuber (1960)	Discrete	Diffuse
Zangwill (1961)	Symbolic	Visuo-spatial
Hecaen, Ajuriaguerra, Angelergues (1963)	Linguistic	Pre-verbal
Bogen and Gazzaniga (1965)	Verbal	Visuo-spatial
Levy-Agresti and Sperry (1968)	Logical or analytic	Synthetic perceptual
Bogen (1969)	Propositional	Appositional

* A publisher's error appears in the original table: 'Left' and 'Right' are in reverse order from their positions above.
Source: Table devised by J. E. Bogen, reproduced from Ornstein (1973:111)
Reprinted with the permission of W. H. Freeman and Company.

Figure 9 Dichotomies without reference to cerebral lateralization

Suggested by	Dichotomies	
C. S. Smith	Atomistic	Gross
Price	Analytic or reductionist	Synthetic or concrete
Wilder	Numerical	Geometric
Head	Symbolic or systematic	Perceptual or non-verbal
Goldstein	Abstract	Concrete
Reusch	Digital or discursive	Analogic or eidetic
Bateson and Jackson	Digital	Analogic
J. Z. Young	Abstract	Map-like
Pribram	Digital	Analogic
W. James	Differential	Existential
Spearman	Education of relations	Education of correlates
Hobbes	Directed	Free or unordered
Freud	Secondary process	Primary process
Pavlov	Second signalling	First signalling
Sechenov (Luria)	Successive	Simultaneous
Lévi-Strauss	Positive	Mythic
Bruner	Rational	Metaphoric
Akhilinanda	Buddhi	Manas
Radhakrishnan	Rational	Integral

Source: Table devised by J. E. Bogen, reproduced from Ornstein (1973:120)
Reprinted with the permission of W. H. Freeman and Company.

encounter and Bogen's apposition and proposition are seen to offer a sufficiently grainy description of the psychological responses in question to demand reference.

The first of these is Deikman's definition of *action mode* and *receptive mode* (1973:67–85), as the two primary modes of organization which explain psychological and physiological variables in states of consciousness.[18] Of the action mode he says it is 'object oriented thought' in which

Sharp perceptual boundaries are matched by sharp conceptual boundaries, for success in acting on the world requires a clear sense of self-object difference.

In contrast, the receptive mode is a state organised around the intake of the environment rather than manipulation. The sensory-perceptual system is the dominant agency.

Other attributes of the receptive mode are diffuse attending, paralogical thought processes, decreased boundary perception, and the dominance of the sensory over the formal. The receptive mode is aimed at maximising the intake of the environment, and this mode would appear to originate and function maximally in the infant state.

Deikman concludes that,

in the course of development the action mode has priority to insure biological survival. The receptive mode develops also – but it occurs as an interlude between increasingly longer periods of action mode functioning. This developmental preference for the action mode has led us to regard the action mode as the proper one for adult life, while we have tended to think of the more unusual receptive states, as pathological or 'regressive'.

(1973:69)

Although this conclusion may be broadly accepted, particularly the implicit criticisms of our expectations of adults, it must be said that other reasons than developmental ones for perceived 'preference for the action mode' can and will be offered. Quite obviously too, Deikman's analysis of which mode 'has priority in biological survival' is not being supported here. 'Blind' action, with only limited awareness of phenomenological environmental change, could surely be no more relied on to ensure survival than the alternative of what might be termed 'informed passivity'.

Whether the preference in question is seen to be part of a developmental process, or a result of cultural pressure, or biologically adaptive or not, Deikman's criticisms seem valid enough, and his two modes will be returned to later, although the action mode may be seen to be more aptly labelled 'preparation for action' mode. Ruddock's bipolar extremes of ritual and encounter will also be returned to, but he also suggests that dichotomies concerning differences between what he refers to as *'instrumental objectives'* which require a narrowing of consciousness, as against purposes which are *'multiple and simultaneous'* (Ruddock 1980:43–4), can be subsumed under Liam Hudson's (1967) useful terms *convergers and divergers*.[19] This is of particular interest because it is part of Hudson's thesis, and consistent with Ruddock's view, that both modes, convergence *and* divergence, are kinds of *defence*.

Hudson's major discovery was that arts specialists displayed verbal biases, and scientists numerical and diagrammatic biases. Being critical of the adequacy of existing mental tests and, more specifically, Getzels and Jackson's (1962) terminology of 'High Creatives' as well as the very notion of creativity tests, which he saw as begging as many questions as intelligence tests did already, he devised tests of convergent and divergent thinking which he called 'open-ended tests'.

In general terms, those displaying a science bias tended to score lower on the open-ended tests, but higher on the IQ tests. These he refers to as convergers. Divergers, by contrast, achieved higher scores on open-ended tests, not such high scores on the IQ tests, and displayed a preference for arts subjects.[20] Arts specialists, he concludes, are on the whole divergers; and physical scientists, convergers (Hudson 1967:56). Perhaps most usefully, Hudson's research highlights the fact, which he stresses, 'that the academically successful boy is distinguished not by his intellectual apparatus, but by the use he sees fit to make of it. This is a finding which runs counter to some of the most persistent of our assumptions about the nature of intelligence' (ibid.:43). Importantly, he considers the belief that 'the higher the I.Q. the better' to be false, and emphasizes that it is the measure of *bias* which produces really striking discriminations between convergers and divergers, not the measure of level.

In however subtle or oblique a manner, it seems inevitable that dichotomies describing how environmental information is dealt with, as well as discussion of biases in abilities, become related to aspects of personality. For instance, in his description of convergers and divergers Hudson talks of the 'characteristics' of subjects, their attitudes and their proneness to self-expression or not, and he even caricatures each type. Interestingly, he does this in highly complementary (and defensive) terms: 'the converger takes refuge from people in things; the diverger takes refuge from things in people' (ibid.:102–12). Ruddock's concern with the relationship between perception and personality is obvious,[21] as are Deikman's. He makes reference to striving and non-striving attitudes as aspects of his action and receptive modes whilst citing colourful and contrasting, but some would say arbitrary, examples: of the meditative monk and of lovers engaged in sexual intercourse as being in receptive modes – that is, receptive to environmental stimuli – as opposed to the cab driver negotiating traffic, exemplifying the action mode (Deikman 1973:70–1). But the task now is to make new connections: between asymmetry of brain function, with which the chapter began; conscious and unconscious modes of processing; degrees of suggestibility; so-called

Figure 10 Dichotomies

Intellect	Intuition
Convergent	Divergent
Intellectual	Sensuous
Deductive	Imaginative
Rational	Metaphoric
Vertical	Horizontal
Discrete	Continuous
Abstract	Concrete
Realistic	Impulsive
Directed	Free
Differential	Existential
Sequential	Multiple
Historical	Timeless
Analytic	Holistic
Explicit	Tacit
Objective	Subjective
Successive	Simultaneous

Source: Table of dichotomies reproduced from Springer and Deutsch (1981:186)
Reprinted with the permission of W. H. Freeman and Company.

'cognitive style'; and personality. It is necessary to relate these to one another in order to go on to describe the new model of individual style, which will eventually be seen to be a model of organic style *per se*.

Springer and Deutsch (1981), whose work on asymmetry of brain function has already been quoted, offer their own table of dichotomies, which is reproduced above (Figure 10). Four of them already appear amongst those offered by Bogen (Figures 8 and 9), but even after allowing for that fact, their list, together with the earlier tables, provide us with over forty dichotomies relating to differences in human experience and behaviour. With reference to their own list Springer and Deutsch comment, 'Although these terms are quite varied, they do seem to have something in common. Perhaps, as some have suggested, they correspond to the separate processes of the two cerebral hemispheres' (ibid.:186).

These authors were cited earlier as having drawn attention to the tendency of researchers into cognitive style to relate their findings to these same processes, and Geoffrey Squires (1981), whose list and brief summaries of the main cognitive styles to be found in the literature are reproduced in Figure 11, also makes this point after remarking that it is possible to detect an urge in some researchers to reduce all of them to one deep style, but adding that 'the evidence for any strong correlation between the styles is still very patchy'. Indicating the 'strongly pluralistic' nature of this kind of research, Squires refers to Messick's identification of nine styles in 1970 and nineteen in 1976, but simply taking into account his own list of twelve major dimensions swells the total number of dichotomies recorded here to well over fifty.

Although the empirical evidence for relating cognitive styles to one another remains less than adequate, when they are viewed as alternative strategies for *coping with and defending against environmental change*, it does become possible to relate them to one another within an APM-A framework. Specifically, this can be done by considering them in relation to changes in level of arousal, and to the kinds of changes which take place in autonomic functioning in response to threat already described in Chapters 1 and 2. All of Squires's list, for instance, can be seen to relate to aspects of, and/or the effects of, at least one of the following key APM-A concepts:

A the scan–focus dimension of attention, in turn related to ANS functioning; to diffuse-sequential processing of information and to degrees of flexibility and control exercised in mental and physical activity;

B need for swiftness and efficiency of action – or not – in response to perceived levels of environmental threat;

C intensity of need for change.

Figure 11 A list and summaries of major cognitive styles

1 Field-dependence–independence. A tendency to see things in context as against a tendency to abstract them from their context.

2 Reflective–impulsive. A tendency to evaluate a response before making it as against a tendency to respond quickly: sometimes referred to as conceptual tempo.

3 Serialist–holist. A tendency to approach things in a linear, step-by-step fashion, as against a tendency to begin with the whole.

4 Breadth of categorization. A tendency to include instances in a category or group as against a tendency to exclude them.

5 Conceptualizing style. To do with the basis for grouping, rather than the size of grouping: three bases are distinguished: analytic-descriptive; categorical–inferential; and relational–thematic.

6 Complexity–simplicity. A tendency to prefer, or be able to process, complex stimulus-situations as against a tendency to prefer simple or well-patterned situations.

7 Levelling–sharpening. The tendency to minimize differences and distinctions as against the tendency to maximize them; often related to memory.

8 Convergence–divergence. The tendency to look for single outcomes against the tendency to entertain multiple possibilities.

9 Sensory modality preference. The tendency to use kinaesthetic, visual, or auditory modes for experiencing the world.

10 Risk-taking–cautiousness. The tendency to take chances as against the tendency to seek certainty.

11 Tolerance for unrealistic experiences. A tendency to accept information that is improbable or unconventional as against a tendency to define out or reject such information.

12 Constricted–flexible controls. A tendency to be susceptible to distraction as against a tendency to disregard it.

Source: Squires (1981:5–6)

An arbitrary classification of the styles listed by Squires in terms of the three classes of APM-A concepts (A, B, and C) above could be conceived of as follows, although it must be emphasized that the aim is to show how the styles can be placed within the APM-A framework and be related to one another, not to make any rigid categorization, as all of them can be seen to relate almost as easily to any of the other two categories:

A
field-dependence–independence
breadth of categorization (narrow or broad)
levelling–sharpening
convergence–divergence
serialist–holist
conceptualizing style (analytic–descriptive; categorical–inferential; relational–thematic)
complexity–simplicity

B
reflective–impulsive
C
risk-taking–cautiousness
tolerance for unrealistic experiences, or not
constricted–flexible controls

N.B. Squire's ninth style, sensory modality preference, is, of course, not a dichotomy.

It is relevant at this stage to note what Cropley has to say about cognitive style:

> Most cognitive styles . . . have in common the property that they involve a dichotomy between, on the one hand, taking the world in in large lumps and, on the other, selectively attending only to chosen portions of the environment. The dichotomy can be restated as being a matter of paying attention to as wide a range of environmental properties as possible, or selecting a few attributes of the environment and concentrating on them and processing them. The latter strategy has the advantage that one can select a few highly related and task-relevant pieces of information and focus attention on them. This makes for ease of coding and necessitates little accommodation (modifying of codes), but that state of affairs is achieved at the expense of losing the capacity to make rapid changes in one's cognitive structures. In other words the highly selective kind of cognitive styles lead to stereotopy [sic] of intellectual functioning, but have an important advantage in that they make life much easier.
>
> On the other hand, taking in as much information as possible involves the risk of cognitive strain, necessitates frequent modification of existing categories, and makes intellectual functioning a more arduous task. However, this state of affairs leads to good pay-offs in that it involves the advantages of being able to change one's existing mental structures very readily, of being able to relate widely different looking data and, in fact, of being in a state highly favourable to the appearance of creative thinking.
>
> (1970:122)

The precise relevance of this fairly lengthy quotation from Cropley should become more obvious as the APM-A perspective is enlarged to include other aspects of individuality, and as an explanation of differences, which itself hinges on differing degrees of urgency in processing information, is offered; but for now it is enough that he stands together 'selectively attending only to chosen portions', 'focus', and 'concentration' against 'taking the world in in large lumps' and 'risk of cognitive strain'; and 'stereotopy' [*sic*] against readiness for change.

It is hoped that by the end of the chapter it will be seen how so-called cognitive style also relates to what were above called first- and second-order needs, and how many of the dichotomies which have been pointed out either fall into one of the broad categories (A, B, C) above, or can be seen as direct or incidental effects of endocrinological changes associated with ANS activity and, crucially, differences in degrees of intensity of response to threat.

3.3 Strategies and attitudes

By considering the phenomenon of cognitive style in terms of individual differences in styles of defence and strategies for coping, we have now reached a position from which it becomes possible, gradually, to introduce a dynamic model of human nature, within which alternative means of defence and coping will be seen to move between the polar extremes of mainly passive and mainly active;[22] but it will be complicated by the element of complementarity which was threatened earlier and by reference to different *kinds* of arousal. Additionally, conscious 'purpose' is to be distinguished from unconscious 'purpose' (see postulates 7, 13, 14, 15, Appendix 2, and Gear 1987), and relative bias towards physical survival will be distinguished from relative bias[23] towards psychological survival, just as the activity–passivity dimension itself is to be qualified as referring to physical *or* mental performance, or both.

Between the polar extremes of activity and passivity, of different kinds, there will also be seen to exist an extraordinarily variable range of possibilities of intensity and kinds of interplay (combinations of *intensity* and *bias*) between excitation and inhibition. In other words, it is to be argued that logically, not only are all mental activity and all physical activity the result of a more or less effective *combination* of excitation and inhibition (or more simply, going and stopping and scan and focus, and all of the kinds of experience and behaviour which may be associated with those functions) but that, in any individual, a characteristic bias may be more or less obvious; and that within a framework of bias, or no obvious bias, *intensity of activity* (or degree of passivity) constitutes another crucial variable.

However, before describing the model in detail there remains just a little more ground-clearing to be done in order to clarify what is *not* meant by some of the terminology to be used. Some of the terminology which is to be used to define a *dynamic model of style* is already well-established and well-understood, whereas other terms have already been used by others in rather special ways which must not necessarily be assumed to be appropriate to their use here. For instance, the terms 'focusing' and 'scanning' have been used above to describe aspects of attention, perception, and memory characteristic of different states of arousal. This naturally leads to the use of the terms 'focusers' and 'scanners' to describe individuals who display a consistent tendency to process information one way or the other: either sequentially and discretely, or making more gross associations and perceiving looser links between items of information, so as to manifest a more diffuse mode of information-processing.

Although Bruner's use of the terms 'focuser' and 'scanner' relates very well to their use here, his use is particular. In experiments in cognitive style and strategies of discrimination between examples and non-examples of particular concepts, those he came to label 'focusers' proceeded by checking single attributes, rather in the manner of a controlled experiment – that is, holding all potentially relevant variables constant, except one at a time – while 'scanners' were apt to make more demands on memory and reasoning skills[24] by remembering several possibilities of key attributes each time, and proceeding by the elimination of whole concepts at once.

More research into this aspect of attention is summarized by Goldstein and Blackman (1978:9), who refer to a number of writers on scanning, in connection with the extent to which an individual compares a stimulus with a standard, and Messick (1976:18–19) makes reference to yet more researchers into the same concept, which he defines as referring to 'individual differences in the extensiveness and intensity of attention deployment' which, he says, leads to 'individual differences in vividness of experience and the span of awareness'.

Another dichotomy of obvious relevance to our major concept of *externalization* is the extremely robust dimension of extraversion[25]– introversion. Although our types will be referred to as externalizers and internalizers (rather than extraverts and introverts) and the theoretical underpinning of the typology is somewhat different, both from that of Jung, who is usually regarded as having first identified the dimension,[26] and from that of Eysenck (1981), whose name is currently most closely associated with it, and whose work has also spawned an enormous amount of research data consistent with APM-A theory.

The original Jungian view of extroversion–introversion held that introversion is manifested by those individuals who derive their motivations chiefly from within themselves, from inner or subjective factors, whereas extroversion represents the attitude of those who derive motivation chiefly from external factors and from active involvement in the environment. Although Jung accepted that dominant attitudes (of either introversion or extroversion) may shift in the course of a life, he also accepted that one of the attitudes can be apparently fixed within an individual, so that it does become possible to talk of types.

Eysenck's adoption of the Jungian dichotomy as one of his dimensions of personality[27] is now viewed as having had as powerful an impact on experimental psychology as Jung's theories have had on clinical psychology. But in contrast to Jung's orientation towards intrapsychic[28] processes (which he calls 'analytical psychology'), Eysenck's orientation is more biological and behavioural.

Typically, Eysenck's extravert is sociable, lively, impulsive, seeking novelty and change, carefree, and emotionally expressive, whilst his introvert is deemed to be quiet, introspective, intellectual, well-ordered, emotionally unexpressive, and value-oriented; and prefers small groups of intimate friends and plans well ahead. It will be useful to remember, though, that the major sub-factors of extraversion are impulsiveness and sociability.

It is because the typology to be used here is not quite the same as that of either Jung or Eysenck that the terms 'extravert' and 'introvert' are to be replaced with the terms 'externalizer' and 'internalizer'. Issue is also to be taken later with the equation of introvert–intellectual and with other notions expressed above, such as the necessarily 'carefree' extravert and the conventionally perceived temporal orientation of the polar-extreme type (for example, the introvert planning well ahead). Other interpretations of research data will naturally also be questioned – both implicitly and explicitly – but in general terms, it will be shown that by simply taking into account *kinds* of sensitivity and *kinds* of distractability (qualities around which a great deal of research revolves), for instance, it is possible to explain phenomena which are difficult to accommodate within existing theory.

The key difference between our position and that of Eysenck or his critic Gray's (1981) position centres on the fact that both of the latter see *introverts* as chronically more aroused than extraverts, who in turn are viewed as chronically underaroused; although as M. W. Eysenck (1981) reports, the evidence for this is not compelling.

Here, *bias* in *kind* of arousal as well as *intensity* of arousal will be taken into account. The suggestion is that it would be far more fruitful to view the *extravert* as *more aroused* than the introvert, and for prime concern to shift from cortical arousal to *limbic arousal*. Indeed, any theory based on hedonistic motivation – as it is stressed APM-A theory is – can hardly fail to view degrees of *limbic* arousal as crucial.

There is plenty of indirect evidence from a number of fields suggesting complementarity between consciousness and unconsciousness. For instance, Freudian concepts of id and ego rest on the concept of a changing balance of dominance and subordination between the two, and, of course, a complementary and dynamic relationship between consciousness and unconsciousness plays a major part in Jungian theory. It is also interesting to note that H. J. Eysenck himself offers an indirect indication of complementarity between cortical and limbic arousal and, incidentally, between conscious and unconscious motivations. In an explanation of different kinds of inhibition (his double usage of which concept, he admits, has caused difficulties), he says,

> it is important not to mix up two contrary and contradictory meanings [of the term 'inhibition']. Cortical inhibition refers to a lowering of arousal in the cortex; this reduces cortical control over lower centres and habit-structures, and consequently leads to less inhibited types of behaviour. Thus high cortical inhibition = uninhibited behaviour. The action of alcohol may make this point clearer. Alcohol is a depressant drug, i.e., it depresses cortical activity, thus disinhibiting lower centres and leading to uninhibited behaviour.
>
> (Eysenck 1981:3–4)

If all that has been said here about limbic arousal and its relationship to behaviour is accepted (Chapters 1 and 2), this statement could be taken to support our hypothesis: that low limbic arousal allows concentrated (that is, focused) cortical arousal, which *may* measure as higher, and that high limbic arousal produces more diffuse, dispersed, and more economical use of cortical arousal (that is, scanning), which *may* measure lower.

It is relevant at this point to mention that Claridge (1981:128–9), in describing various theoretical positions on arousal, refers to Eysenck's revision of his own theory in order for it to be able to accommodate neuroticism as well as extraversion within an arousal framework (when previously neuroticism had been seen as functionally independent of the cortical excitatory process defined as underlying extraversion and introversion). In fact, Eysenck proposed a *second 'arousal' process* to account for variations in neuroticism, which he called *'activation', identified with the limbic system*. Hence two sources of cortical excitation were recognized: 'one concerned with sensory arousal' and mediated by the ARAS, 'and the other, of limbic origin responsible for emotional arousal'.[29]

Two obvious points arise with reference to the new APM-A position: first, it seems much more sound and potentially more productive to relate our behaviourally inhibited and uninhibited types to the physiological system most directly concerned with the motivation of *behaviour*, the limbic system – a move which must, after all, follow arguments that pleasure, pain, threat, and promise play their part in everything we think or do: second, the new position allows an interactive relationship between ARAS, sensory information, limbic arousal/emotion, and cortical arousal and, therefore, a dynamic relationship between extraversion and neuroticism *without* having to resort to Eysenck's separate concepts of 'activation' and 'arousal', or even having to make the rather dubious distinction between 'sensory arousal' and 'emotional arousal' quoted above.

Eysenck's claim, that the extravert is underaroused, is accompanied by an explanation of his apparent need for higher optimal levels of stimulation, simply on those grounds: that because he is underaroused he seeks to raise his level of arousal by exposing himself to arousing stimuli. One is left to wonder why, if this is the case, there appears to be no recorded case of extraversion having led eventually to introversion as a result of this particular form of compensation. The oft-repeated rationale presented here, that increase in arousal equates with increase in need for change, fits neither with Eysenck's view of introversion, nor with his idea of compensatory activity undertaken by extraverts, whom he considers to be underaroused. It does, however, fit with our view of the extravert as the more aroused type; and both the rationale in question and this new view of arousal in relation to extraversion and introversion can still be seen to be consistent with the plethora of data the dimension has spawned.

Our terms for these polar-extreme personality types, externalizer and internalizer, have been used before, but not in a way which is likely to cause any confusion with their use here that this writer has become aware of (see Buck *et al.* 1974).

The centrality of the internal–external dimension of attention has already been stressed, but Shapiro and Alexander (1975:17) also make the point that, although the search for 'fillers' and 'containers', as they put it, has so far failed to 'mirror faithfully' Jung's original insight into extraversion and introversion – the subject of their discussion, which they describe as having been 'that these two possible facets or sides of perception or experience provide the basis for a fundamental difference in personality between people' – the dimension does continue to generate other personality variables which are useful to the understanding of individual differences. They say,

> To illustrate, inside/outside have been taken variously as mental/ physical, which in turn has been rendered as ideas/things, thinking/ acting, and ideas/facts; self/others; inhibition/impulsivity; internal mediation/external reactivity; body/field; internal standards/external standards; passivity/activity; internal/external locus of control; internal/external locus of attention.
>
> (1975:17)

If these polarities do indeed represent aspects of individual differences, and if the model being presented here does, as is being claimed, offer explanations of their major sources, then it should be possible within the new theoretical framework to relate them to one another.[30]

Before finally moving on to the APM-A analysis, at least brief mention must be made of previous attempts to identify SNS/PNS dominance as a source of personality differences. These have been summarized by Van Toller (1979:78ff., 115ff.), who draws particular attention to Lacey (1950) – as having 'tested individuals over a long period of time and concluded that organised patterns of autonomic reaction are shown in similar situations, and that those patterns are repeatable over time' – and to Eppinger and Hess (1915) as the first of five attempts he cites (including that of Eysenck), made between 1915 and 1965, to link personality to the function of the autonomic nervous system.

A related notion to these attempts and to the analysis about to be offered is that identifed by the Soviet school of psychology based on Pavlov's early conception of strong and weak nervous systems. This is discussed by Powell (1979:chap. 4) in relation to the possibility of a neurophysiological model of personality. Powell defines the strong nervous system as 'that which can withstand long and concentrated excitation, or the action of an "ultra strong" stimulus without passing into an inhibitory state' (ibid.:25), and comments on the temptation to equate this with extraversion,[31] if it were not for at least one study (ibid.:30) which has tested this hypothesis, only to produce a negative result. Nevertheless, both Eysenck (1981:10–11) and Gray (1981:271–2) have made the correlation in question.

A more useful hypothetical construct than the rather global ideas of strength and weakness, applied to the complexities of a non-unitary arousal system, could be that of *intensity of activity of the nervous system*. This concept has the advantage of relating to fundamental process: to rates of firing of neuronal cells; to amounts and rates of secretion of transmitters at synaptic junctions, and to the behavioural implications of these neurophysiological phenomena – that is, to the availability and expression of mental and physical energy,[32] amount and precision of movement,[33] and speed of response,[34] all of which have been shown to be significant areas of difference between extraverts and introverts, and have obvious relevance to the definitions which are about to be offered.

An added advantage of such a change of perspective is that by taking into account the balancing role of the PNS, this concept can be seen to apply equally well to the autonomic and peripheral nervous systems and to limbic and cortical arousal, and to allow for a variable relationship between them. If, instead of thinking of strength and weakness (a dimension seen here to hold potentially grossly misleading value-laden overtones, as both of the extreme types will eventually be shown to embody different *kinds* of strengths *and* weaknesses), we think of *relative speeds* of processing *differing amounts* of information, it becomes possible to incorporate a dynamic and complementary relationship between conscious and unconscious information-processing, as well as the bipolar continua characteristic of both cognitive style and the personality dimensions under review into a single model.

We can view the extravert, or our nearly equivalent externalizer, as experiencing both a high degree of limbic arousal (causing him to respond very readily to environmental change at an unconscious – autonomic – level), *and* a high level of cortical inhibition[35] as a concomitant of (1) comparatively heavy demands on mental resources at limbic level, and (2) the consequent bombardment of information the cortex is required to handle because of the same ready limbic response to environmental change. He or she is likely to focus only briefly (too briefly for long-term memory to be effected[36]) on low priority signals, that is, on most of the comparatively large number of signals attended to; to *scan* for items of information most obviously relevant to current purposes, for first- and second-priority signals (see postulate 5, Appendix 2, and Gear 1987), which then receive conscious and/or further unconscious sustained (focused) attention.

Obviously, we do not have unlimited supplies of mental energy any more than we have unlimited reserves of physical energy, and as it has already been established that attentional capacity is limited (Miller 1956), the possibility of overload and dysfunction must exist. It is being argued, therefore, that the externalizer sacrifices *depth* of processing for *breadth* of processing, but with the dominant unconscious mode 'holding' more 'other' significant but less pressing items for greater depth of processing, as and when attentional resources become available.

Urgent intake of information has already been described in Chapter 2 as being associated with the 'need for orientation' response, and is obviously also being regarded as synonymous with the phenomenon of scanning; and just as scanning (or rapid processing) is being regarded as the dominant mode of handling information in the presence of high levels of SNS activity, so is physical activity being viewed as a necessary means of externalizing above tension threshold (that is, overload) excitation. Of course, in evolutionary terms, it seems not just probable but almost inevitable that activity and a scanning mode of attention should have become associated (it being necessary to make rapid assessments of terrain while running, for instance), just as focus and relative relaxation – stopping to think, as it was put earlier – should also have become related.

The *lowest tension threshold type*, therefore, is being described as most active – physically and mentally, unconsciously *and* consciously: quite simply, as the physiologically most active type, with SNS activity already dominant to the point at which physiological changes associated with the orientation response are continuously 'ticking over'.

The inevitable paradox within this explanation is the implication that an incidental effect of a ready response to change, and of paying attention to as much information at once as the system will allow, is that it is necessary for the safeguard/economy of cortical inhibition to be invoked in order for physiological (electro-chemical) equilibrium to be maintained. *Extreme efficiency* in screening as much of the environment as possible, for signs of threat or promise, is seen here to carry an inherent *lack of efficiency* in sustained concentration. Conversely, the more relaxed, *high threshold* internalizer, more prone to focusing than scanning, may be *less* efficient at 'early warning' but be *so* efficient at concentration and retention of information that facts are registered however apparently useless they may seem.

In essence, the externalizer is being described as *more vulnerable* to environmental change than the internalizer – not less so. This is quite contrary to Eysenck's view of his corresponding types. In 1967 he drew similarity between introverts and the 'weak nervous system' type on the basis of characteristics such as greater sensitivity to sensory stimulation; 'relatively low sensory thresholds'; 'low thresholds of arousal'; 'low thresholds of transmarginal inhibition' (response decrements at high intensity); and 'persistent orientation reflexes'.

Typically, research conducted to test this hypothesis (with rather inconclusive results) is directed towards assessing magnitude of OR (orientation response) which, it could be argued, might just as easily indicate not low, but *high* 'thresholds of arousal' *and high* 'sensory thresholds'. To understand this we need only take into account the fact that the introvert/internalizer may *manifest* a more marked response to novel stimuli (or sudden change) than the extravert/externalizer, not because of greater 'sensitivity' but, within the APM-A analysis, because the perceptions of the latter, more highly tuned, individuals include more sub-threshold scanning (see postulate 6, Appendix 2, and Gear 1987) and consequently, greater likelihood of picking up early warning of phenom-enological change.

The externalizer, with the much more fluid attentional/perceptual/memory/arousal characteristics and already described as being in a constant state of readiness for change, can therefore be seen to manifest the less marked response. He or she is less obviously moved by environmental change than those whose attention is more likely to be rigidly held to the matter in hand – and whose awareness of new demands is seen to occur more suddenly as a result – for two reasons. The first is a capacity for shifting easily from one signal to another, arising, incidentally, from greater (more rapid) mental activity, and the second is because of a capacity to make more rapid and more diverse (but possibly less efficient) 'connections' and 'identifications' of environmental events at both con-scious and unconscious levels.

Similarly, it can be argued that the responses of the externalizer extinguish more quickly because his awareness of, and need to process and identify, successive signals is greater than that of the internalizer.

In short, the conventional concepts of 'sensory thresholds' and 'thresholds of arousal', as used by Eysenck and others, are viewed here as being fraught with problems of polymorphism, in the same way as the concepts of 'strength' and 'weakness' have been described as being, when applied to the dynamics of the nervous system. The term 'sensitivity' (within Eysenckian theory conventionally applied to introverts) has been avoided within the APM-A context so far, for the same reason. From what has been said above about vulnerability, it might be thought that if it were used it would be with reference to externalizers. Eventually, however, it will be shown that both polar extremes of personality display sensitivities, but of rather different kinds.

Meanwhile, the term 'vulnerability' is viewed as being much less problematic, and to serve as an explanatory – as will be shown – rather than descriptive concept, just as the phrase 'tension threshold', with its open-ended acceptance of the existing state of the organism and all of its complexities, is being offered as being more useful for the purpose of understanding essential differences between individuals than Eysenck's notion of 'thresholds of arousal'. The latter seems to embody a misleading assumption of unitariness: a view of arousal in terms of level but not of kind, and an inference that we resemble each other in this quality in all but level of facility for its activation and/or intensity.

A much more complex picture of variability is to emerge. It is to be stressed from this point onwards that the human personality cannot be neatly classified as belonging to one of two extreme types; neither can it be adequately described by placement at a point along a bipolar continuum. Not even the identification of individual differences within the orthogonal spaces provided by Eysenck's extraversion and neuroticism dimensions is seen to offer adequate scope for the accommodation of human variability.

The new model is not based on specific traits or tendencies of the person, nor on strict orthogonal dimensions based on particular characteristics, but on physiological process and on the *dynamic interaction* of *kinds* of arousal and their likely effects on experience and behaviour.

All of the APM-A arguments employed so far rest firmly on the belief that above all else man is an emotional being, whose rationality, even at its most informed and sophisticated, is always the result of the fulfilment of an emotional need: the need for orientation. Paradoxically though, the measure of emotion, other than in its most primitive and easily identifiable form (that is, as fear or anger), is fraught with difficulties of classification and identification. For example, to find more than two or three individuals who would make the same fine distinctions between shock and surprise, say, or contentment and happiness, could prove to be exceedingly difficult: the exercise of devising an experiment to *produce* specific emotions in any random group of subjects could prove impossible.

The best-known investigations into fear and anger are those of Ax (1953) and of Funkenstein (1956). Both argued that fear and anger states are characterized by a differential patterning of the activities of the autonomic nervous system, but whereas Funkenstein made an association between anger and noradrenalin, Ax correlated anger and a mixed adrenalin/noradrenalin-like pattern. However, both associated fear with an adrenalin-like patterning.

Others have associated adrenalin variously with apprehension and anxiety, mental pain and discomfort, uncertainty and increased mental activity (Van Toller 1979:98–101). Similarly, increased secretion of noradrenalin has been associated with reactions to unpleasant stimuli, increase in blood sugars (ibid.:98, 105) and to increased activity in rats (Campbell and Singer 1979:49–50).

These findings and others allow us, with some confidence, to make a very simple correlation between the secretion of adrenalin and observable changes in mental activity, and between the secretion of noradrenalin and observable changes in physical activity. They also allow us to begin to move beyond the several concepts of kinds of arousal discussed by Claridge (1981) for instance. The APM-A concept of arousal is founded, essentially, in the notion of increase in the availability of two different kinds of

Figure 12   Intensity and bias of arousal

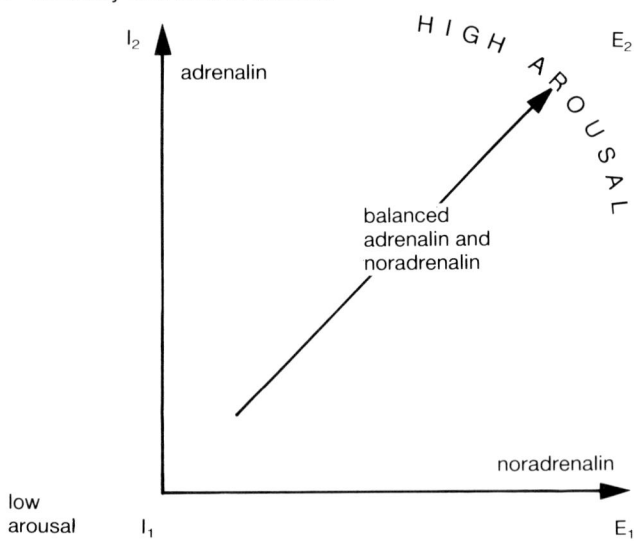

Note: I_1, I_2, E_1, and E_2 will eventually be defined as representing different kinds of internalizers and externalizers.

energy,[37] which in turn promote different kinds of mental and physical activity.

Put differently, we can say that given a relative bias towards SNS activity, an individual may or may not display a *further* bias: towards increase in either mental energy (and activity) *or* physical activity. This is a view which allows us to identify three key aspects of arousal: (1) intensity of arousal, (2) predominantly adrenalin-biased arousal, and (3) predominantly noradrenalin-biased arousal, the interplay of which can be seen to provide for a potentially vast range of variability.[38]

Expressed diagrammatically, this concept offers us the basis of our model as shown in Figure 12.

Intensity and bias of arousal may also be expressed in terms of their incidental effects, that is, as promoting different intensities and kinds of mental and physical activity and, it is being argued, the most fundamental changes in, and characteristic styles of, experience and behaviour.

It now becomes possible to begin to elaborate the model in terms of a typology of individual style, to add definitions of personality, our new hierarchy of needs, and to begin to consider kinds of intelligence and the many different forms of behaviour which fall under the general heading of 'creativity'.

Most obviously, and in the most general terms, it is possible to locate internalizers on the side of low physical activity,[39] implying either relative PNS dominance,[40] in the lower half of the model (I_1), or strongly adrenalin- rather than noradrenalin-biased arousal in the upper half (I_2). Similarly, externalizers can be located on the side on which high levels of physical activity either predominate over mental activity (E_1), or are

Figure 13 Intensity and bias of mental and physical activity

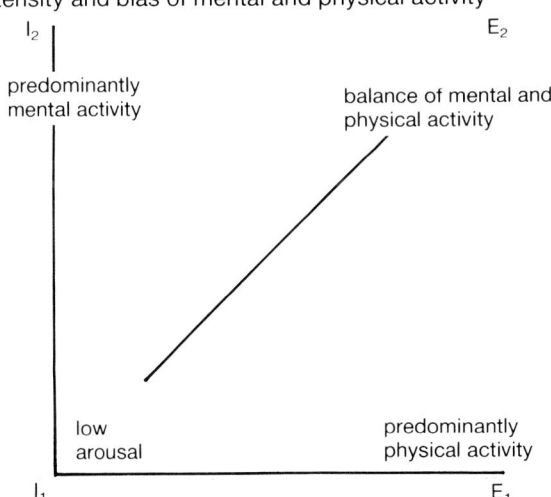

I_2

E_2

predominantly
mental activity

balance of mental and
physical activity

low
arousal

predominantly
physical activity

I_1

E_1

93

Figure 14 Externalizers (E_1 and E_2) and internalizers (I_1 and I_2) viewed in terms of intensity and bias of kinds of arousal and kinds of activity, according to Figs. 12 and 13

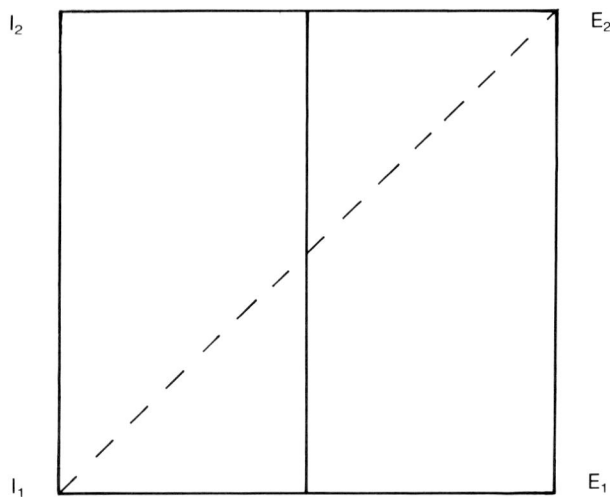

manifest *alongside* intense mental activity as a result of high levels of both adrenalin *and* noradrenalin (E_2).[41]

Instead of simply providing stereotypes to describe the polar-extreme types, the model being developed allows for the possibility of relative degrees of both mental and physical activity; relative degrees of scanning and focus; and of disorganization (or flexibility) and organization (or rigidity) of experience and behaviour, within and between the two major groups. Importantly, as will be discussed in the next chapter, it also allows for the various kinds of activity to be manifested in socially acceptable *or* in socially unacceptable ways.[42] And merely dividing the model again, into four quarters to represent different kinds of externalizer and different kinds of internalizer, will be seen to offer the basis of a potentially much wider range of variability than can be represented either by bipolar continua or by definitions of personality dependent on clusters of traits of the kind offered by Cattell's 16PF scale, for example (Cattell *et al.* 1970).

As a model of fundamental process it can accommodate different possible manifestations of the variable intensities and biases of arousal which it represents, while taking into account dynamic relationships within and between various extremes, the most significant of which are represented by the lower half of the left-hand side of the model, the corner marked I_1 (lowest arousal of any kind and archetypal internalizers), and the top right-hand corner E_2 (highest levels of adrenalin *and* noradrenalin secretion: highest arousal and archetypal externalizers). In the next chapter the same model will also be seen to accommodate the Eysenckian dimensions of neuroticism and psychoticism as well as personality and perceptual disorders such as psychopathy and autism.

Major implications of this model include the fact that, as well as accommodating typical Eysenckian extraverts and introverts, by making reference to kinds, as well as to base levels of arousal, and therefore also – according to earlier arguments (p. 89) – inherent differences in arousability, our dynamic model of style allows for not just ambiverts, but for other quite different categories. It allows for the possibility of extremely sociable, lively (extraverted) intellectuals[43] of the kind we have all met, *and* the kind of *non*-intellectual, unsociable, and inactive extreme opposite types whom we come across in 'real life', but for whose existence there seems also to be no theoretical support in the huge weight of literature generated by the extraversion–introversion dimension.

Figure 15 Some fundamental implied differences within and between the major internal and external adaptive styles

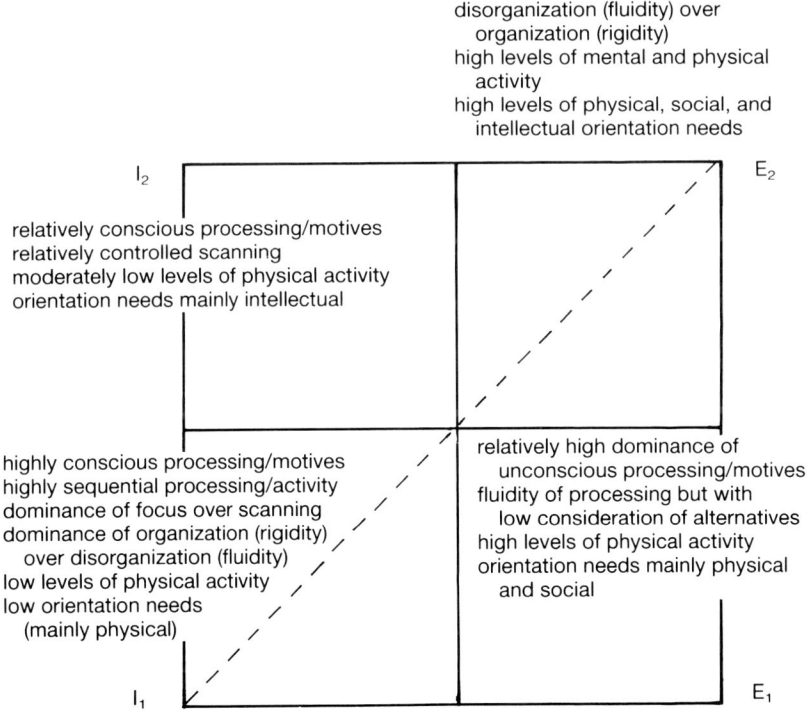

high dominance of unconscious processing/motives
simultaneous processing/activity
dominance of scanning over focus
disorganization (fluidity) over organization (rigidity)
high levels of mental and physical activity
high levels of physical, social, and intellectual orientation needs

I_2

E_2

relatively conscious processing/motives
relatively controlled scanning
moderately low levels of physical activity
orientation needs mainly intellectual

highly conscious processing/motives
highly sequential processing/activity
dominance of focus over scanning
dominance of organization (rigidity) over disorganization (fluidity)
low levels of physical activity
low orientation needs (mainly physical)

relatively high dominance of unconscious processing/motives
fluidity of processing but with low consideration of alternatives
high levels of physical activity
orientation needs mainly physical and social

I_1

E_1

It is being argued that within the broad categories of internalizer and externalizer further differences may be defined: that is, that within each of the two major groups already distinguished by differences ·in levels of secretion of noradrenalin, there exist other extremes – of low and high adrenalin types, and, of course, more or less balanced types in between.

Figure 15 represents chronically underaroused internalizers, low in noradrenalin and adrenalin secretion, and therefore relatively inactive physically and mentally, at I_1; more mentally active internalizers (higher in adrenalin secretion) in quadrant I_2; most mentally and physically active externalizers (highest in adrenalin and noradrenalin) at E_2, and physically active externalizers in quadrant E_1.

However, by invoking our earlier arguments about externalization of neuronal excitation (p. 30), and by referring to the fact that even strong bias towards the release of either adrenalin or noradrenalin includes relatively active release of the other (as both are crucial to SNS activity), I_2s may also be expected to be to some extent more physically active as well as more mentally active than I_1s, but still not, or course, as physically active, or as tuned to environmental change as E_1s or E_2s.

Although multiple continua are being used to cut into and across the model in order to explore and define its dynamics, it has to be remembered that relationships between any one area and the others are conceived as being organic, as merging and melting into one another, and not as existing in isolation. This will become clearer as the model is extended to make connections with other aspects of human variability and adaptability, conventionally subsumed under the headings of motivation, intelligence, and creativity, but which in essence will be seen to refer to *process qualities*, such as *energy, needs, efficiency, originality*, and *productivity*, all of which will be seen to be dependent on different degrees and kinds of arousal.

The most crucial change of perspective which occurs as a result of defining extraverts and externalizers as the *most limbically aroused* types is a change which will be seen to help to make sense of much more than individual differences in major personality traits as measured by Eysenck's famous Inventory (Eysenck and Eysenck 1964). The change in question is that, *instead of being viewed as chronically underaroused, the external types are being viewed as aroused to the point of 'overload'*. The particular vulnerability of the externalizer, therefore, is seen to derive both from experiencing greater impulse to respond to internal and external changes and from greater dependence on the availability of a sufficiently high level of environmental change to meet high levels of need.[44]

Few, if any, would dispute that consideration of levels and kinds of need is of just as much importance to the consideration of motivation as it is to the study of personality. Obviously, needs affect *all* decision making and all action, whether they (the needs or the decisions) are experienced consciously or not, and, incidentally, our model of style should help to clarify why most major theories of motivation are also major theories of personality:[45] all refer to needs, either explicitly or implicitly.

Most direct references to needs, by theorists whose work is applied to the investigation of both motivation and personality, are those of Maslow, already mentioned, and Murray. Murray (1938) actually says that people differ according to their needs: that needs organize the way people think, feel, perceive, and act – sentiments wholly in accord with all that has already been, and remains to be expressed here. However, whereas Murray attempts a conclusive list, of twelve 'viscerogenic needs' and twenty-eight 'psychogenic needs', we are to attempt no such list – only the hierarchy of needs which has already been presented (see Figures 4 and 5).

Orientation needs are, by definition,[46] highest at highest levels of arousal, but what were labelled in the last chapter as first- and second-order needs cannot simply be attributed to low and high levels of arousal respectively without qualification, nor can they (quite) simply be attributed to internalizers and externalizers respectively, although such an application would be appropriate to the polar extremes represented in Figure 15 by I_1 and E_2.

The qualification which has to be made obviously concerns kinds of arousal but, more particularly, whether orientation is towards the physical, social, or intellectual environment, or all three.[47] Differences in levels of need will also be seen to relate to degrees of apparent dominance, or not, of physical survival needs over psychological survival needs, and to different kinds of temporal orientation – that is, levels of anticipation experienced by the organism.

Again, the most dramatic differences in orientation towards the concrete and abstract lie on the diagonal axis in Figure 15 between low arousal (I_1) and high levels of adrenalin *and* noradrenalin arousal (E_2). However, first- and second-order needs are to be placed on the model as rising on a vertical axis, because of their relationship with increases in mental activity. Although the horizontal plane (running from internal to external: from low noradrenalin arousal to high noradrenalin arousal) represents increase in orientation needs, all such needs are seen to be biased towards the concrete, with increases moving from interest in the physical world to more social interaction rather than towards ideas and more abstract interests, the latter being represented by the vertical plane.

In phylogenetic terms, it was argued that higher-order needs evolved as needs for greater social awareness and co-operation, as well as a need for greater ingenuity, were demanded in response to increased environmental threat. And in Figure 3 this shift in awareness was also shown to have phenomenological and ontogenetic relevance, while now it is being defined as a human variable. On the model this gives us first-order needs below

Figure 16 First- and second-order needs in relation to levels of arousal and first- and second-order internalizers (I_1 and I_2) and externalizers (E_1 and E_2)

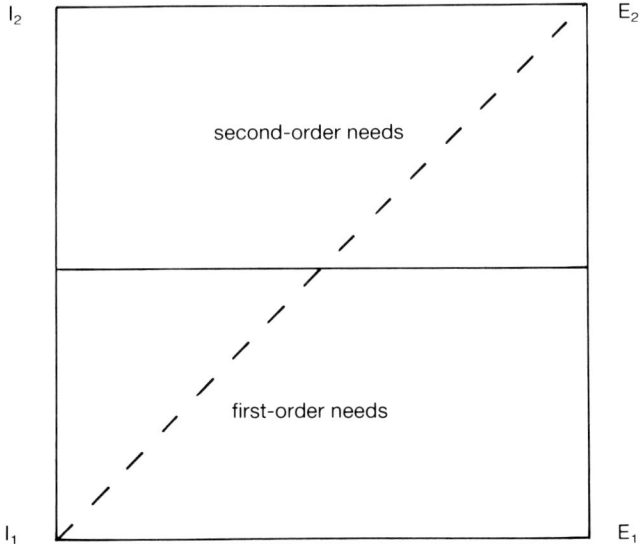

and second-order needs above relating to first-order internalizers and externalizers and second-order internalizers and externalizers respectively.

It is now possible, by considering the implications of all the information already summarized in Figures 3–16, to begin to draw some conclusions about key characteristics of the major personality types which emerge, and to try to clarify some of the differences and similarities between the APM-A classifications and others to which reference has been made.

Throughout this chapter certain parallels have been drawn: implicitly, between characteristics associated with the extreme internal and external types and contrasting styles of processing identified elsewhere (Gear 1987) which correspond with behaviourist and Gestalt views of learning (postulate 6, Appendix 2); and explicitly between polar-extreme (I_1–E_2) APM-A characteristics and the different processes which various writers and researchers have attributed to the right and left hemispheres of the brain. And most of the dichotomies which have been cited, whether in connection with hemisphericality or cognitive style, as well as relating to contrasting modes of information-processing and learning, can also be seen to relate to the underlying physiological processes described in Chapter 1. Additionally, each of the polar extremes in question (kinds of processing; the various dichotomies; and the extremes of the autonomic nervous system) can be seen, in unitary terms, to lie on the diagonal axis (I_1–E_2) of the model: between low arousal and balanced (adrenalin *and* nor-

Figure 17 Key dimensions of individual style holding in common the polarity I_1-E_2

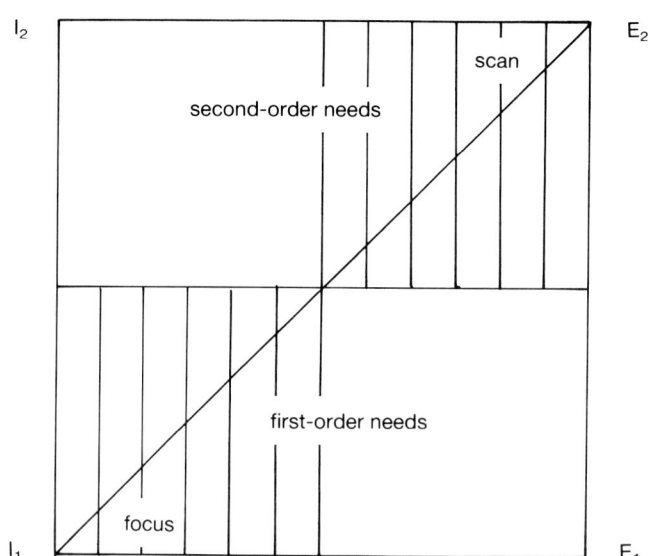

adrenalin) high arousal. On the other hand, other concepts, such as differing degrees of expression of affect and differing levels of need, are seen to occupy different planes and axes corresponding with different aspects and dimensions of the APM-A analysis: most obviously, the inner/ outer dimension and levels and kinds of awareness. These are seen to cut across the model in different directions (see Figure 17), as they are intrinsically about the dominance of one or another kind of arousal (see Figure 12) as distinct from being misrepresented or, at least, grossly simplified, within a unitary, linear model. But all nevertheless hold in common the extreme (low–high) polarity of I_1-E_2 illustrating the simplest possible classification of human variability.

Instead of now drawing on the fifty or more dichotomies and other analyses of polarities which have been cited, and assessing the relationship and degree of appropriateness of each of these to the APM-A model, more useful and comprehensible images of individual style should emanate from summaries of what are being called 'process characteristics'. By concentrating on process and bearing in mind the positive and negative potential inherent in notions of bias, as well as taking into account environmental variables such as the acquisition, or not, of interest or purpose (see postulate 7, Appendix 2, and Gear 1987) it is hoped that some of the problems of polymorphism and the inappropriate attribution of value judgements will be avoided.

Our analysis has suggested that human variability rests on degrees of dominance of one means of processing information, or the other. This has also been defined as incidental to the speed at which the organism attempts to assimilate information and, in consequence, on the amount of information the organism is attempting to deal with simultaneously. In essence, definitions are based on the effects of differing levels and kinds of limbic arousal and consequent intensities and kinds of response to environmental events: not simply in terms of whether active or passive, but if active, whether primarily mentally active or physically active – or both.

It is argued that the externalizer, because of physiological factors which make him or her more susceptible to threat, is driven to become aware of more of the environment at once: that E_1s and E_2s are more vulnerable to, and governed to a greater extent by, environmental change and a need to assimilate and make sense of as much information as possible, as quickly as possible. This requires that they make more 'connections' (and incidentally, more gross connections) than either I_1s or I_2s. Conscious processing is subjected to overload to the extent that (1) attentional styles tend to be broad and shallow, except when directed towards high-priority signals (namely, first and second priority – see postulate 5) or, put differently, attentional capacity includes chronically active sub-threshold scanning, incidentally invoking cortical inhibition to the effect that attention is only easily sustained when arousal becomes specific rather than general; (2) externalizers place greater demands on unconscious processing than internalizers.

These factors imply that, in the conventional language of the personologist, the externalizer is likely to be – like the extravert – sociable, lively, impulsive, seeking novelty and change, emotionally expressive, but, contrary to Eysenck's interpretation, *not* necessarily 'carefree'. Additionally, we can say of externalizers that they are likely to be less predictable in thought and action than internalizers and that, although less 'suggestible' in terms of conditionability (which follows from experiencing higher levels of cortical inhibition), they are likely to be more 'suggestible' when the term is taken to mean being open to alternatives. Because of their more highly developed 'early warning system' (p. 90) they are also likely to be more 'intuitive'. From all that has been said already about arousal and disorganization of behaviour, externalizers may also be expected to be generally less controlled in their thoughts and actions. From this it is tempting to assess externalizers as less efficient, and, in the broadest terms, this might be so. However, just as Liam Hudson has pointed out that academic success appears to depend more on the use a person sees fit to make of his or her intellectual apparatus, than on measures of kind, and as we know from research into arousal and performance that efficiency depends on the nature of the task (Broadhurst 1957), the conclusion being drawn is that the notion of efficiency is not a simple one.

By contrast, the internalizer – of whom we are saying that attentional capacity operates under less pressure of urgency, being less susceptible to change either as a source of continual distraction or as a source of necessary feedback – obviously manifests less emotional involvement with the physical, social, or intellectual environment: he is likely to seem more restrained, to be 'cooler' than the externalizer, to be essentially more organized, more controlled, and less active. Adjectives applied to the introvert, such as 'quiet', 'well-ordered', and 'emotionally unexpressive', are seen to describe the internalizer equally well, but others of Eysenck's terms, such as 'intellectual' or 'value oriented', are clearly true of some internalizers but are seen to be just as likely to be true of some externalizers; just as his term 'carefree' cannot be confined to one physiological type (other than in the most general terms: to those whose limbic *under-* arousal is of a chronic nature).

So far, only characteristics likely to be common to all predominantly internal or external types have been used in our definitions, and all of the concepts used so far have been intimately related to APM-A processes. More detailed description leads us into potentially very lengthy discussion, because the implications of all that has been said above are no more simple than the analysis.

Although there is insufficient space here fully to define variability within and between the two major groups, or the complexities which arise from polymorphic language to describe polymorphic beings, certain issues have been raised. For instance, because it has been said that the externalizer makes more 'connections' than the internalizer, that must not be taken to imply that all externalizers are necessarily more 'imaginative', say, than *all* internalizers. Imagination itself is polymorphic and obviously subject to style. It does imply two things, however. First, that in addition to second-order externalizers (E_2s) showing *more power of imagination* than first-order internalizers (I_1s), they are more likely to display different *kinds of imagination* from second-order internalizers (I_2s). This is because although I_2s and E_2s are defined as experiencing high levels of mental activity, the *greater consciousness of external change and physical activity of external- izers* puts them in a better position (1) to acquire a greater store of sensory experience (though not, of course, to acquire a greater repertoire of ideas transmitted by others) than internalizers, and (2) in the case of second-order (E_2) externalizers in particular, to be more frequently *stimulated* into mental, as well as physical activity. The E_2 externalizer is seen, therefore, to be more likely to *confront and recognize more 'problems'* of however small a scale and to *respond actively to them*. Second, the more gross processing style of externalizers can mean that associations which are made are likely to be more random, and therefore more 'original', than those of internalizers.

On the other hand, E_1s, because of their physical rather than mental bias, are not viewed as necessarily more imaginative than I_2s. Being lower on mental energy, their possibly richer stores of sensory experience are less likely to be 'worked on' mentally than the less actively acquired experience of the polar-extreme I_2s represented by the upper (adrenalin-rather than noradrenalin-biased) half of the model. A major point, however, is that although I_2s are viewed as potentially just as apparently mentally active as E_2s, their styles of processing are likely to remain less urgent, more focused, and therefore biased towards more strict sequence and tighter organization, so that such imagination as is displayed by second-order internalizers is likely to be of a markedly different style from that of second-order externalizers. This key point will be taken up again in Part 2.

Other important questions of polymorphism surround the conventional linking of the terms 'sequential' and 'logical'. Although thinking might still be deemed to be logical when it is so narrow as to be simplistic, what might be termed 'defensible logic' has to take into account complex relationships between as many factors to do with its formulation as possible. The fact that there is a very obvious relationship between simple sequence and logic does not mean to say that (1) a similar relationship does not exist between complex sequences and logic, or (2) (and even more pertinently) that simple logic does not itself depend on more complex and diffuse insights. These same arguments can also be applied to other concepts, such as 'analysis' and 'rationality', and can be seen to be an extension of the Hughlings Jackson argument (p. 75) about the *use* of words not being the same as the *possession* of them. Clearly, the potential for organizing perceptions does not imply at all that such perceptions are *available* and ready for organization.

Other confusions and stereotypes exist, and are perpetuated mainly by our gross tendency to think in terms of mutually exclusive alternatives. They are also perpetuated, it has to be said, by oversimplified theory of most aspects of human psychology: theory which either divorces itself from process, or regards process as unitary.

Mention has already been made of some of the problems associated with the term 'sensitive', and the need to take into account kinds of sensitivity. It is now relevant to add that externalizers, with their greater consciousness of the relationship between themselves and their surroundings, being more tuned to change and more vulnerable to threat and (as the more impulsive) also more vulnerable to promise, are motivated into active scanning of their environments with the effect of being most sensitive to the *general tone* of situations rather than to specific details, as well as being apt to display 'sensitivity' as a result of their more open emotional expression. By contrast, internalizers, being more relaxed and more passive in attitude, with fewer urgent psychological needs of their own, are likely to display more obvious sensitivity towards the needs of others, providing, of course, that their own acquired purposes (and concomitant acquired needs) do not come to dominate attentional capacities.

Any implication which might be read into the above that externalizers are more observant than internalizers must again be qualified, with the by now almost routine response that the external and internal types can each be said to be more observant than the other, but *in different ways*. For example, while externalizers may be picking up generalities and broad features of a given physical, social, or intellectual situation, assessing relationships *between* aspects of the whole, the internalizer is likely to be focusing on and retaining detail.

Finally, issue has to be taken with the notion of the 'carefree' external type and that of the 'intellectual' internal type. The emotionally responsive, highly communicative external type may well give the appearance of being 'carefree', in its loosest possible sense, but the apparent paradox being identified is that his or her external behaviour (responsiveness) derives from underlying experience of threat. Whether it is consciously acknowledged or not, it is being argued that a high level of general arousal is in itself threatening, representing as it does a potential loss of focus/integrity. Because externalizers make more connections than internalizers, it is argued that their concomitant high levels of anticipation make them inherently more prone to anxiety and to the active recognition of problems than their more passive opposite numbers (who are perceived to be tuned to the *recognition of opportunity* rather than challenge).

As for intellectuality, it should have already become clear that the view being expressed here is that complexity of mind does not depend *simply* on the acquisition of knowledge or, alternatively, on the ability to perceive relationships between items of information: the former being identified as a strength of focusers, or internal types, and the latter as a strength of scanners (externalizers). Absorption in a particular field of enquiry may just as well lead to sufficient depth of knowledge for complex associations to become possible for the most sequential of thinkers as, conversely, strength of affect, interest, or purpose may develop to the point at which focus is achieved in the most diffusely organized mind.

The classification of internal types as being 'more likely to be' intellectual, without qualification, can be seen to be just as gross a distortion of probability as it is to exclude mention of external types from the same category. A good long-term memory is no more equivalent to the ability or motivation to think constructively, or adequately even, any more than being sociable and lively, with a rather better short-term than long-term memory, denies that possibility. As will be shown, internalizers and externalizers both come in a whole range of levels of intellectual ability, although clearly manifesting different biases in styles of thinking and performance.

It is being stressed that neither extreme mode represents the *only* possible means of achievement of particular physical or mental goals. Similarly, very few characteristics are attributable to just one personality type. Traits are being viewed as having *complementary forms* at least, *maybe more*. The immense sophistication of the autonomic nervous system clearly provides the human organism and the human species with an inordinately complex system of complementarity and homeostasis, in which balance itself can be achieved in many different ways and many different kinds of strength and weakness compensate each other.

Although personality types are conventionally described in fairly positive terms, such politeness is viewed here as rather misplaced, because both the predominantly focusing style of the internalizer and the predominantly scanning style of the externalizer can operate to functional *or* dysfunctional effect. The same processes which have been defined as resulting in greater *flexibility, versatility, responsiveness, and existential awareness* in the externalizer, in extreme cases (or times) may be manifested in *restlessness, instability, confusion, or anxiety* – let alone the fact that it is possible to be flexible, responsive, or aware to a fault, so that direction, focus, and concentration are all but lost. Similarly, the unquestionably valuable qualities of *stability and control*, which are seen here to be among the more obvious attributes of the internalizer, might just as easily develop into the extremes of *obsession, ritual, bigotry*, and other manifestations of *rigidity of thought* and *action*.

Finally, although it is not accepted that any absolute value judgement can be placed on the benefits or drawbacks of the incidental effects of either extreme mode, it can be said that possession of both modes in even balance, and at an optimal level of intensity, obviously provides for the greatest possibility of adaptation for the *individual*. Coan, after investigating the concept of the 'optimal personality', arrives at a very similar conclusion.

> The finding of overall significance here is that variables commonly regarded as components of the optimal pattern do not covary [co-vary] in such a way to support the notion of a common general factor . . . we might do better to stop thinking in terms of one optimal personality pattern and to think instead in terms of a variety of patterns that are desirable for a variety of purposes, each pattern being ideal when viewed from an appropriate perspective.
>
> (Coan 1974:198)

He goes on to argue that 'flexible exploration and organisation are both essential for growth', and that 'the optimal mode of living combines organised functioning with some flexibility and openness to experience' (ibid.:225–9).

3.4 Kinds of efficiency

Coan's conclusions can be shown to apply equally well to the concept of intelligence as to personality and, incidentally, to provide a useful platform from which to consider the relationship between these and the other kinds of individual difference under discussion.

Just as there is no one definition of personality to which all psychologists would subscribe, there are no generally accepted or standard definitions of either intelligence or the closely related, but even more arbitrary, concept of 'creativity'. Even the much quoted circular statement which says that 'intelligence is what intelligence tests test' merely testifies to the difficulty of finding any single, adequate definition of such a highly variable attribute. There is obviously not only one way of being intelligent: consequently definitions are arrived at which are open to a great deal of criticism. To slightly different purpose from that served by their inclusion here, David Pyle (1979) has compiled a variety of definitions by a number of psychologists well-known for their work in this field, which are shown in Figure 18.

Figure 18 Definitions of intelligence compiled by Pyle (1979:3)

Binet: to judge well, to comprehend well, to reason well.

Spearman: general intelligence which involves mainly the 'eduction of relations and correlates'.

Terman: the capacity to form concepts and to grasp their significance.

Vernon: stresses a simple and non-specific definition, such as 'all-round thinking capacity' or 'mental efficiency'.

Burt: innate, general, cognitive ability.

Heim: intelligent activity consists in grasping the essentials in a situation and responding appropriately to them.

Wechsler: the aggregate or global capacity of the individual to act purposefully, to think rationally, and to deal effectively with the environment.

Piaget: adaptation to the physical and social environment.

The most easy to criticize are those definitions which list specific abilities, because, not surprisingly, lists which do emerge are usually far from conclusive. Binet's definition, for instance, appears to ignore many kinds of ability which might be deemed to be necessary attributes of intelligence – for example, the ability to communicate effectively; to solve problems; and to take effective action. Similarly, Terman's definition ignores behaviour. This must be regarded as a serious omission in connection with a concept which depends entirely on perceived differences in behaviour between individuals, and on the measurement of performance, for its very existence.

Burt, too, seems to omit a great deal. Quite aside from what must be regarded as a gross assumption which his definition embodies, about what proportion of intelligence is innate, and what learned (currently the subject of the major controversy in the field), he too disregards completely the necessity for a definition of intelligence which includes any reference to effectiveness of action within the physical and social environments.

It would seem that the most useful definitions are the non-specific, process-centred definitions such as those of Heim, Wechsler, and Piaget; each of which allows for the possibility of there being different ways of achieving the same successful end. The APM-A definition is, simply, *the ability to cope effectively with new situations,* and one of the major points being made is that, as a species, we embody an enormous range of variability in *kinds of effectiveness* and, therefore, also in kinds of situations – from moment to moment as well as from day to day – we can best cope with.[48]

In arguing that no particular set of personality traits can be identified as constituting a 'general dimension of ideal v. non-ideal characteristics' but that a balance of flexibility and organization is the most fundamental requirement for the individual to attain personal fulfilment, Coan (1974) is using concepts which have already been given some prominence here. Further, both personality and intelligence may be said to be about ways of achieving successful adaptation to changing environmental demands: personality may be said to be about consistencies in *styles* of adaptation, and intelligence about *degrees* and *kinds* of efficiency.

The point can be best illustrated by reference to the model, which can now be extended to refer to individual style in a much more holistic way. It can be seen how areas usually considered to be separate – namely, personality, intelligence, creativity, and cognitive style – hold very important implications for the others to the extent that, if they are viewed in isolation, serious and unrealistically rigid constraints are likely to be placed on both the interpretation of research and the development and testing of theory.

Obviously, the greatest likelihood of balance of kinds of mental and physical activity, which must also include the greatest possible availability of scanning and focusing capacities of attention, must lie in a position at the centre of the model; but except for a microscopic proportion of the whole, even at the centre of the model different biases of kinds of energy and kinds of activity still exist. Only at the absolute centre will scan and focus, implying flexibility *and* control of thought and action, be in even balance.

Some of the differences between individuals represented by areas of the model other than the simple extremes of I_1 and E_1 have been identified already (Figure 15 and p. 101). Now, by elaborating the earlier description,

Figure 19 Examples of kinds of intelligence (see also Figure 15)

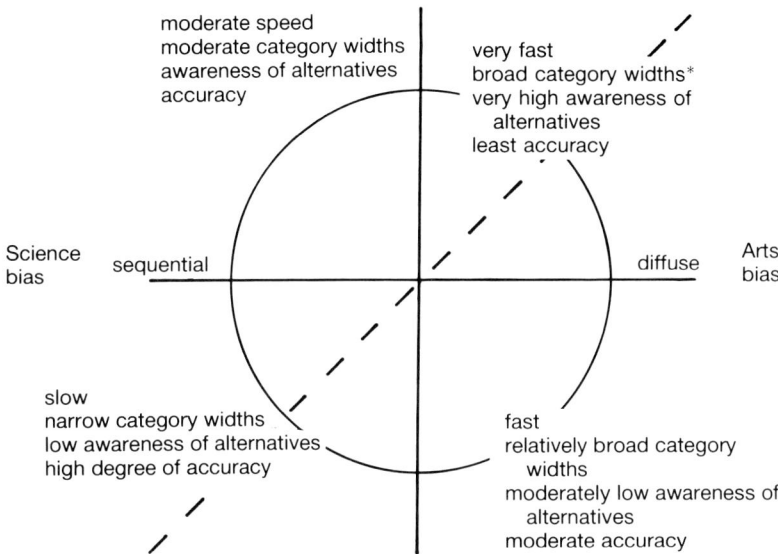

* The term 'category width' is being used to imply perceptual *and* conceptual boundaries.

and applying it to the centre of the model only (to extract a 'detail', as it were), it becomes obvious how, even in a relatively neutral and balanced area, biases are still likely to operate: a fact which is of course quite consistent with our knowledge that a group of subjects achieving identical scores on an IQ test, for instance, are hardly likely to have done so in identical ways, any more than identical scores on any other psychological tests would be expected to have been achieved by identical performances.

Given that speed and accuracy are the major criteria used in the design of intelligence tests, and given also that types of internalizers and types of externalizers have been described in terms of energy and organization of activity, it is easy to see how these qualities (speed and accuracy) may differ within the margins of tolerance imposed by the test even between those individuals achieving the same high score.

It also becomes even more obvious now, how those individuals represented on the model by concentric circles of ever-decreasing intelligence, usually described by two categories of intensity (unintelligent or stupid) and two of bias (careless or slow), in fact fall into an extremely variable matrix of styles.

The constraints of limited definitions, if not distortions, which arise from

Figure 20 Examples of kinds of 'unintelligence' related to classroom stereotypy

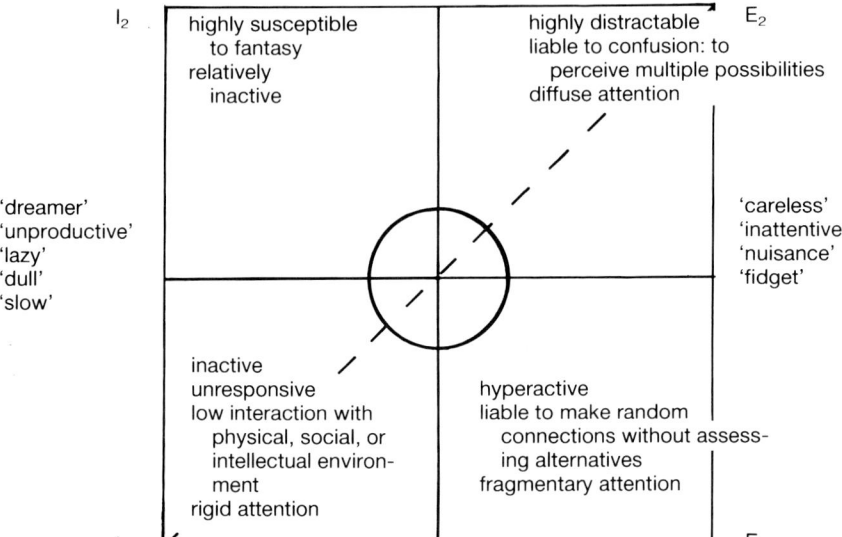

imagining that the entire range of human variability can be described in unitary terms – that is, in terms of continua – have already been mentioned, but in the field of intelligence the tendency to think in unitary terms, simply along a dimension of intelligent to unintelligent, is even stronger: oddly enough, although we seem to have such difficulty in defining it, not only do we measure it, but we measure it in terms of degree, which in turn is expressed in number! What is more, despite growing acknowledgement of biases in intelligence which are reflected in tests designed to identify verbal or numerical skills, or acknowledge and identify arts or science bias, little if any acknowledgement is made of kinds of 'unintelligence'.

Just as Liam Hudson has linked aspects of personality with particular modes of thinking and abilities (although he claims only to have linked the area of creativity research and research into arts/science differences), it is suggested that a much more fruitful approach to the definition of, and subsequent compensation for, inefficiency of performance might be to consider more gross and general characteristics of individual style. It is not uncommon, for instance, for a psychologist to attribute learning difficulties to a 'personality problem', but any attempt to be more precise than this is hindered by the fact that no unified theory of personal style relating personality to kinds of efficiency or *potential* has been available for reference. Such crucial links can, however, be made.

Unavoidably, some links between what is conventionally referred to as personality and other specific aspects of individual style are already established. The area in which such connections are made fairly consistently is that of creativity research. Even the folklore of the artist makes innumerable references to a variety of personality traits associated with the capacity for original thought and productivity. The artist is most frequently viewed as social deviant, in one form or another, and the inventive scientist too is frequently conceived of as a trifle dotty, if not quite mad.

The very fact that creativity has long been regarded as special and rare, having been variously associated with genius, magic, and madness, suggests that in its most marked form it is not 'normal', that, in a sense, a degree of abnormality within the individual is a prerequisite for its manifestation; and obviously, 'originality' by definition implies a departure from the normal. We really should not have needed Getzels and Jackson's (1962) research to show us that high IQ does not necessarily indicate high creativity, when the object of the IQ test is, after all, to elicit a *predictable* response.

A great deal of debate in the creativity literature, in common with the literature on personality and intelligence (and, indeed, with literature concerning many of the other aspects of mind being linked here to arousal and adaptation), centres on what precisely is meant by the term in question. Much of the problem seems to derive from the fact that, as with all other human qualities, none of us is quite devoid of creativity, although many claim to be. Some are clearly more creative than others, but we all have ideas, at some time; all of us are faced with the need to be inventive – especially when truth is painful – and aesthetic decision making is part of everyday life. This writer is actually expressing the view that from moment to moment life is *essentially* a matter of aesthetic choices: most obviously, we all have to decide what to wear each day and more frequently still, select branded goods (mostly packaged to have some kind of emotional appeal) to eat, to groom ourselves, to decorate and maintain our homes, to display our 'good taste', or otherwise be identified positively in particular ways.

However, whatever else creativity is, or is not, it *is* essentially about novelty and productivity, which, in common with all other experience and behaviour, is about ideas and action: creativity is distinguished by being about more – of both, but not necessarily in equal balance.

There exists a huge amount of literature on the subject of creativity, but traditionally, and usefully to our purpose, writers tend to describe it in terms of person, process, and product. Very importantly, however,

Shouksmith (1970:103) quotes Mooney as adding the need to consider environmental factors, which Messick (1976:12) calls 'creative press' referred to here earlier, slightly less prosaically, as 'the ghost around the machine'. That 'person' is a very important pointer to a creative mode of information-processing has been emphasized by many researchers and writers. Freeman *et al.* (1971:15) quote Anne Roe as having found personal differences 'more crucial than differences in intelligence', citing 'fairly high intelligence and a very high degree of persistence and motivation' as being 'more characteristic of the most eminent scientists than very high intelligence with rather less persistence'. And these connections will be seen to be extremely pertinent to our placing of creativity within the new dynamic model, and to the relationship between the key areas of human adaptation which the model emphasizes.

Arieti (1976:347) quotes Taylor as also emphasizing the importance of intellectual, motivational, and personality factors, and Arieti (ibid.:52) himself emphasizes the need for libido or energy (as, of course, did Freud (1922)). Other references to the person include countless references to the need for flexibility and almost as many mentions of qualities such as dominance, self-confidence, fluency, openness, and, probably more surprisingly to some, only slightly fewer to 'femininity of interests'. In referring to masculine and feminine modes of functioning Messick cites Silverman's definitions of Logos and Eros and McKinnon's findings that feminine elements contribute to male creativity and masculine elements to female creativity (Messick 1976:chap. 6). This is a notion which will be seen to fit very nicely with the definition which is to be offered. However, whereas Messick apparently interprets these findings as suggesting some *similarity* between the two modes, which is intensified in creativity, the APM-A interpretation implies that it is the coincidence of *complementary* traits which is so effective.

As well as relating very obviously to literature on intelligence, personality, and motivation and even to questions of 'maleness' and 'femaleness', the creativity field also relates very easily to the ever-growing literature generated by research into cognitive style. We have already seen what Cropley has to say about cognitive style and creativity (p. 82). Bruner (1956) makes a similar correlation between width of categorizing and creativity, and Wallach and Kogan (1965) also express the view that creativity involves the use of broader category widths. Usefully too, after his references to the difference between 'taking the world in in large lumps' and 'selectively attending only to chosen portions', Cropley goes on to say,

A cognitive variable which is closely related to category width and also to cognitive styles involving readiness to accept the maximum amount of information from the external world, is that of risk taking.
(1970:123)

A greater tendency to take risks is yet another factor in a mass of evidence which leads to the conclusion that the archetype defined by researchers into creativity and, incidentally, by folklore and legend, is to be found mostly among second-order externalizers (E_2s), represented by the upper right-hand quadrant of the model: 'mostly', because, as has been stressed, boundaries on the model are not viewed as rigid; on the contrary, differences are a matter of kind and intensity and, as will be fully discussed in Chapter 5, creativity comes in different styles and intensities too.

By definition, the creative (or more obviously creative) individual is active rather than passive. He or she is, after all, productive, and an active and positive response is made to the environment which itself, within the APM-A framework, implies more tendency to scan than focus: this is a view which research into creativity reinforces by its findings about broad category widths. In addition, research indicates that other qualities which have been associated above with the active/scanning mode of attention and diffuse rather than sequential processing can also be correlated with creativity – for example, making unusual associations, flexibility, 'openness', and energy. Further, what Stein says (1974:6) about the concept of novelty being central to all definitions of creativity, and that 'potential for change within the individual' is an essential prerequisite, is entirely

Figure 21 Adaptive style in relation to traditional views of male and female traits

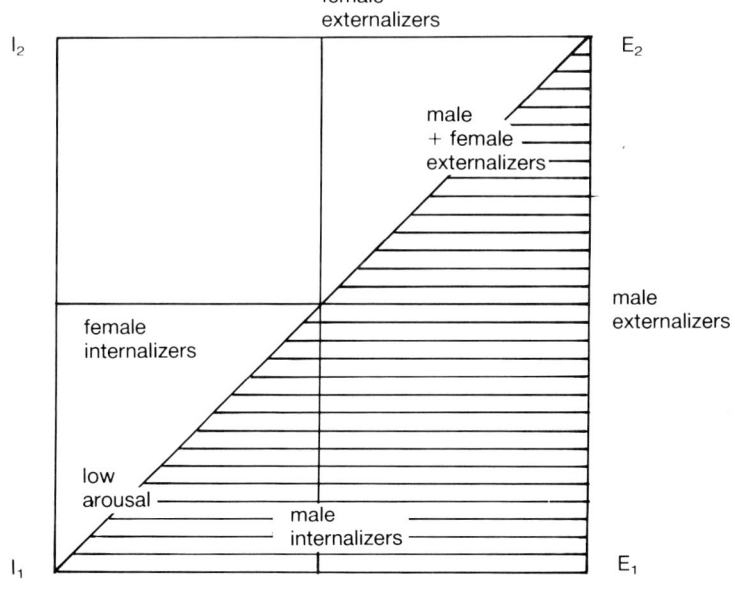

consistent with the APM-A linking of creativity with high limbic arousal. Thus greatest potential for creativity exists in areas of the model where both kinds of arousal, and therefore availability of ideas *and* action, are either relatively or very high. This implicates second-order externalizers (E_2s) most obviously, but it must also include some second-order internalizers (I_2s) and some first-order externalizers (E_1s). However, any more detailed discussion of variations in styles of creativity than this must wait until Part 2.

If we now consider Silverman's definitions of Logos and Eros, to cite just one of many possible summaries of consistently perceived differences between male and female mental processes, we can see that the same portion of the model E_2 also incorporates both male and female traits, which many regard as necessary to creativity. Logos (masculine) traits are viewed in terms of 'disconnection: compartmentalisation, and analytic separation and refinement'; to be described as 'objective, active, tough minded, analytic, rational, unyielding, intrusive, counteracting, independent, self-sufficient, emotionally controlled'. Conversely, Eros (feminine) traits are seen in terms of 'wholeness and relatedness, intuitive perceptions of sensitivities to the feeling component of situations', to which Silverman ascribes the following adjectives: 'subjective, passive, tenderminded, diffuse, sensitive, impressionistic, yielding, receptive, empathic, dependent, emotional' (Messick 1976:95). There is an obvious relationship to be perceived here between Silverman's contrasting modes and differences defined by others to which attention was drawn earlier: that is, contrasting characteristics associated with the different styles of processing attributed to the two halves of the brain, on the one hand, and the various correlations which have been made above with biases in the release of the neurotransmitters adrenalin and noradrenalin, which serve as the basis of our model, on the other.

The argument being developed is certainly not to suggest that all males are externalizers and all females internalizers, or vice versa. It is, however, to suggest that there are sound evolutionary reasons why there should be cognitive and emotional differences between men and women, and to support the notion that there are *degrees* and *intensities* of 'maleness' and 'femaleness': that men and women differ significantly in hormonal secretions, beyond the obvious and conventionally acknowledged differences in secretions of testosterone and oestrogen.

Less obviously, and in evolutionary terms, it would follow that the male and the female of the species are likely to have developed different biases in kinds of arousal and differences in kinds of orientation needs. Quite simply, by considering the evolution of the role of male as hunter, defender of territory, and therefore as aggressor under threat, and taking into account that as such he will have needed to make frequent and swift physical responses to environmental change, it can be seen that arousal is likely to have been biased towards the release of noradrenalin – associated with anger by Ax (1953) and Funkenstein (1956). On the other hand, the evolution of arousal in females, relatively helpless under physical threat, encumbered with young and unable to flee or fight, is likely to have become biased towards the experience of fear and the secretion of adrenalin: towards the dominance of mental rather than physical activity[49] (see pp. 92–3).

Indeed, the likelihood of the original differentiation of the biases of kinds of arousal having evolved from sexual differences and roles, which in turn were imposed by periods of female indisposition, and eventually reinforced by the evolution of more positive and stable sexual roles, seems extremely high. Viewed in this way, it can be seen that greater conscious control over experience and behaviour, attention to physical survival, and readiness for action (the male mode)[50] is likely to have become differentiated from a less conscious and less routinized mode deriving from greater emotional need for security and, incidentally, to sometimes necessarily less direct and more ingenious responses. This would serve to explain many identifiable general differences between male and female thinking.

In sum, different kinds of effectiveness of action are being said to derive from *different degrees and kinds of control*, offering *more or less rigidity* or *flexibility* of *perception and behaviour*, and it is this greater or lesser capacity for *conscious* control which is being defined as the biologically determined element of individual style, whether with reference to what we commonly refer to as personality, intelligence, or creativity. However, 'control' is not a simple concept, as was pointed out earlier. Because mental energy is a limited commodity, it has been argued that either limbic *or* cortical activity is likely to dominate mental functioning to some extent, and that people differ, above all, in this respect. It is important, though, to take account of the fact that we can no more *necessarily* summon the 'will' to be *less* controlled or focused in our experience or actions than we can to be *more* controlled, if that is not our physiological style.

Neither the unwillingness of introverts or internalizers to take unnecessary risks, nor their generally better long-term memory can be attributed to a *conscious* effort of will (which is not to say that they may not be reinforced that way), any more than a 'willingness' to take risks is regarded here as an entirely apt descriptive phrase in connection with the more imaginative and productive external types and their manifest needs for change. The one group can no more 'help' having a good memory (often retaining information of no conscious interest), than the other can resist much of their more spontaneous behaviour and greater inclination to 'have a go'.

This is not simple pedantry, but an important distinction which is being made in the definition and understanding of human beings which, as well as holding a number of implications for educational policy – to be taken up later – is about the importance of taking possible *biological and unconscious differences* into account. This does not imply that either dysfunctionally low or high levels of control are not modifiable by learning, but it is to say, importantly, that the experience and behaviour of some is more easily modifiable than that of others.

3.5 Processes of adaptation and problems of definition

Before moving on to applying the model to other matters of style – namely, styles of pathology and cultural and artistic styles – we can usefully summarize some of the major principles and changes of perspective which have been described, either implicitly or explicitly.

Essentially, all of the areas of individual style which have been under discussion in this chapter are being seen as aspects of the adaptive process, and all of them are viewed as manifestations of the degree of urgency, or not, experienced by the organism, in response to environmental change.

The evolution of the organization of the two complementary styles of information-processing into the left and right hemispheres of the brain has been viewed here as a macro response to macro change: an incidental effect of species-wide heightened sensitivity of response and concomitant greater need for orientation, which has been referred to as a move to higher-order needs including, it has been argued, the crucial need (for psychological survival) 'not to know'.

Now, the intimate relationship between what we are calling first- and second-order needs, and the conscious and unconscious processes inextricably bound up with lateralization of brain function can be made rather more explicit, as can the relationship between individual learning and what has been called 'species learning'. All can be seen to have in common the key notions of selection and reinforcement[51] – as do all of the other aspects of adaptation which have been discussed so far – and all have to do with decision making, conscious or otherwise, imposed, to lesser or greater degrees, by environmental factors.

Quite obviously, whether or not decision making or selection occurs as a result of conscious choice or so-called 'free will', or whether responses are passive and determined, rests primarily on whether or not alternatives are consciously perceived; second, on whether or not the organism is in a position to make a selection; that is, is equipped with the relevant factual or phenomenological information on the one hand, and an adequate degree of physiological balance, on the other; third, and most importantly, the organism has to be in possession of some kind of criterion or criteria from which to be able to make a judgement. The most primitive criterion available to us is the comparison to be made between 'self' and 'not self' (Weir 1977:3). Once more this is a process which can be seen to operate at all levels of organic organization,[52] and it is clearly the most basic kind of assessment of familiarity or unfamiliarity which can be made.

Comparison-making and the recognition of sameness and/or difference or, put differently, match and mismatch as the most fundamental tool of perception, has been described here as operating either simply or sequentially, or in more complex ways which identify more apparently random and less obvious similarities and differences. Whether or not the arguments presented here about their evolution are accepted, it would be exceedingly difficult to deny their logical conclusion, which is that our potential for perceiving and knowing of alternative interpretations of situations, and for finding alternative solutions to problems, and therefore for the exercise of 'free will', is greater now than at any earlier stage of our evolution. However, advances which have been made towards greater awareness and freer exercise of choice as a species can be shown to be by no means adequately represented by a steadily rising graph, any more than any individual may be guaranteed to exercise such freedom as may be available to him or her at any particular time.

In the most general terms, APM-A theory implies that all kinds of decision making (selection, by another name) belong within a hierarchy related to levels of arousal. In Figure 3 (p. 47) it can be seen that levels of awareness (called 'levels of minding') are also levels of decision making, as it were: from determined to, at least, less determined. Consistent with the high degree of paradox to which, it has been suggested, the human organism is victim, human beings emerge both as autonomous, that is, free (within certain well-marked parameters related to the availability of energy) and, as learning animals, subject to environmental influences as well as to extraordinarily high belongingness needs. We are thus also very much determined, both as a species and, to varying degrees, as individuals, by our physical, social, and intellectual environments.

In short, now that individual differences have been explored a little, a spectrum of kinds of activity described by the rigidity–flexibility continuum can be seen to exist *between* individuals as well as having the phenomeno-logical, ontogenetic, and phylogenetic applications shown in Figure 3. But yet another, and extremely important, application of the continuum can be added. This describes the difference between phylogenetic and ontogenetic extremes; that is, the difference between the most rudimentary kind of species learning and our potential as individual learners.

The simple principle of 'trial and error' can be seen to apply just as much to the most primitive form of species adaptation (learning) as it does to part of the repertoire of individual learning (adaptation). Selection, choice, and decision making at species level depend as much on the concept of reinforcement as they do in the most rudimentary form of learning in the individual, as described by the behaviourists. But the notion of *species* learning by reinforcement implies not just one, but two forms of adaptation. One form of 'trial and error' is manifested quite simply as the 'survival of the fittest', so that those individuals best equipped to deal with prevailing conditions survive to procreate; the other results in the most successful biological characteristics of the species being reinforced over aeons of time to produce apparently quite rigid responses commonly referred to as 'instincts'.

However, quite apart from fuelling what has already been criticized above (see note 11) as a rather meaningless either/or debate about 'nature' or 'nurture', the use of the term 'instinct' obscures what must be a vast range of rigidity and flexibility of response, which then remains totally unacknowledged in any typical discussion of which behaviours are apparently 'innate' and which 'acquired' (as if any were not, providing we take a sufficiently long-term view). For instance, it is surely a gross assumption to imply that what might be termed long-term (evolutionary) species 'habits', such as depth perception, presumably laid down over millions of years and common to species other than primates, is no more rigid an 'instinct' than the much more recently 'learned' (typical) male response to the more curvaceous (usually) female shape; after all, fatty pads of the kinds of which breasts and buttocks are made are a relatively recent refinement evolved, oddly enough, in response to a kind of social demand (Lancaster 1975:82). Although it is unlikely that such a successful stimulus to procreation is ever likely to be 'species forgotten', it is not unlikely that social changes such as changing male and female roles, potential economic parity between men and women (so that a woman's sexual 'capital', as it were, may become as complicated as a man's) and so-called 'unisex', could – given a sufficiently long period of evolution – modify its impact and its power to sell practically anything.

In contrast, however, to what happens at species level, the human individual, in common we are led to believe with chimpanzees and other primates (see Hilgard and Bower 1975:253), is in possession of the fundamental means of deduction (essentially the ability to select from alternatives) as well as that of induction, which of course trial and error represents. Further, the two extreme means of information-processing available to us, which are so closely bound up with the notion of 'levels' of consciousness both within the species and the individual, and which are being taken to underlie differences in individual style, differ in ways beyond those already described. The same analysis which implies such differences in style as have already been defined above, also suggest that the types of processing underlying the polar extremes (I_1–E_2) and all of their dynamically related variables, differ both in their temporal orientation and in their fundamental approaches to problem solving.

It is being suggested that the one means, the kind defined by the behaviourists, operates chiefly by *reference to past experience*, and the application of this to situations which are either simple repetitions or complications of past events, or resemble them very closely; whilst the other, described by the Gestaltists, is geared to the *anticipation of future events* from currently available 'clues' by drawing on any acquired information which is even loosely related to the anticipated, or existing, problem.

We have, therefore, a direct, simple, and fairly rigid approach to problem solving which, in evolutionary terms, has been enhanced by the simultaneous availability of a more complex and indirect means, but the two means are likely to be manifested in the individual with an identifiable bias towards one or the other (see postulate 6, Appendix 2).

The one means functions to solve problems as the need (or developed purpose) arises, being always organized and ready for action, while the other operates in a more anticipatory and more autonomous way, within which readiness consists essentially of a state of looser organization; a state of flexibility. The latter is most evident in those whose (mainly unconscious) experience of threat (in itself a future-oriented concept) is greatest. The orientation of this other mode is essentially towards the solution of new problems.

This *difference in temporal orientation*, between concern primarily with the past and concern primarily with the future, is being seen as one of the extremely important differences which relate to molar characteristics of individual style: most obviously to the extremes of I_1–E_2. It is also being seen as a concomitant of manifest variability in degrees of passivity and activity, and in the next chapter will be related to levels and kinds of vulnerability to 'abnormality'.

Research correlating better long-term memory and introversion and better short-term memory and extraversion has already been cited, and has relevance again here as another indication (intimately related to span of attention, degrees of focus, and levels of arousal) of individual differences in temporal orientation and consequent differences in behavioural responses. This key difference is yet another which can help to identify some of the over-simplifications embodied in readily accepted stereotypes of human variation.

The equation which emerges from relating span of awareness to anticipation and to relative needs for externalization is that greater *im*pression (a term being used to encompass long-term memory, suggestibility, and effective socialization, or, more simply, the absorption of information) takes place most effectively when need for *ex*pression is relatively low, that is, when the organism is relatively limbically relaxed, so that facility for focus is high, unless an existing state of arousal is already specific to (focused on) the information in question.

On the other hand, where needs for expression are high impression is either a slower process, requiring frequent repetition (or other kinds of reinforcement), or has to be accompanied by higher levels of affect in order for long-term retention to be effected. By taking account of the relationship between degrees of impression, needs for expression, and levels of limbic arousal we may also begin to understand why compulsory education is apparently such an unsatisfactory and unsuccessful experience for so many (in Chapter 6 it will be argued 'most') of those who undergo it. However, more full discussion of the implications of this analysis must wait until after a few more complexities have been unravelled.

Up to this point, the relationship between increase in arousal and changes in perception has been described as moving in a relatively simple and straightforward fashion from focus to scan, from relatively simple to more complex experience, and from reactivity to flexibility. In the next chapter this relationship will be shown to be rather more complicated, with the introduction of a third stage: of maladaptively high levels of arousal leading to the narrowing of perceptual boundaries taking them back to focus. However, before closing the present discussion of individual differences, which in the space available is no more than a brief outline of the new perspective, clear indication has to be given that by no means all of the possible permutations of ways of perceiving are being covered here. But first, a little more about the most extreme modes.

Our successful orientation depends on achieving some consistency in perceiving similarities and differences, and patterns and sequences, among environmental phenomena, but frequently our ability to do this offers security at the expense of deeper understanding. One example of this is a too ready classification as 'different', as is conventionally the case in considering the relationship between species and individual adaptation, for instance, which can be seen to create problems of definition just as serious as our more obvious and robust tendency to generalize (even among those schooled not to) and to over-simplify. The one tendency can be seen to be more of a problem for internalizers and the other for externalizers.

From all of the evidence we have it can be assumed with some confidence that the perception of differences is primarily the task of the left hemisphere (in most people: see p. 72ff.), whose characteristic style of processing is described as discrete and sequential, among other things (Figure 10), and related to the style of internalizers who, with their higher tension thresholds, can 'afford' to perceive differences – which carry an inherent threat. On the other hand, the perception of similarities appears to be governed by the right and a greater urgency of processing, to produce a more diffuse style as more 'connections' are made: a trait being associated with externalizers for whom, it has been argued, orientation needs are higher, and for whom the perception of similarities, rather than differences, is therefore likely to provide security.

The association of the perception of differences with a more relaxed and passive state, and the perception of similarities with the experience of greater tension and urgency, also follow from adopting an historical point of view. According to Razran (1971), the oldest, most primitive stage of evolution is essentially a non-urgent, reactive state; a state which also represents the simplest means of maintaining integrity, differentiating self from non-self and remaining distinct from and uncontaminated by alien organisms. The sophistication of this – originally non-anticipatory state – patently operates to maintain the integrity of not just cells and groups of cells, but complex organisms, individuals, and groups of individuals.

The recognition of sameness can also be seen as a *complication of the recognition of differences*. The identification of sameness can be seen as the means of distinct classification from one another of familiar kinds of difference, to the effect that the perception of what might be called classes of same-differences evolves. To this it can be added that a capacity for perceiving greater familiarity under threat, as a means of achieving greater emotional security, is a valuable instrument of homeostasis.

We can now add to our typologies, therefore, that the one extreme mode is likely to be more inclined to achieve objectives by the *recognition of opportunity* and the avoidance of emotional involvement, essentially by maintaining and conserving the status quo and own well-marked boundaries and classifications of the world; the other, fired by an inner experience of urgency to respond to stimuli, is likely to be more inclined to *anticipate possibilities*, to welcome change, to be active, combative, and to achieve objectives by confrontation: to approach rather than to avoid.

It must not be assumed though, that because political systems great and small – that is, those of individuals and those of nationalities – necessarily reflect the stylistic extremes of thinking available to us as a species, that individual style and biological tuning cannot be at variance with apparent ideological bent. It has to be borne in mind that allegiance to political parties and to particular politicians is offered for many emotional reasons other than the need to express or identify with a fundamental *modus operandi*: entire families are known 'always' to vote in a particular direction, and when times are very insecure really powerful leadership displayed by *any* faction is likely to gain support. Complexities abound, and whereas the point has been made more than once that access to a balance of both modes of functioning is of obvious benefit to the organism, it is now necessary to acknowledge the possibility of more than one kind of balance.

So far in this chapter discussion has centred on different kinds of arousal and their implications for styles of thinking and feeling, and 'balance' has been conceived in terms of (1) the release of neurotransmitters promoting both mental and physical activity, which is represented on the model by the line I_1–E_2 dissecting the right angle at I_1, and (2) a complementary relationship between limbic and cortical arousal, or rather, between high limbic arousal and high cortical inhibition (p. 86); that is, high limbic arousal = high cortical inhibition (resulting in conscious scanning) and low limbic arousal = low cortical inhibition (allowing conscious focus). The former condition is represented on the model to differing degrees by I_2, E_2, and E_1, and the latter by I_1, so that (1) and (2) are both represented as being in balance at the centre of the model.

The model does not, however, take into account the possibility of a variable PNS/SNS relationship but is based on the relatively simple notion of the gradual dominance of SNS activity over PNS activity, as arousal increases. In order to give as complete a picture of ANS activity as possible it would be necessary to place various overlays of possible patterns of 'balancing' PNS activity over our existing relatively simple model of increase in intensity of different kinds of SNS activity only. Variation in intensity and bias of aspects of SNS activity must surely be compounded by variations in patterns of SNS/PNS interaction. This implies that interaction may be even, forming a simple hyphenated pattern, as it were, of SNS/PNS activity (of low *or* high intensity), or uneven, providing a bias in the form of a dot–dash, rather than dash–dash pattern, so that SNS activity is either under- or over-compensated, again at different possible intensities. These complications obviously increase the potential range of variability in autonomic functioning accommodated by the APM-A model, but to explore it fully would require numerous diagrams, and probably more than one volume.

Most importantly, though, this opens up other concepts of 'balance': in particular, the concept of an even patterning of SNS/PNS firing at different intensities, and therefore a balanced range of abilities available at different levels in different individuals, rather than very high-intensity SNS activity *necessarily* implying dysfunctionally high SNS dominance. It suggests that as well as the moderately aroused, moderately active individual at the centre of the model being an 'all-rounder', we can also accommodate a very highly (limbically) aroused, highly active, and extremely successful individual who can also be described as an 'all-rounder': not just apparently equally at ease with both the arts and the sciences in the way in which the best architects, as one example, appear to be, but able to make a significant contribution to both fields in the manner of, say, Jonathan Miller, as one of the well-known living examples, or rather more notably still, Leonardo da Vinci.

However, holding to the simpler construct, we already have an adequate tool of analysis to be able to draw a number of conclusions about individual style and to allow many more issues pertaining to questions of style to be raised in the following chapters. Above all, by relating species to environment, mind to body and conscious processes to unconscious processes, it is possible to arrive at a *basic language* which can be applied to all aspects of the person, and relate them to one another.

From the arguments about interactive processes which have already been put forward, it follows that if we are subject to something called cognitive style (pp. 80–3), now apparently an established aspect of human variability, then we must also be subject to an 'emotional style', an 'attentional style', a 'memory style', and 'styles of arousal'. The term 'individual style' is being used to suggest all of these things, and more. It is being used to describe what might be called an individual's *adaptive style*. It is also being used to bring together all of the major concepts of human psychology under discussion.

It is surely in the interests of a fuller appreciation of the *complexities* of human functioning (so that the whole person can be taken into account) and in the interests of better communication that, instead of talking only in terms of personality, motivation, intelligence, and creativity, which are all global and highly polymorphic terms that some regard as having become devoid of meaning, discussion centres on certain key concepts, which concern *essential* areas of difference between people.

Some process characteristics and process dimensions have already been identified (pp. 95–6) and to these can be added other key concepts of style which are in part biologically determined (species learned over millennia, but variable within certain tolerances) and in part attributable to specific environmental conditions (individually learned). It is stressed, therefore, that all of the global terms we normally use in description of people incorporate *both* species and individually acquired aspects, and all may be defined in terms of intensity *and* bias.

What we call 'personality' may simply be regarded as the *sum of individual adaptive style*: discernible consistencies in individual behaviour composed in part of ante-natal and post-natal physiological tuning (see note 11 (a)) and concomitant levels and kinds of need, and in part of acquired habits of maintaining integrity, with variable emphasis on psychological and physical survival. Similarly, it is equally important to keep in mind that 'motivation', otherwise referred to as 'drive' but with very little consistency of meaning (although the former is often taken to mean acquired interest and the latter an 'innate' source of responsivity), is not just measurable in terms of 'low' or 'high' but may also be perceived to be biased towards the generation of mainly mental or mainly physical activity. To speak in terms of 'intensity and bias of energy', for instance, and for reference to be made to tuning *and* to environmental factors can be seen to allow for much specific discussion of what incites an individual into action, than simple reference to 'level of motivation'. By reference to the model and to the new hierarchy of needs it also becomes possible to make predictions about the kind of stimuli to which response is most likely to be made.

The APM-A model also indicates much more constructive ways in which to talk about intelligence and creativity. When we refer to 'intelligence', questions of levels and biases relate essentially to *degrees and kinds of efficiency*, while 'creativity' is defined as being fundamentally about ideas and action – that is, *degrees and kinds of discernible novelty* (so-called 'originality') and/or *degrees and kinds of productivity*.

By using what are being called 'process terms', it would seem to be possible to avoid a great deal of the miscommunication and many of the omissions which patently arise from reliance on the gross terms in question. They are, admittedly, frequently accompanied by definitions, but rarely by definition founded in sufficient depth of analysis to gain any degree of general acceptance. Besides facilitating communication, the use of knowledge of APM-A process as a tool of analysis also offers a kind of check-list. For example, in addition to what has already been said above about it being possible for discussion to take place at a 'grainier level', we could also expect exploration of human experience and behaviour always to take into account both inner and outer, and both conscious and unconscious, elements and influences. The APM-A view also suggests that, in considering any environmental phenomena or human activities, however improbable or microscopic they may be, there are always both similarities *and* differences to be perceived, and that classifications other than the ones we make most readily ourselves are more than just 'possible'.

Clearly, the conscious adoption of an alternative mode of perception could be a fruitful exercise. Because our own styles usually consist of one kind of bias or the other does not mean to say that the opposite mode cannot be developed consciously and with practice – but first it has to be properly understood. It is not being suggested that individual style is amenable to complete re-education, but it is suggested that a person's adaptive repertoire can be extended.[53]

It would seem that unconscious attempts at 'compensation' commonly take place in the form of partnerships of many kinds, and in most political systems; but because of lack of understanding of psychological homeostasis and its effects on perception, many of them are very clumsy. Because neither extreme mode operates to the total exclusion of the other, in theory, potential for seeing the other's point of view always exists, but at worst, differences in perceptual styles are so great that polarization takes place, and instead of the stimulation and roundness of view to be provided by the availability of different modes, the see-saw lurches from dizzy heights to resounding thuds, so that no common experience or meeting place seems possible. It is as if there is an optimal distance yet to be discovered between the possible biological extremes of perception: a kind of golden section of human relationships to be defined along the various continua, in order for harmony to be attainable between individuals, groups, and nations. Such a discovery would have to incorporate notions of optimal levels of threat and promise but, most importantly, it would also have to allow for at least phenomenological polarizations, because without the facility for conflict and disorganization, there is no facility for reorganization, new beginnings, nor positive response to change.

Just as it was said earlier that *Homo sapiens* are a biological response to the environment, so are we all as individuals, but we respond to different degrees, and are frequently victim to our own inner environments as well as to the inhospitalities of the outside world. These 'inner worlds' governed by physiological process are to be defined as determining our potential for so-called 'normality' and 'abnormality', as well as for psychological and physiological survival.

That there are stylistic differences to do with abnormality as well as normality must be accepted; that similar styles of abnormality may result in accolade or institutionalization, depending on which 'tools' happen to be to hand, is more difficult to accept for some, but this is the case to be argued next.

Individual style and psychopathology

Summary

Chapter 4 sets out to relate so-called 'abnormality' to 'normality' and to stand neuroses, psychoses, suicide, and criminality, as well as other kinds of experience hitherto regarded as inaccessible to scientific investigation (such as religious and aesthetic), within the new perspective.

The current state of psychiatry is criticized on a number of grounds, including its methods of diagnosis and classification. However, alternatives are offered. By pegging conditions such as phobias, obsessions, paranoia, schizophrenia, and other neuroses and psychoses on to the model in terms of 'normal' and 'stressed' locations, a *basis for a new system of classification* is offered which includes *severity*; *kind* of condition; likely *underlying biochemical states*; and reference to 'normal' *adaptive style*. The idea of the need to identify 'stressors' or 'markers' is seen to be inadequate; rather, it is argued, it is necessary to diagnose *levels* of susceptibility to different *kinds of disorientation* in order for therapy to provide *means of orientation*; that is, means of 'relocation' and regaining 'direction' specific to the needs and adaptive style of the individual. The plethora of available therapies and an alternative way of viewing them are discussed, and it is explained why a simple eclectic approach is inadequate.

More criticism is made of Eysenck's theories and tests – his theory of criminality and tests of N (neuroticism) and P (psychoticism) in particular – and an analysis is offered of the advantages and disadvantages of Gray's modifications of these and Eysenck's theory of E and I (extraversion and introversion).

An initial step towards relating cultural phenomena, the subject of Part 2, to the *dynamic model of style* is taken by discussing some theories of social change put forward by Zurcher, Adler, and Harrington, respectively. New models introduced include a *model of biological alternatives*, which refers to alternative human potentials, and a *simplified, unitary model of regression*.

4.1 Styles of madness

One of the central themes of this book is that certain identifiable aspects of human nature can be observed operating at all levels of biological organization. The most crucial and obvious of these has already been identified as the process of maintaining integrity (2.4), for which some means of orientation is necessary, so that even the simplest organisms and cells manifest tropism.

It is, therefore, particularly significant to note a curious phenomenon currently evident in the field of psychiatry. Both as a field of knowledge and as an area of practice dealing with mental and nervous disorders, it is itself showing signs of disorientation and confusion. In short, some of the most pressing issues in psychiatry (Bean 1983) are issues which can be seen to be axiomatic to its own integrity and 'survival'.

Psychiatry itself (taken here in its most general meaning to include psychopathology) lacks an established identity. There are many alternative models, but none which offers a general framework to hold together growth and change in its own system of functioning. Similarly, the larger and even more fragmented field of psychology can also be perceived as manifesting signs of crisis (Westland 1978). Both fields can be seen to be in need of what, it is to be argued, all good therapies offer by one means or another: orientation.

In psychiatry the most serious of the theoretical controversies appear to strike at the very roots of the discipline. They centre on questions to do with (1) whether or not there is such a condition as mental illness (Ineichen 1979:chap. 1), (2) the imprecision and inadequacies of current diagnostic procedures and categories (Ward *et al.* 1978), and (3) to what extent 'cure' is possible (Clare 1983:156ff.).

To provide a context within which these key issues can all be considered within the attempt to make better sense of psychology in general, maladaptive mental states will be related to adaptive mental states by reference to three, in particular, major APM-A concepts. These are the intimately related concepts of *vulnerability*, shown in the last chapter to underlie the second concept – *individual style* – and, third, psychological needs as *orientation needs*. The first of these, vulnerability, is a concept found in psychiatric literature, but not apparently deemed at all significant, so far, to any of the other aspects of individual style referred to in the last chapter.

Most significantly, it is a concept referred to by different authors in a volume (Barrett 1979) which reports and examines advances in relating stress and disorder during the 1970s. One of the contributors, Zubin, in summarizing discussion of 'life events, vulnerability, crises and episodes [of mental disorder]', actually foresees the possibility of vulnerability itself being the focus of a symposium (ibid.:279). He sees the primary question facing investigators to be that of why the same life event stressor leaves some individuals untouched while in others it leads to either a crisis or an episode. This is precisely the question this chapter sets out to answer, together with another: namely, to what kind of disorder a vulnerable person may be predisposed. Consequently, as well as defining sources of vulnerability we will also be defining *kinds* of *vulnerability*. Zubin goes on to propose that, once we have discovered the 'markers' which differentiate the vulnerable from the less vulnerable,

> the contingent life event triggers necessary to transform the latent vulnerability into an episode can be determined and therapeutic intervention instituted for preventing either the initial episode or any subsequent episode. After the triggering events are found, families of patients as well as patients themselves can be taught to avoid the occurrence of the noxious events or desensitize the patient to their occurrence if they are inevitable.
>
> (Ibid.:288–9)

The view to be explained here is that 'triggering events' in themselves can*not* be avoided *in toto* because these 'events' comprise our perceptions of our physical, social, political, economic, and cultural environments. They are inherent to the human condition. Further, it is argued that most often it is an agglomerate of internal and external stressors (any one of which, alone, may be easily tolerated) which precipitates disorientation and/or breakdown.

Discussion of what Zubin calls 'the modification of conditions which lead to the psychopathology' will be the subject matter of Chapter 6, but will be seen to amount, rather, to the need for a paradigm change: a need to adopt a quite radical change of view of what a person is and, in turn, to consider the implications of a different view for what kind of education system may best further the cause of orientation for most people.

However, identification of the 'markers', by extending the APM-A model of adaptive style and potential to include maladaptive styles and potential, *is* the business of this chapter.

Klerman (1979a:151) has already argued that, as a concept common to biology, ethology, psychology, and physiology, the idea of adaptation should have relevance to theoretical and clinical problems in psychopathology. He also cites Adolf Meyer's attempt (see Lief 1948) to build a science of psychobiology and his emphasis on the continuity between normal experience and clinical disorder. But Klerman confines his argument to depressive affect having an adaptive function as a signal for social communication; equating separation and the loss of maternal bonds among mammals with human sadness: stages of anxiety, agitation, protest, and increased psychomotor activity, followed by a phase of social

126

withdrawal and decreased motor activity (Klerman 1979a:152). In fact, by taking into account *variability* as well as adaptability, other so-called illnesses than depressive affect can be made sense of within an evolutionary perspective.

APM-A theory actually indicates the existence of *styles of neurosis* similar to those arrived at in a totally different way – from clinical observations – by David Shapiro (1965), and these are referred to throughout the rest of the chapter. It is because Shapiro's descriptions derive from clinical experience, but are nevertheless coincident with the APM-A analysis, that they are used here. However, his rationalizations are not coincident with the APM-A view and are criticized, also in order to clarify the new position.

Shapiro arrived at his conclusions about the possibility of describing general characteristics and consistencies of style amongst neurotics from working with psychological tests, particularly the Rorschach test.[1]

He eventually describes how both 'normal' development and neuroses always proceed through existing cognitive forms, or what he calls 'initial organising configurations' (biological predispositions to particular ways of perceiving and thinking). But at this point Shapiro's curiosity seems to have dissipated, as he simply attributes these configurations, which occupy such a critical place in his analysis, to innate variability, whilst at the same time attributing *to* them the control of tension thresholds (Shapiro 1965:117ff.).

Although APM-A theory provides a very different analysis and leads to very different conclusions about the processes underlying the styles which Shapiro describes so brilliantly, his descriptions relate so closely to our existing model that it is possible to endorse with enthusiasm his view that,

It is only when we understand the style and the general tendency of the individual's mind and interest that we can reconstruct the subjective meaning of the content of an item of behaviour or thought . . . Without this understanding, we run the risk – and it holds for therapists and testers alike – of seeing only textbook meanings, possibly correct, but far removed from the sense and tone of an individual's experience.

(Ibid.:18)

Agreement can also be expressed with most other things he says, but, quite contrary to his analysis, in Chapter 3 cognitive styles were defined (as neurotic styles will be) as *manifestations of variability in tension thresholds*, which in turn are viewed as incidental to *variability in patterning and intensity of ANS activity* rather than, as Shapiro suggests, tension thresholds *arising from* innate cognitive structures.

In order to provide a theoretical underpinning for the existence of styles of neurosis (without which, as Shapiro says, such consistencies as can be observed 'will only have the status of clinical impressions'), and in order also to be able to identify styles of other kinds of 'madness' and in turn to be able to relate these to our model, it becomes necessary to return to and extend some of our earlier arguments. One of the new aspects of style which will be seen to emerge is that neurotic styles, in common with cognitive styles, display particular temporal orientations.

In Chapters 1 and 2, evidence was offered to support the idea that at high levels of arousal attention becomes more diffuse: that more gross and less obvious associations are perceived, and that initially, we scan, rather than focus, in our efforts to achieve orientation. In essence, the argument is that arousal, by virtue of concomitant increases in energy levels, offers access to what we call imagination and greater capacity for problem solving. This position has yet to be elaborated in discussing various kinds of neuroses and psychoses, but we must also consider evidence of a different kind: evidence which suggests that at very high levels of stress, panic leads to narrowing of attention – sometimes with tragic effect.

Making this point, Norman quotes Bachrach (1970) on diving behaviour and how panic seems to override certain aspects of training:

> For example, it has been reported that in all of the deaths attributed to diving in California the diver was found still wearing his weight belt despite the attempts in diving courses to make jettisoning of the weight belt automatic in emergencies. This woman . . . drowned while diving for golf balls . . . When her body was recovered, she was wearing her weight belt, and in addition, was still clutching a heavy bag of golf balls.
>
> (Norman 1976:64)

Norman (1976:64–5) attributes this phenomenon to the Yerkes–Dodson curve, and rationalizes that attention becomes more narrowly focused as arousal increases, providing, at first, an improvement in performance; but, with ever-increasing levels of arousal, attention becomes more narrowly focused, until it eventually proves detrimental to performance.

The logical conclusion to be drawn from Norman's interpretation is that disorientation associated with fragmentation of conscious attention is most likely to occur at lowest levels of arousal – if not during sleep! In fact, we know that such states are associated with anxiety and high arousal.

In Chapter 2 the dynamics of attention and performance, particularly the scanning and focusing functions of attention, were described as being somewhat more complex than Norman indicates, with organization of behaviour depending on an optimal balance of the capacities in question, according to the degree of flexibility demanded by the nature of the task. We know, for instance, that some tasks require relative rigidity of attention and the exclusion from consciousness of environmental change, as in a complicated but highly mechanical task such as repairing a watch, while other occupations of a much more existential nature, such as teaching or chairing a meeting, demand much more flexibility of approach. Such tasks demand a much less focused mode of attention in order for the unexpected to be accommodated or even for tactics to be changed entirely, in order to take advantage of unpredicted outcomes of action.

The point being stressed is one already made above. This is that we do not either scan *or* focus to the total exclusion of the other mode (however much it may feel like it): that the chemical transmitters most closely associated with these states of consciousness always operate in a compensatory manner. But above all, increase in arousal will at first, however briefly, initiate attentional activity associated with searching and, for reasons already explained in Chapter 3, this takes a diffuse form in some individuals, while in others the 'search' is always conducted in a more sequential and focused manner.

From the arguments put forward in the last chapter it now becomes possible to see how some types of individual are physiologically more vulnerable to disorientation. They experience higher orientation needs and already display greater disorganization of behaviour than others. Further, by referring back to Figures 15, 19, and 20 we can also see that different kinds of dysfunction have already been associated with all of the definably different kinds of internalizer and externalizer. But in order to relate major forms of neuroses and psychoses, as well as the rather more serious 'abnormality' manifested as suicide (which, incidentally, will eventually be defined as adaptive), to our model, it is necessary to explain the kind of narrowing of attention accompanying states of very high arousal to which Norman has referred.

By pursuing earlier arguments concerning variability of patterning of ANS activity (1.2, 3.3, and p. 120) and bearing in mind the compensatory nature of the PNS in response to the SNS, it is not at all difficult to imagine that given a sufficiently threatening situation and concomitant intensity of SNS activity, a state of panic may eventually be reached which represents a massive imbalance of neuro-chemicals. Compensatory response in the form of PNS activity is therefore likely to be equally dramatic. As the internal condition (of excitation) becomes at least as threatening to the organism as the perceived external conditions, it is likely to change the experience of frantic mental searching for a solution to a seemingly hopeless situation to sudden focus on to some *apparently* vital detail.

The adaptational value of attention finally narrowing under severe stress can be seen to be psychological as well as physiological. Most obviously, anxiety – if not mental agony – is likely to be alleviated to some extent as attention narrows and fewer 'connections' are made, allowing an opportunity for the organism actually to regain balance, or, in the case of panic being well justified, for the subsequent horror to be minimized.

Klerman's summary of stages of anxiety moving through increase in activity (which, it has been argued, always involves physical *and* mental activity, however biased towards one or the other it may be), followed by social withdrawal and decreased psychomotor activity, has already been quoted above. Similar observations of extreme anxiety resulting in withdrawal (which also necessarily implies a narrowing of perceptual and conceptual boundaries) have been made by Pavlov (Hilgard and Bower 1975:73) and, rather more recently, by Seligman (see Miller *et al.* 1977). But whereas Pavlov labelled his observation 'protective inhibition', Seligman's experimental model is called 'learned helplessness'.

Various items of physiological evidence implicating chemical transmitters of the adrenergic and cholinergic systems fundamental to the APM-A model – namely, adrenalin, noradrenalin, and acetylcholine (see 1.2) – will be introduced as specific pathologies are discussed, but it must be made clear that this is not to imply that particular physical correlates of mental conditions necessarily indicate physical aetiologies. On the contrary, the view to be put forward is that certain patternings of ANS activity do predispose particular types of individual to more or less vulnerability of particular kinds but that, most often, interaction of biological predisposition and unmet needs (which may be due to environmental deficiencies, past or present) precipitates those extremes of perception and behaviour usually referred to as psychopathology: that the physiological correlates may either precede *or* accompany psychological changes. Just as the same life stressors do not precipitate psychopathology in approximately 20 per cent of those deemed at risk, and approximately one-third of those *not* deemed so by the same criteria *do* experience some form of 'illness',[2] it must be emphasized that not all of those we may define as physiologically vulnerable will necessarily be so unfortunate. By no means all are likely to encounter environmental conditions likely to compound their vulnerability to the extent of developing clinical symptoms. Implicit in results obtained from the use of life-event scales is the need to take both physiological *and* environmental conditions into account.

This brings us to the third and most central APM-A concept in our attempt to provide a backcloth against which better sense can be made of psychiatry: *orientation needs.*

It is to be argued that 'mental illness', 'mental disorder', 'abnormal behaviour', and any other kind of psychological crisis experienced by, or attributable to, an individual can always be described in terms of disorientation. Mental states experienced as, or perceived to be, maladaptive are so defined because of their behavioural manifestations. But indications of *loss of shared experience* (of time, space, people, places, things, and their significance or priority value), and to a greater or lesser extent, the 'reality' which this constitutes are not always as obvious as the loss of efficiency or other impairment of effectiveness within the individual's social or working environment usually taken to signal the onset of mental problems. This is because we all have at least some awareness of the uniqueness (as well as shared nature) of our perceptions and tolerance of isolation, and levels of need for the kind of reassurance to be gained from authentic communication (for which quite a large measure of shared experience is of course essential) have already been defined as variables (pp. 58–63).

Levels of vulnerability will be seen to arise from biological tuning and intensity and kinds of need (Figures 4 and 5) on the one hand and availability of means of understanding and tools of expression on the other. The latter (environmental) condition will be seen either to compound, or to compensate for the former (physiological) condition. But the crucial 'marker' of vulnerability *is* taken to be biological tuning, which determines (at least initially) both level and kinds of need for orientation, and level of need for expression. Obviously, if these needs are relatively low, tolerance of the limitations of unsympathetic environmental conditions is likely to be relatively high.

Support for a view of maladaptive states as states of disorientation is offered both by an increasing weight of physiological evidence implicating the chemical transmitters most closely associated with the orientation response[3] and by the accepted significance of 'stressors' in the onset of mental problems. The critical importance of orientation needs (as defined in Chapter 2) is also implicit in lists which have been compiled to indicate the differences in circumstances between those most likely to respond favourably to treatment and those others for whom the prognosis is not good. As one would expect (if such lists hold any validity), there is a very close inverse correlation between them: namely, in the more fortunate group, a first illness with an acute onset of response to massive and understandable stress; well-established personality; social competence; supportive social networks (Clare 1983:139); in the less fortunate group, a genetically determined predisposition; early life experience of loss; the presence of certain personality traits, particularly inter-personal dependency; inadequate repertoire of learned social skills; the absence of social supports in the individual's environment (Klerman 1979b:138–9). All of these factors can be seen to relate directly to the degree of orientation a person has already, or is likely to be able to achieve.

Klerman, already cited as one who believes in the value of the concept of adaptation, draws the conclusion that 'the adult depressive episode represents a vain attempt on the part of the individual to adapt. Clinical depressions are maladaptive outcomes of partially successful attempts at adaptation' (1979a:156). Maybe it will turn out to be more precise and theoretically more fruitful to suggest that such episodes represent maladaptive outcomes of attempts to defend and maintain psychological integrity under threat.

Whereas Freud identified the nine defence mechanisms of sublimation, regression, fantasy, identification, projection, rationalization, reaction formation, dissociation, and conversion hysteria, it has already been suggested within the new perspective that everything to do with mind can be identified as having to do with defence, and that *all* of its identifiable modes and mechanisms of classification and means of planning for action can be defined as defence mechanisms. The details of this position must wait for a volume to itself, but for now it can be said, and few would disagree, that anxiety is a defence; habits of perception (as well as behaviour) are defences; vigilance is obviously defensive; and the predominance (or overactivity) of any of these functions can very easily shift an individual into the practice of 'abnormal behaviour' and the accompanying experiences of isolation, guilt, embarrassment, and/or other forms of mental discomfort.

We must also always bear in mind that so-called 'normal' ways of perceiving and behaving – requiring, as they very often do, varying degrees of pretence, conformity, and other manifestations of inauthenticity in order not 'to offend' or to continue 'to belong' – appear positively lunatic to those whose biological tuning leads to more expressive styles; especially when outcomes are sometimes even worse than those they are intended to avoid, and would become quite unnecessary were we to develop the potentials for better means of understanding, and better means of communication, which are now well within our grasp.

4.2 Fears and phobias

The logical extension of our previous argument that everything to do with mind has to do with defence is that everything we experience and do also relates, however indirectly, to fear and anger; these being the emotions most obviously representative of the flight/fight response. This position is actually implicit in the contents of the last chapter.

By defining variability in modes of experience and behaviour as hinging on the different biases of limbic arousal associated with fear and anger, the view of mind as a highly complex defence mechanism is endorsed. Given also that 'mental illness' becomes more and more closely identified with the physiological correlates of these two emotions (see note 3), we already have the most fundamental and direct as well as the simplest possible connection to be made between normal and abnormal behaviour,

Figure 22 Different kinds of potential for 'abnormal' experience and behaviour, with so-called 'weak personalities' located in the lower left-hand side of the model (see also Figs. 15, 19, 20)

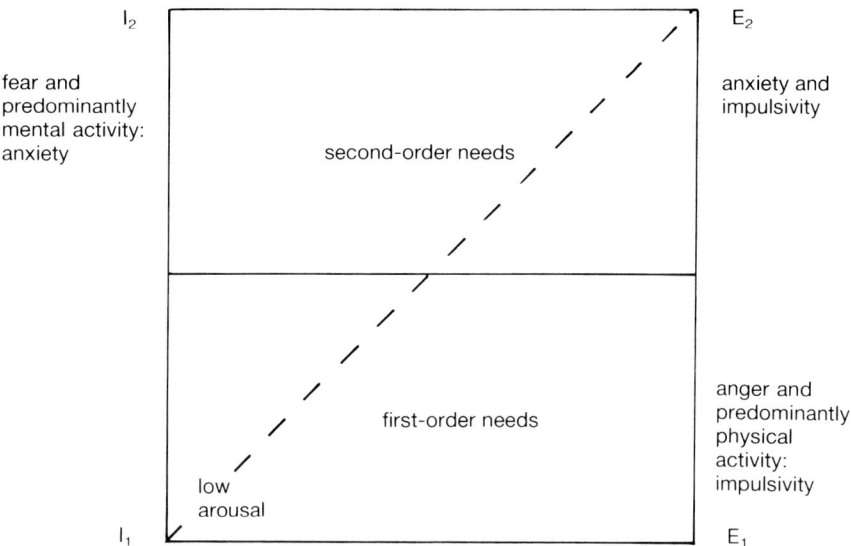

I_2

fear and
predominantly
mental activity:
anxiety

second-order needs

E_2

anxiety and
impulsivity

first-order needs

anger and
predominantly
physical
activity:
impulsivity

low
arousal

I_1

E_1

whether the norms in question are taken to be statistical or as emanating from cultural expectations.

In order to relate conventional descriptions and classification of abnormality to the APM-A model, we shall first consider the significance of fear – that is, the mental conditions and processes represented by the top half of the model; then the relevance of aggression (represented by the right-hand side of the model and already directly related to the idea of externalization of excitation) to various kinds of abnormality. Finally, abnormalities associated with those types of individual referred to by Shapiro as 'weak personalities' will be located in the position of lowest arousal of either of the kinds (adrenalin or noradrenalin) in question, on the bottom left-hand side of the model. In this way we will see that the 'markers' of vulnerability sought by Zubin are subject to variability in just the same way as any other identifiable aspect of individual style.

We shall also see the relevance in each case of Shapiro's immensely perceptive and useful descriptions of style and how these can be understood in terms of, and related to, the larger APM-A perspective. He identifies four styles of neurosis: obsessive-compulsive; paranoid; hysterical; and impulsive. Because the general modes of deployment of attention characteristic of each of these styles have already been described in APM-A terms in Chapter 3, Shapiro's definitions of neurotic styles from clinical observation will be seen to provide a very valuable means of relating the new model to 'abnormal' experience and behaviour, even though the view of his theoretical stance is a critical one. But in order to account for these more extreme manifestations of the APM-A process, we must remember the fact that the model of style illustrated in Figures 14–21 is relatively a very simple conception of the range of variability available to the species.

It was suggested earlier that in order to represent human variability more adequately, a whole series of models, or at least a whole series of overlays for the original model, would be necessary to illustrate even a quite narrow range of possible variability of SNS/PNS patterning and activity. It was also explained that the model as it stands represents only a simple pattern of gradual increase in SNS dominance as arousal increases. This conception must now be extended to accommodate alternative relationships between the biases, of varying degrees, towards adrenalin or noradrenalin and compensatory PNS activity; that is, to accommodate the complexities of the interaction of two possible kinds of variability in bias rather than one. But by making brief reference only and confining ourselves to Shapiro's descriptions of neuroses, and plotting these on to the APM-A model in the first instance, the extension of the original conception – to account for an even greater range of variability – will be at least a little simpler than it sounds.

Three of Shapiro's styles will eventually be located in the upper half of the model – the obsessive-compulsive, the paranoid, and the hysterical – and it will be seen that as styles of attention, perception, and memory they move fairly obviously (and in the above order) from one side of the model to the other. They move from the exercise of extremely narrow focus to the deployment of extremely diffuse attention; from rigidity to flexibility; from concern with the specific to concern with the general; from concern mainly with facts to greater concern with feeling; from close organization of experience and behaviour to evident disorganization of experience and behaviour; and from interest in and memory for technical detail to practically no memory for detail at all. In fact, the three styles in question will be seen to occupy places along bipolar continua which, by now, should have acquired a certain ring of familiarity.

The first of these styles, the obsessive-compulsive style, is seen above all to display extreme rigidity of attention and a deliberateness of action, which is reflected primarily in a general tendency to persist in a course of action until after it has become irrelevant – or even absurd. This characteristic of rigidity may also be reflected in a stilted social manner, a stiff body posture, or both, in addition to other inflexible characteristics of behaviour (Shapiro 1965:24).

Shapiro describes the obsessive–compulsive's narrow range of attention as being comparable to the kind of rigidity displayed by those suffering from organic brain damage – 'gripped or passively held by a more or less immediately manifest or concrete aspect of a situation or task' – and goes on to say,

> although sharp [attention] is in certain respects markedly limited in both mobility and range. These people not only concentrate, they seem always to be concentrating . . . .
>
> Specifically, this is a mode of attention that seems un-equipped for the casual or immediate impression . . . [which] allow[s] one to be 'struck' by even that which is peripheral or incidental to its original, intended focus of attention or that may not even possess a clear intention or sharp focus in the first place. . . .
>
> The sharp but narrowed focus . . . misses certain aspects of the world even while it engages others quite successfully.
>
> . . . he must go after and get the facts – and will get them straight – but he will often miss those aspects of a situation that give it its 'flavour' or 'impact'. . . .
>
> Every action, every direction is weighty, heavy with deliberateness . . . .
>
> Thus, preoccupation with technical details takes the place of recognition and response to the actual person or event.
>
> (Ibid.:26–8, 37, 50)

In contrast to the belief of the author of these descriptions, which is that the 'normal' person's attention shifts in direction and in intensity quite smoothly, APM-A theory indicates that 'normality' itself is highly variable in this respect. It is being argued that the extent to which an individual can deploy attention in a flexible manner varies more significantly than any other aspect of his or her psychological bearing.

In fact, *all* of the process characteristics that Shapiro describes have already appeared in one or other of the descriptions of commonly observed experience and behaviour cited in the last chapter. All are representative of an extreme mode, and it is suggested that the differences between, say, Ruddock's ritualistic teacher, Deikman's cab-driver in action mode, or Hudson's converger and Shapiro's obsessive–compulsive have more to do with intensity of arousal than bias (of the kinds already defined on the model), and more to do with content than form; in other words, Shapiro's 'abnormal' style has more in common with the APM-A model, than not.

However, the new theory does concur with Shapiro's criticism (ibid.:5) of the Freudian position with reference to explanations based exclusively on early acquired drive *content* and libidinal development. But Shapiro fails to perceive the full significance of the relationship between content and form. Most obviously, as has already been pointed out, he disregards the possibility of tension thresholds being an intrinsic part of form, but further, he fails to recognize the influence which form actually exercises over content: for instance, over whether interest is in the concrete or the abstract, or both.[4] Additionally, he does not perceive that 'abnormality' does not necessarily represent 'hypertrophy' of 'normal' processes but may represent 'normal' processes operating on a content which is inappropriate to the attainment of social approbation within a given environment. The latter point, in particular, will be elaborated later.

Moving on to the paranoid style, we will not see here any obvious expression of an extreme example of any of the bipolar continua referred to in Chapter 3. Rather, this style will be seen to be extreme only in terms of intensity. Shapiro's paranoid scans and focuses, *both* to an extreme degree. To complicate matters further, the paranoid can be seen to belong to one of two identifiable types, of which neither, apparently, provides easily distinguishable components of a general style. One type is furtive, constrictive, apprehensive, suspicious. The other is rigidly arrogant, more aggressive, suspicious, and megalomanic. The paranoid style is also, incidentally, the only neurotic style regarded by Shapiro as involving any serious loss of reality. He attributes this to a characteristic mode of perception which assimilates only expected content while dismissing what is not relevant to the prior supposition.

The style is characterized by a directed search – that is, focused searching, or what might even be called 'focused scanning':

attention . . . is . . . not only unusually acute and intense, but also unusually active. It is not the carefully studying and measuring attention of the obsessive–compulsive, but an actively scanning and searching attention.
. . . never passive or casual, never simply wandering . . . it is attention that is rigidly intentional.

(Ibid.:58, 59)

Significantly, Shapiro observes:

Thus [he] . . . can be at the same time absolutely right in his perception and absolutely wrong in his judgement.

(Ibid.:61)

He also describes this type as 'hypersensitive' and 'hyperalert', and as being always in a condition of 'hyperintentionality', which also has the effect, Shapiro says, of making expressive behaviour seem not 'the real thing' but, rather, whatever the tactics of a situation call for. He refers very graphically to lack of spontaneity, lack of expressiveness, and lack of self-revelation as manifestations of an 'internal police state', and by doing so, incidentally, implies the very high degree of threat experienced by this kind of individual (ibid.:73ff.).

Finally, we turn to the description of the hysteric who – as in the case of the obsessive–compulsive – should remind us of a type of individual already encountered in the last chapter: one interested in 'not facts, but impressions. These impressions may be interesting and communicative, and they are very often vivid, but they remain impressions – not detailed, not quite sharply defined' (ibid.:111).

Shapiro describes the attentional mode of the hysteric as global, diffuse, impressionistic, and certainly not technical (see references to lateralization of brain function cited earlier). He then confirms something we might suspect from our acquaintance with Hudson's work and the fact that hysterics are clearly not convergent in their style of thinking. He tells us that the hysteric is not good at mathematics and, with a low capacity for concentration generally, does not search as much as is 'struck' by environmental information (ibid.:113). We may also be reminded at this point of Deikman's receptive mode – of 'diffuse attending, paralogical thought processes, decreased boundary perception, and the dominance of the sensory over the formal'.

In discussing this more 'fuzzy' mode of attention, Shapiro makes direct reference to the hysteric's quality of memory, and makes a very important point about the fact that the Freudian defence mechanism most often associated with hysteria is repression. He suggests from his observations of the very low level of factual knowledge displayed by hysterics, together with their low capacity for concentration, that their style is actually conducive to forgetting.

The validity of any particularly close association between *active* repression (however unconscious or automatic) and hysteria can be brought further into question if we amplify Shapiro's suggestion with conclusions drawn from the APM-A perspective. We can add that the style of the hysteric is likely to be unsympathetic to the acquisition of factual, detailed information because of a characteristic already attributed to externalizers, particularly second-order (E_2 type) externalizers (with whom shared characteristics have already been implied): namely, the experience of an urgent need to take in as much of the environment as possible at once and, therefore, greater dependency on unconscious processing.

Just as the Freudian defence mechanism of projection, which is so obvious in paranoics, can be seen to be an *incidental effect* of extraordinarily narrow attention (so severely and continuously biased towards the assessment of the security of their own position within the social environment that no other possible motivations can be seen to exist than those which already dominate their consciousness), so can repression in hysterics be seen to be an *incidental effect* of a general mode of perception. Concomitant psychological conflicts (between conscious and unconscious perception) can be viewed in a similar way: as arising from inadequate conscious processing, and therefore also from inadequate conscious accommodation and understanding of information crucial to the psychological security of the individual. Uncomfortable changes in orientation may eventually be required in order for the new information to be accommodated, and may be all the more reluctantly undertaken as the acquisition of new, related information increases.

But the principal argument being put forward is that *all* of the processes so evident in abnormal behaviour, mental illness, or whatever other category we use for states maladaptive to current environmental conditions, are processes which go on in all of us more or less actively, but are not obvious, or often apparent, until manifested in an extreme form.

It is argued that we all harbour something of the obsessive, with occasional bouts of habitual attention given to some self-imposed or other goal; the compulsive, by smoking, drinking or, without the complications which arise from the ingestion of stimulants or depressants, stepping over lines on the pavement or dressing in a certain order; the paranoid, a tendency identified as commonplace by Saul Bellow's formulation of 'just because everyone is talking about me doesn't make me paranoid'; and the hysteric, in the form of at least occasional lack of concentration and/or the occasional emotional outburst under stress: mass identification with characterizations of which probably accounts in large measure for the success of actor John Cleese.

It would seem that it is because Shapiro's descriptions are based on clinical observations – that is, on individuals in whom particular processes are manifested in extreme form – that they do not so much just echo the various kinds of work cited earlier (concerning lateralization of brain function and cognitive and perceptual styles); they seem to cut right across these fields in such a way that they can be very easily pegged on to the APM-A model.

It is possible now to view the obsessive–compulsive, paranoid, and hysterical styles moving in the order in which they have been discussed, from left to right (in the direction of increasingly intense and more generalized experience and expression and increasing dominance of unconscious processing) in the upper half of the model (which represents high levels of mental activity) except for one problem. The extremely high degree of focus characteristic of the obsessive–compulsive places him in the lower half of the model (see Figure 15), but this is inconsistent with his very high degree of physical activity.[5]

However, an extremely comfortable fit does occur if we view the neurotic styles discussed so far in terms of our I, I/E and E types – under stress. This gives us an *original location,* along the diagonal indicated in Figure 17 as defining the bipolar continuum taken as the simplest possible representation of human variability, *and a second position*: stressed, but maintaining the original pattern of SNS/PNS activity at a higher intensity, rather than that relationship being changed to necessarily greater SNS dominance, as the original model assumed.

The hypothesis is *not* that apparently maladaptive states always occur as a result of these particular kinds of changes taking place, or even that the patterns of events in question necessarily lead to identifiably obsessional, paranoid, or hysterical behaviours. For instance, there exists a very wide range of likely significant variables such as those cited by Clare, above (p. 131), which in general terms could be said to refer, on the one hand, to the capacity of the individual to understand and cope with stressful situations, and on the other, to his or her access to channels of communication and expression.

Similarly, it is not being argued that *only* the kinds of change in ANS activity already described are likely to work to sinister effect. Human potential for the development of mental anguish in self, or infliction of the same on others, is acknowledged to be considerably more rich and varied. But before other possible kinds of hindrance to effective mental function-

Figure 23 Examples of possible extreme differences in manifestations of more or less intense patterning of ANS activity, when I^3, IE^3, and E^3 are taken to be stressed (exaggerated) patternings of ANS activity and potential examples of obsessive–compulsive (o–c), paranoid (p) and hysterical (h) neurotic styles respectively (with I^3 remaining PNS dominant, IE^3 manifesting very intense PNS and ANS activity, and E^3 heavily SNS-dominant), while I, IE, and E represent so-called normal styles

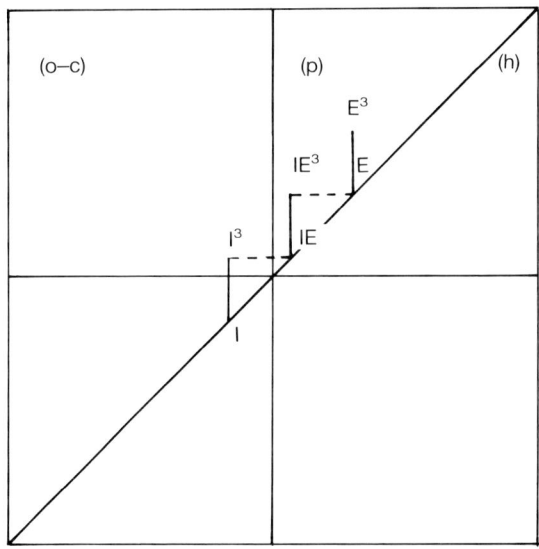

ing are discussed, Figure 23 illustrates first, the marked difference in the likely effects on experience and behaviour (according to the analysis offered in Chapter 3) of different patterning of SNS/PNS activity in relatively close positions on the model. These are exemplified by differences between the 'stressed', or exaggeratedly active, but still PNS dominant, I^3 position and the highly SNS dominant IE position; and between the stressed, extremely high level of SNS *and* PNS activity represented by the IE^3 position and the very highly SNS dominant E position. Second, the figure also indicates how I^3, IE^3 and E^3 could be taken to represent possible examples of intense limbic arousal combined with more intense and, therefore, exaggerated SNS/PNS activity to produce the symptoms of the obsessive–compulsive, paranoid, and hysterical styles of neuroses respectively.

Bearing in mind that the IE/IE^3 positions could be plotted in a number of other locations which would still represent a relative balance of SNS/PNS activity, they could equally well be placed slightly to the left or slightly to the right of their locations on Figure 23. This would, of course, offer two slightly different clusterings of attributes related to the paranoid style which, in turn, concurs with Shapiro's observations of two identifiably different paranoid types (see p. 136 of this text) of which neither offers an easily discernible separate style, but both reflect characteristics consistent with the APM-A model.

Many of the continua used by Shapiro in his definitions of neurotic styles actually coincide with those already used in APM-A explanations – for example, scan–focus; rigidity–flexibility; specific–general; concern with facts – concern with feelings; organization of experience and behaviour – disorganization of experience and behaviour; good memory for detail – poor memory for detail – and yet others of the concepts intrinsic to the APM-A view of how increases in arousal are manifested in different levels and kinds of awareness can be seen at the same time both to extend Shapiro's descriptions and to be reinforced by them.

The most obvious of these underlies his references to concern with facts as opposed to concern with feelings. This relates very closely to our earlier association between levels and kinds of arousal, levels and kinds of need, and likely degrees of involvement with the physical, social, and/or intellectual environment (see Figure 15): whether orientation is primarily towards the concrete or primarily towards the abstract.

The interest of the obsessive–compulsive is described in terms of attention given to, or gained primarily by, the physical world: as being attached to technical details and facts to the extent that the 'flavour' or 'impact' of a situation is very often missed. To quite different effect, the consciousness of the paranoid is seen to be dominated by a continuous assessment of his own standing in the community or group, so that he is 'in general extremely aware of power and rank, relative position, superior and inferior, who is boss and who is obliged to take orders, or who is in a position to humiliate whom' (Shapiro 1965:85), while the attention of the hysteric, although highly responsive to stimuli emanating from both physical and social sources, is seen to be consumed by ideas, nostalgia, and fantasy – that is, turned towards a rather individualistic, exaggerated world of highly subjective impressions.

This is, of course, quite consistent with the APM-A view of the obsessive–compulsive as an intensely aroused but extreme PNS-dominant type; the paranoid as displaying relatively balanced, but intense, ANS activity; and the hysteric as a highly aroused extreme SNS type. It is also wholly consistent with the different levels and kinds of need and awareness already attributed to rather more moderate manifestations of these states in the last two chapters.

The second APM-A concept which both expands Shapiro's descriptions and, at the same time, is reinforced by them, concerns conclusions which have been drawn about individual style and temporal orientation. As different temporal orientations have already been associated with relative dominance of PNS or SNS activity (see p. 117), relative differences in orientation should also apply to neurotic styles. Such differences are in fact implicit in Shapiro's descriptions.

The obsessive–compulsive can be seen to have what might be called a past-based view of the present and future. He is described as carrying through his already formulated intentions – however irrelevant or even absurd they may have become. He is shown to be unable to respond to the immediate, to the present set of circumstances, or to anticipate phenomenological change. He is viewed as habit- and ritual-bound and therefore also implicitly bound to the past, displaying a future orientation only in as much as he experiences compulsion: to continue with his ritual practices and already formulated goals.

The paranoid, on the other hand, is seen to be dominated by anticipation of future happenings, but with his expectations nevertheless solidly rooted in a particular fixed view of his own relationship to other people and events.

The hysteric, by contrast, displays a much more marked bias.

He does not seem rooted in a sense of factual being and history, in firm convictions, and a sense of the factual, objective world. Instead, he is actually 'carried away' by the immediacy of his responses to and the ease with which his whole awareness is captured by vivid impressions, romantic provocations, transient moods of his own, or the fantasy characters that, for whatever reason, appeal to him. . . .

The hysterical person's emotional behaviour or ideas do not seem to the observer to be anchored in real and deep interest, a long history or an abiding purpose.

(Ibid.:120–1)

Within our analysis the quotation above labels the hysteric as highly future-oriented, not simply because of his lack of 'deep interest', 'long history', or 'abiding purpose', but because even the present, to which he responds so readily, is not registered as more than a fleeting impression before he is 'carried away' by response to something new. He is characterized by the same urgency of processing which has already been described as typifying the externalizer. His style is highly dependent on unconscious processes continuing the task of monitoring incoming data, as conscious awareness is subjected to overload in the attempt to take in and assess as many as possible of the perceivable threats and promises (both of which are intrinsically future-oriented concepts) in his immediate environment.

This point brings us to another significant difference between individual styles (neurotic or otherwise) of defending against, and coping with environmental change, and a third instance of the usefulness of the APM-A perspective to amplifying neurotic typologies, to relating them to 'normal' states, and to broadening our understanding of both.

Shapiro's descriptions emphasize the differences between the compulsive's 'intended focus', 'clear intention', and actions 'heavy with deliberateness'; the 'directed searching', the 'actively scanning and searching attention', and 'hyperintentionality' of the paranoid (who is nevertheless seen to be 'hypersensitive', 'hyperalert', and much more perceptive than the narrowly focused obsessive–compulsive); and the contrasting 'global' and 'impressionistic' mode of the hysteric who does not search as much as is 'struck' by environmental information.

These differences are, again, consistent with the kind of differences which APM-A theory would lead us to expect to occur as a result of relative dominance (or not, in the case of the paranoid who displays signs of a fairly balanced access to both) of conscious or unconscious processing of information: characteristics already associated with intensity of limbic arousal, and consequent relative dominance of PNS and SNS activity respectively.

All three styles can be interpreted as manifestations of fear, but each has to do with fear of a different kind. Key differences, which all relate to the conscious–unconscious dimension, to levels of awareness, and to kinds of temporal orientation, are associated with the extent to which fears are specific or general; whether they are of the known or the unknown; and whether they are of the 'real' or of the 'unreal'.

Threats endured by the paranoid, for instance, are much more general than those which consciously motivate the obsessive–compulsive. The fears of the paranoid are expressed as suspicion of anyone he perceives to have any direct or indirect influence or control over him (which usually includes everyone), while the security of the obsessive–compulsive is bound up with the known, and with the performance of his *specific* rituals and habits of behaviour. He consciously confronts and manages his fears *through* his practices – in stark contrast to the hysteric, whose entire *modus operandi* is characterized by uncertainty and a readiness to accept anything as possible. But, by contrast, the really serious fears and conflicts of the hysteric are dealt with mostly at an unconscious level and are not usually the direct cause of the visit to the psychiatrist.

The role of memory style in these differences is obviously very important. In each case, the first of the pairs of alternative kinds of fear mentioned above can be most readily associated with the obsessive–compulsive, and to the dominance of a clear long-term memory, and the second of each pair to the hysteric's more 'fuzzy' world of inaccuracies, of not very much detail consciously registered, and to an urgently acquired breadth of sensation coincident with a more effective short-term, than long-term, memory.

The paranoid, once more, can be seen not to display any obvious bias, but to have a style embracing all of the alternatives in different ways. He appears to employ sufficient breadth and flexibility of attention to be 'absolutely right in his perception', as Shapiro puts it, but then to impose such a rigidly organized frame of reference over what he perceives that his judgement becomes highly distorted.

There are, however, other abnormal perceptual states which exemplify even wider extremes than those which have been discussed so far. Two of these are represented by the highly conscious, easily communicable reactions to the real world of the phobic, and the quite different, extremely individualistic and much less consciously problematic *un*reality of the schizophrenic.[6]

The phobic's perceptions and reactions arise as much from habit as those of the obessive–compulsive, although his problems are usually even more highly specific. Phobias are actually categorized as fear of a specific object; fear of a specific situation (often a place); and fears of a more abstract but still very specific kind, such as illness or death (Melville 1979:170). The attentions of the sufferer are clearly directed towards the real world and its contents: whether towards spiders, snakes, open spaces, or practically anything else essentially 'known', or rather, remembered, from a previous encounter in one form or another. But the threat presented to the phobic by the already encountered, but still unfamiliar, does not produce the experience of fascination which was defined earlier as emanating from what is perceived to be a manageable threat. The phobic object or situation is consciously and unequivocally recognized as presenting an *un*manageable threat.

In extreme contrast, the schizophrenic is not at all characterized by consistent reactions to real objects, places, or events. His interests are likely to be much more abstract – in religion, philosophy, spiritualism, or power (Crowcroft 1967:39). Unlike the phobic, although well-acquainted with fear, because the real and the unreal merge to become indistinguishable to the schizophrenic, his psychological problems are far more generalized and remain mostly unacknowledged by himself. His fears are much more labile, often attaching to random perceptions, or to imaginary or distorted situations: essentially to what seem to everyone else to be wild impossibilities.

4.3 Ways of seeing

The examples of phobias and schizophrenia also offer us useful examples of contrasting levels of pathology. Whereas the phobic is able, most often, to cope with his condition by simple avoidance strategies or, if this is not possible, usually responds extremely well to behaviour modification techniques, the prognosis for the schizophrenic is not nearly as good. According to Tsuang (1982:75ff.) only about 20 per cent make a complete recovery. Of the remainder, around 40 per cent become able to live outside hospital, but their ability to function effectively is still likely to be seriously impaired.

Of all of the so-called abnormal states to be discussed in this chapter, the experience of the phobic will be seen to represent one of the simplest conditions and the one likely to be associated with lowest levels of arousal (in the absence of the phobic object or situation), while schizophrenia will be seen to represent potentially extremely complex manifestations of very high levels of ANS activity.[7]

Levels of arousal were related earlier to different degrees of simplicity and complexity, in connection with levels of needs (p. 97), and similarly, intensity of arousal has been related to high levels of anticipation and concomitant capacity for imagination (see Figure 3). Further, in the last chapter it was explained that because our model of style represents increase in arousal in two directions (horizontally and vertically), quadrant E_2 represents the compound effects of the interaction of both kinds of increase.

By eventually plotting our other extreme conditions on the model, and considering them in relation to those already placed (however arbitrarily), it will be seen how the notion of regression – indicating changes in experience and behaviour to more primitive styles – ties in with the APM-A view of *increase in pathology associated with increases in limbic arousal and relative dominance of the more archaic (than cortical arousal) system.*

An important effect of increases in relative dominance of the more primitive kind of arousal over cortical arousal is that various kinds of 'loss of reality' may alternatively be viewed as increases in autonomy of the perceptual process but, of course, not always to the benefit of the individual concerned.

In comparing obsessional–compulsive and paranoid styles Shapiro tells us,

> the paranoid style is, in every instance, the more extreme, the less stable, the more tense and antagonistic, the more openly occupied with instinctual conflict, and, in a word, the more psychologically primitive.
> . . . the paranoid style may be regarded as a more primitive transformation, in the mathematical sense, of the obsessive–compulsive style.

> (Shapiro 1965:107)

On the kinds of loss of reality experienced in each condition he describes the obsessive–compulsive as being characterized by an unlikely mix of doubt and dogma, but explains this as deriving from the fact that both doubt and dogma arise from lack of conviction and that 'a sense of conviction . . . – a sense of truth, in other words – involves a breadth of attention' (ibid.:51), whereas doubt and dogma both depend on what he calls a 'technical-indicator style of thinking' (narrow focus) of which the obsessive–compulsive's ritualistic behaviour is symptomatic.

For the paranoid, however, the 'loss of the world as it apparently is' is seen to be much greater than that for the compulsive person. Shapiro talks of 'a biased seizing of "significant" clues from their context' and of delusions containing 'kernels of reality' wrenched from their context so that they sometimes seem quite convincing (ibid.:65–8).

The idea of regression from one pathological condition to another, more serious one, being accompanied by shifts in attention from the physical to the social environment (which is implicit in Shapiro's conclusions) or from the social environment to more abstract phenomena, is reinforced by what Arieti tells us about the phobic being likely to move towards the more serious condition of paranoia when his attention turns from things to people (Arieti 1981:40); by Shapiro's observations that 'in practice psychotic paranoid conditions almost always involve schizophrenic elements' (Shapiro 1965:68); and by a large body of research which shows that schizophrenic patients frequently regress from paranoid to non-paranoid forms (Magaro 1980:58–9, 143).

But before we plot these regressions on to the model according to their APM-A styles, a very brief digression must be made in connection with the crucial question concerning whether 'reality' is actually lost or found; and another – to be returned to later – about the more or less subtle differences between the two possibilities. Eventually a very striking pattern of increases in pathology, which can be clearly associated with increases in scanning functions of attention, as well as with earlier analyses of the relationship between arousal and changes in style, will be shown.

There are now well-established links between creativity and schizophrenia (Prentky 1980:47ff.). One key work on creativity, at least, has been written by an eminent clinician (Arieti 1976), and a great deal of the considerable amount of debate surrounding the 'disease' has centred on its creative elements. Therefore, in considering the positions of all the various kinds of neuroses and psychoses under discussion in relation to one another on the model, it is particularly interesting to note that the kind of loss of reality so vigorously expressed by the hysteric is described by Shapiro as 'theatrics', 'dramatic exaggerations', and 'acting': thus providing a very obvious theoretical link between the neurotic condition of hysteria and the considerably more serious psychotic condition of schizophrenia – sufficient to confirm the positioning of both in the quadrant of the model (E_2) already associated with creativity.

It is also highly relevant to note a number of other kinds of relationship which can be forged between conversion hysteria, in particular, and schizophrenia. Sedgwick (1982:257), for instance, quotes Maleval's complaint that the modern framework for the diagnosis of schizophrenia has excluded the possibility of observing a psychosis which is hysterical in nature: 'the introduction of the concept of schizophrenia authorises not so much the disappearance of the hysterical delirium . . . as the expulsion of hysteria from the terrain of madness.'

Relevant too, is the fact that Szasz, in his major classic (1972) denying the notion of mental illness, explores the idea of hysteria as indirect communication – by 'iconic body signs'[8] – and the protective function of the use of allusion. Interestingly, he defines the more primitive type of logical operation of the hysteric in terms of the Von Domarus principle,[9] as does Arieti (1981:69) with reference to *both* schizophrenia and creativity. And whereas Szasz refers to the protective function of indirect communication in hysteria (the prevalent form of 'madness' in the nineteenth century), Laing (1967:85) addresses the question of why schizophrenics (the 'madmen' of the twentieth century) have to be 'often brilliantly, so devious, so adept at making themselves unremittingly incomprehensible'. Within the APM-A analysis this suggests that for the schizophrenic the process of withdrawal and concomitant move towards a world devoid of shared context and away from organized conceptualization is more advanced than in the hysterical patient.

Finally, we can now map the following arbitrary (although hardly more so than current diagnostic practice) but significant relationships between neuroses, psychoses, and increases in limbic arousal on our model.

Bearing in mind all that has been said about potential differences in patterning of ANS activity and the differences which have been hypothe-

Figure 24 Relative positions of phobics (ph): obsessive–compulsive (o–c), paranoid (p), and hysterical (h) neurotic styles; paranoid schizophrenia (ps) and non-paranoid schizophrenia (s), in connection with increases in cognitive disorganization

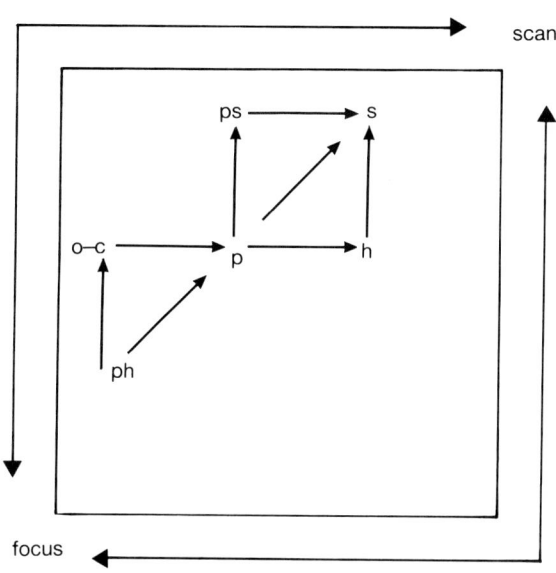

sized between the various extreme conditions in question, both Figures 23 and 24 also serve to illustrate Crowcroft's argument that 'perhaps, people can be graded, from "normal enough" to neurotic, and from neurotic through to psychotic. Nevertheless, a difference in degree can amount to a difference in kind' (1967:26). Further, Figure 24, in conjunction with Figure 26, can be seen to illustrate the point that whereas many theorists interpret certain characteristics of the schizophrenic as emanating from his or her failure to relinquish childish behaviours – which Arieti (1981:41) sees as a 'readoption of immature ways of thinking and acting' – these behaviours are much more likely to be simple manifestations of the greater spontaneity and expressiveness already associated with limbic arousal in Chapter 3.[10]

These characteristics are among many which relate the experience and behaviours of the schizophrenic to those of the archetypal creative individual.[11] Arieti (1976:21–2), however, also defines a particular difference between the two modes of perception: that creatives are able to fuse what he labels 'paleologic thinking' (from the Greek *paleo*, meaning old), to which both kinds of individual in question are seen to have ready access, with the 'usual logical mechanisms of the mind', while schizophrenics are apparently unable to make this 'laborious synthesis' (ibid.:67).

Other theorists take a much more extreme view and perceive *no* difference at all between creativity and schizophrenia. David Cooper (1980), for instance, sees the real danger of schizophrenia as being the threat it poses to social control, and sees this as the reason for its 'repression'. Following Laing (1967), he goes so far as to suggest that madness should be taken right out of its clinical context to be viewed as creativity instead.

Ronald Laing gained simultaneous fame and notoriety for the promotion of this particular point of view in the sixties, and even raised the possibility that the schizophrenic may be someone unable to suppress normal instincts in order to conform to an abnormal society. Laing, in fact, seeks to understand the schizoprenic in 'existential social terms' by focusing on the existential meanings of experience.[12] He views the schizophrenic as a visionary, as one who can see the 'ultimate truth'[13] and as one who 'breaks through' rather than 'breaks down'.

Unfortunately, neither Laing nor Cooper identifies a fundamental problem inherent in the position they adopt: the Catch-22 situation which arises from the fact that it is this very prized uniqueness of vision itself which renders the schizophrenic incoherent. The schizophrenic's particular version of the truth is so far removed from the shared perceptions of others – the consensus – that it is also intrinsically incommunicable. Creatives can clearly be labelled as such only when they manage to retain sufficient contact (however tenuous) with the perceptions of others to be able to communicate their ideas adequately, and for these to be perceived to be in some way valuable.

The legendary fine line to be drawn between the genius and the madman can be seen, in APM-A terms, to be not just fine, but exceedingly wavy – if not sometimes broken. Sometimes, and in phenomenological terms, creativity and madness can be seen to be rapidly alternating conditions rather than mutually exclusive states of being. Similarly, the 'laborious synthesis' can be seen to be indeed laborious to those archetypal creatives who, by (APM-A) definition, experience 'orgies of identification' (as yet another of Arieti's graphic expressions has it) which cannot be 'switched off' (or on) to order, and for whom the demands of 'multiple and simultaneous purposes'[14] can make the necessary degree of focus extremely difficult to maintain.

As a species we have, however, discovered diverse and more or less socially acceptable ways and means of facilitating the particular kind of orgy to which Arieti refers. We know, for instance, that some abusers of amphetamines experience symptoms which are indistinguishable from those of schizophrenics (Tsuang 1982:37), and Aldous Huxley's well-known experiments with mescalin (whose chemical composition, most significantly, is very similar to that of adrenalin) led him to liken bad experiences to a state of 'schizophrenic hell' while also acknowledging other experiences of 'heavens', 'inexpressibly wonderful, wonderful to the point, almost, of being terrifying' (1977:44) (which, incidentally, also provides more support for the APM-A definition of pleasure – as being composed of *both* threat and promise; see 1.3).

Most interestingly, with reference to earlier discussions of control and degrees of organization of experience and behaviour, Huxley refers to the drug's effect on relaxing cerebral control in terms of 'Mind at Large' seeping past the no longer water-tight 'cerebral reducing valve': phrases which could equally well be applied to our definition of the less dramatic, but urgent processing of the externalizer, or the original hypothesized move to higher-order needs of *Homo sapiens*, effected as heightened experience of threat and urgency broke down rigid control, producing more labile processing of information and more flexible behaviour.

But in addition to these evocative descriptions of his journeys through what he calls the 'Door in the Wall'[15] (after H. G. Wells) and back again (which use of metaphor is also reminiscent of Laing's descriptions of the mind-expanding return journeys of those schizophrenics who eventually manage to communicate their reorganized perceptions), Huxley also discusses the power of real versions of the kinds of gleaming and brightly coloured images of his vivid mescalin experiences, to give access to quite sober, if not puritan, minds to the 'doors of perception'.

He draws attention to the traditional use of rich materials, brilliant colours, gleaming and glittering objects, flame and light in religious rituals and ceremony, which are all used to 'transport' consciousness away from the actual, the concrete, and the banal, on to fresher and more exciting levels of experience.

If we think in terms of the evolutionary associations of such imagery – in terms of what glints and gleams, for instance – indicating things hard, sharp, and most often dangerous, as in tooth; claw; the eyes of a large animal, or enemy, in the dark; the hard edge of wet rock; or moon-shine on unknown depths of dark water; it is not at all difficult to see why such symbolism evokes a change in consciousness, particularly when we draw on arguments with reference to arousal and changes in attention which were presented in Chapters 1 and 2.

The notion of altered states of consciousness being induced phenomeno-logically by consciously or unconsciously experienced fear in response to various kinds of symbol is developed in the next chapter, but for the purposes of the current argument, it is important to note that sometimes the source of a chosen means of elation can be seen to be a direct and/or consciously experienced physical threat rather than changes produced by 'purely' psychologically induced psycho-physiological responses to more subtle (and therefore more easily managed) hints of danger.

A fairly obvious example of deliberate interference with usual pattern-ings of biochemical functioning is offered by religious fasting undertaken in order to become more receptive to insight or to achieve other spiritual goals which, in the light of the APM-A analysis, may well be literally 'spiritual' in terms of the effects of endocrinal secretions.

This example also happens to be one cited by Huxley (1977:118), who also makes a fairly dramatic point about the historical coincidence of highest religious excitement (Holy Week) with a period of low vitamin levels resulting from long voluntary fasting during Lent, and diminished food supplies in the last phase of harsh medieval winter-times.

In fact, all of the 'ways of seeing' being discussed are dependent on direct or incidental intervention in the APM-A process by the manipula-tion of levels and kinds of external (environmental) or internal (physio-logical) threats; and all can be seen to hold important implications for understanding religious ceremony and ritual,[16] itself, besides other things, a means of coping with fear: primarily, with fear of death.[17] Possible examples abound. One which can be very easily related to the direct experience of fear is the practice of baptism by total immersion. Its adoption is easily attributable to changes in consciousness effected by the inherent threat of being pushed under water by someone else (however much trusted that person is, and however contractual the arrangment), being countered by powerful feelings of elation at being able to breathe again.[18]

Another insight into effective aids to visionary experience offered by Huxley (1977:112ff.), centres on the effects of CO_2. In particular, he comments on the value of yogic breathing exercises (which after a time result in prolonged suspension of breath) and the effects of chanting, shouting, and singing by various religious sects, to which we can now add 'and football crowds', to induce feelings of excitement and elation. Moreover, psychic changes and mystical experience among sportsmen themselves are now also an increasingly recognized and researched phenomenon.[19]

Other ways of manipulating consciousness and achieving access to greater imaginative power involve deliberate and volitional interference with the attentional process itself, and are usually referred to as one or another form of meditation. The same principle of altering levels of experienced threat, most often in terms of level of informational input, can, however, still be seen to apply. And in some forms of meditation various devices to aid contemplation are used to help achieve 'a fully rested and relaxed body and a fully awake and relaxed mind' (Wallace and Benson 1973:258) in order for conscious control to be relaxed sufficiently for 'free' experience to take place.

However, while the meditator becomes susceptible to new, but autonomously conceived (albeit, in the case of those already heavily indoctrinated in a particular dogma, with a rather biased kind of 'autonomy') ways of seeing and behaving, the hypnotic subject necessarily surrenders autonomy to another. It would seem, in APM-A terms, that suggestibility is achieved, in the latter case, by the regulation of sensory input to well within the parameters of adaptation-level; by offering an essentially monotonous input composed of monotonic speech levels often combined with requests to attend to some changing – but highly predictable – visual stimulation. The effect of this steady input of entirely manageable sensory stimulation apparently relaxes the individual, lowering, rather than increasing, arousal, producing a condition conducive to a positive response to suggestion.

This APM-A definition derives in part from findings which indicate differences between introverts and extraverts in their capacities for short-term and long-term memory, for which a simple formula has already been offered (pp. 117–18). It was suggested that greater need for *ex*pression (as promoted by higher levels of limbic arousal in the externalizer) leads to less *im*pression and vice versa: that the better long-term memory and greater suggestibility of the introvert (where suggestibility is taken to imply easier assimilation of information and easier socialization, rather than openness to possibilities), could be attributed to lower limbic arousal, a consequently less urgent style of processing of environmental information, and more rigidly focused attention.

Differences between the relative autonomy of perception of both the schizophrenic and the creative, as opposed to the suggestibility of the hypnotic subject, are clearly open to a similar explanation. Later, after briefly considering other commonly experienced changes in states of mind, we shall come across another similar example while discussing Shapiro's fourth neurotic style (impulsive) in relation to other kinds of individual whom he categorizes as 'weak personalities'.

Obviously, not all shifts in states of consciousness are precipitated either to order, or to propitious effect. Instead of providing excitement, elation, deeper insights, and/or a positive move towards more abstract interests, an increase in limbic arousal and accompanying changes in attentional capacity (which, it has been argued, allow the greater consideration of possibilities rather than actualities) may work to negative effect. It may reveal to the individual concerned a *lack* of possibilities, and either a future devoid of purpose (see postulates 7, 13, Appendix 2) or, conversely, a future full of intentions ('purposes') but no means. This situation may well produce feelings of helplessness and hopelessness, characteristics generally associated with the more or less gradual shutting down of activity (and in APM-A terms, narrowing of focus) and withdrawal from social intercourse typical of the depressive.[20]

The kind of withdrawal and narrowing of interests in question can be just as marked, and sometimes work to just as tragic effect as the psychological 'cutting out' and withdrawal in panic of Bachrach's divers referred to above (p. 128). But the total giving up and withdrawal represented by an act of suicide is conscious. It demands positive action – although to negative effect – and patently takes place at a stage of despair at which the sufferer still feels that he can *actively* arrive at a solution to whatever unsatisfactory situation he finds himself in. Suicide demands a certain amount of effort combined with constructive thinking of a kind of which, ironically, the really severely depressed individual may no longer be capable.[21]

The act itself may arise from what may be perceived to be altruistic motivations,[22] allowing others out of an unbearable situation as well as self, but even when suicide cannot be seen to be of direct benefit to others, it is still rather difficult to argue that the act of withdrawal that such a gesture represents is not adaptive for the individual concerned.

Adaptation and selection are intrinsically about death as well as life, and the case for the priority of psychological survival needs over physical survival needs has already been put in Chapter 2. It is, however, relevant to note two things with reference to suicide and orientation needs – the latter of which have already been defined as being dependent on various kinds of communication and feedback for their fulfilment. The first is the phenomenal growth of the Samaritans' 'befriending' movement since its inception in 1953,[23] and the second, the fact that however coldly and rationally (apparently) an act of suicide is undertaken, it is usually deemed to have happened while the 'balance of the mind was disturbed'.

The reasons for this brief departure into the areas of depression and suicide are manifold. The first is to reinforce the notion introduced earlier in the chapter of the possibility of excessively high levels of limbic arousal eventually changing perceptual style back from scanning to focus. In previous chapters narrow focus and low levels of physical activity have been associated only with low levels of limbic arousal, but the possibility that this state may be arrived at via excessively high levels of arousal, as was argued in the case of Bachrach's diving example, is clearly reinforced by the literature which associates stress and depression.

Additionally, various items of biochemical evidence can be interpreted as supporting our general model of pathological style. For instance, Whitlock (1982:23), summarizing anatomical and biochemical factors in the aetiology of affective disorders, suggests that the balance of evidence tends to favour a 'disturbance of noradrenergic control of the hypothalamic-pituitary axis, which in its turn may be modulated by influences from the limbic area of the brain'. While acknowledging that the heterogeneous nature of affective disorders implies that their explanation *solely* in terms of neuro-anatomy and biochemistry is likely to be inadequate,[24] he nevertheless cites a proposal made by Janowsky *et al.* in 1972 as the first indication of the cholinergic mechanisms playing a significant role in the aetiology of affective disorders. Their proposal was that an imbalance between adrenergic and cholinergic mechanisms, resulting in excess or defect of available noradrenalin, could explain some of the phenomena of mania and depression. Simply, Whitlock explains that current theory holds that depression is a consequence of physical depletion of noradrenalin at receptor sites in the brain, and that mania develops when there is an excess.

Goodwin (1974:249), however, believes that as a total explanation of all severe depression the catecholamine hypothesis is not adequate, and that the most consistent correlate with catecholamine activity may be *psycho-motor activity*, rather than the presence or absence of depression. He cites findings which suggest that mania and depression are *not* polar-extreme manifestations of the same mechanism, but that manic patients are very often depressed (ibid.:243).

Obviously, not all depression develops into a clinical case,[25] and many would argue that milder conditions may more aptly be described as sadness.[26] This represents another example of the not just thin, but wavy and broken, line separating 'normal' and 'abnormal' processes, first defined above as existing between schizophrenia and creativity. For instance, the aetiology of mania could lie in either externalization of excitation (due to any of a variety of stressors) which, for some, may serve to stave off a condition of clinical depression completely,[27] while another case could be rooted in physiological instability of patterning of adrenergic–cholinergic activity – to psychological as well as to psychomotor effect.[28]

A second important reason for considering the intimately related topics of depression and suicide[29] is to reinforce yet another notion introduced earlier, in Chapter 2: a view of the tendency of the human organism to contemplate (at least) self-destruction as a means of escape from psychological threat, as an adaptive tendency. This is a tendency which will assume even more importance in the next chapter.

Third, we can assess the phenomena of depression and suicide as being no more unitary, simple, or susceptible to easy definition or classification than any other manifestation of the APM-A process. We have seen that although a strong case exists for describing schizophrenia in terms of a continuum moving from paranoid to non-paranoid types, with even a condition of paraphrenia in between (Magaro 1980:131), the question of whether it is one disease or many remains unresolved (Crowcroft 1967:41). Similarly, our model indicates that there exists a no less complex range of conditions covered by the term 'depression'.

In fact, R. E. Kendell, in his review of 'contemporary confusion' in the classification of depression (1976), makes this point very forcefully. He insists on the need for researchers to pay more attention to questions of validity, and to use classifications accompanied by unambiguous operational criteria of the terms they employ. In response, it is suggested that a *process model*, such as the one being developed, offers such a possibility: a classificatory system with the potential of accommodating enormous complexity, but which is also simple in conception and relates directly to 'normal' processes.

In an earlier paper Kendell and Gourlay (1970) argued that neurotic and psychotic depressions occupy a continuum, with the less severe neurotic depressions at one end and the more serious psychotic conditions at the other. But it has already been stressed that although any condition can be described in terms of intensity (or in this case, 'severity'), bias – if not biases – must also be taken into account. In this instance it implies that variability in style of neurotic depression *and* variability in style of psychotic depression are as inevitable as the existence of neurotic style, cognitive style, styles of creativity, styles of intelligence, and, as has also been suggested above, styles of unintelligence.

Chodoff has already pointed out the need to take account of the fact that personality structure has a bearing on depressive illness 'not only by providing possible predisposing factors, but also by colouring the depressive illness itself, so that hysterics will have hysterical depressions and obsessives will have obsessive depressions' (1974:58).

We must therefore conceive of continua, rather than of a simple continuum: of as many possible roads to depression and suicide – or beyond that possibility (see note 21) – as there are roads to madness, in connection with which fact it is also important to acknowledge that depression can be either active or inactive,[30] or both.[31]

Suicide is no more susceptible to easy classification than depression (or any other aspect of 'normal' or 'abnormal' psychology discussed so far), and questions of style manifested by suicidals go well beyond choice of instrument.[32] In addition to the inevitable difficulties which arise from the dead being unavailable for interview, and the consequent need to rely on whatever evidence is available in order to establish whether death was accidental or deliberate, survivors of apparent suicide attempts do not, and often cannot, furnish all of the answers concerning intent. This problem has now been formalized in a dichotomous model of suicide in recognition of the fact that many hospital patients designated 'attempted suicide' had no such intention, but instead were performing an act of what is now known as 'parasuicide' (Farmer 1979:19ff.).

To complicate matters further, while most theorists now regard suicide and parasuicide as distinct phenomena, Farmer draws the tentative conclusion that the two are quite intimately connected. He argues that it is the availability of lethal instruments which determines the numbers of actual suicides (ibid.:36). Others simply argue in support of the continuum view on the grounds of level of intent – that the will to survive may or may not exceed the will to die (Katschning *et al.* 1979:154ff.) – but Farmer argues that a primary division on the criterion of fatality may be less appropriate than yet another possible division between the impulsive and the planned suicide.

Of course, by following this line of argument we can, if we wish, create innumerable other categories of suicide related to the ineptitude (or not) of the planners. As this would take us on yet another journey through the literature on IQ, creativity, personality, cognitive style, motivation, and abnormal psychology . . . to arrive back at the intercourse principle (postulate 15, Appendix 2) and our model of individual style (which obviously apply as much to styles of inflicting self-harm and possible self-destruction as to anything else we do), the rather predictable conclusion being drawn is that Farmer is indicating a potentially very fruitful line of enquiry.

This leads to the fact that a discussion of depression and suicide also allows us to present more evidence in support of the significance of our key notion of externalization (of beyond threshold levels of neuronal excitation), but before we examine Farmer's ideas in connection with the intercourse principle in particular, brief notes can be added about (1) the controversial use of ECT (electro-convulsive therapy) in the treatment of depression, and (2) the phenomenon of autism, which can be seen to represent yet another kind of withdrawal.

Both the biochemical evidence and what might best be described as the folklore pertaining to the use of ECT are consistent with a conception of depression as being essentially a condition of withdrawal from stress via excessively *high* levels of arousal – rather than as a simple condition of low arousal.[33] On the one hand, Whitlock discusses the implication of acetylcholine in depression, and presents a review of the evidence which supports the idea that ECT lowers the level of acetylcholine in the brain (Whitlock 1982:15–16): an idea which is also consistent with our 'compensation hypothesis'. On the other hand, legend has it that to be effective ECT should promote a 'fit', or at the very least, observable muscular contractions,[34] and this is a notion which fits rather nicely with both Janet's thesis (see note 27) and conclusions drawn above about catecholamines and motor activity (p. 153).

Given the potential variability of patterning of ANS activity which may (according to the new model) underlie depression, and given also the variability of its possible physical aetiologies (for example, structural brain damage, drugs, childbirth, vitamin deficiencies, and inherent biochemical changes associated with physical diseases: see Whitlock 1982:155ff.), it is hardly surprising that ECT remains such a highly controversial form of treatment; or that its use in the early stage of a depressed phase of a manic-depressive illness can promote hypermania (Crowcroft 1967:135).

A number of the concepts which have been under discussion here are brought together by Kinsbourne (1980) on the brain-basis of subjective experience and, in particular, with his comments on autism. He reviews evidence from a number of sources to offer an explanation of autistic behaviour in children which is coincident with the explanation which arises from the APM-A analysis, and which also embodies our central concepts of *change, thresholds, tolerance, externalization,* and *withdrawal.* He explains behaviours such as the avoidance of exposure to change or to rich stimulation, as well as initiation of repetitive spinning, whirling, or head-banging movements in terms of discharge of central activation (arousal) and the avoidance of overarousal; so that in the case of information avoidance failing to combat overarousal, it is discharged by indulgence in stereotypic behaviours (ibid.:169–70).

Autism, therefore, appears to represent an alternative style of with-drawal and discharge, and an alternative means of combating arousal to those manifested by either clinically depressed patients or manic-depressives.[35] In the latter cases compensatory changes in patterning of ANS activity appear to take place either as a result of the failure of, or as alternatives to, behavioural mechanisms of the kinds exemplified by autistic children.

Finally, applying our 'energy model' of style and the vital concept of externalization to Farmer's theoretical position on suicide and parasuicide, we can offer the possibility that whether or not death actually occurs as a result of a suicidal gesture probably depends very much more on *available energy* – the degree of vigour invested – and the *kinds of materials* the individual is used to handling (as well as the relative dominance of the wish to die) than on Farmer's more bland hypothesis which refers simply to the availability of tools. This would serve to explain more precisely both the fact that men are likely to be more effective in their attempts at self-destruction than women as well as well-established differences between men and women in choice of instrument (Farmer 1979:19–32).

Thus, the intercourse principle not only offers an explanation of why, during a still active phase of feeling helpless and hopeless, the need to 'do something' results in turning energies towards self when apparently no other possibility of doing anything exists; it also endorses Farmer's suggestion of the need for a classification of suicide which acknowledges the part played by impulse.

4.4 Deception and violence

Reference to acts of impulse brings us, at last, to Shapiro's fourth category of neurotic styles: a general style and variants which he labels 'impulsive styles' (Shapiro 1965:134ff.). It also marks a shift from the theme of altered states of consciousness touched on above, to a theme of *alternative* states of 'being' and the possibility of similar styles of abnormality resulting in accolade *or* institutionalization.

Now that Shapiro's first three styles have been located in the top half of our model and these, in turn, have been related to other kinds of neuroses and psychoses, as well as to less extreme forms ('normal' manifestations) of the APM-A process, his fourth category of neurotic style and its variants, as he defines them, will be seen to fill in, as it were, the lower half of the model.

It will also be seen (as we should by now have come to expect) that as much confusion, overlapping of classifications, and fairly indiscriminate use of blanket terminology are apparent in conventional efforts to define those pathological conditions which, by APM-A definition, have in common low levels of consciously experienced anxiety,[36] as those already located in the upper half of the model in positions indicating high levels of anxiety.

The styles of experience and behaviour to be discussed now will be seen to hold much more obvious implications for, and more obviously reflect, levels of social stability than the styles which have been discussed hitherto. This is especially so as it is argued that those individuals who display extreme impulsivity or extreme passivity are apt to be more of a problem to others who attempt to engage with them or, sometimes, just happen to be near, than to themselves.

While at a descriptive level Shapiro's final classification coincides perfectly with the relevant typologies which emerge from the APM-A analysis, and which belong in the lower (as yet undefined in pathological terms) half of the model, at an explanatory level the APM-A definition differs quite markedly. In addition to the fundamental theoretical difference between Shapiro and Gear already identified at the beginning of the chapter, the new model allows us to tease out much more precisely underlying similarities *and* further differences between what Shapiro sees as variants only of the impulsive style, and to be able to redefine his two major variants as identifiably quite separate in their extreme forms.

The new model also allows us, once more, to move beyond the obscurity and confusion created by blanket terminologies (which sometimes overlap with one another, or simply cover different ground from the same term used elsewhere by someone else) by making consistent reference to *process* rather than to its various possible manifestations.

This way we can place pathologies in the same general framework as normal (socially tolerable) styles and states, in order, eventually, to enable us to assess much more accurately what kinds of intervention and compensation may be necessary for the 'abnormal' to be able to function more effectively (and acceptably) within the 'normal' (dominant) social milieu.

One of the most striking aspects of Shapiro's identification of the formal qualities of his general impulsive style is the close correspondence between the qualities he identifies as typifying impulsives and the urgent style attributed to the first-order externalizers (E_1s) identified in the last chapter.

> impulsive action is speedy; it is typically quick in execution, and, more important, it is speedy in the sense that the period between thought and execution is usually short . . . it is usually abrupt or discontinuous in contrast to normal activity, which ordinarily seems to follow from avowed or at least perceptible aims or visible preparations. To these two characteristics, we may add a third, perhaps more basic one. Impulsive action is action that is unplanned. This is not to say that it is necessarily unanticipated. . . . But anticipation, such as anticipation of the next snowfall, is by no means the same thing as planning. Each of these characteristics – speediness, abruptness, and lack of planning – seems to reflect a deficiency in certain mental processes that are normally involved in the translation of incipient motives into actions. The translation here of motive or inclination into action seems to 'short circuit' certain active mental processes.
>
> (Shapiro 1965:139–40)

Shapiro discusses these formal qualities in relation to a general deficiency in integrative processes, and therefore also a 'deficiency in the integration of whim or impulse with a pre-existing organisation of stable and continuous aims and interests' (ibid.:143). He also discusses them in relation to the fact that the kinds of individual in question do not apparently look much beyond the immediate concerns of their own lives and often lack durable emotional involvements, to the extent that family or even personal career goals are usually not strong or occupying. It is chiefly these motivational deficiencies – an 'attenuation of phases prepara-tory to action', and lack of 'active, searching attention' (ibid.:163, 149) – which lead Shapiro to bracket impulsives together with passive characters whom he labels 'weak', and to view the latter type of person as representing a variant of the impulsive style. His view that the 'essential congruence of the two groups is suggested in a general way by what is conspicuously absent in both of them, namely planned, sustained activity associated with a sense of deliberateness' (ibid.:169) is perfectly consistent with what our model suggests; however, within our analysis that is where the similarity ends.

The theoretical position adopted here leads to a view in which the perfunctory and insufficient pursuit of information in following an argument, or in making a judgement, evident in both the impulsive and passive types, emanates from quite different sources and therefore has quite different implications for other aspects of their personal development and expression. True, the gesture of 'giving in' has certain properties in common with the active expression of an urge or the pursuit of a whim: all can be seen to happen as a result of the 'short circuiting'[37] of integrative processes which Shapiro identifies.

However, on the one hand the 'primitive and bare' content of the impulsive individual's spur to action can be seen to derive from excessively high levels of physical drive (energy) and from the compulsion to *act* overriding a less urgent need for sustained processing of information and the consideration of alternative responses. On the other hand, the 'primitive and bare' and unenriched considerations of the passive individual (whom we may view as a first-order internalizer) who gives in readily to, or, as our interpretation suggests, is energized *by* the motivations of others, are seen to derive from his own exceedingly low level of mental *and* physical energy. All of his needs are low. He is both mentally and physically relatively inactive, but, following points made in Chapter 3, simply to label this type in terms of 'weakness' can be criticized as being potentially very misleading. This particular type of individual can be viewed alternatively as being very strong indeed. Being so apparently blind to alternatives and possibilities, and indeed to most kinds of future concern, apart, perhaps, from very concrete and rather rigidly planned short-term objectives usually directly related to the business of satisfying immediate physical needs, this type of individual also remains enviably free from anxiety and therefore relatively immune to the experience of any form of 'troubled mind'.

Another point of disagreement with Shapiro arises from his argument that even recklessly impulsive actions are the outcome of *some* kind of integrative process (by which he implies an alternative, but equivalent in complexity to the 'normal' integrative process), rather than from what he regards as the only alternative possibility: that they 'are simple eruptions of instinctual energy in which executive apparatuses and functions are inoperative'.

He argues that this

> would be difficult to support theoretically for any person, and, if such a thing occurs in any one, it is certainly not in the case of nonpsychotic people. On the contrary, it is exactly the characteristic of impulsive people that neither are they helplessly immobilised by surges of instinctual energy nor do they explode chaotically. They *act*.
>
> (Ibid.:143)

If we accept that eruptions of energy do not have to be so gross as to 'helplessly immobilise' or 'explode chaotically' but that they may be relatively minor, rhythmical, and virtually continuous; and if we also argue that executive apparatuses and functions do not have to become *totally* inoperative for there to be a marked absence of 'planned and sustained activity associated with a sense of deliberateness', but that processing (or 'executive functioning') merely has to take place to a more shallow extent; and if, further, we argue that it is precisely *because* the impulsive individual is practically always involved in some kind of activity (thereby continuously externalizing his energies) that *major* eruptions of energy are unlikely to occur, it becomes perfectly simple to support the position which Shapiro regards as untenable. It can be done easily in terms of the depth-processing arguments already put forward (postulate 4, Appendix 2), combined with our notion of tension thresholds and is entirely consistent with the APM-A position: that the deficiency of integrative processes observable in impulsive individuals derives from the effects of biased and minimal processing; that is, processing which is only partial and in which scanning is heavily dominant, rather than emanating from an intrinsically different source. Similarly, passive individuals are also seen to manifest the effects of partial and biased processing, but to manifest a deficiency in scanning rather than in focus.

This difference in point of view again rests on the fact that Shapiro accepts what he calls the 'innate organising and form-giving configurations of psychological apparatus' of the 'initial organising configuration' (ibid.: 179) as a variable *per se*, which, in turn, leads to his failure to define crucial underlying differences between passives and impulsives. By contrast, the APM-A analysis regards differences in cognitive structures (or rather, styles) as arising from more fundamental physiological factors; namely, from what has been described as tuning (1.2).

Important differences to be perceived between Shapiro's weak, passive characters (being re-classified as first-order internalizers: I_1s) and his impulsives (first-order externalizers: E_1s) which emerge from our explication, include the fact that the attenuated motivation which they hold in common is seen to emanate essentially from *differences in levels of energy*, and therefore also *differences in levels and kinds of need*.

The passive type, being viewed as mostly energized by the influence of others, does not have the excess energy (or even a continuously high level of energy) to be expended, neither does he suffer from the apparent mental disorganization displayed by the impulsive type, or make such apparently random associations between items of information. He will also usually have a better long-term memory. Paradoxically, our analysis also indicates that although the passive type may be motivated only by others to indulge in activities superfluous to immediate and basic needs, it also indicates that he does not actually *need* others in the same way as the impulsive character: that he is much more likely to interact with things or places rather than with people or ideas. In marked contrast, our analysis indicates that the impulsive type *really* interacts, or engages, only with other people (see Figure 15).

Shapiro's other variant of the impulsive style is the psychopathic character (ibid.:157) whom he regards, in many respects, to be 'the very model' of the impulsive style. Besides discussing the psychopath's lack of moral values and conscience in connection with his general mode of thinking, together with other such deficiencies which occur in the absence of an integrated context of interests and aims, he also discusses the 'glibness, fluency and ease' of the psychopath's insincerity. He describes the psychopath as never saying what he 'really thinks' or 'really means', but as lying in order to 'get by'.

Oddly, Shapiro does not refer at all to the insincerity and lack of interest in truth manifested by his 'weak' type, who may also be observed lying to 'get by'. This can be seen to be a serious omission if we recognize interest, or not, in 'truth' – and different kinds of interest in truth – as constituting perceivable and important differences between people concerning qualities commonly referred to as openness, directness, or authenticity or, in more active terms, as having an 'enquiring mind' or being 'full of curiosity' or 'needing to know'.

For instance, in the former case, of the usually quite obvious lack of regard for truth displayed by the psychopath, who lies in order to 'get by', dishonesty can be seen to be a direct outcome of an urgent style of processing combined with the urgency of the kind of situation which he or she is apt to get into; while in the latter case, of Shapiro's 'weak' type, lack of interest in truth (as opposed to its studied and active avoidance) can be defined as deriving from a similar lack of *breadth* of attention, which Shapiro attributed to those manifesting his obsessive–compulsive style.

Before discussing the significance of apparent concern for truth, or not, to the definition of style, and the different kinds of lack of engagement it may represent in more general terms, one further, but important, criticism has to be made of Shapiro's classification of impulsive styles. This demands a fairly long but highly relevant digression into the field of criminology, but eventually Shapiro's simplification of psychopathy will be seen to be no less justifiable than that of one of the major theorists in the field. Just as it has been argued that Eysenck's powerful extraversion–introversion paradigm fails to accommodate the richness of 'normal' human variability, so will it be argued eventually that neither do his added dimensions of neuroticism and psychoticism accommodate a credible range of variability of so-called abnormal experiences and behaviours. The conclusions he draws about the relationship between crime and personality, in particular, will be seen to disregard many different kinds of criminal, and his fundamental position on arousal will again be seen to be potentially (but with much more serious implications in this case) very misleading.

The criticism being levelled at Shapiro's perceptions of the psychopathic personality as 'the very model' of his own impulsive style is that it reflects only a very narrow view of psychopathy, when the literature on the subject indicates a very wide range of behaviours covered by the term.

Mannheim (1965:263ff.) reviews both the changing history of the concept and a complex of current academic and statutory definitions. He details early emphasis on 'moral weakness', from which position it was conventional to regard 'if not every criminal as a psychopath, at least every psychopath as a criminal', and discusses current typologies, in which the criminal psychopath represents only one of many types of psychopathic personality. Mannheim mentions Kurt Schneider as having distinguished ten different types of psychopath, and Henderson as having contented himself with three (ibid.:264). Most interesting from the position being adopted here is the fact that Henderson's three types are (1) the predominantly aggressive, (2) the predominantly inadequate, and (3) the predominantly creative, only the first two of which he associates with criminality.

However, a definition by the McCords (cited by Harrington 1974:35) strikes the most familiar note, and, incidentally, it seems to be the nearest to Shapiro's 'impulsive style': 'an asocial, aggressive, highly impulsive person who feels little or no guilt and is unable to form lasting bonds of affection with other human beings', but the McCords regard the psychopath as being too preoccupied with his own insecurities to be creative, while others say that the last thing the psychopath worries about is being insecure.

More confusingly, Harrington contests the assumption that psychopaths do not make lasting bonds of affection (ibid.). He draws attention to the fact that psychopathic types certainly do display loyalties – particularly to other gang members. Harrington also points out that in 1952 the American Psychiatric Association dropped the designation 'psychopath', replacing it with 'sociopath', so 'lumping together many varied types of criminals, sexual deviants, drunkards and even unsavory politicians into one mass', and since 1971 and another rearrangement, the psychopathic tent covers 'antisocial persons' (ibid.:16).

Citing many other definitions and classifications, Harrington eventually distinguishes between psychopathy as an illness, possibly caused by mild brain damage; as a means of survival – a functional process in response to many possible kinds of pressure; as a deliberately adopted style of 'romantic bravura', after Bogart as Sam Spade and more recently 'infatuation with James Bond'; and as a revolutionary tactic 'in the form of bombing shooting brick-throwing urine- and feces-hurling hatred of police authority' (ibid.:39–41).

After both Mailer's and Glenn's views of the psychopath as the 'new outlaw able to deal coldly with reality . . . [as] best fitted for our culture', he clearly also regards psychopathy as a *dynamic process*, and discusses at length the possibility of psychopathy as a medical aberration, likely to become unimportant while a

> headlong free-form style derived from it may be about to *turn into the norm?* And in this sort of predominantly psychopathic society, the sober, rational examiners who devise such classifications would be judged abnormal. Worse, we could be laughed at, with our learned papers used as paper airplanes.
>
> (Ibid.:191)

By contrast, it is also important to remember that Harrington also identifies psychopaths who are obviously not identifiably 'deficient' in their 'integrative processes', or, at least, who force us to acknowledge the existence of different levels and kinds of deficiency. He cites Cleckley's concept of the 'successful psychopath' as a conception of a part-psychopath: a concept which emerged strongly in the late 1940s and 1950s of 'brilliant, remorseless people with icy intelligence, incapable of love or guilt, with aggressive designs on the rest of the world' (ibid.:17).

At the other extreme his identification of a kind of psychopathy with the somewhat meaningless syndrome of mild brain damage (MBD)[38] also indicates a key overlap with the literature on delinquency and criminality and, relevantly, with the literature of the educational psychologist. The term 'MBD' is, of course, yet another blanket term, and both the APM-A analysis and a study of the syndrome by Schrag and Divoky (1981) suggest that it is also extremely misleading. It does not actually refer to any identifiable damage, but to a phenomenon which becomes more and more obviously manifest in our school and post-school populations. The phenomenon can be seen to relate, in turn, not only to Harrington's prognosis of what might become statistically normal, but also to aspects of cultural style to be discussed in the next chapter.

Harrington quotes from a general conversation about psychopathic behaviour with Dr Thomas P. Detre and Dr Henry Janecki:

> He is always going somewhere . . . but they will also be *more bored* [italics in the original text] than the average person. They have to constantly escalate in order to get a kick out of life. And at times they escalate to the point of being arrested. Have you ever seen a psychopath sitting down quietly in a chair? They always wiggle. Sure, they dissipate tension with greater ease. They get what they want

more quickly. But though they dissipate tension, it recurs faster than in normal people.

(Harrington 1974:211–12)

On the subject of MBD, behavioural neurologists Pincus and Tucker have this to say,

The most common symptom of MBD may be described as inappropriate, poorly controlled behavior, a shortened attention span, and an intellectual deficit . . . the child, seemingly driven by some internal force, is constantly on the move, touching and handling objects, often quite briefly and to no discernible purpose. Such behavior is maximal in anxiety-provoking situations and unfamiliar surroundings. . . . The distinction between a normally active child and a hyperactive child is largely a matter of clinical impression, and it may be made on the grounds of impulsive rather than excessive activity. . . .

Attention span is characteristically altered in MBD, so that affected children cannot concentrate on anything for a sustained period. . . .

Impulsive behavior, poorly controlled behavior may be destructive. . . . It may also involve aggressive acts.

(1978:166–7)

The similarities in these descriptions hardly need pointing out, but perhaps even more striking is the fact that Pincus and Tucker comment that 'virtually any minor abnormality ascribed to MBD can be seen in normal children of the preschool age group'. They also review a study which attempted to correlate hyperactivity and neurological abnormality, but comment that 'It thus seems probable that such activity, inattention and impulsivity in children do not result from brain damage but rather are non-specific aspects of a behavioural disorder'.

They conclude: 'Since etiology is so often in doubt, and there have been no entirely convincing longitudinal studies, a really clear picture of MBD cannot be drawn' (ibid.:166–71).

Of particular interest within the APM-A perspective is the fact that amphetamines and other 'alerting' drugs have the paradoxical effect of calming these children down; but it is precisely the controversial and widespread use of amphetamines and amphetamine-type drugs, in addition to behaviour modification techniques and psychological testing, and the apparent growth of an ideology which views non-conforming children as 'maladjusted', to which Schrag and Divoky respond with outrage. They regard MBD as a term used by the medical profession to denote a *belief* only, that brain damage exists in hyperactive children, although no empirical evidence exists to support that belief. Neither have these children been found to be in any way biologically impaired (Schrag and Divoky 1981:9).

The same quietening effects as occur in cases of MBD (which is, incidentally, sometimes diagnosed simply on the grounds that the effect of amphetamines is positive) are described by Eysenck as occurring in criminals (1970:chap. 8). He also advocates the administration of amphetamines, in order to render criminals more easily conditionable. This fact also brings us back to the fundamental difference between his theoretical position and the one being established. Eysenck actually labels these drugs 'introverting drugs' (ibid.:173) and recommends their use on the grounds of a posited connection between extraversion and antisocial behaviour – as well as with brain damage, deficiencies in processing, and criminality in general. His position rests on findings which indicate the extravert's greater need for stimulation and the greater difficulty experienced by extraverts in learning social inhibitions or, more accurately, the greater difficulty experienced by those who attempt to teach such inhibitions to extraverts.

Eysenck's belief that extraverts suffer cortical inhibition on account of their chronic (and unqualified) *under*arousal, and his introduction of different kinds of arousal into his theory only in order to accommodate neuroticism as well as extraversion within the same framework, have both already been criticized (pp. 85–7). Because he views extraverts as underaroused, Eysenck rationalizes that their sensation-seeking activities arise simply from their need to compensate for underarousal, and his explanation of the effects of amphetamines on extraverts is equally simple: that stimulants have an introverting effect because they stimulate.

Although the evidence does suggest that amphetamines have a paradoxical and introverting effect on extraverts, this fact is obviously not the same as evidence substantiating Eysenck's fundamental assumption about general levels of arousal in relation to extraversion–introversion. The disinhibition of cortical activity cannot simply, or reasonably, be taken to be the equivalent of raising arousal. It could, however, reasonably be taken to represent a change in *dominance* of *kinds* of arousal; that is, from limbic to cortical.

It has already been argued, particularly with reference to manic depression and suicide, that increase in arousal does not simply increase scanning, or increase focusing functions of attention in a unitary fashion, as different researchers hypothesize, but that changes in these functions follow a similar inverted U-curve to that which accompanies performance in relation to arousal. Now, by relating to each other (1) a high degree of focus and measurably high levels of cortical activity (as well as relative PNS dominance); and (2) heavy predominance of scanning and both cortical inhibition and high levels of limbic arousal (sufficiently high levels to threaten cortical overload); and by taking into account the compensatory relationship (as well as the antagonistic relationship referred to by Eysenck) between SNS and PNS activity, other possible interpretations of the effects of amphetamines on extraverts arise.

One possible interpretation is that this kind of drug may artificially disinhibit (increase) cortical activity, to the effect of artificially lowering limbic activity. Eysenck's own indirect references to complementarity between the cortical and limbic areas of the brain, in which he employs the reverse example of the effects of a cortical depressant (alcohol) 'disinhibiting lower centres' (by which he surely means 'increasing limbic arousal', after explaining the term 'cortical inhibition' as 'lowering arousal in the cortex'), were quoted in Chapter 3, and actually reinforce the alternative interpretation (to his) of the effects of amphetamines on extraverts.

What is being argued here is that biochemical interaction is likely to take place, within which the artificial maintenance of high levels of cortical activity inhibits the intake of environmental information, and that this happens as a reciprocal and reflex response, mirroring the kind of natural relationship between low intake (relatively narrow breadth) of information and high levels of cortical activity[39] which was suggested throughout Chapter 3.

However, Eysenck's theory of criminality is only one of many theories and many schools of theory (see Mannheim 1965:vols. 1 and 2; and Emshoff *et al.* 1981) and in his review of literature relevant to the hypothesized link between criminality and extraversion, Wayne Morris (1979) actually quotes Black's conclusion that 'Eysenck's theory is not adequately supported by the studies as regards criminals, although there is some evidence that on the whole psychopaths [as opposed to criminals in general] may be extraverted neurotics' (ibid.:122). He also quotes Passington's conclusion that the 'impulsivity component of the extraversion factor may differentiate criminals from normals and that it may be possible to separate subgroups of delinquents and criminals, some of which are higher on extraversion whereas others are not' (ibid.:123).

Most relevantly to the APM-A position, Morris cites Sheldon (ibid.:122) as having proposed two types of extraversion: extraversion of affect and extraversion of action. In turn, this relates to what is being seen to be one of the major flaws in Eysenck's theoretical stance.

Although Eysenck acknowledges that there are inherent difficulties in equating emotionality with ANS activity, as he does when he refers to difficulties which arise from the specificity of SNS and PNS activity in relation to predicting and measuring the effects of arousal (Eysenck 1970:78), he ignores further possible specificity – actually *within* the SNS division of the ANS. For instance, he ignores the different roles and effects of adrenalin and noradrenalin in ANS activity on which the APM-A model is based.

When we take these key differences into account, the fact that experimental studies of autonomic reactivity in psychopaths (particularly by Hare 1970) has led to the hypothesis that psychopaths may be deficient in anticipatory anxiety, can be seen *not* necessarily to support the hypothesis that psychopaths have a lower level of autonomic arousal than 'normal' as, for instance, Brendan Maher (1980) in his discussion of experimental psychopathology implies.

On the contrary, deficiencies in anticipatory arousal can be taken to imply differences in SNS activity: that arousal is simply very heavily biased towards anger/aggression rather than towards fear, consequences, and the future – that is, towards a predominantly physical rather than a predominantly mental response. One item of research, at least, directly addresses the question being raised and endorses the need for a model of individual differences which acknowledges this key possibility. It shows that of a sample of Broadmoor patients 24 per cent had an excess of noradrenalin over adrenalin (Woodman 1980). Most strikingly, this hormonally imbalanced 24 per cent contained 57 per cent of the patients who were convicted of crimes which resulted in death.[40]

The possibility that the classic impulsive/aggressive psychopath (as opposed to the other alternative of a brilliant, calculating individual of exceedingly high intelligence) can be categorized as a first-order externalizer, or, in Sheldon's terms, as an 'action' (as opposed to 'affect') type of extravert, seems to be supported by a great deal of research. But both the broad field of criminology and research into delinquency are far more complex and cover a much greater range of more or less sophisticated activity, as well as more or less suggestible (easily conditioned) types of individual, than Eysenck's theory (the best-known personality theory of crime and the best-known biologically based theory of personality) is able to accommodate.

With reference to Eysenck's implication of learning problems in criminality (1970:chap.6) it is relevant to consider Mannheim's conclusions on the subject of mental deficiency and crime (1965:vol.1, 277): 'However divergent may be the views on the delinquency of mental defectives, it is beyond doubt that the dull and backward group of subnormals has a far higher delinquency rate than persons of average intelligence', and to consider this point together with the fact that we have already argued a case for acknowledging *kinds* of unintelligence (see Figures 19 and 20).

It is also extremely important to take account of the fact that not only extraverts (or externalizers) have learning difficulties. Introverts (and internalizers) have their own particular kinds of difficulty: namely, difficulties which we have already associated with lack of breadth of attention, which in turn, by our analysis, can be associated with deficiencies in *understanding*, as opposed to difficulties in habit formation (which is the only kind of difficulty identified by Eysenck). The kinds of deficiency being identified are, admittedly, less *obviously* antisocial, just as being essentially inactive makes for a 'low profile'.

However, this does not render the internal type immune to temptation, as our discussion of Shapiro's weak character or Cleckley's icy-cold psychopath implies. To more sinister effect, under certain circumstances, his or her characteristics may eventually earn Bach and Goldberg's label 'crazymaker' on account of the difficulties experienced by others in their attempts to make relationships.

On the other hand, Mannheim (ibid.:332) quotes Frank's opinion that a recidivist is as likely to be produced through ease of conditioning (into the mores of a criminal peer, or family, group) as through difficulty: a position obviously supported by the social learning theorists (see Goldstein *et al.* 1981:413–14). And over twenty years ago Mannheim (ibid.:287) referred to 'the growing scepticism, not to say complete despair of the possibility of finding any psychological differences between the personality make-up of offenders and non-offenders'.

This coincides with the view being expressed here: that criminal behaviours, whether taken to be relatively quietly perpetrated acts of fraud, or obviously impulsive and/or violently antisocial acts, are as representative of our efforts to 'cope and defend' – in psychological and physical terms – as any other kind of human behaviour. The reason why 'the academic quest for the criminologist's stone no longer enjoys any credibility' (West 1982:119) is seen, therefore, to be because criminal behaviour is a *biological alternative*. The argument is that it represents a whole range of behaviours which are rather less altruistic than average, and that because of certain biochemical rather than – but possibly including – genetic factors, some individuals are more susceptible than others to criminality being triggered by any one of a number of different 'life-events'; but, most importantly, not if the individual is offered, or gains, an alternative repertoire of behaviours which are appropriate to his or her APM-A style.

As a result of the well-known Cambridge study of delinquency, and after summarizing various theories, West (1982) adopts an eclectic approach. He identifies an 'hereditary disposition', under which he places characteristics such as low IQ, impulsivity, and aggressive temperament as being conducive to a 'delinquent personality', which he then exemplifies in terms of characteristics like rebel, truant, alienated, heavy drinker, hedonistic, gang leader, and possessor of antisocial attitudes. These factors, together with 'political and economic forces and social traditions' – such as bad home environment, membership of minority group, poor social circumstances, precipitating events, and opportunities for crime – are all ultimately seen as interacting to produce the delinquent act (ibid.:129).

Embodied in this approach is at least a potential framework for acknowledgement of the key concept being defined – the concept of antisocial behaviour as an *alternative* response – as well as a tacit acknowledgement of the significance of concepts such as 'vulnerability' and 'stressors' which have assumed such importance above.

Some forms of crime and social deviancy are obviously more or less *active* than others. Other forms of crime clearly demand more or less *planning*, intellectual involvement, and access to sophisticated resources. Further, some kinds of crime (and criminals) are more or less difficult to hide and/or are more socially tolerated. For the latter reason alone it is easy to understand a simplistic bracketing together of criminality and extraversion of the kind Eysenck recommends, and, after all, a seemingly obvious fact supported by research findings is that 'delinquents appear consistently more rebellious and less conformist in a wide range of contexts' (West 1982:61). But delinquency refers to only one area of criminality, and rebelliousness and non-conformity (which, as we have seen, are also characteristics of creatives) refer only to the more 'active' APM-A styles.

Within the APM-A view criminality is simply an alternative channel of expression, not the outcome of a genetic predisposition,[41] and the high levels of activity which are so easily related to criminality are also characteristic of more controlled personalities. This fact was highlighted earlier in our discussion of obsessive–compulsion and paranoia. Then it was emphasized that when we take both bias *and* intensity of ANS activity into account, need for activity and expression can override even quite high degrees of control.

Some of the implications of these arguments for understanding artistic and cultural styles are discussed in detail in the next chapter. Immediately relevant are questions concerning the notion of a common process underlying behaviours deemed to be socially acceptable or not, as one implication of the intercourse principle introduced in Chapter 1, which suggests that styles of criminality can be as rich as those manifested in art.

The evidence for artistic and criminal potentials existing within the same individual and for artists experiencing more than momentary bouts of deviancy – as well as their well-documented 'moments of madness' – is quite strong. In addition to Henderson's conception of a creative type of psychopath, Mannheim refers to links between criminality and creative genius, and cites various examples from both the arts and the sciences of creative individuals found guilty of criminal offences (1965:vol. 1, 279–81).

However, while it is fairly commonplace for the famous to gain notoriety, only rarely do the notorious seem to gain fame. One of the best-known living examples is former gang-leader and convicted murderer Jimmy Boyle. Having passed through periods of his life unable to express

Figure 25 Examples of alternative forms of expression of physical and mental energies, with 'religion' and 'sport' exemplifying mental and physical biases repectively, and 'creativity' and 'madness' seen as productive and destructive manifestations of either. All are also seen to be alternatives to criminality of different kinds

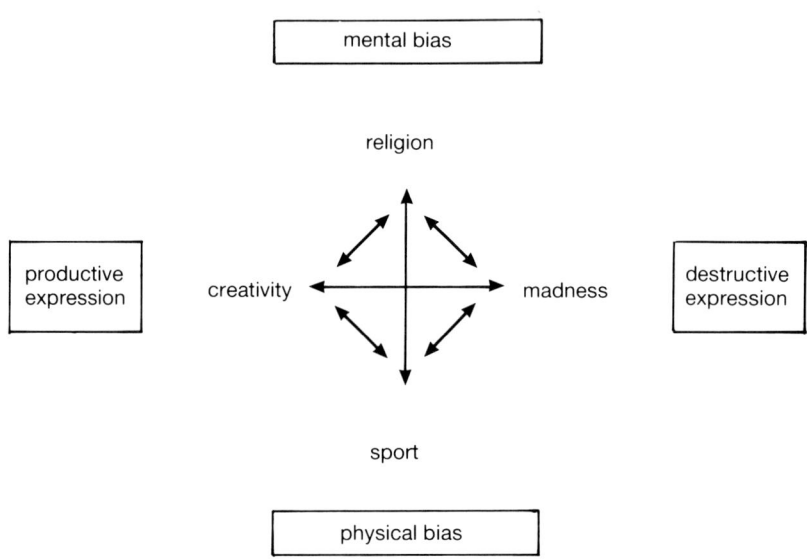

his feelings even orally, he now talks eloquently and movingly about finding a creative outlet for his energies through sculpture in particular. He speaks of the turning point in his life being when he was given a lump of clay while in prison. Most relevant to our argument is the fact that he is emphatic about the value of this as a positive vehicle for the expression of his energy. On turning to the medium of carving he draws a parallel between cutting away pieces of wood and 'finding things inside' at the same time as his own hard exterior was being removed, so that he was able to experience a similar sense of discovery about himself.[42] Outlets for his energies now include setting up and working in drug addiction units.

The current activities of Jimmy Boyle also make him an exemplar of the 'saint or psychopath' syndrome, explored to some extent by Harrington (1974:20, 208, 227–8), and this alternative, together with others to which attention has been drawn – artist–madman, artist–criminal, criminal–genius, and what might be termed 'hysteric–cleric' (see pp. 148–50 above) – all make very good sense within an energy model of human nature. All, together with sport – an example not discussed but one which cannot be ignored completely – represent high energy (mental or physical, or both) states. Whether or not the use to which energy is put has positive or negative outcome is seen to depend wholly on environmental factors. It is seen to depend largely on family and peer group influences (of which, ultimately, peer group is seen to be potentially stronger)[43] and whatever 'tools' of expression may come to hand.

Figure 25 illustrates some examples of manifestation of these more obvious alternative behaviours.

4.5 Sensation seeking

The concept of phenomenological environmental change has already been identified as underlying changes in states of arousal and the quality and direction of attention. For this reason it has also been seen to be crucially important to the analysis and understanding of human experience and behaviour in general. Similarly, perceived, actual, and anticipated change have been identified as the ultimate sources of threat to the organism and an explanation has been given of why the degree to which an individual either tolerates, or actively seeks, change is an established human variable (Zuckerman 1979:43ff.).

In turn, these differences have been incorporated in a hierarchy of needs which takes into account relatively stable differences *between* individuals, in what constitutes optimal levels and kinds of environmental feedback, as well as phenomenological change in these needs *within* individuals.

An extremely important contribution to our knowledge of relatively stable variability in what are referred to within APM-A theory as 'feedback needs' has been made by Marvin Zuckerman (1979). His Sensation Seeking Scale (SSS) originated as a measure of individual differences in what constitutes an 'optimal level of stimulation' but, in fact, identified needs for varied, novel, and complex stimulation rather than for simple, intense stimulation in one sensory modality or another. From this, Zuckerman has propounded a theory which identifies sensation seeking as a biologically based activity with a strong genetic influence but with analogues in exploratory and social behaviours in other species (ibid.:chap. 13). He suggests that brain amines and enzymes influence arousability, limits of arousability, underestimation of risks, and overestimation of positive reinforcement in novel situations.

In the light of all that has been said above about impulsivity, which correlates strongly with SS (ibid.:181), and the marked attenuation of integrative processes that both can be seen to reflect, it is surprising that Zuckerman's position implies that a similar weighing of alternatives takes place in high as in low SS scorers, as if all individuals make similar conscious and/or unconscious assessments of possible outcomes of action. He sees the major difference between their behaviours as resting on how accurate an assessment is made of the potential risks and rewards, rather than on the adequacy of the duration and/or completeness of the process itself.

The APM-A analysis, on the other hand, suggests that thresholds of risk tolerance are higher in the high SS scorer as an incidental effect of speed of processing and urgency of response. Within this new analysis risks are seen *not* to be underestimated, but as intrinsic to the satisfaction of very deep-seated unconscious needs; that is, as providing greater sensation of environmental feedback. Similarly, rewards are viewed *not* as being overestimated, but as assessed according to their value for satisfying the demands of these particular kinds of need.

In our attempt to establish a model which both acknowledges and accommodates greater variability in style than existing models, but which, at the same time, systematizes (and therefore simplifies) classifications and relates them to normal states, there is another highly relevant point to be noted. We must take into account that the range of behaviours to which the SS refers represents greater variability in style than a specific correlation with impulsive extraversion (ibid.) or other correlations which have been found (with measures of egocentric extraversion, for instance) might suggest. It is argued therefore that (1) choice of means of satisfaction can itself be seen to reflect other general perceptual and behavioural tendencies; and (2) the range of different findings about high SS scorers places them in more than one discrete area of the APM-A model.

Correlations have been established between sensation seeking and aspects of extraversion, and SSs have been found to be non-conformists and risk-takers (ibid.) ruled by their own needs, but it has been shown to be possible to locate predominantly (to different degrees) external types over at least three-quarters of the model. This holds the important implication that some SSs may be high on both internal *and* external characteristics but with external characteristics still dominant. In terms of general style, therefore, individual SSs may differ considerably in characteristics other than the SS trait.

For instance, many of the findings cited by Zuckerman echo findings cited by researchers into creativity, and even correlate with creativity personality scales and innovative thinking tests (ibid.:240) as well as identifying tendencies to indulge in 'primary process' thinking (ibid.:245). Other findings relate very strongly to commonly acknowledged characteristics of the psychopath. In fact, in tests of psychopathological tendencies, sensation seeking has been shown to relate to mania and other character disorders of the psychopathic variety (ibid.:181).

In short, some of the findings cited by Zuckerman place the SS in the top half of the model, and others in the lower (right) half (see Figures 15, 19, and 20). In addition, the range of activities indulged in by SSs can be seen to be described along key dimensions already associated with different levels and kinds of arousal.[44]

The argument being put forward emphasizes that SSs manifest styles which can be identified as the outcome of a range of differences in intensities and biases in what has been identified as biological tuning to change. It is argued, therefore, that the SS phenomenon may be better understood within the context of other data by regarding it as primarily adaptational. Within this context, not only may it be regarded as having the strong genetic influence that Zuckerman perceives, but the same phenomenon could just as well result from pre-, peri-, or post-natal tuning, or from a much later adjustment to environmental conditions, in common with all of the other behaviours classified as normal or abnormal which have been discussed so far.

Zuckerman's conception of sensation-seeking behaviour as being a normal trait based on an appetite that is a normal part of the mammalian nervous system, but which takes place 'beyond the optimal level of arousal', together with the strong potential for self-harm inherent in the broad range of behaviours which identify SSs, suggests the existence of kinds of 'regression' within the bounds of normality, in addition to those kinds of regression which have already been associated with abnormality.

It becomes possible to present a very simple unitary model of regression which, nevertheless, identifies a certain sequence of events as being common to so-called pathological and non-pathological states (see Figure 26).

Although this gross simplification of processes of ineffective psychological defence – or disorientation as the result of unfulfilled orientation needs – does not account for individual differences in coping and defending

Figure 26 A simple, unitary model of regression which acknowledges changes in levels of engagement with the physical and social environments and heightening of both cognitive and sensory feedback needs (and, therefore, also of 'sensuality') as SNS dominance increases. See also Figures 4 and 5

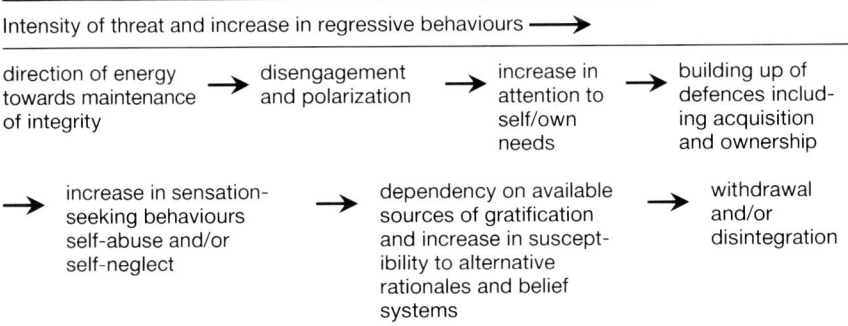

Intensity of threat and increase in regressive behaviours ⟶

| direction of energy towards maintenance of integrity | ⟶ | disengagement and polarization | ⟶ | increase in attention to self/own needs | ⟶ | building up of defences including acquisition and ownership |

| ⟶ | increase in sensation-seeking behaviours self-abuse and/or self-neglect | ⟶ | dependency on available sources of gratification and increase in susceptibility to alternative rationales and belief systems | ⟶ | withdrawal and/or disintegration |

behaviours, it can be seen to relate very strongly, in general terms, to descriptions by others of what can be viewed as regressive mutations of style.

Two quite separate identifications of such phenomena have been made by Louis Zurcher (1977) and Nathan Adler (1972). Zurcher assigns descriptive labels to four modes of self-concept defined in a measure called the Twenty Statements Test (TST), and conceives of the possibility of individuals gaining autonomy by learning to shift between modes, thereby achieving mutability. He sees this capacity for mutability as offering the greatest effectiveness in dealing with the demands of a rapidly changing society. Adler, on the other hand, identifies an increase in the incidence of a particular personality type. He labels this the 'antinomian personality' and views it as a pathological response to social instability.

Zurcher's modes shift between what he calls the *physical self,* the *social self,* the *reflective self,* and the *oceanic self.* The first two modes are defined as having some anchorage in the social structure and as 'consensual', whilst the latter two modes are seen to be 'non-consensual' and as indicating 'some disjuncture between the individual and society with likely pathological consequences' (ibid.:10). The physical self is viewed as a 'sub-social' state of being, with behaviours meeting adult expectations at a minimal level or below; the social self as representing more socially effective ways of behaving; the reflective self as more free and variable; and the oceanic self 'so free and variable that . . . [those manifesting this mode] frequently violate the norms of the situations in which they found themselves, behaving in bizarre and extravagant ways' (ibid.:47).

Zurcher points out that an individual can manifest all four kinds of self-concept with one mode temporarily preferred over the others, depending on particular sets of circumstances; but that it is more likely that a person comes to favour one or another as a result of socialization.

It is on the basis that the social self has, in the past, been reported as the dominant self-concept among members of American society, while more recently the reflective self has become more commonplace, that Zurcher argues the case for the desirability of mutability. He sees the phenomenon of rapid social change in the United States as thrusting significant numbers into troubled reflective states of mind. He sees the same circumstances, however, as providing an option either for the development of the integration of all four modes into a 'purposeful and adaptive wholeness', or for accelerating the development of even more limiting forms of self-concept than that already represented by his oceanic mode.

A similar shift in what was defined in Chapter 1 as biological tuning – which, it is being suggested, underlies the phenomenon of the apparent supersedence by Zurcher's reflective self of a former dominance of the social self in American society – can also be seen to underlie the increase in incidence of the type of personality Adler labels 'antinomian'.

He chooses the term 'antinomian' to imply repudiation of established institutions, the centrality of anti-rational values and gnostic ways of knowing, as opposed to 'cognition as a way of knowing and orienting to the world': to imply the centrality of what he calls 'direct and personal illumination' by inspiration and intuition (1972:xix).

Zurcher, Adler, and Harrington (whose book *Psychopaths* was first published in the same year as Adler's identification of antinomianism and five years before Zurcher's concept of mutability) all offer extremely valuable insights into changes in individual style in response to increases in social instability. But there are some obvious questions raised by their different perspectives: questions such as whether or not they are all describing the same phenomenon; to what extent their explanations of changes in style coincide; and whether the perceived increase in reflective and oceanic self-concepts, in antinomianism, and in psychopathy, can also be related to Zuckerman's concept of sensation seeking.

Full answers to these questions cannot possibly be furnished here; but in order to bring questions of cultural style – the subject of the next chapter – into the new perspective, as well as to amplify some of the general conclusions being drawn about individual styles and psychopathy, they must be considered, if only briefly.

The answer to the last question is the easiest to attempt to provide. The different concepts identified by Zurcher, Adler, and Harrington can be, and are being, placed under the same sensation-seeking umbrella, and many of the behaviours associated with the tendencies they describe are actually mentioned specifically by Zuckerman.

The short answer to the second question, about differences in explanations, is, again, fairly simple. Apart from references by all three authors to the significance of social change, and reference by both Harrington and Adler to the absence of adequate institutionalized means of personal expression, the rationales are quite different.

Zurcher's emphasis is on the notion of self as process rather than object, and is centred, therefore, to a much greater extent on our potential for mutability and the desirability of training for mutability, rather than on its precipitating factors. For him, rapid social change *per se* currently results in 'uncontrolled adaptation' and, more often than not, in 'defensive fixation upon one (or less than all four) of the self-concept modes' (1977:250).

Harrington's rationale which, as we have already discussed, defines psychopathy alternatively as an illness, as a means of survival, as a deliberately adopted tactic, and as a revolutionary tactic, also takes account of the fact that not only do many individuals diagnosed as at least part-psychopaths rise to eminence, but that the psychopathic ideal has also become accepted. His view of the dominant style he perceived at the beginning of the seventies (which clearly also includes some characteristics which fall into Zurcher's descriptions of reflective and oceanic modes) was of psychopathy as adaptive rather than maladaptive: as embracing the possibility that lack of feeling may be regarded as a boon because it relieves pain, and that we may even come to see abrupt, conscienceless behaviour as a means to mental health.

Adler does offer a specific theory in explanation of antinomianism, besides expressing the opinion that 'In a secular, naturalistic world that fails to institutionalise the range of roles which other cultures make available, some individuals are forced into deviance and pathology' (1972:104).

Zurcher would seem to endorse this view (in addition to endorsing Adler's expression of the need to view self as gerund – as process – rather than material category), but as a psychoanalyst Adler offers a rationale which is limited by the psychodynamic concepts of individuation; differentiation; body–object relations; and body–ego as a matrix for the cognitive ego.

Essentially, at the nub of Adler's explanation is a concept entirely coincident with the APM-A analysis: that under stress we strive to 'stabilise and reconstitute the self' (ibid.:88) although the APM-A concept of maintaining psychological integrity is seen to imply that and very much more besides.

However, whereas within our perspective sensation-seeking behaviours are viewed as an expression of shifts to needs for higher levels of sensory feedback in order to maintain orientation, as a response to a psycho-physiological demand, Adler's analysis is quite different. Although he refers in similar fashion to a 'tuned organism', he regards the increase in sensory needs as an expression of the narrower function of the manipulation of 'self, sensibility and body image' (ibid.:106). Thus the process he defines is rather more psycho-physical than psycho-physiological. Resort to drugs, sexual hyperactivity, and participation in religious cults and psychotherapies which involve physical contact with others are all viewed by Adler as attempts to adjust body image and to manipulate relationships between the 'phenomenal self and the field' (ibid.:chap. 5); that is, between inner and outer worlds in order to establish *body* boundaries.

Adler stresses the need to construe self as process, but instead of going on to centre his arguments on the *perceptual process and its relationship to physiological process and behaviour,* he combines a process definition with only one aspect of man's perception – an object–relations view of his body image.

On the one hand, Adler does make frequent reference to the perceptual process, describing changes in response to stress in strikingly similar terms to those used here:

experiences become syncretistic, global and diffused, the threatened person undoes himself.
    As ways of adjusting to stress, pathologic behaviour – like a radarscope – involves hypervigilance, an incoherent, inconsistent scanning of the environment.
    Hypersensitivity and dropping out are attempts to reorient and stabilize the threatened self.

(Ibid.:102, 60, 105)

On the other hand he attaches the significance of these changes to what is seen here to be just *one* incidental effect of heightened psychological needs.

Shifts in degrees of objectivity and subjectivity, on which Adler's theorizing rests, can be explained in quite different terms and according to the same principles which have been identified in relation to variability in needs for sensory stimulation: that is, within the same framework which has been used to explain relatively stable individual differences.

Similarly, the shift from rationality to increase in sensuality, which Adler links with increase in subjectivity thus: 'The failed rational, cognitive modes based on sight and objectifying are displaced by subjective, intuitive styles and modes of perception that rely on the primitive tactile sense of pressure, temperature, texture, and pain' (ibid.:93), has already been related (in terms of heightened responsivity and feedback needs) to increase in psychological security needs (see Figure 15 and pp. 60–63). The narrow psychoanalytic position on security needs and the significance of oral, anal, and genital areas and orifices during childhood only, has also already been criticized (note 10, Chapter 2).

In short, increase in subjectivity can be explained in terms of increase in SNS activity, which has already been associated with increase in levels of emotional responsivity, increase in sensuality and an increased capacity for abstract thought (section 4.3 and Figures 4 and 5).

The prime question posed earlier, concerning whether or not Zurcher's least functional reflective and oceanic selves, the various kinds of psychopaths identified by Harrington, and antinomianism are all references to the same phenomenon, has already been answered in part. In APM-A terms there *are* large areas of overlap between the states of consciousness and the changes in behaviour they each identify. Just as Harrington's very wide interpretation of psychopathy can be seen to refer to a quite disparate range of styles on the APM-A model, so can Adler's label of antinomianism (covering 'polymorphous perversions') be seen to cover a *range* of characteristics – some having a more intellectual bias, and others being more physically oriented – rather than just one kind of predisposition of personality.

We can also add that, despite certain differences in emphasis made within the three perspectives, each identifies a shift along the simple I_1–E_2 dimension of the new model (see Figure 17): all identify a move towards cognitive disorganization and away from rigid perceptual and conceptual boundaries. For instance, Zurcher refers to the concept of an oceanic self being characterized by freedom and variability (1977:47), Harrington refers to a psychopathic 'free-form style' (1974:191), and Adler to 'oceanic merging' and 'undifferentiated oneness' (1972:104).

4.6 Disorientation and breakdown

The final arguments to be presented in this chapter are in support of the need for a theory and a model of psychopathology which allow both more systematic classification and diagnosis of counter-productive mental states and behaviours *and* accommodate much greater variability in their manifestation, while holding potential for offering insights into social and cultural instability (a prime aim of Chapter 5) as well as individual instability.

This is not simply a call for a general eclectic approach as, for instance, recommended by Thorne (1973:445ff.) in his 'Eclectic psychotherapy': a therapy which can be seen to be based on no particular view of man and, therefore, nor on any particular view of what a healthy, effective human being is.

It has already been argued elsewhere (Gear 1987) that synthesis of existing theories alone, even when they may seem to embody all of the major concepts of a potentially unifying point of view, does not automatically offer greater explanatory power, and that it may be necessary to adopt an entirely new position in order to make sense of all available data within a general context.

In the case of neuroses and psychoses and other forms of maladaptive experience and behaviour, there are already theories which centre on many of the concepts important to the new position, but by no means all. There are theories of neurosis based on some aspects of learning (adaptation) – for example, the conditioning and modelling theories; theories based on the concepts of expectation and anticipation – such as attribution theory with reference to the former and social anxiety and social competence theories in the case of the latter; theories which refer to defence – for instance, the psychoanalytic theories; theories which concentrate on stylistic differences – like the trait theories; and others based on physiological process (see Gossop 1981:chaps. 5–8).

As it would be possible to imagine a separate list emphasizing other mechanisms of mind – perhaps starting with the non-existent Justification Theory followed by, say, Mutually Exclusive Categories Theory (MECT) – it is fairly obvious that (1) potential for the fragmentation of a theoretical understanding of the human species is not yet entirely exhausted, and (2) synthesis would take us nowhere. It would still omit many of the mechanisms of mind which can act as a source of either orientation *or* disorientation.

In some ways the understanding reflected in current psychotherapies is rather more cohesive (as might be expected, as therapists do deal with real people) than that reflected in the theories, and it is possible to see some kind of disorientation–dependency model underlying all of them. Interestingly, Nathan Adler (1972:117) has pointed out that the proliferation of new 'antinomian therapies' can itself be seen to be symptomatic. He says,

> Modish ideologies of self-actualization and self-realization encourage experimentation with drugs, sexual hyperactivity, and spiritual exercises in the name of new life-styles to counter the loss of boundaries, the identity confusion and diffusion . . .

to which we can add that it may also be significant that the theories themselves can be seen to represent a general move to more abstract, holistic, and existential modes of thinking. This, too, can be seen to be symptomatic.

A prime example of what is meant by the suggestion that available therapies actually embody a disorientation–dependency model of mental disorder is the Freudian psychoanalytic approach, a central tenet of which is that happiness derives from love and work. We are, however, now in a position to place a different interpretation on these long-held values – values which are seen here to be dangerously confusing, given the very imprecise nature of the terms 'love' and 'work'. A definition in orientational terms of the benefits they *may* bestow can also help us to see that there are substitutes.

Clearly, the experience of love and participation in work have been found to provide orientation and focus. Both can be seen to provide a variety of different forms of sensory and cognitive feedback (defined as necessary to the maintenance of orientation), and both can be seen to provide 'purposes' of different kinds, namely, short- and longer-term aims which, it has been argued, are necessary (to some more than others) for psychological survival. For clinical purposes, however, 'love' could be replaced with a complex of other more specific and, arguably, much more helpful concepts including 'authentic interaction', and, similarly, work with 'purposeful means of expression'.

Other more or less random examples of therapies which embody the disorientation–dependency model in question include Adlerian psychoanalytic therapy, and, much more recently, Ellis's Rational Emotive therapy (RET) and Gestalt therapy. In the first case the person experiencing psychopathology is viewed as 'discouraged' rather than 'sick' (having either never developed, or lost, courage with respect to meeting life tasks) and is, above all, regarded as a 'becoming' individual. This approach obviously places very high value on the development of autonomy, with its most important aims listed as: encouraging the patient to have faith in self; to be a co-operator; to be a contributor to a better society; to be a person who feels belonging and at home in the universe and is actualized (Mosak and Dreikurs 1973:25–83).

Although the newer therapies continue to place different degrees of emphasis on the various needs defined as orientation needs in the APM-A hierarchy (to the total neglect of some), the tacit underlying principle of orientation is unmistakable. For instance, Ellis's RET (1973:200) rests on the importance of the patient's belief system. It is designed to enable the individual 'to observe, to understand, and persistently to attack his irrational, grandiose, perfectionist *shoulds, oughts,* and *musts*'.

Reality therapy aims at the individual being able to 'face reality', to fulfil his or her own needs without harming others, and at the crux of this example is the need for the individual to accept responsibility for his or her own behaviour (Kemplar 1973:251). The implicit references to autonomy and orientation are again fairly obvious, and many other examples could be cited. Gestalt therapy emphasizes what has been called in APM-A terms the 'need to know'. It aims 'to bring discordant elements into self-disclosing confrontation' (Glaser and Zunin 1973:2), while Encounter therapy also stresses the importance of self-understanding, and pays obvious attention to sensory feedback needs (Schutz 1973:401–43).

A recent plea for a unifying structure within psychology and psychotherapy has been articulated by David Pilgrim (1983). His perception of psycho-therapy as a potential source of unity in a field which he sees as containing no stable paradigms seems to be well founded in the light of the fact that, *together*, the current range of available therapies seem to refer, in one way or another, to most of the kinds of need identified within the new analysis.

Pilgrim, in common with Zurcher and Adler, stresses the need to consider human beings as subjects rather than objects, but he takes the argument further. He presents a case for the need to 'up-end established dogma' and, in particular, he criticizes the severe limitations of what he sees as an 'unhealthy obsession concerning how far they [the adherents of academic psychology] are or are not "scientific"'. Essentially, he is critical of what he calls 'a scientific mythology which in fact takes almost no account of our actual experience in psychotherapy' (ibid.:10).

Quite apart from the inherent limitations of employing scientific means only to gain understanding of a species composed of both arts' and science's modes of exploration – acquired, incidentally, as a result of the employment of both means having proved successful so far – Pilgrim's views can be endorsed on other, theoretical grounds. For instance, attention has already been drawn to the confusion and fragmentation which arises from the kind of blind empiricism which proceeds without sufficient account being taken of interactive aspects and dimensions of the adaptive process, and/or which grossly oversimplifies the range of human variability.

Eysenck's dimensional model of personality was criticized in the last chapter on both counts. Incidentally, a good example of the value he places on the 'status of a science' is contained in his discussion of 'Models and explanations' (1981:chap. 1), in which he stresses the view that the psychology of personality must be regarded as *only* scientific. However, we have already seen that scientific models, when subjected to theoretical analysis, are just as vulnerable as theory is when subjected to scientific testing. The only reasonable 'status' which can be accorded to either the arts or science mode is as an alternative means of 'knowing'. It is surely only when there is some degree of coincidence between the outcomes of the two modes that any real question of status arises, and then it has to do with the status of the *knowledge*, not the means.

In the most fundamental and general terms Eysenck's theory was criticized above for its failure to take sufficient account of the interaction of cortical and limbic arousal, so that emotion is seen to have no part to play in individual differences (although emotion *is* seen to have a part to play in neuroticism). Similarly, it oversimplifies the relationship between excitation and inhibition which are seen to be mutually exclusive, in contrast to the APM-A view, in which the possibility of high intensity of *both*, as well as the possibility of overall bias, is accommodated.

Interestingly, Graham Powell (1979) arrives at very similar criticisms, among others, from the standpoint of a neuropsychologist. He, too, criticizes Eysenck's assumption that excitation and inhibition are reciprocal or mutually exclusive. He also criticizes two other assumptions: 'that a quickly (slowly) developed potential will be strong (weak), and that a quickly (slowly) developed inhibitory potential will dissipate slowly (quickly)'. He makes these criticisms 'on the basis of a lack of explicitly stated empirical evidence' (ibid.:8), and produces figures illustrating other possibilities of kinds of excitation and inhibition from the limited range that Eysenck's theory embodies. One simplified version of these, Figure 28, is very similar to the APM-A figure in the last chapter (Figure 17) which illustrates a similar point: about alternative kinds of excitation and inhibition for which Eysenck fails to account.

In fact, Eysenck's best-known critic (on different grounds from any

Figure 27 Types of individuals defined by certain aspects of excitation and inhibition (I=introvert cell, E=extravert cell), reproduced from Powell (1979:7)

				Excitation			
				Develops FAST		Develops SLOW	
	Develops	Strength	Dissipates	STRONG	WEAK	STRONG	WEAK
INHIBITION	FAST	HIGH	FAST				
			SLOW				E
		LOW	FAST				
			SLOW				
	SLOW	HIGH	FAST				
			SLOW				
		LOW	FAST	I			
			SLOW				

mentioned so far), Gray (1981) modifies the theory to bring the limbic system into the explanation of both personality and neuroticism. He does this by rotating the neuroticism dimension through 45° and adding two

Figure 28 Simplification of Figure 27 reproduced from Powell (1979:8)

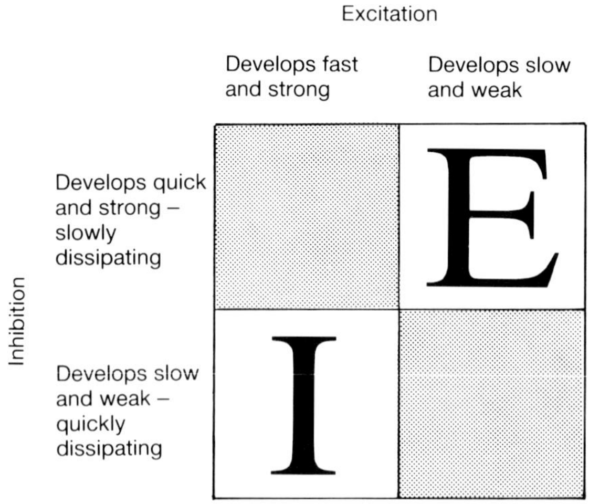

other dimensions: anxiety and impulsivity (see Figure 29). This clearly brings it much nearer to the APM-A model but, in addition to problems identified by Powell (1979:23–4) – mainly concerning lack of empirical evidence – and others identified by Zuckerman (1979:52–3), there are still more.

In essence Gray argues that the socialized behaviour of the introvert cannot be properly accounted for by the simple blanket reason that introverts are better at conditioning. He says that they condition better than extraverts only under certain conditions, and that they do not differ in the capacity to condition *per se*. He sees the vital difference being in

Figure 29 Proposed relationships of (1) susceptibility to signal of reward and susceptibility to signal of punishment to (2) the dimensions of introversion–extraversion and neuroticism. The dimensions of anxiety and impulsivity (diagonals) represent the steepest rate of increase in susceptibility to signals of punishment and reward respectively. (After Gray 1970)

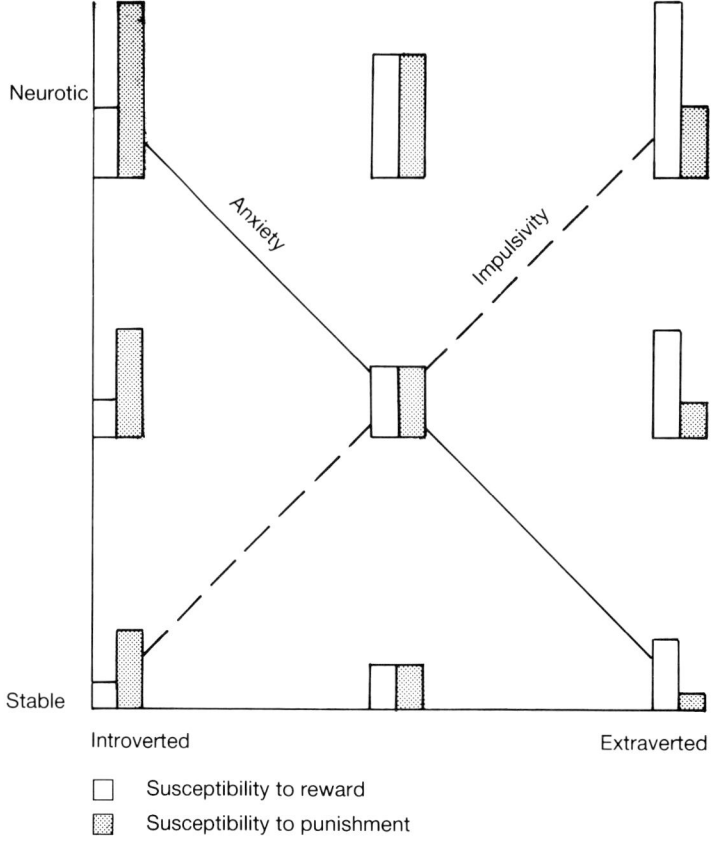

susceptibility to *punishment* and *fear*, so that the introvert's effective conditioning is dependent on the degree of threat encountered. He points out that psychopaths (high E) behave with little or no apparent thought for punishment consequences, whereas dysthymics (high I) are extremely fearful.

Our position is also that differences in susceptibility to punishment, fear, and threat are crucial to differences in individual style (including psychopathological styles), but to very different effect.

In view of all that has already been said about polymorphism, about the need to take account of conscious *and* unconscious aspects of the APM-A process, about differences in orientation towards the concrete and the abstract, and towards the specific and the general, the idea that introverts are simply more susceptible to punishment, fear, and threat seems quite inadequate.

We may say that introverts are more or less susceptible to different *kinds* of punishment, fear, and threat (and, indeed, promise) and in different *ways* from extraverts, but we must acknowledge at least as much *complexity in these vulnerabilities* as has been identified earlier in this and the last chapter. It has already been argued, for instance, that external types are more susceptible to unconscious and more general fears and threat than internal types who, in turn, are seen to be more vulnerable to more conscious and specific fears (see section 4.1).

In fact, the new position indicates that predominantly external types are more tuned to the *unconscious anticipation* of threats and the *recognition* of *problems*, while predominantly internal types are more tuned to make *conscious* use of past experience to minimize emotional involvement: to the *recognition* of appropriate (to particular purposes) *opportunity*.

This position allows us to hypothesize alternatively that the affective value of punishment is usually greater for introverts because their *expectations* of engagement with aversive stimuli are comparatively low. Consequently, such stimuli are likely to hold more specificity and greater novelty value. Similarly, it can be argued that the affective value (that is, specific emotional impact) of rewards is likely to be greater for extraverts, whose characteristic mode is biased towards the unconscious expectation of more challenging stimuli.

The most obvious advantages and disadvantages of Gray's model are summarized below. From the APM-A position it is seen to have two major advantages over Eysenck's model:

1 The accommodation of neuroticism and personality within the same explanatory framework as a result of acknowledging a role by the limbic system in personality (although introverts and extraverts are still described in terms of cortical arousal only).

2 The introduction of the dimensions of impulsivity and anxiety as 'lines of causal influence', so that E–I and N are seen to be secondary consequences of their interaction, rather than E, I, and N themselves being seen as causal. This is closer to the APM-A position, in which the physical energy dimension includes impulsivity, and the mental energy dimension includes anxiety.

Problems are, however, still manifold. We can add the following to the separate criticisms of Powell and Zuckerman mentioned above.

1 Shifting Eysenck's neuroticism axis through 45° so that E and I reflect *relative* strengths of impulsivity and anxiety, and increments in N reflect *joint* strength (increments of impulsivity and/or anxiety) holds implications that (a) anxiety does not necessarily have a role to play in neuroticism (thus ignoring the unconscious dimension) and (b) that introverts are unequivocally more prone to anxiety than extraverts, when it has been argued here that there exist low-energy internal types who remain enviably free of troubled minds and external types high in physical *and* mental energy prone to impulsivity *and* anxiety (Figure 22).

2 Adopting 'anxiety' as one of two causal dimensions denies acknow- ledgement of complications such as the difference between conscious and specific anxiety, and unconscious and general anxiety (see section 4.1).

3 Although Gray's model shifts away from E, I, and N as causal influences *per se*, the causal influences he suggests are still specific traits, i.e. particular manifestations of process, rather than aspects of process itself. Further, because the traits he selects carry certain negative overtones his model still does not provide an adequate framework for the accommodation of both normal and abnormal states. For instance, it presupposes that highly impulsive extraversion is necessarily pathological when, from our alternative position, pathology can be seen to be just one alternative (see Figures 22, 25).

4 Gray's modification of Eysenck's model still precludes the possibility of the coincidence of high levels of excitation *and* high levels of inhibition, and continues to ignore possible variability in patterning of hormonal secretion. Both of these criticisms, together with the fact that both Eysenck's and Gray's models are static, dimensional models, are seen to limit their capacity to represent an adequate range of human variability: both models, therefore, can only reinforce extremely simplistic concepts of people and society.

It is ironic that Eysenck's E–I and N are so intimately connected with

Galen's ancient, but nevertheless perceptive, categories of melancholic, choleric, phlegmatic, and sanguine, which were based on the potentially much more dynamic idea of the 'humours', primitively associated with the dominance of one or another biochemical product such as blood or bile. It also seems ironic that it is claimed that Eysenck has 'developed a theoretical model for explicitly linking diagnosis with aetiology in the expectation that this will lead to a more systematic approach to treatment' (Nias 1976:238), when his most recent addition to his dimensional model, P (psychoticism), seems more adequately to describe psychopathy: 'the P+ personality is solitary, troublesome, cruel, lacking in feeling, lacking in empathy, hostile to others, sensation-seeking, and liking odd and unusual things' (Eysenck and Eysenck 1976:202). He currently argues that E–I is on the way to becoming a paradigm in Kuhn's (1970) sense. It is maybe more accurate to suggest that it has already served as an extremely powerful and heavily value-laden paradigm which has influenced the interpretation of a great deal of research in quite widely separated fields, including educational psychology. It has fallen into everyday use, but with often confusing and negative effects because of its inadequacy to describe real people.

However, the seductive power of psychoanalytic explanations in terms of object-relations and individuation, as well as the value-laden 'explanatory' extraversion–introversion dimension (with 'introverting drugs' being used to 'remedy' criminality and 'brain damage'), is easily understood when we recognize that separateness, ease of conditioning, sequential thinking, and focus can all be associated with *low levels of psychological need*. These qualities carry with them lower levels of emotional expression, lower levels of dependency, and fewer demands on others or the environment. Consequently, within most social and institutional settings they are perceived to 'do better' and/or to 'be nicer', which, in reality, can be interpreted as meaning that they are the most easily (economically) served – or shaped – members of the group. It can be argued that the same members, therefore, also provide the most economical standard or norm.

One of the discernible incidental effects of this phenomenon, combined with the fact that neither primary nor secondary educational systems yet exist to serve fundamental needs of human organisms (only to encourage the acquisition of particular forms of 'knowledge'), is that in times of rapid social change and increasing social tension growing numbers of people either do not ever achieve effective means of orientation, or are highly susceptible to disorientation.[45] Until we can disseminate a credible view of human nature which provides at least a fundamental understanding of self and others, even identities which *are* found can very easily be lost, when particular roles change or rationales break down.

The fundamental point being made is an extension of the major argument of this chapter: that so-called 'normality' and 'abnormality' cannot reasonably be regarded as mutually exclusive states of existence, or adequately be explained by separate models, theories, or dimensions. One of the logical extensions of this position is that because information and experience gained in helping the manifestly disorientated has obvious relevance for the prevention of disorientation, there is a very strong case to be argued for education and psychiatry to be viewed as intimately related, rather than quite separate fields of enquiry and practice.

Whereas ideas drawn from the therapeutic methods of Alfred Adler and, more recently, Eric Berne and Carl Rogers have permeated other institutions, including education, formal connections between the two fields, as areas of academic enquiry whose findings may be consciously and directly applied, are not apparent.

But before discussing a concept of education as orientation (in Chapter 6), and before that, some of the cultural manifestations of the continuous effort to maintain – or achieve – that condition, the briefest possible outline of some of the most obvious implications of a disorientation–dependency model of mental disorder is set out below.

First, classification, diagnosis, and therapy would be rooted in definitions of sources, degrees, and kinds of disorientation and dependency and the development of understanding of self, variability of needs in others, and the establishment – or reinforcement – of a repertoire of means of expression and communication.

Second, testing and case-history building would centre as much on identifying *potential* as limitations, and their fundamental aims would be to establish a *stylistic profile* and particular *kinds* of vulnerability. This would be done by defining attentional, perceptual memory (that is, emotional and cognitive) styles, as well as styles of movement and gesture, in order to assess levels, and kinds of use, made of both mental and physical energy both currently and in the past.

More specifically, the diagnosis of style and degrees and kinds of disorientation would include practical tests as well as other tests and measures. Besides observation of facial and body movements and gestures, for instance, other very simple practical tests (such as folding a piece of paper into a given number of squares, say, or filling in more or less complicated shapes with a pen) would give very strong indications of such things as rigidity/flexibility of response; speed and/or precision of activity; levels of control/disorganization; and the degree to which movement is task-specific or 'superfluous'.

Third, the therapist would be seen to have a counselling/tuitional role and, as well as attempting to define other process aspects of style such as degree of 'future orientation'/anticipation, would aim to define *levels and kinds of need* and *unmet needs*. These would have to be (1) as perceived by the client, and therefore most likely in terms of cultural and social expectations, and (2) as perceived by the therapist according to the revised hierarchy of needs which may be met in *alternative* ways.

Processes of diagnosis and therapy would, in fact, be interactive and ongoing processes, rather than diagnosis being regarded as a discrete and finite stage of affixing one or more highly arbitrary labels. An important aspect would still be defining attitudes; prejudices; values; particular life-stage; educational and social backgrounds; relationships with significant others; and investigating possible sources of stress in a fairly conventional manner, but with a difference. Constant aims would involve reducing the perception of threat and identifying sources of conflict and stress in *process* terms with reference to the individual's *own* psychological needs and perceptual and conceptual *style*: in sum, systematically to provide means of orientation and alternative ways of coping and defending which are rooted in understanding of self and others, and in awareness of the key significance of stylistic (as well as circumstantial) limitations and potential.

Part 2

Homeostasis and heterostasis: balancing and changing

Introduction

Having discussed some of the major psychological implications of the tendency of the human organism to seek homeostasis, it becomes necessary to take account of the fact that as well as striving to maintain internal balance we are also heterostatic: growing, stimulus seeking and self-actualizing. Whereas theories of personality and motivation usually suggest that we are either homeostatic *or* heterostatic,[1] the position being adopted is that our experience and behaviour are actually subject to the influences of both processes and that these processes too are interactive.

Part 1 described and explained relatively stable differences in the ways individuals strive to achieve psychological homeostasis, and these in turn were attributed to variability in patterns of electro-chemical activity associated with the orientation response. In Chapters 5 and 6 the task will be to bring questions of lifelong growth and irreversible kinds of development – that is, the longer-term dynamics of human functioning, in addition to individual differences on the one hand and more or less temporary adjustments in tuning on the other – into the same perspective.

Emphasis will shift from the subject of individual differences *per se* to a consideration of some of the cultural manifestations of the diverse changes in levels and kinds of psychological needs which, it has been argued, take place in response to mounting conscious and/or unconscious tension (disorientation). In short, the notion of style as the expression of a particular pattern of physiological, as well as psychological, orientation will be developed to show how the various hierarchies and models introduced in Part 1 can also be applied to variability in broader – cultural – manifestations of human adaptation.

In Chapter 5, examples of these variations and changes will be pegged on to the existing model of style by making direct comparisons between specific and well-documented styles of art; namely, between some of the rich variety of styles expressed in the visual arts in the nineteenth century and the various 'isms' of twentieth-century European and American art history.

Finally, in Chapter 6 the APM-A perspective is offered as a theoretical basis for the adoption of a lifelong developmental view of human modes of learning and expression: as an argument for the integration of the various sectors of the education system (which is not to argue for any less *variety* of provision) and for other radical changes in its structure, its methodology, and the view of humanity it currently reflects.

In order for these arguments to be presented, a means has to be devised to relate style as it is expressed in the products of behaviour, including those we place in the highly arbitrary category of 'art', to the kinds of experience which underlie the behaviour itself. Therefore, the initial problem to be addressed in Chapter 5 will be how to provide tools of analysis of artistic style which not only relate to the perceptual process but which can also be applied equally well to art and non-art.

Although what follows could be said to represent an attempt to demystify art, similar to that which related 'ineffable experience' to 'ordinary experience' in the explanation of religious experience and ritual in Chapter 4, demystification does not necessarily imply devaluation. For example, while it is to be stressed in Chapter 6 that the human species must eventually divest itself of *belief* in myth and legend (including religion) in favour of 'belief' (that is, confidence) founded on knowledge, in the species itself, this is not to say that myth and legend have no place in our culture at all or, for instance, that we should stop telling stories. It is only to suggest that we recognize their limitations when confused with reality.

Similarly, although an explanation of art is offered which relates it to other kinds of experience, one of the conclusions of this book is that both participation in the arts and the arts mode of perceiving are grossly undervalued.

Chapter five

Nineteenth-century refuges and twentieth-century prospects

Summary

The functions of this chapter are manifold. The simple aims are to show the relevance of APM-A theory to the better understanding of artistic and cultural styles, creativity, and aesthetic experience in general. However, in order to achieve these broad aims – for which it is essential to consider some specific, well-documented shifts in style – it is necessary, first, to establish a simple, but widely applicable, *means of classification* which allows (1) artefacts to be related to psychological process, and (2) the APM-A model to be used to define links between micro (information-processing) and macro (social and cultural) processes.

Other tasks essential to achieving the general aims include (1) identifying basic elements of art; (2) defining and locating concepts such as 'classic' and 'romantic' within the APM-A perspective; (3) considering the complex relationship between the classic–romantic dichotomy and that of objectivity–subjectivity; (4) differentiating some other, related, ideas from the APM-A view; (5) making some important distinctions (for example, between 'style' and 'preference' and what are called 'attention' reactions' and 'preference reactions'); and (6) distinguishing between the shared and different APM-A experiences of what Kreitler and Kreitler (1972) labelled 'creating' and 'spectating'.

Among the many ideas and findings which are seen as relevant to the APM-A position two contributions, in particular, from quite different fields, are seen to hold special significance. The first is the introduction to the field of aesthetics of two key concepts by Appleton (1975): namely, 'prospect' and 'refuge'. The second is research, most closely associated with Lindauer (1984), into the phenomenon of physiognomy – the perception of expressive meanings.

Eventually, some systematic comparisons of style are made by reference to five key concepts, and alternative APM-A interpretations are made of significant changes in style during the nineteenth and twentieth centuries.

The chapter ends with a critical look at certain views of cultural 'pathology' and the presentation of a new diagnosis.

5.1 Principles and processes

Before any kind of comparison can be made between different artistic and cultural styles, fundamental decisions have to be made concerning what constitutes a stylistic feature. This of course is not a new problem in itself. Heinrich Wölfflin (1950), for instance, adopted certain 'objective criteria', namely, five opposed dynamisms;[1] but our problem differs in two obvious respects from that addressed by Wölfflin.

First, in order to extend the APM-A model for it to apply fully to the field of 'aesthetics'[2] a classification system has to be devised which relates artistic style and preferences (which will be distinguished[3]) to other psychological processes.

Second, the same means must be capable of relating art products and aesthetic experience to kinds of experience and behaviour traditionally regarded as quite different, as belonging to the class of ordinariness.

Richard Wollheim (1978) has made some 'programmatic remarks' on identifying the 'primes of style' (a term he borrows from literary criticism) which seem to express similar felt needs. He draws an important comparison between two quite different kinds of description. One, the orthodox *taxonomic* view of which he says,

1 it picks out all the interesting, significant, distinctive, features of the artist's work; and
2 it groups them conveniently;

and the other, a *generative* view of style which he describes as follows:

1 it picks out those elements of the artist's work which are dependent upon certain processes or operations characteristic of the artist's activity; and
2 it groups these elements into stylistic features accordingly, i.e. according to the process on which they are dependent.

(1978:9)

He makes the significant point that 'to take a generative view of style is to imply that style has a psychological reality', and adds, 'any adequate view of style must reflect or pick up on the conceptual equipment of the artist' (ibid.:9, 10). This is wholly consistent with the APM-A view, and although Wollheim offers no specific solution to the problem of style himself, he does offer some examples of different styles of expression which will be returned to later.

Before attempting to define any 'primes of style' from the new perspective, or attempting to explain some of the processes which underlie preferences and changes in preferences, it is necessary to define the relevance of two important, but very different, contributions to the field of aesthetics in general. These are research into physiognomy[4] on the one hand, and Appleton's (1975) prospect-refuge theory on the other.

Neither of these contributions actually comes from the field of philosophy where key contributions might be expected to be found. The reason for this (while it is not argued that psychology and philosophy are wholly independent, and although the approach being adopted is essentially arts-based) is that similar 'impediments to progress' are identified as those recognized by Berlyne.[5]

The APM-A stance rests on the postulate that all human decision making is fundamentally aesthetic (postulate 10, Appendix 2): that it always involves the exercise of preferences. Therefore enquiry into the nature of aesthetic experience and behaviour is seen to be best conducted within the same framework as enquiry into any other aspect of experience and behaviour.

Although Berlyne was making this latter point as long ago as 1971, the view is by no means yet universally held; but *Aesthetics and Psychobiology* does remain one of the best-known contributions to the psychology of art which, incidentally, also contains an excellent overview of developments in the field up to that date.

Berlyne's own approach is exclusively scientific and empirical. But in seeking to understand the biological origins of art he deals at length with research findings about arousal, exploration and the perception of environmental information which happen to be consistent with the APM-A synthesis. The new perspective also overlaps with Berlyne's position in recognizing that pleasure may derive from variable mixes of arousal-increasing and arousal-modulating stimuli, rather than depending on the perception of the one kind or the other. Berlyne calls these mixes 'arousal jag', meaning a temporary rise in arousal which is then reversed; 'arousal boost', a pleasurable rise; and 'arousal boost-jag', which refers to overlapping classes of experience (1971:136).

On the subject of expressive style Berlyne makes important observations and cites useful findings (ibid.:chap. 13) but, surprisingly, his own classificatory system relates directly not to psychological *processes*, but to the kinds of *information* transmitted by particular historical styles, and his discussion of individual differences eventually switches away from styles to preferences.

Another major contribution to the field was made by Kreitler and Kreitler (1972), the year after Berlyne's. The Kreitlers' work differs in that they offer an 'encompassing theory' specifically about the 'spectator of the arts'. They contend that a major motivation for art is tensions which exist in the spectator of art prior to his exposure to the work of art. The work of art mediates the relief of these pre-existing tensions by generating new tensions which are specific.

Thus, the resolution of the specific tensions implies relief also for the diffuse tensions with which they have combined. The resolution of these tensions is attended by pleasure.

(Ibid.:19, 22)

From the APM-A position the role of the spectator is viewed as only a reinforcement for the artist's productive efforts, rather than being 'a major motivation for art'. Further, the outcome of being a spectator of the arts is by no means always seen to be tension reduction. Particular works may actually provoke problem recognition and continue to arouse on occasions long after the event: the totality of a work may actually continue to be arousal-increasing, although composed of both arousal-increasing and arousal-decreasing devices.

In fact, Morse Peckham (1967), whose writings are perhaps nearest to the APM-A position in that he deals with some of the same concepts, although very differently, actually holds the opinion that all art *raises* tension. He suggests that it provides 'protected situations' in which disorientation can be savoured: a notion discussed at the end of the chapter.

A more recent theoretical formulation which regards the concept of arousal as crucial to an understanding of the arts is Apter's reversal theory (1982) but, again, the emphasis is on the role of the spectator for whom the perception of ambiguity – and accompanying arousal – are seen to play a central role in the aesthetic experience. Apter's theory is actually more descriptive than explanatory, and is limited by its denial of the significance of both homeostasis and the existence of any relatively consistent personality traits.

A general, but very useful, overview of the psychology of art has been provided by Granger (1979). He takes the writings of Gombrich, chosen for the 'depth and breadth of his knowledge', and considers some alternative points of view in order to provide what he calls 'an initial orientation in the field'; and Gombrich himself offers a more specialized overview, of theories of style, in *Art and Illusion* (1977). Another rather specialized discussion, this time of theories of aesthetics, is offered by Child (1978).

From outside the mainstreams of art, psychology, or aesthetics altogether, Appleton identifies some of the major contributions to aesthetics from philosophy, and in a review of his own theory ten years on (1984a), makes the point that awareness of the importance of the need to gain insight into the nature of human preferences is apparently now especially strong among landscape architects and designers.

The fact that interest in aesthetics is expressed within so many different disciplines can be taken as one indication of its centrality in human experience and behaviour. Brothwell (1976) has produced a particularly useful interdisciplinary contribution, and other more specific contributions have come from the fields of anthropology (Greenhalgh and Megaw 1978a), zoology (Orians 1980), psychiatry (Kalina *et al.*), and environmental psychology (Kaplan and Kaplan 1982), but the setting up of the International Association for Empirical Aesthetics in 1965 has also contributed greatly to its growth as a field of enquiry. For instance, at its most recent meeting in Britain 120 papers ranged in subject matter from the psychology of religion (Beit-Hallahmi 1983) to drug abuse (Adler 1983); while participants included architects, artists, designers, and specialists in literature, as well as psychiatrists and psychologists.

Against this level of interdisciplinary interest it seems curious that aesthetic theory and art history are regarded as quite separate fields by art historians. This is particularly interesting in the light of contributions being made to aesthetics from archaeologists and anthropologists and a fairly recent complaint by Greenhalgh and Megaw (1978b) in particular. They pointed out that at that time there were no courses offered in British universities which applied art-historical disciplines to ethnographic materials, and, further, very little difference in approach to art history was detectable in journals during the last fifty years. In the light of the fact that art history students are exhorted to experiment with water colour for instance (Pointon 1980), in order to become acquainted with at least one medium of painting, it can also be viewed as anomalous that similar significance is not attached to becoming acquainted with either the psychological processes of the painter or the nature of visual art.

The breadth of interest in aesthetic theory existing outside art history together with identifiable problems with the philosophical approach (see note 5) makes it less surprising that Appleton's prospect-refuge theory is the theory of a geographer, rather than a psychologist or professional aesthetician of any other kind. It was actually conceived in response to

the absence of any generally accepted theoretical basis for the aesthetics of landscape . . . [or] . . . any adequate machinery for linking the predominantly abstract generalisations of philosophers with the *details* of actual landscapes.

(Appleton 1975:vii)

The author looks for clues initially in the relationships which can be observed between animals and their perceptual environments and is led to two hypotheses. The first concerns the notion that pleasurable sensations can be linked to experience of landscape favourable to biological survival. This he calls 'habitat theory'. The second hypothesis he calls 'prospect-refuge theory' of which he says, '[it] opens the way to the analysis of landscapes in terms of their strategic appraisal as potential habitats' (ibid.).

Appleton then sets out a system of symbolism which relates pleasurable sensations to the recognition of requirements for biological survival, such as water, food, and shelter, which, in turn, he groups into classifications designated 'prospect' and 'refuge'.

The system is designed specifically to apply to the experience of landscape, but it is an incidental aim of this chapter to show how the concepts of prospect and refuge can serve as rich contributions to art criticism and to the understanding of human preferences in general. But this can be done only if certain complexities, relating both to the techniques of the artist and particular attributes of the human mind which were postulated in detail in Chapter 3, are taken into account. In this way it will be shown how, by reference to psychological process, to human variability as well as adaptability, and to the form as well as to the content of behavioural products, the application of Appleton's central concepts can be extended quite dramatically.

Specifically, in order for a biological approach to aesthetics to be adequate to apply to *Homo sapiens* it must also reflect the significance of what have been called *psychological survival needs* in addition to physical survival needs. For the same system to have more general application it must also move beyond defining the evolutionary significance of symbolism of the contents and potential of landscape only, to make reference to other dynamics of the natural world, including biosocial activity.

Although a hierarchy of attention has been devised elsewhere (Gear 1987) in which priority signals are related directly to physical survival needs, and which is seen to operate regardless of individual differences, it has also been argued that physical survival is not always a prime motivation for anything *other* than attending to a signal, at least momentarily. Situations have been defined in previous chapters in which physical survival needs may be temporarily or permanently superseded by the dominance of psychological survival needs. It follows, therefore, that preferences vary according to the state of the organism in much more complicated ways than the consideration of simple survival needs suggests.

The scope of this chapter is limited to certain changes in style which have emerged as recognizably novel events in our formal cultural history, but it should become fairly obvious how the broad principles of the approach are equally relevant to the analysis of style of individual artists, as well as to other, apparently quite different, manifestations of cultural change which may be reflected in any kind of fashion, from hair-styles to furniture design, or in other mass modes of expression or gaining stimulation.

Obvious examples in our own culture include changing tastes in popular music and dance, and, currently, escalation in the ingestion of alcohol and drugs, escalation in other forms of self-abuse and the abuse of others, and the frequent appearance and disappearance of various kinds of cult activities and beliefs. All can be explained in terms of changes in states of arousal and consequent changes in levels and kinds of orientation needs.[6]

There is no *direct* relationship between all of this and Appleton's theory of pleasure in landscape perception deriving from the symbolic representation of the concepts of prospect and refuge, nor is prospect-refuge theory being viewed as having direct relevance to artefacts, other than the representation of landscape, or to artistic style other than figurative painting and drawing. Indeed, it will be shown how preferences can be expressed for pictures with *no* refuge symbolism in them at all. However, although Appleton's theory in its present form is limited to the analysis of landscape preference – for which, after all, it was conceived – the breakthrough it represents, in this writer's estimation, is that its major concepts are, incidentally but directly, related to the absolutely crucial psychological concepts of 'approach' and 'avoid'.

The only other concepts at all familiar to researchers into aesthetics which may be perceived as bearing a similar relationship are those of 'takete' and 'maluma'. The names refer to two abstract shapes: maluma, a fairly regular curved shape; and takete, a very different, irregular and rather spiky shape (Figure 30). It could be said that both the shapes themselves and their names are 'soft' and 'hard' and/or 'friendly' and 'hostile' respectively, so that the one is seen to invite approach while the other might promote avoidance. To perceive them in this way constitutes a physiognomic response.

Physiognomic perception is defined by Martin Lindauer in Wiley's *Encyclopedia of Psychology* (1984) as referring to

> expressive perception of persons, events, and things. A red patch is not only small in size, among other physically measurable and literal attributes, but it is also 'exciting, hot, and energetic'. Metaphoric, figurative, and symbolic language often capture physiognomic

Figure 30 Takete (left) and maluma: patterns devised by Köhler (1947)

meanings; for example, threatening clouds, wild oceans, forbidding mountains . . .

He also says,

Physiognomic properties are felt to be inherent in the object itself, that is, perceptual rather than associative. A tree *is* sad – it does not just remind you of something sad or make you feel sad.

(Lindauer 1983)

After conducting research into physiognomy himself he has reached the following conclusions:

(1) physiognomy exists in both art and non-art; (2) it can be demonstrated in at least two areas of perception: orientation and colour (i.e. brightness and saturation); (3) distinctions between physiognomic and non-physiognomic stimuli can be shown; (4) so too can differences between physiognomic stimuli; (5) physiognomy is rooted in perception; (6) it does not depend on familiarity; and (7) the roles of learning, memory, and past experience in general are not primary. [He refers of course to individual learning, not to what has been called species learning.]

(Ibid.)

Lindauer also makes the point that there are still some important questions to be answered, such as 'What exactly makes a physiognomic response physiognomic?' He says that a new approach to answering this and other questions he poses might be to move away from conventional approaches to look 'sideways', outside psychology, to what artists do.

The relevance of research into physiognomy to this book is twofold. Besides the indirect support it gives for the idea that there are, in APM-A terms, relatively consistent species-learned emotional responses to certain classes of stimuli, it could also provide a very concrete psychological basis for the analysis of art-form; this could, incidentally, also add to the existing limited range of tests requiring oral or written response to visual stimuli to provide the kind of practical diagnostic tests likely to offer insights into individual style suggested at the end of the last chapter.

Conversely, APM-A theory also holds relevance for physiognomy. It offers some possible lines of empirical research which may answer some of the questions which still exist. For instance, the answer which arises from the new perspective to Lindauer's question 'What exactly makes a physiognomic response physiognomic?' is 'The extent to which it embodies a species learned priority signal' (see Figure 66, Appendix 2); but the production of a detailed taxonomy would require a considerable amount of research, for which Lindauer's suggestion of looking towards art-practice seems very sound. After all, artists not only 'know' (intuitively, if not consciously) that upward-sweeping lines indicate joy; that diagonal lines suggest movement and energy; that red and other 'warm' colours 'advance', while blue and other colours in the 'cool' range 'recede', they also manipulate and moderate meanings, whether their prime motivations are to communicate or not. Artists are also acutely aware of the importance of context in perception, and how the impact of any particular element in the perceptual field can be modified by changes in its surroundings.

The kinds of symbolism in question have fairly obvious roots when viewed from within an evolutionary perspective. In the case of there being a strong association between upward-sweeping lines and feelings of happiness, it seems reasonable enough to believe that *Homo sapiens* was not the first upright primate to externalize positive arousal by hopping around waving unoccupied arms in the air, that is, expressing a powerful surge of excitement without the need to adopt any defensive or aggressive pose.

In the case of diagonal lines indicating movement, experiential knowledge of the law of gravity alone suggests that something we perceive to be not quite upright, or not quite horizontal, cannot stay in the same position for long without support and that some kind of movement is likely[7] – if it is not already taking place. As for the 'advancing' colour red which Lindauer points out is also 'exciting, hot and energetic', blatantly obvious associations can be seen to exist between red and both blood and fire; and both can threaten to spread beyond their immediate locations, that is, to 'advance'. The fact that blue also has strong associations with temperature and spatial relationships – with cool water and distant sky respectively – hardly needs spelling out either, but the implications of these kinds of possible associations are very important if a case is to be argued for the existence of a widely understood (at however deeply unconscious a level) and cross-cultural language of emotion. This is not to argue for the existence of a cross-cultural language of symbolism in any general sense, because although the two possibilities are not *quite* separate issues, neither are they the same.[8]

Both Lindauer (1983) and Arnheim (1966:56–72) outline existent theories of physiognomy which attribute the phenomenon variously to processes which are innate, learned, or perceptual. The APM-A position accommodates certain aspects of all three approaches but without subscribing to the precise details or limitations of any of them as they have been formulated so far. Rather, physiognomic responses are seen to be species learned by means of association; as responses to signs and symbols embodying vestiges of species-learned priority *signals* (of different levels and kinds of threat and promise) found in the natural (including the social) environment. Further, the APM-A process itself is seen to have evolved around the recognition of significant environmental events in such a way that physiognomic perception has become a key aspect of sub-threshold scanning, and exerts a strong influence over all decision making.

Arnheim sees physiognomy as common to all of the arts and as a potential bridge between art and non-art (ibid.:63) as does Lindauer, who also draws attention to its potential as a bridge in another way, by referring to Werner and Wapner's (1952) view of inter-sensory connections between sight, touch, and movement resting on physiognomy.

A great deal is written by art historians, critics, philosophers, and other investigators of art about the use of symbolism; and those with a psychological orientation are inclined to refer freely to particular kinds of stimuli. Signs also warrant some attention – more so from practitioners of the arts – but consciousness of the role of signals in art seems to be comparatively low.

Leach has drawn attention to the need to differentiate symbols, signs, and signals by offering a detailed analysis of their roles in social anthropology (1976:chap. 2). Signals are defined as always being part of a cause and effect sequence, as eliciting a reflex action; a sign has a contiguous (and therefore agreed) relationship with something else; while the meaning of a symbol is not necessarily agreed, and being metaphoric, holds only 'arbitrary assertions of similarity' (ibid.:15).

In the discussion which follows, all symbols, signs, and signals are viewed in terms of potential threat or promise, whose presence or absence have already been identified as influencing what is attended; how we attend; whether attention is sustained in order for exploration and/or learning to take place; and as being a factor in the expression of preferences and taste (see Chapter 1). The focus of this chapter is to be mainly on non-figurative means of expressing threats and promises: on how both are inherent in any picture, object, or building. That is to say that emphasis will be more on the role of *form* as a vehicle of expression and communication, than content.

Communication is to be viewed as only a *possible, incidental* outcome of expression. The fact that a 'message' is received is not necessarily seen to be evidence of either its conscious, or deliberate, transmission; and, as the mental set of the perceiver (spectator) of art is seen to be just as influential as in any other kind of perception, whether the same message is received as may have been sent, is also questionable.

The point being made is that interpretations of what the artist is 'saying' can only be a matter of conjecture (sometimes even to the artist) unless a direct, verbal statement is available.[9]

In fact Gombrich's (1978:65ff.) idea of the possibility of the existence of hierarchies of messages is to be endorsed, with the suggestion that the reading of a picture takes place according to the same fundamental processes as reading any other pattern of visual stimuli, namely, according to two intimately related hierarchies[10] introduced elsewhere (Gear 1987); but since the theoretical framework has been extended to take account of individual differences, a rider has to be added. It has to be acknowledged that the extent to which conscious responses are dominated by what Appleton calls 'naturally determined symbols' as opposed to 'culturally determined symbols' (1984b) is likely to be affected by levels and kinds of arousal – that is, to be itself a variable.

It follows from previous arguments that if cortical arousal is predominant, the strong tendency is likely to be to rationalize, while if limbic arousal predominates there is still likely to be a stronger tendency to react 'with feeling' despite the acquisition of relevant 'cultural tools'.

Whereas Hochberg (1972), in discussing the relationship between 'perception and intention', argues that the symbols of art are not in general arbitrary, the APM-A position implies that they *are*. After the experience of some kind of emotional impact, and the initial classification of stimuli in terms of threat and promise to the organism (first as a member of the species and then as an individual), the conscious reading of them may be highly arbitrary. Both representational and non-representational visual imagery allow similar interventions of guessing about meanings and the same economy of effort which Hochberg tells us happens in learning to read when we are equipped with the 'knowledge of the spelling, grammar, idiom and substance of the text'. But in the case of art problems of interpretation can in fact be exacerbated by the *apparent* obviousness of visual realism. On the other hand, in the absence of recognizable imagery, questions such as 'What is it?' or 'What does it mean?' may be quite inappropriate.

The position being adopted is near to that of Gombrich when he suggests that the physiognomic response represents the 'initial probe', but not when he argues that 'In normal conditions we would not operate with them any longer than necessary to perform the first unstable act of categorisation which serves as a starting point for subsequent probes' (Gombrich 1978:50). In this quotation 'we' are surely art historians or others in possession of rather sophisticated ways of apprehending the world or, at least, individuals experiencing high-order needs and relevant acquired interests in order to be moved to make subsequent probes. The same state-ment by Gombrich also begs the other question raised above: whether other than the most fundamental kind of emotional response is *always* appropriate.

However, the classification of style which follows rests on the assumption that whether or not an intellectual response is always evoked or is absolutely appropriate, physiognomic responses do always play a part and influence perception to a much greater extent than is yet acknowledged.

Variability in responsiveness to physiognomic stimuli follows from the identification of characteristics of individual style in Chapters 3 and 4: specifically, from hypothesized differences in relative dominance of conscious and unconscious processing and differences in emotional responsivity. The assumption is confirmed, however, by findings about greater sensitivity to physiognomic stimuli in artists, psychotics, and children cited by Lindauer (1983), which coincide with the APM-A view of lower tension-threshold types being more vulnerable to priority signals.

Now the argument is to be extended in support of the notion that tension-thresholds differ and change at group as well as individual levels, with the effect that stressors act on the consciousness and unconsciousness of whole communities to produce different kinds and levels of cultural 'pathology'.[11] Particular kinds of change in creative output are to be discussed with special reference to this phenomenon, when evidence of all of the key characteristics of style defined in Chapters 3 and 4 (and broadly summarized in Figures 15, 16, and 17) will be seen to be reflected in the products of behaviour as well as in behaviour itself.

To recapitulate in the most general terms, the characteristics in question could also be classified under the headings of attentional style, perceptual style, memory style, and physically expressive style, which interact with one another reflecting different kinds and levels of energy and the experience of different levels of anticipation and urgency. As experience of anticipation and urgency increase, initially (1) attention becomes less rigid and more diffuse and dominated by scanning rather than focus; (2) perceptual and conceptual boundaries broaden with the effect of processing becoming more fluid and holistic; (3) with greater demands being made on unconscious processes speed of processing takes precedence over accuracy, as well as breadth over depth, so that memory is likely to be better for general ideas than for specific details and facts, and short-term memory better than long-term memory; (4) increase in emotionality, in turn, increases responsivity to stimuli and heightens reassurance needs and subjectivity; (5) increase in physical expression is likely to produce motor disorganization and a 'freeing' or 'loosening' of physical control (see Figures 15, 19, 20, and 26).

For the purposes of this chapter and the application of the model to styles of expression – to things as well as behaviour – five main categories are to be used. Two of these, *abstraction* and *dynamism*, are actually binary. The term 'abstraction' is to be used in opposition to the presence of recognizable imagery, and not in opposition to the more conventional other extreme of realism. This is because there is more than one way in which realism is evident in nineteenth-century European art. The term 'dynamism' is to be used simply to refer to movement as opposed to stability, and primarily as evidence of motor activity. Both of these oppositions, abstraction vs. recognizable imagery and dynamism vs. stability, will be seen to relate directly to the APM-A model and the expression of different levels of mental and physical energy, and both will be seen to be observable in more or less focused forms, as were the different kinds of neuroses and psychoses discussed in the last chapter.

High levels of abstraction are to be taken to imply dominance of process characteristics associated with the extremes of the upper right-hand side of the model (high SNS dominance and high mental energy); while the qualification of 'focused' and/or inclusion of more detailed and recognizable imagery – which may nevertheless be 'fantastic', that is, imaginary – will be seen to relate to processes associated with the upper left-side of the model (see Figure 15). This represents high SNS activity well-compensated by high levels of PNS activity, lending a higher degree of organization and greater conceptual and motor control. Dynamism and strong motor activity clearly relate to the right side of the model, and in previous chapters their dominance has been associated with the lower rather than the upper half.

Appleton's three concepts of *prospect, refuge,* and *hazard*[12] are also to be used as indicators of certain physiological and psychological processes at work, but in a much more specific way: as indicators of the extent of the predominance of physical or psychological survival needs, and therefore also of levels of pathology. But contrary to Appleton's proposal that as a species our preferences in landscape and in representations of landscape are governed by physical survival needs, and therefore by opportunities to perceive a symbolic balance of prospects and refuges, the new theoretical perspective suggests that this may not always be the case: that when psychological needs predominate over physical survival needs preferences are likely to move away from the need to perceive symbolic possibilities of physical refuge to symbolic exposure to physical risk (see section 4.3).

Basically, Appleton's concept of prospect refers to keeping open one's channels of perception, to being able to see; and his concept of refuge to possibilities of '*not* being seen'. His use of the concept of hazard is as simple as it seems, and refers to potential hazards to physical survival. But while Appleton sees these concepts as being conveyed by recognizable imagery, this hypothesis is being extended to suggest that these concepts are also conveyed physiognomically, and by the form as well as the content of particular behavioural products: and therefore in non-representational as well as representational art, and in art other than landscape art.

All five categories of the proposed classification of style will be viewed as vehicles of different kinds and levels of threat and promise, but whereas the concepts of hazard and refuge embody specific and unambiguous potentials for threat and promise respectively (while the concept of a prospect might represent either), it must be understood that signals or symbols of the same could nevertheless be highly ambiguous depending on (1) context, and (2) the particular schemata of the viewer.[13]

Another important consideration is the fact that the overall physiognomic message of any art object may contradict its recognizable content in terms of whether threats or promises (or what kind of mixture of the two) are conveyed, in the same way as in normal social intercourse actions can be deemed to 'speak louder than words'.

In order to clarify how this might happen, and specifically, how it is possible for form to convey meaning, it is necessary to consider some of the specific elements of design at the artist's disposal.

What follows is a rudimentary list drawn from the visual arts, and although some changes in terminology might be necessary for the arguments to apply to other modes of expression, transposition into the languages of literature or music, for instance, would be very simple.

Gombrich has made the point that 'By virtue of their mere existence . . . [any lump or blot] must have a physiognomy, some kind of expressive character, if only we dig deep enough into the layers of our mind that respond to the voice of things' (1978:52). Surely the same is true of *every* kind of sensory experience, so that we read meanings of some kind into every sound or movement as well as all we see or feel.

The basic elements of the visual arts – of which any may be composed of one or more of the others (for instance, line is necessarily also composed of tone and, in the strictest sense, colour) – include *line*, used chiefly to convey movement and perspective as well as horizontality and verticality; *tone*, which refers to the range and intensity of darkness or lightness and is used mainly to convey three-dimensional qualities referred to variously as form, volume, or depth; *colour*, which may carry a very wide range of associations but, above all, warmth or coolness; *texture*, which refers simply to tactile qualities; and *shape*, which, even when negative (part of the background), is always composed of one or more of the other elements.

There are very well-established findings concerning meanings of lines and colours (Kreitler and Kreitler 1972:chaps. 3, 5), as well as others relating to tone and shape[14] which can very easily be interpreted in terms of threats and promises to the organism, either by association with species-learned signals or in terms of coincidence with or deviations from adaptation levels.

A particularly interesting example of research into physiognomic expression in the context of APM-A theory is Poffenberger and Barrows' replication (1924) of Lundholm's early findings (1921) about the expressiveness of lines, but whereas Lundholm's subjects drew lines, Poffenberger and Barrows were interested in the feelings aroused by looking at lines. Their investigations were *supposedly* into line, but it is relevant to a point made above, about our tendency to read meanings into *all* perceivable stimuli, that both used different-sized curves and angles (shapes) in their experiments. However, total agreement occurred about which of them conveyed 'sad', 'quiet', 'lazy', 'merry', 'playful', and 'harsh' (big curves in the first three cases, small or medium curves in the fourth and fifth, and small and medium angles in the last); and moderate agreement occurred with the words 'agitating', 'furious', and 'gentle' (small angles, small angles, and big curves respectively).

Most interestingly in relation to our new model, which is essentially an energy model, Lundholm's original summary of his findings makes repeated reference to the amount of energy particular lines express. He says,

> The downward tendency of a line expresses relaxation, the upward expresses power. The downward tendency expresses faintness, not sufficient strength to keep it up. Going downwards expresses losing of energy. The doleful line droops without energy. If it had force it would have ascended higher. Strength is expressed by going upwards. A joyous line also ascends. Joy is an uplifting feeling. A forceful line tends upwards.
>
> (Ibid.)

After arriving at similar findings about the expressiveness of lines, Peters and Merrifield (1958) come to the following conclusions:

> The *form* of the line is apparently related to the degree of *overt activity* suggested by the word. The more angular or irregular lines are used to express such words as lively, agitating, angry, and furious, whereas a straight line is used to represent the words grave, idle, quiet and hard.
>
> The *intensity* of the line is apparently related to the *intensity, persistence,* or *strength* of the emotional feeling represented by the word. Heavy lines were used to represent such words as angry, furious, and cruel; in contrast, a light line was used to represent the words gentle, delicate, and quietly.

They also make the very important point that there is a logical fallacy in assuming from a fairly general understanding of these devices that individual drawings can be used clinically for the identification of emotional feelings in the subject; for example, that individuals who draw downward-sloping lines are sad. Whilst in full agreement with this point, the present writer suggests that relative *consistencies* in qualities such as the form, direction, and pressure of lines are nevertheless key indicators of style inasmuch as they give information about energy levels and other crucial factors such as degrees of rigidity/fluidity; organization/disorganization; and the general level of control being exercised by the subject, all of which contribute to gaining insight into *individual patternings of orientation response* and likely clusterings of other personal tendencies.

This seems an appropriate point at which to return to Wollheim's remarks on the 'primes of style' and to consider, without further comment, the example he offers of differences in style, in the light of an energy model, and taking account of such key factors as pressure, intensity, organization, and control.

When specific artefacts are discussed with reference to the concepts of abstraction, dynamism, prospect, refuge, and hazard, later in the chapter, it will be seen that some fairly consistent associations can be made between

Figure 31 A quiz taken by Wollheim from a book on graphology, about which he asks the question, 'Has the official answer been arrived at by "stylistic analysis"?' The task was to pair off writer and rectangle, to which the official answer was: no. 1 has been drawn by writer D; no. 2 by writer C; no. 3 by writer B; and no. 4 by writer A. See Wollheim (1978:12–14)

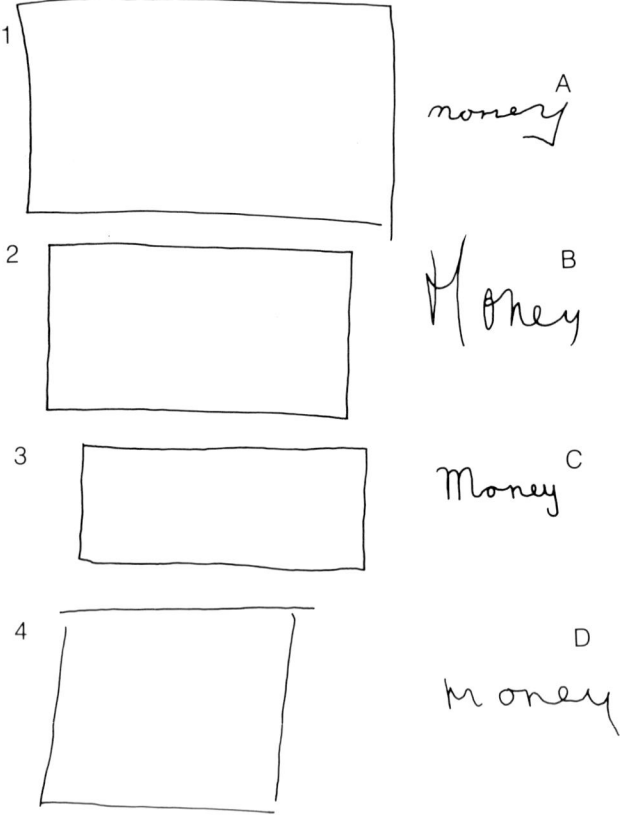

formal qualities and the concepts in question. For instance, unbroken areas of light tone can hardly connote the concept of refuge, whereas unbroken areas of dark tone may do so. On the other hand, high contrast, ungraduated changes in tone are likely to be perceived as 'hazardous'.[15] But however well-established certain findings may be, or however strong a species-learned association is, because context and the state of the perceiver must always be taken into account, no absolute classification system of what constitutes threat or promise to the individual organism is possible even if their most extreme representations do evoke near universal agreement (see postulates 4 and 5, Appendix 2).

Any classification system devised to compare expressive styles involving complex configurations of stimuli is necessarily arbitrary to some extent. Although comparisons between extreme examples may be relatively uncontroversial, in cases where the contrast is much less obvious, classification inevitably becomes more problematic, arbitrary, and subjective. Consequently, particular works can be described only as being more or less 'rich' in their representation of specific concepts (Appleton uses the terms 'prospect-rich' and 'refuge-rich', for instance); or as being prospect, refuge or hazard 'dominant'; or as 'relatively' abstract or dynamic. It is, however, possible to provide examples where some fairly stable associations can be made; for instance, rhythmic, curving lines can be seen to be more suggestive of the concept of refuge than smooth, unbroken, or angular lines, which are more likely to be associated with the idea of prospect. On the other hand, uneven or broken lines carry a fairly obvious association with the concept of hazard, as do very hot, vibrant colours or fragmented shapes and textures. Loose textures and inconsistencies of brushwork or palette knife can, by contrast, suggest 'hiding places' and refuge; but the specific examples of these phenomena offered below, in context, are likely to be more helpful.

Finally, two more clarifications are important to the understanding of the main arguments to be presented. The first of these is to distinguish the concept of *preference* from that of *style*; and the other intimately related distinction which has to be made is between the processes of *perception* and *expression*.

Any investigation into the nature of aesthetics necessarily touches on all four of these concepts, but they are not always distinguished, and failure to do so frequently leads to untenable generalizations and/or inconsistencies and confusion. All four share certain aspects of the APM-A process, and they are all intimately related, but they also represent quite different aspects of aesthetic experience.

Both of the distinctions to be made involve a difference between experience and behaviour, and, of course, in each case the experience is a prerequisite to the behaviour, so that all involve what might be called *attention reactions* and *preference reactions*; but whereas the experience of a preference does not necesarily include behaviour, expression and style obviously do.

Further, the APM-A model suggests that both the perceiver and the producer – or in Kreitler and Kreitler's terms (1972:4), the 'spectator' and 'creator' – of patterns of stimuli labelled 'art' move from unconscious attention reactions to unconscious preference reactions, to more conscious experience and/or behaviour. It is suggested, however, that in the case of the spectator the *conscious* experience of seeking orientation in response to a particular art object is much more likely to dominate reactions and involve a much higher degree of rationalization and justification. This is only in part because of the argument that the artist is highly limbically aroused. It is also because, although a high degree of rationalization *may* be involved in the creation of a piece of work, the roles of patrons, critics, and art historians demand a somewhat higher degree of conformity than that of artist. Cultural expectations and perceptual defence may therefore more easily influence the interpretations and rationales of the perceivers, especially when comment and explanations are required of themes such as the oral, anal, and genital themes of recent art, as will be seen.

Whatever rationales are constructed, fundamental motivations underlying the creation of art (in common with other behaviour) are nevertheless being seen to be orientational, but not only in terms of cognitive orientation. The term 'orientation', as it is used in this book, always includes reference to endocrinological processes.

This is not to deny a complex web of other interactions and influences on the evolution of particular styles, but it is to say that a readiness to *be* influenced, and particular kinds of susceptibility, must pre-exist. It suggests, for example, that the ubiquitous Japanese print, which occupies such an important role in the history of modern art, was actually an opportune vehicle for the expression of a *pre-existing* need for less refuge symbolism in painting. To the point, the incorporation of its most obvious characteristic (its flatness) can be interpreted as having eliminated a requirement for depth, allowing a more two-dimensional (less refuge-rich) rather than obviously three-dimensional patterning of the picture plane.

5.2 Styles of madness

The general case to be argued is relatively simple and will proceed mainly by example, so that a large proportion of the rest of the chapter will be composed of comparisons between the dominant styles of nineteenth- and twentieth-century art. Argument by example is, of course, always open to the criticism that only 'convenient' examples are chosen. However, the examples in question have been selected as being representative of well-documented events in art history and are being used in preference to literally hundreds of other possibilities only on the grounds of their acknowledged typicality and consequent ready availability.

The central problem of art history has been described by one respected writer as the need to determine whatever law remains operative throughout all change (Wöfflin 1950:17). It follows from the arguments contained in previous chapters that if such a law exists it must be biological, and it must have to do with changes in levels of conscious or unconscious experience of urgency in response to changing environmental conditions. That such a law must also relate to changes in the extent of expression of subjectivity or objectivity follows both from the APM-A synthesis and the facts of art history.

In Chapter 3 differences in levels of subjectivity and objectivity between artists and scientists were explained in APM-A terms. But obviously (and according to the APM-A model), artists also differ among themselves in this respect. What is more, in art-historical terms, both the extent to which individual expression occurs, and whether emotional expression predominates over respect for formal qualities or vice versa, are crucial variables. Periods are actually marked by direct reference to this factor; for example, German Expressionism, Bloomsbury Formalism, Classicism, and Romanticism.

The terms 'classicism' and 'romanticism' are actually headings under which all art – and artists – can be more or less loosely characterized and classified, as well as bearing reference to specific movements in art history. They are also concepts which can be understood in terms of objectivity and subjectivity and very easily related to the new dynamic model of style and the contrasting modes of processing on which it is based.

For instance, terms used by Kenneth Clark (1982:chap. 12) to make comparisons between classicism and romanticism bear an extremely strong relationship to concepts familiar from Chapters 3 and 4. He uses words such as 'trim', 'finite', 'consistent', and 'restrained' in description of classical art, while he talks about romantic art as being 'obsessed with the image of movement and escape' and as being 'sensuous' and 'rebellious'.

Wiedmann's discussion of romanticism comes even nearer to the model when he says of the late eighteenth-century Romantic movement:

Romantic art generally cannot be understood without taking account of this passionate involvement with change, process, force . . .

The Romantic's insatiable desire was to be fully and ecstatically alive to the point, paradoxically, of courting sickness, if not madness, for the sake of living more intensely.

. . . the tendency to follow spontaneously instinct, impulse, the force of passion, might be called Romantic vitalism.

(1979:13, 15)

211

However, just as the new model of style is a dynamic model which has been shown to represent a huge range of variability in both 'normal' and 'pathological' styles, a similar degree of variability more obviously exists in the arts. The classic–romantic dichotomy is not, therefore, simply being seen as a reflection of the exercise of objectivity or subjectivity, nor is it being suggested that classicism and romanticism are mutually exclusive. It has already been argued that one mode of processing never operates to the total exclusion of the other, however much it may seem to do so.

The line of argument is actually that classicism and romanticism are no less arbitrary categories than that of art itself – which is being seen to differ from non-art only according to the context in which it is placed and the mental set of the creator and/or spectator. Further, just as classicism and romanticism can be seen to coexist at various times in art history, so are they also sometimes evident within the same individual. For example, Kenneth Clark (1976:36) has said of the painter David that he 'tuned up each form to the concert pitch of the ideal'.

Kreitler and Kreitler (1972:29) use the phrase 'aesthetic distance' to describe a degree of detachment in the spectator of art, which they see as a characteristic which acts to restrain personal involvement 'beyond certain limits', which might otherwise 'impede' aesthetic experience. Within the new perspective this mix of 'involvement' and 'non-involvement', which is undoubtedly an aspect of aesthetic experience, is being viewed instead as a key variable in both the creator and spectator.

Wiedmann (1979:99) makes oblique reference to the possible variability of this 'mix' of objectivity and subjectivity in the creation and perception of art when he discusses the expressionist theory of art underlying the work of the Romantics. He criticizes the conventional view of them as expressing 'no more than a defiant subjectivism, a proud egoticism which recognised no authority beyond the creative self'. His own view of the expression of subjectivity by both the Romantics and the Expressionists[16] is of its merging 'in a mysterious way' with, and being inseparable from, the expression of objectivity in their 'desire to reach beyond the finite self': indicating that even some of the apparently most powerful expressions of subjectivity arise from some interest in objectivity. The APM-A view is that different mixes of involvement and non-involvement occur as an outcome of variability in SNS–PNS patterning, and that different levels and kinds of arousal in turn affect the extent to which symbolic threats and promises affect the organism and, therefore, susceptibility to aesthetic experience in general.[17]

The APM-A definition of aesthetic experience which arises therefore is as follows: the experience of pleasurable arousal and engagement with a stimulus or stimuli which promotes the perception of associations and relationships which are not necessarily relevant, obvious, consciously sought, or actually demanded, by either the state of the organism or current environmental conditions.

After having stressed that such experience may be more or less *obviously* subjective or objective and, in common with all other kinds of experience, always contains elements of both, the subjectivity–objectivity dimension is to be regarded as axiomatic to cultural change. Movement around and between these poles, it is being claimed, always accompanies change, but such movement is by no means random.

From this point of view, romanticism might be viewed as the subjective experience and/or expression of the objective, and classicism as the objective experience and/or expression of the subjective. In turn, the concept of aesthetic distance can be seen as arising from the fact that the specific act of engagement (sustained attention) essential to aesthetic experience is not actually demanded in order to fulfil particular survival needs.

The examples which follow are intended, on the one hand, to illustrate the observation that, in the most general terms, major stylistic changes during the last century and during this century have displayed a movement away from focus and control, through stages of increasing fragmentation, dislocation, and disorganization of both content and form;[18] and, on the other, to present a rationale for this which relates these changes to the physiological and psychological processes already described.

The intention is not by any means to suggest that there has been any simple or linear progression – or regression – of changes in form and content, nor is it to suggest that any very clear-cut or neat distinctions can be made between the complex and overlapping developments which have taken place. On the contrary, what follows is only one cross-section of particular cultural developments, viewed in a certain light, in an attempt to expose the most fundamental motivations of those who created the new styles, and of their spectators who – however indirectly or unintentionally – helped to establish them. In short, the aim is to consider alternative interpretations of major events in art history by referring to some alternative stylistic features.

For example, a very strong stylistic contrast can be perceived between the highly refuge-rich products of Victorian England and the generally much more prospect-rich products of twentieth-century Europe and America. When these factors are stood in the context of theory in which physical survival needs do not always dominate behaviour, such comparisons can be seen to be potentially very significant. This is especially so when the historical contexts themselves provide a contrast in relative dominances of physical or psychological stress. This is to say that, however intense were the threats posed by the Industrial Revolution and however harsh the conditions, sources of stress for the general population are readily identifiable as having had to do primarily with fear, and experience, of physical privations: of poverty, hunger, sickness, and death. Although anxieties will have been an obvious element of everyday life, they will have been specific (focused), and social enmeshment and physical contact with others will often have been all too obvious, providing, paradoxically, high levels of communication and social and physical 'feedback' and concomitant fulfilment of a variety of psychological needs (see Figures 4 and 5).

By contrast, in the second half of the twentieth century, while physical hardship in the western world is still more prevalent than generally acknowledged, vast numbers of people, if not on prescribed drugs to ameliorate the direct or indirect effects of psychological stress, are taking non-prescribed drugs or showing other signs of psychological unease.[19] Most relevantly, people very often profess not to *understand* their own self-destructive behaviours, or their depressions or (general) anxieties, and neither do family or friends when a person can be seen to 'have everything' – providing orientational needs are not taken into account.

It is not difficult to understand why psychological orientation (seen to be dependent on the fulfilment of psychological needs set out in Figure 4) should be more difficult to achieve during the current technological upheaval than formerly. It is necessary to take account only of *rates* of social and other change, alongside more obvious sources of orientational difficulties which arise from increase in levels of information to be processed and in the degree of specialist knowledge very often required to understand how even everyday items work. These and many other factors can be seen to contribute to increases in levels of general (unfocused) arousal and unconscious experience of threat.

Without attempting to define closely a law which seems to crave definition – a law not quite the same as 'the attraction of opposites', but which might be called the *law of external compensation* – it appears that we very often seek or create in the external world compensation for unconsciously perceived internal psychological and physiological de-ficiencies.[20] The theoretical position which has been defined, together with the evidence of art history, certainly support the idea that we seek and create external and sometimes symbolic 'prospects' and challenges under conditions of loss of internal focus or perceivable (psychological) prospects. Within the context of art history it is being suggested that preference for high prospect-dominance occurs under conditions of psychological disorientation and predominance of psychological over physical survival needs.

Conversely, under predominantly physical stress, when internal focus and psychological organization remain intact, perception and preferences are dominated by the seeking and/or creating of real or symbolic refuge; and when the organism is relatively physically and psychologically stable, preferences are more likely to be expressed for prospects and refuges in balance.

All that has been said above might suggest that a simple relationship obtains between classicism, objectivity, focus, and prospect-dominance on the one hand, and romanticism, subjectivity, and refuge-dominance on the other. After all, each of the first group has been related to either PNS dominance or PNS compensation, and each of the second to high SNS activity; and in many cases the juxtaposition would be quite valid. But it also has to be remembered that it was argued in the last chapter that a high degree of focus may derive from either a very relaxed *or* a highly stressed state, and corresponding differences in kinds of focus are apparent in the arts.

There is a kind of focus – clarity of form – which may be expressed in classicism or romanticism in which the concepts of prospect and refuge are both well-represented; and another, more evident in the classical mode, and seemingly symptomatic of very high psychological tension, in which refuge symbolism does not play an important part, if any at all. The romantic mode can also become less refuge-rich, but conscious concern with nature, the organic, mystery, emotional expression and concomitant inconsistencies[21] rather than consistencies ensures that it never becomes quite devoid of refuge symbolism in its formal qualities.

Before moving on to more systematic comparisons of style which will move across the model in the same order as the discussion of pathologies in the last chapter and show a similar pattern of regression, it is relevant to consider briefly some of the commonalities that Wiedmann (1979) perceived between the specific movements of Romanticism and twentieth-century Expressionism.

First, his descriptions of the characteristics of both the Romantics and the Expressionists are highly suggestive of high arousal and of SNS dominance, which makes them very easy to relate to the model – with the twentieth-century Expressionists occupying the more extreme position, of course. In addition to Clark's apt terminology quoted above, Wiedmann also refers to characteristics already associated with style in previous chapters. He refers to the Romantic need for 'motion' and 'constant mobility'. He says 'Setting everything in motion, the Romantics . . . could indeed nowhere find stability and peace' (1979:12). He also refers to the fact that they were 'intoxicated with unity'; to their desire for 'the synthesis of the arts'; 'their longing to hold and embrace the world'; and their concern with love. The relation to externalization, motor expression; scanning and holistic thinking, and high order (reassurance) needs, which have all been associated with high (SNS dominant) arousal, could hardly be more obvious.

Second, some of the characteristics Wiedmann describes are also symptomatic of stages of regression as they were defined in Figure 26. The quotation about Romantics paradoxically courting sickness is but one example. He makes references to their 'desolation and despair' and 'longing for immediacy' as well as to increase in dominance of unconscious processes: most significantly, he refers to the Expressionists' strong attraction to the primordial (see p. 217) which he says leaves a wide field for speculation and enquiry.

He rejects speculation that the work of the Expressionists, with its usually dramatic and apocalyptic form, may have been an expression of premonition of the First World War, on the grounds that no evidence exists in support of the notion of the artist as prophet or seer. Instead he suggests,

> Whenever old forms and symbols have become stale, when life has retreated to the surface of things, when man finds himself a stranger to his fellow men, to himself and to the universe in which he lives, a compelling urge drives him to seek out the chthonian, the primeval. Memories and instincts deeper than thought thrust him towards a chaos from which he hopes to wrest a new cosmos, a new sense of being and belonging.
>
> (1979:214)

In this passage the references to change from focus to scanning, 'when life has retreated to the surface of things'; to increase in orientation needs 'when man finds himself a stranger'; and to increase in dominance of unconscious processes, 'instincts deeper than thought' are slightly more oblique, but nevertheless apparent; but Wiedmann is offering what is merely a *description* of changes in psychological process, as explanation.

Conversely, the 'violence and fury' these painters created on canvas *can* be seen to have 'foreshadowed the fury and destruction of events to come' but not in a way which suggests that the artist is in any way a prophet of specific events. It has been argued, rather, that he is an *'anticipator'* and *highly susceptible to general arousal.* From this point of view, and given awareness among artists of growing political tensions and unconscious and/ or conscious reactions to them, violence, fury, and increasing primitiveness of style can be seen to be an outcome of organism–environment interaction consistent with APM-A theory.[22]

The regressive nature of Expressionist and other, more recent, art will be discussed again in other contexts; but whereas Wiedmann attributes 'imitation' of primitive forms to 'a return to mythic origins' which, he points out, can be observed sporadically throughout history and particularly during periods of cultural transition or when civilizations reach a marked degree of complexity, *urgency of execution* and *externalization of high levels of physical energy* are seen to offer a more likely explanation.

Figure 32   Emil Nolde: 'Candle Dancers'

© Nolde Stiftung 1989

Examples of the attraction to the primordial by German Expressionist painters described by Wiedmann. The quality of line and the shapes should be compared with those of Penck in his painting 'West' below.

Both the Expressionist work and that of Penck (1980) is high in dynamism and, at a physiognomic level, prospect and hazard symbolism; but the recent work is both more abstract and even lower in refuge symbolism.

The lack of refuge symbolism is attributable mainly to flatness (the two-, rather than three-dimensional quality), and the hazard symbolism to strong tonal contrast, angular shapes, and diagonals. In the Nolde, both hazard and prospect symbolism are also obvious in the content.

Figure 33   A. R. Penck: 'West'

217

5.3 Fears and phobias

Although different interpretations are being placed on specific developments in nineteenth- and twentieth-century art history from those of Wiedmann, for instance, his belief in the significance of cultural transition and high degrees of cultural complexity in the production of stylistic change is shared. This is because the most fundamental kinds of emotion – fear and anger – are being associated with the frustration of basic psychological needs seen as likely to occur under these conditions.

A very early connection between the emotion of fear and aesthetic experience was made by Edmund Burke (Boulton 1958). He arrived at his conclusions long before empirical findings about the limbic system or arousal could have guided his thinking into a more precise formulation than his 'philosophical enquiry' represents; but even without the advantage of the body of knowledge which exists two and a quarter centuries later his approach can be seen to have embodied fewer 'impediments to progress' than many since.

Burke associated experience of the sublime with the mechanisms of pain and fear and the perception of beauty with pleasure, which in turn he associated with sex (ibid.:57, 42).

Although empirical psychologists are unlikely to involve themselves with concepts quite as abstract as the 'sublime' and the 'beautiful', they have had a great deal to say about fear and sex, as well as other sources of unpleasantness and pleasantness, and in the last three decades specific connections have also been made between aesthetics and the mechanisms of arousal.

In his documentation of the interaction of some of the social, scientific, and cultural changes of the nineteenth century Klingender (1972:chap. 5) compares Burke's conclusions on the sublime and the beautiful, published in 1757, with those of Uvedale Price in *An Essay on the Picturesque*, first published in 1794. The latter was an attempt to hone theories of the picturesque conceived by the artist and traveller, the Reverend William Gilpin. Klingender (1972:73) makes the point that however persuasive Burke's arguments about the sublime and the beautiful were, it was not surprising that Gilpin and Price should soon need to add the 'picturesque' – the forerunner of the Romantic movement – to Burke's incomplete view of aesthetic experience.

He notes that Burke's concept of the beautiful is 'neat and smooth' and Gilpin's idea of the picturesque is 'rough and ragged'; but in fact Burke adds to the criteria of comparative smallness and smoothness others such as gently deviating lines, lightness, and delicacy (Boulton 1958:109–17). By contrast, he says of the sublime, 'All general privations are great, because they are all terrible.' He refers specifically to vacuity, darkness, solitude, and silence (ibid.:71): to conditions, it should be noted, which were associated two centuries later with the findings of arousal-producing sensory deprivation research as summarized by Zubek (1969).

Within the APM-A context, what Burke calls 'the experience of the sublime' can be viewed as having to do with feelings of arousal attributable to what has been called 'manageable threat', and what he calls 'the experience of the beautiful' as having to do with arousal deriving from the conscious or unconscious perception of identifiable promise.

Klingender expands his remarks about Gilpin's and Price's alternative ideas about the picturesque and the 'rough and ragged' by referring to Gilpin's advice to gardeners. It included hints to break the edges of a walk; to mark the garden well with tracks; and to scatter stones. Similarly, he offered advice to painters of landscape about the attractiveness of folded drapery and/or tattered rags if figures were to be introduced; the charm of ploughed fields; as well as castles, palaces, cottages, mills (especially when they were ancient or battered); and the attractiveness of such things as the intricacy of the wheels and woodwork of watermills (Klingender 1972:74).

The refuge-rich nature of both the forms and the recognizable imagery of these recommendations can hardly be missed, being full, as they are, of inconsistencies, recessions, hollows, shadows, and other potential 'hiding places'. The contrast of this with Burke's near obsession with threatening and promising *prospect* symbolism makes it even more impressive. More impressive still is the apparent need experienced by both Gilpin and Price to *compensate* the bias expressed by Burke. No wonder they perceived his omissions so clearly when their own bias, and needs, were diametrically opposed, in this respect.

The complementary nature of the contributions of Burke on the one hand, and Gilpin and Price on the other, is just as intriguing in the light of Berlyne's (1971:chaps. 11, 12) identification of complementary arousal-raising and arousal-modulating devices as it is in terms of the complementary nature of prospect–refuge theory. It is also interesting in this context that Greek forms were generally considered to be beautiful and Gothic forms picturesque, and that the former are typically prospect-rich and the latter refuge-rich.

The tension between the formal and the expressive, which the contrast between Greek and Gothic forms represents and which, with slightly different emphasis, is also that between the geometric and the organic, takes the discussion back to the highly significant, underlying, but many-faceted concepts of objectivity and subjectivity.

These key concepts actually provide discernible patterns within the tangle of nineteenth- and twentieth-century art history. They are like irregularly twisted pairs of contrasting threads moving closer together or further apart, and sometimes overlapping with other pairs of a more or less similar kind.

One example of this kind of contrast is provided by the different kinds of concern with realism characteristic of Victorian painting. One particularly striking form is that of the painters of the Pre-Raphaelite Brotherhood.[23] Their positive obsession with detail and truth to nature is epitomized in Millais's painting 'Ophelia', for which his model, Lizzie Siddell, was required to pose for hours lying in a bath of water with insufficient warmth from the candles 'heating' it to stop her catching pneumonia.

This was quite a different form of realism from that of another group, who dedicated themselves to the practice of a kind of 'social realism' with the intention of drawing attention to the misfortunes of the poor. They tackled subjects such as poverty, death, seduction, and deserted children, but as Christopher Wood points out (1976:17), the extent to which their themes were factual was limited by the social conventions and inhibitions of the time and the necessary 'liberal coating of sentiment or humour to sugar the pill'. But it was not their concern to reproduce accurate detail so much as to convey prevailing conditions and moods.

Gaunt describes the nineteenth century as a new age,

[having] come into being in the period of storm and stress – physical, emotional and ideological – marked by the end of the eighteenth century and the beginning of the nineteenth. It was shaped by war, by political and industrial revolution and revolutionary ideas, and by social change.

(1972:7)

The two different styles of painting in question can be seen to represent contrasting modes of 'coping and defending' against change. One, the Pre-Raphaelite mode, can be seen to be objective expressions of highly subjective interests, and a striving to reproduce accurately the minute details of often medieval subject matter; the other, to be subjective expressions of particular aspects of society. They are not such polar-extreme expressions of objectivity and subjectivity as those which produce classic or romantic forms, but represent different patternings ('mixes') of underlying processes.

Although the Pre-Raphaelites were involved in a rebellion against the academic establishment of the time, their work is also conventionally regarded as a 'retreat' from the worsening social conditions and unrest of the 1840s: a *retreat* to a world before the High Renaissance and away from stylistic conventions to a nostalgic, medieval world of myth and legend, brilliant colour, and incredibly detailed natural forms. The rationale of the Pre-Raphaelites may have included a rejection of schools and formulas, but their obsessiveness about 'truth to nature', involving an almost surreal degree of focus and sometimes farcical efforts to achieve it, amounted to

Figure 34 William Holman Hunt: 'The Hireling Shepherd' (Pre-Raphaelite)

Refuge symbolism dominates both content and form. In the content it is provided most obviously by the group of trees, the pose of the figures (and the lamb on the lap), folded drapery, and undulating landscape. In the form it is provided by overlapping shapes; a very strong, three-dimensional quality deriving from well-modelled natural forms, and both aerial and linear perspective; a generally stable composition of strong verticals and (predominantly) horizontals; and the extreme detail offering a very strong variety of tone and rich, deep textures.

Figure 35 Frank Holl: 'No Tidings from the Sea' (Social Realism)

Refuge dominance is again very obvious in both content and form. As well as there being partitioned spaces, huddled figures, and heavy shadows, there is also folded drapery and even the insides of shoes. The form of this picture also contains overlapping shapes, linear perspective (offering depth), and a very stable composition; and although there is relatively little fine detail, the looseness of the brushwork itself provides a certain depth of texture.

replacing one set of rules with another. All of this is consistent with characteristics associated with the left side of the model.

The alternative 'realistic' mode involved a *confrontation* with prevailing conditions rather than a retreat, and reflects characteristics associated with the other side of the model. Although quite energetic efforts were very often made to reconstruct elaborate scenarios in the studio, this was more in the interests of creating an atmosphere than creating facsimiles of specific objects. The aim was to reproduce the *general* tone of situations; and their style was, on the whole, much looser and freer than that of the painters of the Brotherhood. It was just as rich in refuge symbolism, but in a different way (see p. 222).

Differences between these two groups mirror differences concerning characteristics associated with approach and avoidance behaviours which have already been described in the previous two chapters, and which are observable again, in a much more obvious form, when the total impression of nineteenth-century art is viewed against developments since the turn of the century. By the latter half of the twentieth century the relative differences between objectivity and subjectivity actually diminish, as subjectivity of approach in the production of art in general becomes much more obvious and prevalent.

What can be observed indicates mass increase in general, unconscious, anticipatory arousal and a concomitant shift in tuning of APM-A processes: an observable shift in adaptation-level. The period under discussion ends, appropriately, with a movement euphemistically labelled 'Hot Art'[24]. It is irrational, saturated with emotion, makes frequent reference to biological functions, and has favourite motifs of dismembered nudes, vampires, skeletons, vultures, and a variety of other kinds of physical and biological debris.

5.4 Ways of seeing

Before looking at twentieth-century developments in more detail, mention should be made of some of the many other nineteenth-century conflicts and contrasts relevant to relating artistic style to the dynamic model. They are William Morris's Arts and Crafts Movement (Harrison 1981:13–14), instigated in response to his perception – and that of others – of the role of art and design in relation to the division of labour and the potentially degrading effects of the latter on both society and art; the conflict between the perceived 'morality' of Gothic forms as opposed to the 'paganism' of the classical Greek style (Pugin, first published 1841); and the conflict between narrative art and the English Art for Art's Sake Movement (Farr 1978:chap. 1) which produced the scandalous trial of Whistler vs. Ruskin in 1878, in which Whistler was awarded one farthing damages in compensation for Ruskin having accused him of 'flinging a pot of paint in the face of the public' (Gaunt 1945:80–96).

The lack of popular success of Morris's undertaking is conventionally attributed to its impracticality and the fact that hand-made objects could not compete in price with machine-made goods (Farr 1978:chap. 3); but this argument does not really stand up to scrutiny as an explanation of the difference between expressed public taste and that of Morris and his associates. If simplicity of form *had* been in tune with current taste, its machine production would have been even easier – and more profitable – than the production of the complicated style of goods which *were* machine-produced and sought after. It seems more likely that the accumulation of the 'overblown', the bizarre, the complicated, and the novel actually satisfied certain unconscious needs which have been discussed in full in Chapters 3 and 4.

The fact that the novelty and complexity in question took particular forms makes this even more likely. They were not typified by angularity, for instance. On the contrary, the mass-produced ornaments of the time were characterized by their roundness, by a certain sculptural quality within which there were very often quite deep hollows and niches which, when perceived physiognomically, were extraordinarily rich in refuge symbolism.

Similarly, although Greek forms were utilized throughout the nineteenth century, as Richard Jenkyns (1980) goes to some lengths to point out, it is also the case that the Victorians seem to have had some difficulty fitting the 'trim', 'finite', 'consistent', and 'restrained' forms of classicism into their scheme of things. Even the most objectively conceived forms were frequently contaminated with certain (subjectively conceived) extravagances in order to render them more acceptable – and more refuge-rich.

The sheer energy and ingenuity of the Victorians was nowhere better exemplified than in the contents of the Great Exhibition of 1851 (see Bibliography) which, as well as emphasizing the degree of flux taking place at the time, also served to highlight polarities in the kinds of response elicited by so much change. At the one extreme Prince Albert and his followers were extolling the virtues of competition and 'progress' for mankind, and at the other both Ruskin and Morris, among other distinguished members of the intelligentsia, anticipated its consequences as being an inevitable increase in materialistic values and the propagation of 'bad taste'.

For anyone whose first criteria of 'good taste' included fitness for purpose and simplicity of form there was plenty to worry about: Gothic bookcases; Egyptian-style steam-engines; a stove in the shape of a suit of armour; ingenious new uses for old materials, and elaborate uses for new ones such as gutta-percha (the PVC of the Victorian era, used to imitate other materials) and papier mâché. But inventive madness did not stop at understandable experimentation with new materials and new techniques. The general atmosphere of excitement led to the production of such things as a 'life-preserving portmanteau' which could be rowed if the need arose, and other items (significantly) *combining* features.[25] In addition to fairly moderate flights of fancy, such as a combined flower-stand and bird-cage, quite astonishing devices were exhibited: an alarm-bedstead, for instance, whose front legs folded underneath as the alarm went off in order for the sleeper to be thrust into a standing position, it was hoped, where a cold bath could be placed at choice.

The psychological processes underlying these kinds of bizarre elaborations have already been discussed in Chapter 4. They were defined as being common to both creatives and schizophrenics, and just as different levels and kinds of schizophrenia were referred to above, so can different levels and kinds of cognitive organization be identified from considering works of art. Art produced in the last two centuries is particularly rich in examples; but whereas even the most extreme imaginative leaps of the Victorians still remain at least rooted in the 'real' world, this is not true of the products of the twentieth century. These include examples which can be compared to the processes of both paranoid and non-paranoid schizophrenia (which display more and less cognitive organization respectively).

Prime examples of contrasting levels of cognitive organization are the movements of Dada, which became most clearly identifiable at the height of the First World War, and Surrealism, which appeared shortly afterwards and has continued to exist in some form ever since. Relevantly, Dada is regarded as having been more of a state of mind than a movement, and Surrealism more of a life-style – based on a belief in the importance of inexplicable coincidence (Osborne 1981:141, 529): and whereas the apparently less cognitively organized art form of Dada has no clearly definable boundaries, or beginning even, the tighter cognitive organization of the Surrealists is apparently reflected in the fact that it was originally also 'the most highly organized and tightly controlled of all of the artistic movements of the twentieth century' (ibid.:528). Maybe it is more than coincidence that one of Salvador Dali's best known paintings is called 'The Persistence of Memory'.

One of the conscious motivations for Dada was to show to the public the irrelevance of poetry and the plastic arts in what the Dadaists perceived to be a rotten, bourgeois society; and although the origins of its name (a French word meaning 'hobbyhorse') are still disputed, with some saying it was simply representative of childishness and foolery, a contemporary poet said it 'expresses the primitiveness, the beginning at zero, the new in our art' (Ades 1974:12).

Figure 36 Georg Grosz: 'Funeral Procession' (Dada)

In common with most Dada painting, this is very low in refuge symbolism but very high in prospect and hazard symbolism. The buildings provide both prospect and (weak) refuge symbolism and evidence of the concept of hazard is obvious in the content. The prospect and hazard symbolism are both reinforced in formal qualities by the strong diagonal lines, high tonal contrast and violent colour (black, red, and yellow). The painting is obviously highly dynamic and relatively abstract. Evidence of low cognitive organization – and motor control – is apparent in the lack of detail and recognizable imagery beyond the immediate foreground, and the relatively 'busy' composition.

226

Figure 37 Salvador Dali: 'Autumnal Cannibalism' (Surrealist)

© DEMART PRO ARTE BV 1989

The paintings of the Surrealists are as rich in their symbolic references to the concepts of prospect and hazard and as low in refuge symbolism as those of the Dadaists; but content and representational imagery (although it may not always be possible to name what is represented) play a more dominant role than form in this respect than for the Dadaists.

The 'symptoms' of Dada are similar to some of those manifest in recent Hot Art.[26] Both make frequent expressions of nihilism and violence and often refer to processes of decay and waste. For instance, the Dada manifesto of 1920 began,

TO THE PUBLIC
Before going down among you to pull out your decaying teeth, your running ears, your tongues full of sores.

227

Before breaking your putrid bones.

Before opening your cholera infested belly and taking out for use as fertilizer your too fatted liver, your ignoble spleen and your diabetic kidneys.

Before tearing out your ugly sexual organ, incontinent and slimy.

Before extinguishing your appetite for beauty . . .

(Ades 1974:3)

Dada was clearly identifiable on an international level – as Hot Art was at the time of writing – and as well as the movement 'borrowing' from other forms such as German Expressionism, one of its practitioners, Jean Arp, provided a strong link with the Surrealists through his experimentation with 'automatic' drawing.[27]

The fact that the Surrealists were influenced by Freud's *The Interpretation of Dreams*, published in 1900, is generally accepted, but the question of the reasons for their high degrees of susceptibility to that particular influence is never raised. The suggestion being made is that theirs is only the most direct and obvious expression of an increase in the dominance of unconscious processes which started long before their production of dream-like imagery; and that their particular susceptibility to influence by Freud nevertheless demanded patternings of orientation response capable of relatively more control of imagery and technique than that generally displayed by the Dadaists, for instance.

The general trend outside Surrealism shows a gradual loosening of form traceable back as far as the 'atmospheric' paintings of Turner, early in the nineteenth century, and evidence of increase in expression of limbic arousal can also be seen to exist in apparent changes in levels of motor expression. It moves from the gentle stroking of the canvas with a brush, through dabbing, slashing, cutting and pasting, splashing, and pouring, to the extremely sensual exercise of applying the paint with the whole naked and writhing person.[28]

The movements of sculptors have become even more gross, but then not quite as much motor control had been expected of their craft since ancient Greece. This physical expression has increased to the point recently where it has not been unusual for work to spread across acres of land demanding, presumably, hundreds of hours' walking, and sometimes climbing, in addition to the usual exigencies of making.[29]

At the leading edge of art history, as it were, evidence of increase in SNS activity in its creators – and presumably also in its spectators/ reinforcers – becomes more and more apparent as the nineteenth century wears on and as twentieth-century developments take place. But all the time, although the general tendency can be seen to be different kinds of move towards more and more extreme characteristics represented by the right side of the model, relatively cognitively organized, but nevertheless

Figure 38 Puvis de Chavannes: 'Poor Fisherman' (Symbolism)

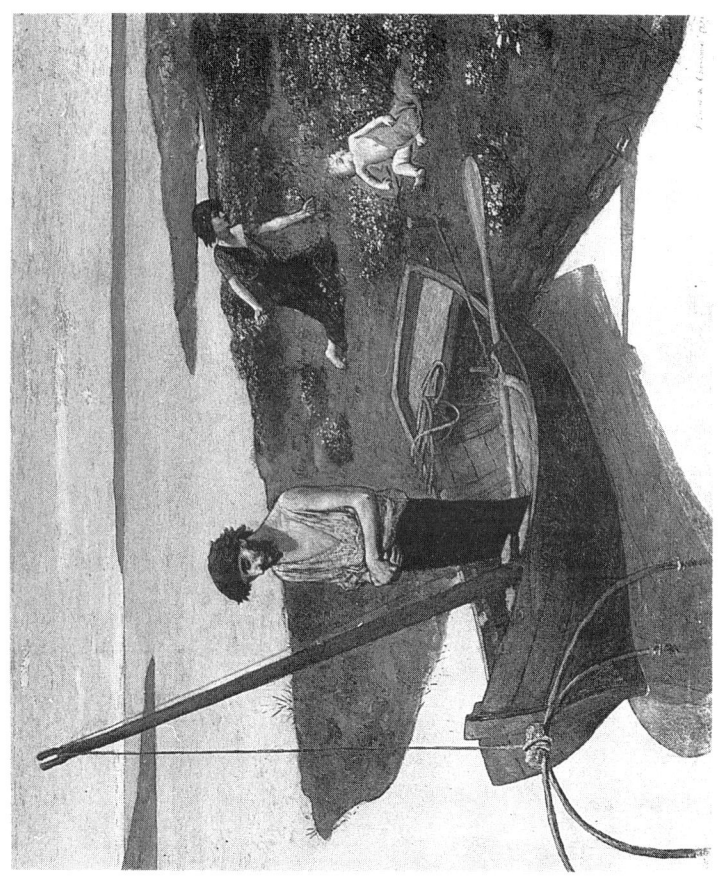

An example of a form of Symbolism in which content is composed of discrete entities and seen to reflect comparatively rigid perceptual and conceptual boundaries. It contains both prospect and refuge symbolism in content and form, but despite the strong diagonals in its composition it is still very low in dynamism and abstraction.

Figure 39   Gustave Moreau: 'Salome Dancing' (Symbolism)

The work of Moreau provides examples of the more diffuse style in which boundaries between shapes beyond the immediate foreground are not well-defined; and greater use of graduated tones and atmospheric effects provides much more refuge symbolism than the contrasting style typified by Puvis de Chavannes. By contrast, however, Moreau's work typically incorporates a high level of hazard symbolism: in this case in the use of very 'hot' colour (reds and oranges) and glinting textures.

Figure 40 Pablo Picasso: 'Seated Nude' (Cubism)

© DACS 1989

This picture offers an example of the highly fragmented and dislocated style of Analytical Cubism in which dynamism and abstraction are both obvious; prospect and hazard symbolism are high, but refuge symbolism low: tendencies being viewed as typical of twentieth-century art.

extreme modes – either with some figurative content, or displaying a 'hard-edge' technique or geometrical form – coexist with the much more loosely organized styles.

Sometimes complementary forms occur within the same movement. The Symbolist movement of the 1880s and 1890s provides one example, and Cubism, which is usually taken to have happened between 1907 and 1920, provides another.

The many diverse strands of Symbolism[30] are usually divided into French Symbolism and Pre-Raphaelite Symbolism, and it is the characteristically erotic and exotic French work which is expressed in two quite distinct ways. In the one form, which is strongly related to the later, relatively organized style of Surrealism, high focus and definition produce a relatively 'hard-edge' effect. In this mode objects and people are seen as wholly discrete entities with strong boundaries between them. The other style of Symbolism is diffuse, and atmospheric effects prevail.

In the case of Cubism the contrasting modes are not as obvious to the non-specialist, but their names are just as appropriate to the APM-A model as the terms 'discrete' and 'diffuse' used above. They are called 'analytic' and 'synthetic': all four concepts were associated with different degrees of urgency of processing in Chapter 3 and all were related to differences in breadth of perceptual and conceptual categories.

Analytic Cubism refers to a form which had to do chiefly with separateness and the breaking down of an image into fragments, while Synthetic Cubism was concerned primarily with wholeness. It started with a whole image, with which other ideas and/or materials were then merged or superimposed. In this example the same group of painters underwent a development from the Analytical to the Synthetic form.

Coincidental with these happenings in France, other more or less controlled styles were evolving in other parts of Europe. In England the relatively objective and analytical style of Bloomsbury Formalism was being promoted by Roger Fry and Clive Bell,[31] followed shortly afterwards in Holland by a movement of highly conscious objectivity, called De Stijl, founded in 1917 by Piet Mondrian.[32]

In strong contrast to these new ideas about what art should be at the turn of the century, in France the so-called 'wild and dangerous beasts' – the Fauvists – were doing moderately shocking things with colour; an art described particularly well as 'an art of maximum statement, [of] . . . crashing, undifferentiated oppositions of pure colour' (Russell 1981:54), and in Germany, even these excesses were surpassed shortly afterwards by the beginnings of Expressionism.

5.5 Deception and violence

Those who experienced the social and political 'storms and stresses' of the

Figure 41   Juan Gris: 'Violin and Fruit Dish' (Cubism)

An example of Synthetic Cubism in which rounder forms and overlapping shapes and textures provide marginally more refuge symbolism than in Analytical Cubism, but in which high levels of dynamism, abstraction, and prospect and hazard symbolism still prevail.

Figure 42   James Abbott McNeill Whistler: 'Nocturne in Blue and Gold'

Figure 43 Jackson Pollock: 'Number 23'

nineteenth century could hardly have anticipated the worse upheavals to come, or how the whole pace of life could change as a consequence of new forms of transport and communication. Neither could those who ridiculed and scorned Whistler's 'Nocturnes'[33] (see p. 234) as being not serious works of art have imagined the artistic revolution which was to follow his involvement in what amounted to a trial of 'Art for Art's Sake'; or that Ruskin's famous insult containing the phrase 'flinging a pot of paint' could ever bear reference to the acceptable form of artistic expression the New York Action Painters[34] made it into half a century later.

In the last chapter deception and violence were particularly strongly associated with the lower half of the APM-A model. Deception was discussed in relation to both low levels of both physical *and* mental energy in the one case, and to high levels of predominantly physical energy in the other. In the first case, deception was discussed as an incidental effect of a very simple, pragmatic, but highly controlled mode of coping and defending, and in the latter, as a quite different, very *un*controlled form of pragmatism.

As evident creativity has been defined as requiring relatively high levels of mental *and* physical energy associated with the top right-hand (E_2) quadrant of the model, in the light of analysis offered in Chapters 3 and 4 the fact that Gombrich (1977) has devoted a book to arguing that all art is illusion (with the implication that artists are primarily concerned with deception) may seem anomalous. In pursuing his argument, Gombrich rejects the common conception of the artist possessing an 'innocent eye' (sometimes called a 'naked eye') which enables him to bring 'fresh vision' to bear. He argues that the innocent eye is a myth, and he does this on the perfectly reasonable grounds that all seeing involves knowing. On these grounds he concludes that the artist can only 'make' and 'match', that is, manipulate clues until resemblances occur. However, striving to match reality – or an abstract idea – still requires active exploration in order to identify essential features; and while it is likely to be a misconception that the artist has to *rid* himself of knowledge in order to see 'innocently', this is not to say that the artist's 'innocence' is non-existent. It can simply imply that his or her perceptions are less susceptible to habit than those of others (as in fact has been argued as being the case for externalizers).

The APM-A analysis suggests that the reason why the artist is constantly confronted with conscious decision making: decisions to do with what should be emphasized, where best to locate a focal point, or which elements of his extremely arbitrary medium are more or less important, derives not from less, but from more – unresolved and fluid – 'knowledge'. This strong awareness of alternatives combined with a certain spontaneity of expression is very likely to be perceived by those with more rigid

Figure 44   Depictions of violence by Goya

Francisco Goya: 'What more can be done?' (1810–20)

Francisco Goya: 'This is worse' (1810–20)

perceptual and conceptual boundaries as a kind of innocence.

To return to the urgency-of-processing argument: the archetypal artist can be seen to be less likely to assimilate his surroundings in terms of conventional meanings. In part this is because of greater awareness of background 'noise',[35] as it were, and in part because of lower conditionability. For the highly SNS-dominant type of artist, in common with the schizophrenic, the 'real' and the 'unreal' are likely to be much less easily distinguishable. Perceptions are likely not to be confined to the same 'coded' messages perceived by others. In perceiving more environmental information, rather than less, and having to make more choices between alternatives, his perceptions may at times contain what are considered to be essential features – the essence – and at other times be apparently very remote from the actual precipitating stimuli.

The history of modern art is often regarded as the history of the imagination, but in our context this idea takes on a different shade of meaning as it becomes possible to identify a similar shift from interest in the concrete to interest in the abstract to that which has already been set out in Figure 3.

From the new position it is also possible to see the history of art as a history of motor expression (see p. 35) and of relative degrees of control demanded of, and exercised by, the artist.

Violence has always been expressed in the arts, and it would be a difficult, if not impossible, argument to sustain to say that the depiction of violence has become more explicit during the nineteenth and twentieth centuries. For example, it would be difficult to imagine more explicit representations of violence than some of Goya's pictures of physical mutilation (see p. 237). To argue that the depiction of violence has become more widespread would be much easier – to which the neologism 'video-nasty' offers some testimony; but the argument to be undertaken, that violence has steadily become part of the form as well as the content of art, is relatively simple.

This is not to suggest that every development towards freer motor expression has had to do with the expression of violence. On the contrary, the pointillism[36] of Seurat, for instance, was a highly controlled and relatively gentle form of dabbing rather than stroking of the brush, in celebration of sheer pleasure. The suggestion which is being made is that physiognomically expressed violence in the arts has actually occurred most obviously at fairly specific times during this century, and usually during periods of rapid technological change and/or high political and economic tension.

Most strikingly, the years immediately following the first powered flight (1903) and into the First World War were years of turbulence in art. Starting with and including the developments in Europe mentioned above, these events coincided with more general upheaval and revolutionary change in the form as well as the content of the arts than either before or since. Further, the kinds of attention, perception, memory, and motor activity reflected in the major styles of the time are suggestive of particularly high levels of SNS activity.

Figure 45 Christopher Nevinson: 'The Arrival' (Futurism)

Figure 46 Wyndham Lewis: 'Composition' (Vorticism)

Major art styles became more subjective, more spontaneous and more primitive in colour and line. Increase in dominance of unconscious processing is evidenced in less dependence on the observation of detail or accurate memory; distortion of imagery; the depiction of irrational associations; and lessening of motor control.

Both Dada and German Expressionism are prime examples of the kind of loosening in style in question; but it can be argued that Dada, at its height during the First World War, manifested the more psychologically sinister symptom of withdrawal of the kind described in Chapter 4 (4.3). It was nihilistic as well as violent. Ades quotes from the diary of Hugo Ball, one of the movement's poet members,

> What we call Dada is a harlequinade made of nothingness in which all higher questions are involved, a gladiator's gesture, a play with shabby debris, an execution of postured morality and plenitude.
>
> (1974:5)

It actually stood for the repudiation and abolition of art itself.

Just a little earlier (1913) the term 'Vorticism' was coined by Ezra Pound, and applied to the work of a group of English painters led by Wyndham Lewis, who broke away from the Bloomsbury Formalists. Their work was both the first move towards abstract art in England and, physiognomically, some of the most violent in Europe.

They were strongly influenced by the earlier Italian social and cultural movement of Futurism (which also influenced German Expressionism to some extent). The 'violently revolutionary art' of the Futurists was intended to 'destroy the cult of the past' (Wees 1972:12). But despite violent intentions expressed in their manifesto with 'We wish to glorify War – the only health giver of the world' and 'We shall sing the love of danger, the habit of energy and boldness' (ibid.:15, 88), its rationale included the exaltation of modernity. This was symbolized by the steam-engine, the motor car, and the aeroplane and implicit ideas of motion and speed, so that the recognizable imagery of Futurism was mostly non-violent, unlike its physiognomy; but whereas many round forms were still a feature of Futurism, they are much less evident in Vorticism (see pp. 239–40).

Vorticism was characterized by the juxtaposition of abstract and mostly angular geometrical shapes, apparently as expressions of sheer physical energy and violence *per se*. The fact that the shapes used by the Vorticists were extremely angular might be taken as additional evidence for a relationship between *angularity* and *urgency*. An example of this association is the simple exercise of drawing a wavy line composed of well-rounded forms and then observing what happens when the exercise is performed at speed.

Wees quotes various comments about the general mood just before the war and then adds his own: 'There was a dynamism in the air fraught with a sense of dire things to come'; 'Long before there was any shadow of war,

I remember feeling . . . that something *had* to happen'; 'The world, I think, was mad then.'

> The 'very militant years' of 1910–14 were the germinating period of Vorticism, and the last summer produced the movement in full bloom. Declaring, 'The artist of the modern movement is a savage', the Vorticists appeared at exactly the right moment. They epitomised the times in the cover of their magazine: a huge black 'BLAST' on an electric, pinkish, purple background. Because of the violence and the noise, few people noticed at the time that the Vorticist movement also gave to the times an aesthetic and a body of painting, sculpture and writing that transformed violence into art.
>
> (Wees 1972:16)

The physiognomy of Vorticist painting and sculpture does indeed suggest the transformation of very high anticipatory arousal and accompanying high levels of predominantly physical energy into art. It is also relevant that members of the Italian movement, which extended such wide influence, were anticipators to the extent of actually labelling themselves 'Futurists'. They were also apparently as addicted to change, motion, and other kinds of risky pursuits, as individuals defined as experiencing excessively high anticipatory arousal in the last chapter.

The increasing absence of refuge symbolism in the paintings of the German Expressionists, the Futurists, the Dadaists, and, most obviously, the Vorticists, began a trend which has been continued in a number of different forms. These can be placed under the broad headings of geometrical abstract art and non-geometrical abstract art. Under the non-geometrical heading it is possible to place the biomorphic imagery[37] of Surrealism, which spanned the crucial years between 1918 and 1939 – as a formal movement – and which, as well as being prospect- rather than refuge-dominant, is extremely rich in hazard symbolism. While geometrical abstract art includes De Stijl and Russian Constructivism,[38] which appeared at the end of the 1914–18 war, both were major precursors of American Abstract Expressionism of the 1950s and 1960s, whose particular significance to this book is that it included the phenomenon of Minimalism.

The phenomenon itself was not new. It had appeared under a different name and a different rationale in the expressive output of one painter, at a much earlier stage. Colour, line, and content practically disappeared from painting for the first time when the Constructivist, Malevich, exhibited 'White Square on a White Ground' in 1918, the year after the Russian Revolution: it was one of his 'White on White' series of Suprematist compositions of 1917–18.

In the 1960s, however, Minimalism became widespread. In common with most terms which describe art movements the meaning of the term is very broad, but it refers chiefly to the exercise of minimal 'art-work', which mostly also implied minimality of content so that it could be given an alternative name of 'the blank canvas syndrome'. It is pertinent that Edward Lucie-Smith (1980:20) on Minimalism of the 1960s and 1970s makes the point that although it is generally called avant-garde it is actually 'deeply conservative'.

The same can, of course, be said of the De Stijl movement which was taking place in Holland at the same time as Malevich's Suprematism; but it was less extreme: it retained more content and it was more stable (see pp. 244–5).

This in itself is significant because both Mondrian and Malevich were seeking pure, ultimate forms but from polar-extreme positions. Mondrian's expressed aim in De Stijl was to 'create as objective as possible representation of forms and relations. Such work can never be empty because the opposition of its constructive elements and its execution arouse emotion' (Herbert 1964:116). Malevich, whose canvases became devoid of refuge symbolism, and almost devoid of prospect and hazard symbolism at the same time, writes,

> Under Suprematism I understand the supremacy of pure feeling in creative art.
>
> Objectivity, in itself, is meaningless to him [the artist]; the concepts of the conscious mind are worthless.
>
> Feeling is the determining factor . . . and thus art arrives at non-objective representation – at Suprematism.
>
> It reaches a 'desert' in which nothing can be perceived but feeling.
>
> (Ibid.:93, 94)

He goes on to make reference to the perceptions of others of what he was actually producing. This also relates very nicely to the next point to be made. It makes indirect reference to processes which are being seen to underlie his rationale: 'Yet the general public saw in the non-objectivity of the representation the demise of art and failed to grasp the evident fact that feeling had here assumed external form' (ibid.:96).

Edward Lucie-Smith's conclusion about the conservative nature of Minimalism is wholly consistent with the interpretation which arises from the APM-A context. Whereas Dada was a conscious expression of nihilism, the phenomenon of Minimalism is being viewed as an example of unconscious expression of hopelessness and helplessness, and evidence of PNS over-compensation of the kind referred to in the last chapter (4.3), in which prospects are no longer perceived and neither they, nor refuges, are any longer sought.

In what was certainly the first, and is probably still the only, attempt to overview what amounts to a vast range of extremism expressed in the art

Figure 47   Kasimir Malevich: 'Suprematist Painting. Yellow Parallelogram on White Background'

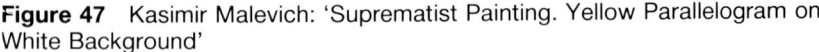

Figure 48   Piet Mondrian: 'Composition with Red, Yellow and Blue' (De Stijl)

of the 1970s, and in addition to using headings such as abstraction, illusionary art, figurative art, and various forms of minimalism, Lucie-Smith's (1980) classifications extend to erotic heterosexual, erotic feminist, kinky, homo-erotic, happenings, absurd architecture, absurd machines, new technology, and cultural colonialism.

What he actually describes as typifying recent art, of course, together with the contents of the exhibition of 'New Art at the Tate' to which the critic Marina Vaizey (1983) applied the terms 'fearsome', 'crazy', 'powerful', and 'nightmare', among others, is a wider range of symptoms of limbic

245

Figure 49 Robert Longo: 'Sword of the Pig'

Figure 50 Joseph Beuys: 'Fat Battery'

Figure 51 R. B. Kitaj: 'The Rise of Fascism'

Figure 52 Barry Flanagan: 'A Aing I Guiaa'

arousal than have ever coexisted in art before. Michael Compton, who prepared the New Art exhibition, perceived it as holding 'Qualities of deadpan wit and irony . . . alongside extreme and direct expressions of sexuality, anxiety, hostility and violence and all that is most disturbing'

Figure 53 Claes Oldenburg: 'Soft Drainpipe, Blue (Cool) Version'

(1983:17). He and Alan Bowness, the gallery's Director, along with critics, nevertheless see current trends as positive and welcome, and in the case of Bowness, as 'despite the economic climate . . . an exciting moment' (1983:6). Critics and artists alike may disagree about the application of any of these specific terms to the accompanying illustrations, but collectively they provide some examples of the kind of descriptions offered by Edward Lucie-Smith, Marina Vaizey, and Michael Compton.

Attention has already been drawn to the powerful role of perceptual defence, and the likelihood of it remaining more intact among 'spectators' than 'creators'. In this case, perhaps it is an overwhelming emotion of relief that art is still perceivably alive and kicking, despite the many expressed fears to the contrary, which apparently obscures its chilling physiognomic messages in *response to,* not *despite,* our social, economic, and political environment.

5.6 Sensation seeking

All of the discussion in this chapter so far has concerned the artist's special sensitivity to change and different levels and kinds of response to more or less disorientating experience. It has also been about the fact that artistic style, embodied in products of behaviour, is just as dependent on relative urgency of processing, levels of mental and physical energy, and concomitant rigidity or fluidity of perceptual and conceptual boundaries (according to a focus–scan–focus inverted U-shaped curve – see pp. 128–9) as are 'normal' and 'abnormal' individual styles. Additionally, it has been claimed that the art product also offers a kind of barometer of levels and kinds of imbalance of SNS–PNS activity in its physiognomy, particularly in its expressions of need for predominantly prospect or refuge symbolism. It can also be seen as a barometer in its reflection of sensation-seeking behaviour (see section 4.5).

The major difference between creators and spectators is being seen to be the same as the major difference between any individuals or groups of individuals: difference in needs. At the most fundamental level the difference between creators and spectators is being seen as the greater need for expression in the former; but it is not being suggested that this is a simple difference. Both creating and spectating are actually always composed of complex interactions of the perception of arousal-raising and arousal-moderating stimuli and activity, whatever the total outcome of either kind of experience may be. Although the *prime* motivations of creators and spectators may be complementary – to express mental and physical energies and to gain stimulation respectively – the experiences of making and perceiving art are seen to be composed of micro interactions of excitements and relaxation similar to those described earlier as being essential to any pleasurable activity or experience.

Art is, however, one of the pursuits more obviously concerned with sensations and sensuality, and its degree of concern with sensation

251

Figure 54 Janis Kounellis: Untitled

Figure 55   Guiseppe Penone: 'Breath'

Figure 56 John Walker: Untitled

Figure 57 Georg Baselitz: 'Adieu'

Figure 58 Stephen Cox: 'Gethsemane'

provides yet another indicator of different levels of limbic dominance, particularly in the contrast between the relatively moderate sensation-seeking motivations evident in nineteenth-century art and the comparative risk-taking apparent in more recent art.

One of the most obvious examples of what can be regarded as sensation-seeking behaviour in the visual arts in the last century exists in the prurient imagery created by William Etty under the guise of neoclassicism. The inclusion of corset marks on the thighs of his models, and other less than 'ideal' details, was hardly consistent with ideas of classical restraint. Most other examples are also fairly obvious and sexual, and neoclassicism in particular became a vehicle for Victorian eroticism, which included the photography of the 'naughty nineties'. This was regarded as an aspect of *fin de siècle* decadence, epitomized in the work of Aubrey Beardsley, who was one of the originators of Art Nouveau.[39]

Gaunt says of Beardsley's work:

The decadent lines were decadent in that they formed an elaborate and sterile system, as if of symbols whose meaning and purpose had ceased to exist or were profoundly hidden. They were decadent in another sense: that is they were full of troublesome suggestions of the sub-world of vice, of exhaustion and excess. It was an inner existence that Beardsley had put down on paper, of sexual images and fantastic literary reveries. He had a sort of innocent familiarity with evil, he communed with the leering dwarfs, the bloated epicene figures that peopled the depraved landscapes and grotesque interiors designed by his pen, as a child might talk with fairies. He invented a mythology which could only be explained by that other mythology of modern times – psycho-analysis.

(1945:139)

He makes the following comments about the Aesthetic movement (otherwise known as the Art for Art's Sake movement), which include incidental references to the fascination of juxtaposed threats and promises (see section 1.3), and the greater obviousness of the inclusion of threatening imagery at the time:

What was gross and vile as well as what was savage and barbarous might be made to yield its quota of beauty: and any means were justified in achieving that result. There was even a sort of religious exaltation in choosing the necessary martyrdom of vice, a saintly courage in exploring sin, a religious belief implicit in the defiance of religious rule.

The craving for sensation, the fastidious and patrician research for strange refinement, the jealous cultivation of art as a thing removed

from the common affairs of men constituted the prevailing
atmosphere.

(Ibid.:12, 16)

Art Nouveau was but one aspect of the Aesthetic Movement. French
Symbolism, mentioned above, which occasionally 'borrowed' the sensuous
flowing lines of Art Nouveau, was another. Part of the extreme relevance
of Symbolism to this chapter lies in the fact that its most obvious feature
– when viewed from within the APM-A perspective and in addition to its
two distinct forms discussed above – is the variety of ways in which it
combines very obvious and concrete threats and promises in its content,
and abstract ones in its form. One of its characteristics is its frequent
reference to the *femme-fatale* image. No combination of threat and
promise could be more obvious than in the notion of the 'deadly woman':
besides the many depictions of Delilah and Salome, danger and beauty are
combined in the form of 'she-monsters' or cruel sphinxes and images of
beautiful women with knives, snakes, or other dangerous animals, or in
hazard-rich landscapes.

Philippe Jullian says of Gustave Moreau's work,

Moreau gives birth to an endless procession of treacherous queens,
excessively beautiful martyrs and gilded Gods.

(1973:37)

On Symbolist art in general he says,

Angels – there were hosts of them for they represented 'souls', a role
which explains the frequent ambiguity of their smiles, the equivocal
swelling of their hips. Many Symbolists preferred the supernatural to the
divine; with the Decadent Movement, fairies also invaded the studios
either in medieval disguise . . . , or ready for dinner at Maxim's . . .
There were the disturbing sorceresses of Levy-Dhurmer and the ghouls
of Lenoir.

(Ibid.:49)

At a physiognomic level combinations of threats and promises are fairly
obvious in the Symbolists' use of colour, line, tone, texture, and shape.
Obvious examples are their frequent juxtapositions of brilliant reds and
blues, and the heightening of the effect of red by placing it next to its
complementary, green.[40] Other devices include high contrast created by
painting hard, smooth textures, glinting out of diffuse backgrounds, and
brilliant lights puncturing dark shadows.

During the 1880s the cultivation of the senses became such a conscious
pursuit that it produced a phenomenon which became known as 'synaesthesia'. Attempts were made to develop means of alerting all of the

Figure 59 Herbert James Draper: 'Ulysses and the Sirens' (Neoclassicism)

Very obvious combinations of symbolic threats and promises and evidence of the concepts of refuge, prospect, and hazard are all conveyed by the content, and echoed in the form, of this picture.

senses at once, and these led to claims of being able to taste or smell colour, for instance.

There are kinds of 'synaesthesia' apparent in the 1980s: for example, the railway-train passenger looking out of the window, wearing headphones, and chewing or smoking and drinking at the same time so that stimuli are impinging on all of the senses at once. The popularity of the Sony-'Walkman' which allows the brain to be bombarded with aural stimuli while walking out of doors – or cycling, to add to the risks – is surely also evidence of heightened sensory needs: but the prime example is the 'Pop scene' itself.

Formerly, this simply referred to popular music and dance, but during

Figure 60 Studio competition: book covers, 1898 (Art Nouveau)

Reproduced from *Art Nouveau* by A. Melvin, Academy Editions, London.
Strong refuge symbolism is conveyed mainly in the formal qualities of the designs.

the last decade or so it has become a much more interactive form. It has become a powerfully visual as well as aural phenomenon; it demands a high degree of novelty in the images of its participants, and gross forms of motor expression; and as the Pop scene grows older, so do its participants. It is no longer a pursuit of the very young only. It holds much more widespread appeal.

However, to return briefly to changes nearer the turn of the century, and to a gradual change in the form of Art Nouveau, Bevis Hillier says, 'The new masculinity, which was partly a reaction against 1890s "decadence", had a bracing effect on the decorative arts. The old, sinuous "curvilinear" Art Nouveau was superseded during this decade by a new "rectilinear" Art Nouveau' (1983:44). Hillier perceives this 'new masculinity' as having emanated from the jingoism of the time, the 'Edwardian code of honour', the Boy Scout movement, and the activities of the suffragettes, but masculinity has already been defined as a hormonal condition and related to other matters of individual style for which explanation has already been offered (pp. 112–13), and changes from round to angular forms have already been seen to be part of a phenomenon affecting parts of Europe untouched by any of the influences Hillier mentions, other than jingoism.

The changes Hillier describes eventually produced the extremely widespread applied art form of Art Deco, and whereas up to now examples of important changes in style have been culled mainly from the fine arts, or so-called High Art, the applied arts can no longer be ignored. Since the Arts and Crafts movement of the 1860s, the proliferation of Guilds and Associations which accompanied it, the setting up of the provincial Colleges of Art and Crafts, and the spread of mass production, more general aspects of art and design have become highly significant to expressions of changing 'tastes'.

Art Deco, which Hillier (ibid.:83) describes as a 'promiscuously eclectic style', actually appeared as an identifiably new style in the mid-1920s bearing influences as far-flung as 'mock-Egyptian exoticism', the Russian Ballet, pre-Columbian and other American Indian art, and African tribal art; all of which contributed to the net effect of extreme angularity. Its strong geometrical forms are perhaps best evoked by reference to the fan-shaped mirrors of the 1930s and 1940s, or the ubiquitous, and very Egyptian sun-ray motif, apparently perceived to be most suitable to the design of wireless cases and glass front-doors.

By the mid-1930s and up to the Second World War Art Deco developed to a stage at which its prospect-rich physiognomy can be very easily related to the concepts of sensation seeking and the wilful exposure to risk. Its angularity became dominated by diagonals, or very steep curves of different sizes linked together, stepped shapes, and strident colours. It usually included a garish orange, or red and black (which were,

Figure 61 Oliver Bernard: Prismatic entrance to the Strand Palace Hotel, London (Art Deco)

incidentally, the colours used by Hitler at the Nuremberg rallies, and also fashionable at the time of writing this book) and, for the first time, asymmetry.

The 'riskiness' being attributed to Art Deco is particularly well exemplified in the popular porcelain or bronze figurine of the time. This was usually a scantily and/or glamorously clad female in shiny silk or satin wearing *one* glove or *one* stocking and posed in some kind of 'impossible' position, on one toe, or leaning at a precarious angle, and always poised for action of one kind or another. The style was obviously syncopated and 'jazzy', expressing what seems to have been an almost irresistible urge to interrupt the continuity of forms and shapes, reminiscent (relevantly) of the outcome of Eysenck's perseverance tests among extraverts. It was essentially daring. Everything seemed to be at an angle, including hats and

Figure 62   Bridget Riley: 'Arround' (Op Art)

Figure 63   Richard Long: 'A Line in Bolivia, Kicked Stones' (2nd version)

hemlines. Similarly, the physiognomy of the fabrics which were used were extremely rich in hazard symbolism; either high contrast and shiny, or bearing motifs like lightning flashes, other 'broken' forms, or 'dazzle'.

Interestingly, Art Deco has never really gone away. It persisted in more utilitarian forms into the 1940s, gave way to the so-called 'Contemporary' style of the fifties, after which the swirling forms of Art Nouveau re-emerged with 'satanism' and the birth of the 'drug scene' in the sixties, only to turn back into an Art Deco revival in the seventies. Its unique and significant feature of marked asymmetry has recently returned in the form of lop-sided hair styles, the single ear-ring, odd coloured sleeves, and the deliberate wearing of odd socks.

Meanwhile, back in fine art, the brash forms of Pop Art of the sixties gave way to Body Art and Performance Art (hardly distinguishable from drama); Bridget Riley dazzled us with Op Art (see p. 263); difficulty was experienced in separating painting from sculpture; some thought painting was dead; and the making of sculpture sometimes became difficult to distinguish from a geological field trip (see p. 263). There was Conceptual Art, Theoretical Art, and Photo Realism – and all before Edward Lucie-Smith's amazing catalogue of art in the seventies.

On the Pop scene stars apparently named after bodily functions, effluent, and indictable offences, such as Dick Vomit, Johnny Rotten, and Sid Vicious, heralded the arrival of Punk. The relationship of Punk to Hot Art (see Figures 49–58) could be appreciated fully only by witnessing how the gallery visitor with pale yellow hair, white face, black lips, black cross in one ear, perhaps wearing a short black shiny skirt and black stockings with irregularly shaped large holes in them, and pointed shoes, merged into the high-contrast, nuclear-flash, ghoulish backgrounds of the pictures on display. The whole ethos, which could be called 'destructivism', could also be experienced in only slightly different but 'synaesthetic' form on a regular basis on television pop-video programmes, during which most of the emblems of Symbolism, Futurism, Vorticism, Dada, Surrealism, Art Deco, and Hot Art can still occasionally be experienced at once.

Whereas earlier in the century there was a move from refuge-rich curves to prospect- and hazard-rich angularity, and violence entered the physiognomy of the visual arts, in recent years, with a return to more figurative art, violence has returned to the content and remains in the form.

There is another phenomenon which is highly relevant to an endocrinological model which takes account of research suggesting that the female of the species is more prone to fear, and the male to anger/aggression. This is the phenomenon of 'unisex', epitomized in a figure of popular culture known as Boy George. If it is accepted that adaptational adjustments in tuning to change create changes in patternings of hormonal release, and that release of adrenalin and noradrenalin are not completely independent however much the one may predominate over the other, it follows that extreme polarity between the sexes should also diminish as secretion levels rise.

Earlier in the century there were trends which could be associated with masculinity which Hillier describes above, and in the 1930s and 1940s strong angularity entered female fashion; and although women continue to 'borrow' forms of dress traditionally regarded as male and seek male privileges, the current trend is not only for those males not belonging to any of the recognized 'tribal groups' to 'borrow' more colourful and draped styles from female fashion, but for this to be taking place against a backcloth of escalation in female violence.[41]

On the one hand, the physiognomic messages given out by 'punks', 'skinheads', and 'bikers' alike were all highly aggressive, but the aggressiveness of punks was far more confined to form than, for example, the obvious functional associations to be made with large boots – all the better for kicking with – and difficult-to-hold smooth heads; their spiky hair, pointed toes, and black, yellow, and red colour schemes offered the most powerful example of human beings giving out biological messages of aggressive display.

On the other hand, there are other indications of breaking down of boundaries, fusion, and synthesis, associated with the upper half of the model. These include the increasing tendency towards dialectic thinking and interdisciplinarity referred to by Crook (1980) and a decreasing difference between so-called 'High Art' and 'kitsch' (popular art) which Waldemar Januszczak (1985) found particularly striking at the 1985 International Contemporary Art Fair.

5.7 Disorientation and breakdown

It is hardly surprising that even in 1967 Morse Peckham should have come to the conclusion that art is about disorder, not unity, as is commonly believed. He actually concluded that its prime function is to expose man to the experience of disorientation in protected situations. He says,

> Man desires above all a predictable and ordered world, a world to which he is oriented, and this is the motivation behind the role of the scientist. But because man desires such a world so passionately, he is very much inclined to ignore anything that intimates that he does not have it. And to anything that disorients him, anything that requires him to experience cognitive tension he ascribes negative value. Only in protected situations, characterised by high walls of psychic insulation, can he afford to let himself be aware of the disparity

between his interests, that is, his expectancy or set or orientation, and the data his interaction with the environment actually produces.

(1967:313)

However, there are two sentiments expressed in this statement which require comment. If Peckham's first sentence implies that the capacity to offer prediction and orientation is the sole prerogative of the scientists, this is certainly not in line with APM-A theory (see Chapter 3). Second, it is disputed that negative value is necessarily ascribed to anything which disorientates, as people clearly enjoy engaging in a wide range of disorientating experiences to the extent of creating social problems.

Although Peckham deals with some of the same concepts dealt with in this book – for example, energy, orientation, and style – the conclusions he draws are rather different. For instance, he sees orientation as deriving solely from the process of acculturation. The other important difference is just as fundamental. Although Peckham has usefully drawn attention to the fact that art is not only about unity, neither is it simply about disorder; and although it does not necessarily provide orientation for the spectator, the motivations for its production *are* being seen as orientational. It has proved adaptive because it provides orientation – and disorientation – in a number of different ways which are more complicated than merely furnishing reaffirming and reassuring pictures of the world and its belief systems, as it did in the past.

One of a number of problems with Peckham's approach is that he fails to account for acceleration in changes in style, and the only explanation offered for the move towards abstraction is that since the function of art changed in the nineteenth century the artist has been free to explore the medium itself, rather than produce what he calls 'iconicity'.[42] This is a fairly conventional argument, but it does not explain the 'blank canvas syndrome', for instance, or the recent return to more figurative content.

In Peckham's view the *role* of the artist assumes greatest importance. The demands made on the artist by the public are seen to promote change (ibid.:261). Not only does this imply that the behaviour of people notorious for their disinclination to conform is controlled by others, it also ignores the frequent expressions of contempt expressed by gallery visitors, as well as the greater number who stay away, for most of what is new in art.

In fact, Peckham conceives of a four-faced pyramid with art on one face and scientists, philosophers, and 'valuators' (spectators and critics) occupying the other three (ibid.:121); so that changes in art derive, apparently passively, from changes in the other fields.

This is actually one of a group of favoured kinds of explanation prevalent in art history. There appear to be three main kinds. There is the 'cross-fertilization' type of explanation of which Peckham's is an example, and which is generally safest as there is obviously always 'evidence'; then there is the 'external demand' type of explanation in which 'the times' or a particular event is seen to demand a 'fitting' kind of art; and finally, there is what can be called the 'spontaneous eruption' type of explanation to which Peckham's phrase 'non-functional artistic dynamism' bears some reference, but in the hands of less imaginative writers is reduced to a suggestion that the artist, or group of artists, became tired of what had gone before, or that a particular style could not 'be taken any further'. But all of these kinds of explanation beg other questions. 'Cross-fertilization', in the form of interaction with other fields as well as other practitioners, obviously does take place. There are indubitably 'external demands' made on artists, as on everyone else, and need for change – the 'spontaneous eruption' – is a fact of life. *But why are artists susceptible to one particular kind of influence and not another? How do we know when a style is 'fitting' or not? And why does change, if for its own sake, take particular forms?*

These are the questions which have been addressed above and to which a process model does provide answers. There *are* discernible patterns underlying changes in behaviour. The specifics are by no means predictable, but art-process characteristics relate to the dynamic APM-A model and the various hierarchies associated with it, in the same way as other kinds of experience and behaviour. All have to do with environmental perception and organism–environment interaction, which has been defined above as being subject to the 'intercourse principle'.

It has also been argued that art is not only an indicator of cultural tension, but that it also offers indications of levels and kinds of tension; and further, that the variable kinds of response to agglomerates of life-stressors observable in individuals also occur at macro level.

One of the implications of this position is that the concept of 'cultural convergence' has a much wider application than is conventionally understood. It usually refers to members of the same culture arriving at similar answers to the same problem quite independently of each other. This can be understood in APM-A terms as individuals perceiving the same problem and with access to relevant data, also sharing similar orientational styles, that is, active sub-threshold scanning and unconscious processing, so that a high proportion of relevant 'clues' is picked up at an early stage in the problem's general recognition and as soon as appropriate information becomes available. A kind of cultural convergence can also be perceived in process terms at cultural levels, when *shifts in styles of thinking* take place across the arts and sometimes in science and philosophy too.

This other kind of cultural convergence arises from what might best be described as 'simultaneous *increase in limbic dominance*'. This describes a change in orientational style (tuning) affecting thinking and behaviour in ways which have already been described. For example, it is being claimed that Einstein's theory of relativity (published in 1905) was *not* a *causal* factor in the development of Cubism, as is frequently suggested, but that awareness of relativity and readiness to acknowledge alternative ways of seeing were part of a more general move among artists and theoreticians to a dialectical mode of thinking.[43] In this mode consciousness of *dynamic oppositions, relative and changing truths,* and *abstraction,* are particularly high.

This kind of awareness existed in individuals before and since, but in the years just before and after the turn of the century there was a positive explosion of ideas which continue to have very powerful effects. It is also being viewed as significant that the unconscious mind was 'discovered' at this time too.

At the end of *Beyond the Tragic Vision,* in which Peckham describes what he calls 'the quest for identity in the nineteenth century', he discusses the stage of thinking at which Nietzsche arrived and expresses the belief that the Nietzschean vision may prove serviceable far into the future. Peckham decides that in proclaiming that God is dead and finding 'a resolution to the problem to keeping the antinomies, the contraries, the irreconcilable opposites of life, forever apart' (1962:368) Nietzsche solved the problem of the nineteenth century.

The antinomies in question were comedy and tragedy (which is supposed to give a profounder view of human life). Nietzsche viewed both as outgrown, and suggested instead that man is neither adequate (as comedy reassures him he is) nor inadequate (as tragedy confirms), but is a creator of value, order, meaning, and a sense of identity himself.

Peckham's speculation that the nineteenth century 'may have been, in terms of high level and advanced culture, an age of transition to the last stage of stylism, to the Nietzschean vision' (ibid.:371) may well prove to be true in the light of the regression which has taken place since, but the conclusion being drawn is that the species has a very great deal of growing up to do, before a similar level of synthesis to that achieved by Nietzsche can be attainable by more than a tiny proportion of the population of this planet.

Evidence of the *in*ability of those whom the education system is deemed to have served well, to achieve autonomy of the kind Nietzsche recommends, is freely available.

The art historian Rookmaaker tells us in *Modern Art and the Death of a Culture* how the 'feeling of our time' echoes what is written in the Bible.

> As we walk through a modern art gallery, do we see the sky vanished like a scroll that is rolled up, the sun becoming black as sackcloth, the moon becoming like blood, the stars falling down . . . ? God is not dead, nor the world a closed system: He, the Creator, He who loves mankind even to the sending of His Son to die, He not only came in Old Testament times with His righteous anger and judgement

upon men who forgot Him and walked in their own sinful ways, He will do so in our times too . . . There is a God to be feared.

(1970:219–20)

Similarly, evidence of our continued inability to overcome the trap of mutual exclusivity in our thinking, which Nietzsche overcame with reference to at least one issue, still abounds even among those who theorize about thinking. For instance, Crook (1980:399ff.), discussing 'dialectics in the behavioural sciences', talks about the irreconcilability of reductionism and dialectic thinking. He sees reductionist thinking being replaced by a dialectic mode whose explanations recognize 'oppositions to forces operating to create change through time'. He refers to reductionist thinking as tending to reify processes into static principles. But just because, as he says, 'it becomes easier to topple the old barricades between the classically defined sciences and to work in the intermediate domains' (ibid.:400) and dissatisfaction with behaviourist principles is leading to other 'more conceptually elaborate theories', this does not make what has been called 'explanatory reductionism' redundant. Neither does the identification of underlying processes necessarily deny acknowledgement of complexity at other levels, as has been stressed.

The Nietzschean ideal is also being delayed (at least) because of another problem which he could not possibly have foreseen. We now have two more 'Gods' to contend with, namely Freud and Marx. Both have identified crucial concepts, but in doing so have also created extraordinarily strong paradigms whose influences on interpretations of literature, social and economic history, and art history, tend to alternate and have powerful effects on the theory and practice of both psychology and education.

Their influences are so powerful that both of them militate strongly against free thinking, and together they sometimes even create yet another either/or dichotomy.

The attitude of the leading art critic Peter Fuller (1980) is not unusual. He draws attention to the limitations of Marxist interpretations of art history, but elsewhere expresses his perceptions of the relevance of biology to art principally in terms of the effects of the particularities of infant–mother relationships on the imagination.

Faber addresses questions to do with the relationship between culture and states of awareness from within the same paradigm. He identifies the fact that 'the way in which we perceive the world determines crucially the way in which we feel about it, and in it' (1981:13), and stresses the need for changes in awareness but, disappointingly, his argument is set in the psychoanalytical mould. Consequently, he sees the solutions to our cultural problems as lying in the achievement of mystical detachment and altered states of awareness of this kind. He concludes,

As perceivers, we must strive to understand as completely as we can the psychodynamic forces that have produced our ordinary consciousness. Additionally, we must work to fully understand the methods by which deleterious, pathogenic materials can be removed from the perceptual life of the organism as a whole . . . What psychoanalysis has long relegated to the periphery of its concern, namely mysticism, the occult, the desire and need to alter one's awareness, must be brought to the centre.

(Ibid.:270)

In turn, Badcock also recognizes the 'madness of modernity' from within the psychoanalytic framework. As he refers to modern art and literature as 'an externalisation of psychological states which is unmistakably schizoid and which bears all of the signs of a psychotic conflict with, and flight from, reality' (1983:135), it is interesting to note that, the Freudian diagnosis over half a century earlier was of the milder form of neurosis, rather than psychosis. Badcock actually perceives 'a new and in many ways unprecedented trauma of incalculable consequences [which] has broken on the human race' and 'pathology that is no longer confined to the individual neuroses but is increasingly becoming that of an entire civilisation' (ibid.:171). His solution is simple:

I see no reason why the later years of secondary, or the first years of tertiary education should not be in part devoted to giving young people insight into themselves through sensitive education in psychoanalytic psychology.

(Ibid.:170)

Apart from this representing at best a cosmetic approach only to reducing the problems spawned by a chronically inadequate education system, it is worrying from other points of view for those of us who, despite Freud's enormous contribution to psychology, regard the basis of psychoanalysis as theoretically crude (see also Leach 1976:96).

Although no exception is taken with Badcock's argument that the need for change lies in the education system, much more radical change is seen to be required than he suggests.

The APM-A view is also coincident with Faber's, when he stresses the need for changes in states of awareness, but although a capacity for 'mystical detachment' might be a very good habit to cultivate, the conclusion being drawn is that a change in states of awareness has to include a new view of man. Further, it has to be one in which his potency is no longer seen to derive either from God, his mother, his sexual organ, or his class identity. It is also vitally important that the new view of 'man' includes radically different views of woman and child which emphasize the similarities as well as the differences between all three categories.

The key point being made is that, when the interactions of emotion and reason and the complexities of human variability and adaptability are taken fully into account, it can be seen that social control is not maintained *only* by the manipulation of capital and the possession of knowledge, but primarily, and at a more fundamental level, by the manipulation of *emotion* and the withholding of *understanding*.

At the end of *Aesthetics and Psychobiology,* Berlyne overviews a very large number of findings which identify a wide range of 'uses and functions' of art (1971:chap. 16). They include the important fact that art exploits stimulus properties in such a way that attention can be effectively controlled and learning promoted. General headings, other than learning, include expressive behaviour, exploratory behaviour and rehearsal, play and entertainment, catharsis (inducing strong emotions) and personality improvement, occupation of surplus energy, and provision of functional pleasure and experience – that is, by enjoying and practising what is adaptational, keeping relevant equipment efficient.

All of these 'uses and functions' constitute orientational behaviour and all can be related to the revised hierarchy of needs (Figures 4 and 5); but the practice of art actually provides opportunities for achieving a functional level of orientation in special measure. Both the arts and the sciences are exploratory activities, but the fact that the arts involve free expression makes them a *special basis for interaction* with the physical and social environments according to the intercourse principle introduced in Chapter 2. They are therefore seen to offer special opportunities for achieving self-understanding, understanding of others, and effective means of communication, which are seen to be more crucial aims of education than current priorities.

There seems to have been tacit recognition among primary school teachers for a very long time that the arts modes offer special opportunities for the achievement of basic orientation at both sensory and cognitive levels (see Figure 4). Now it is to be argued that (1) without a minimum level of orientation (for which some require more sensory input than others: see Chapters 3, 4) neither a sufficient degree of focus for the practice of the sciences nor the effective practice of life can be achieved; (2) in order for an education system to produce a mentally healthy society it must pay attention to actual stages and kinds of cognitive development of individuals, rather than equating age with stage and stage with unitary measures of performance.

Chapter six

Understanding and expression

Summary

This chapter raises questions about what *meanings and values* we place on different ways (styles) of attending, perceiving, remembering, and behaving. In so doing it indicates some of the implications of APM-A theory for how we view people and society, and briefly explains a possibility for what is seen to be one of its most important applications: a theoretical underpinning for a particular view of lifelong education.

It is actually a call to view ourselves and our potentials differently, and to question where and how we locate notions of 'good' and 'evil'. It is also a plea for us to 'grow up' as a species and come to terms with ourselves as not only biological, with biological needs but also as sensual, emotional, and hedonistic beings with the means of fulfilling associated needs *non-abusively* – to ourselves or others.

It is stressed that art's ways of 'knowing', as well as science, offers means of 'understanding, prediction, and control' which, as was argued in Chapter 3, are also unreliable: that it is only by striving for what is called *bi-modal knowledge* that we can 'know' – as best we can.

Attention is drawn to the shared exploratory nature of learning, science, *and* art, as well as to what are perceived to be some major flaws in the education system. Radical changes are suggested which, it is argued, could produce a more stable society and a more authentic form of democracy, as potential outcomes of a process exemplified in an alternative model to the unitary model of regression introduced in Chapter 4 (Figures 26, 64).

6.1 Changing paradigms

The implications of adopting a new view of human nature amount to the possibility of being able to adopt a different view of knowledge and a different view of society: a paradigm change.

In accepting, and providing a theoretical underpinning for the fact that we are not, for instance, either free *or* determined, not shaped *or* shaping, but that we are both competitive *and* co-operative, as well as being all of the other things which are so often seen to be mutually exclusive alternatives but are actually subject to individual and temporal variability in degree of dominance, the really important questions are identified as those which concern the extent, the ways, and the circumstances in which the various aspects of our nature manifest themselves.

Viewing the species in terms of (1) *psychological* variability and adaptability with reference chiefly to mechanisms for *psychological survival* which, nevertheless, are seen to emanate from and interact with mechanisms for physical survival; (2) psychological *potential* rather than psychological limitations, as is currently most usual; and (3) as having *alternative potentials* has important implications for how we judge the 'abnormal', the 'inadequate', and those we designate 'pathological'. But more powerfully still, it may affect how we come to see our various kinds of social institution. For example, it may affect how we view the primitive incarceration in prisons and mental institutions of those we may come to see as having exceptionally high and/or unmet orientation needs. We may come to view bad *as* mad, and mad as disorientated, and to regard the mad-or-bad issue which underlies so much of our legal decision making, for instance, as itself inane.

This might, in turn, lead us to question the whole notion of moral ethics, to consider the validity of locating problems as necessarily within the individual, or within human nature, and also to question whether we should actually be attempting to identify predispositions to psychopathology or criminality; or, on the other hand, whether we should be much more concerned with identifying levels and kinds of need and considering in more positive terms the alternative kinds of potential these indicate. By continuing to subscribe to beliefs in inherent and mutually exclusive forces of 'good' and 'evil', in 'original sin', or, along with Lorenz (1974), that evolution has gone wrong, we are not only expressing heavily blinkered vision, we are propagating notions of human passivity and, at the same time, escalating the need for organized (if not armed) social control, in the attempt to fit reality into the myth.

6.2 Growing up as a species[1]

It was suggested at the end of Chapter 5 that closer links should be forged between psychiatry and education. The extension of this idea is that the achievement of orientation should become a prime aim common to an educational/developmental model of psychiatry and what might be termed a mental-health model of education.

The title of Gauguin's 'spiritual masterpiece', 'Where do we come from? What are we? Where are we going?', painted immediately prior to his suicide attempt, provides a useful example of a plea for orientation which can be seen to be just as appropriate to the current state of tension within western culture as it was to the personal despair of Gauguin in 1897. It is, of course, *possible* to imagine worse situations than having an unfulfilled desire to know where we have come from, what we are, and where we are going; one of them, quite obviously, is being given conflicting answers, but worse still, is being subjected to conflicting propaganda from what seems to be the same source (which, for the sake of argument, can be called 'conventional wisdom') when none of it seems quite to match reality.

The apparent identity crisis which may currently be perceived at species level, and the concomitant lack of positive direction or adherence to any unified system of self-knowledge, has already been said to be analogous to the kind of disorientation experienced by the teenager: to a familiar syndrome of self-doubt and energetic displays of unconvincing sureness of purpose, as old frames of reference are discarded before new ones are found to take their place. To potentially more sinister effect, Badcock's diagnosis (p. 270) is consistent with the possibility that as a species we could be confronted with the pre-schizophrenic condition defined so graphically by Gregory Bateson as 'double-bind' (1973:178ff.). As it becomes increasingly difficult for us to discriminate accurately between different orders of messages received from our cultural, ideological, and socio-political environments, appropriate response becomes equally difficult. We seem to be caught in the psychologically dangerous situation in which different orders of messages patently deny one another; a situation which, for many, holds potential for despair.

We have a work ethic, but for millions no work. We have an accompanying establishment call to Victorian moral values, against the polar-extreme media-vision of life composed of sexual athletics and sadistically violent heroism. More pernicious, it can be argued, is the more covert conflict between, on the one hand, our knowledge of ourselves as sentient and sensual beings responsive to rewards and punishments, and on the other, the bad name attached to pleasure which makes us flinch at calling ourselves hedonists.

The argument to be pursued is that it is only through the radical change and integration of the education system that these conflicts can be resolved and belief in myth and legend can be replaced with widespread understanding and confidence in the species, and, above all, self. However, first of all, decision-making adults must come to understand, examine critically, and make comparative and dispassionate study of the alternatives, in order to effect structural, curricular, and methodological changes, primarily in the secondary section of education; which, in turn, will require some changes in the adult sector and, to a much lesser extent, in primary provision as well. But above all, it will be necessary for us to 'grow up' and confront what patently seem, to most people still, to be the unsavoury facts of life.

It has already been pointed out that hedonistic motivation is not at all the same as, or necessarily leads to, hedonistic outcomes of action. On the contrary, caring for and furnishing the needs of others holds its own vitally important gratifications and, as Hans Selye's very useful concept of 'altruistic egotism' (1974:62ff.) suggests, psychological pleasures and pains are complex indeed. In sum, the position which has been adopted is that, being biological, we have biological needs; being human, we have human needs; being also sensual, emotional, and hedonistic, we have needs for sensual, emotional, and pleasurable experiences.

In evolutionary terms and in terms of individual development, it has been argued that our rationality arises from our emotionality, and that we learn when situations we find ourselves in hold sufficient threat or promise for us to need, or to want, to find out more. It is of paramount importance, though, to recognize that the 'threats' must be perceived to be surmountable – as challenges – for us not to withdraw completely. This emphasizes the vital importance of the need to acquire a positive self-concept and the need for opportunities to identify as many things as possible that we *can* do.

It is suggested, therefore, that we need curricula based on the human organism rather than on subjects, and on what have been called *process characteristics* (p. 121). This implies the need for provision for children and adults which reflects our extremely high needs for understanding and expression, for feeling and doing, as well as for the acquisition of facts. It must promote fulfilment of the essentially human need to answer more complicated questions of 'how' and 'who' in addition to those stimulated by the simple, lower-order, Pavlovian 'What is it?' response, and to do so in other than purely factual terms and not within the confines of a knowledge-based curriculum. After all, we do now have ample evidence to suggest that, for some, the acquisition of new knowledge demands the prior existence of a much wider frame of reference than it does for others.[2]

6.3 An art and a science of everything

An essential component of a process-oriented curriculum would have to be the provision of opportunities for the conscious recognition of our various mechanisms of mind, in order for us to be able to recognize and hone such skills and capacities as we possess, to attempt to overcome their dysfunctions, and to be able to exercise some degree of compensation when necessary (see p. 122). It is, incidentally, interesting and important to note that many of the exercises identified by de Bono (1982), and the processes defined by Feurerstein (1980), are intrinsic to participation in the arts.

Furnishing answers to what are being regarded as the key questions of 'Who am I?' and 'What can I do?', or in Gauguin's terms, 'What are we?' and 'Where are we going?', must start with differentiation and comparison making, whether we consider the psychoanalytic approaches of object-relations or individuation, or adopt the rather more 'grainy' information-processing view of how we assimilate environmental information. Establishing what we are *not* is a very important aspect of establishing what we are. This requires the acquisition of experience through *inter*action, and exposure to a rich variety of *other* possibilities.

In his speech accepting the Nobel Prize for Literature in Stockholm in 1983 William Golding made the following comments about the novel. He said,

> the novel stands between us and the hardening concept of statistical man. There is no other medium in which we can live for so long and so intimately with a character . . . No other art, I claim, can so thread in and out of a single mind and body, so live another life. It does ensure that at the very least a human being shall be seen to be more than one billionth of a billion.

Without in any way wanting, or venturing, to disclaim what William Golding says, it has to be added that other arts do allow us to enter other worlds and other identities in different ways, and in ways which offer greater sensory involvement, the importance of which in the development of 'mind' is increasingly recognized by neuro-psychologists. It has already been argued in the last chapter that participation in all of the arts offers the means of orientation in every sense of that word, and the same is true of other art forms: from vital sensory feedback and stimulation (which we now know actually promotes growth in the nervous system), to insights into alternative modes of perception and behaviour, which offer whole ranges of possibilities and the very stuff of concept formation.

Involvement in the arts offers opportunities for what might be called *chained symbolizing and hypothesizing* and the pains and delights of continuous sensory and emotional involvement in problem solving. It requires that we move through constantly changing symbols, from hypothesis to hypothesis, and from the solving of one problem to the recognition of the next, which, from the evidence Davis (1981) presents (see p. 14), could be deemed to provide participation in the most human possible kind of endeavour. Although it was argued in Chapter 5 that the practice of the arts provides a special basis for interaction and orientation, the arts and the sciences actually hold these and other processes in common at a fundamental level. Both, for instance, offer us means of understanding, predicting, and controlling phenomena, although, as it was pointed out in Chapter 3, these are conventionally regarded as being the sole prerogative of scientific method. The two different means of knowing – the one predominantly deductive and the other predominantly inductive – are both means of coping with and defending against environmental change.

If we consider the arts mode to be that in which the characteristics of right-hemisphere processing are dominant, and the science mode that in which those of the left-hemisphere dominate (see pp. 72ff.), the arts mode can be seen to be generally the more risky means of understanding, predicting, and controlling.[3] Importantly, it can be seen as a general anticipatory mode of imaginative speculation which serves to alert the individual, the group, or the community to positive and negative possibilities which, by their very nature, may be unpredictable with any degree of accuracy. At the same time, as the mode which allows perception of the greatest range of possible interpretations of items of information, and the greatest awareness of possible relationships between them, it also offers an enhanced holistic and dynamic means of knowing by *understanding*: knowing by the ready perception of, and response to, clues provided by indirectly associated information and awareness of covert as well as the overt possibilities.

On the other hand, scientific method allows us to be able to predict and control events with immense precision; but only certain kinds of events, and often at the expense of fragmentation and at the cost of the kind of interpretive and theoretical limitations and confusions which arise from the unitary measurement of polymorphic phenomena (Gear 1986).

The arts and the sciences are, clearly, complementary modes of understanding, predicting, and controlling which embody different kinds of costs and benefits and different means of orientation for the individual, the community, and the species. But the arts offer the most obvious access to all three of the prime means of orientation which have been defined in this book: a means of knowing, a means of expression, and a means of gaining stimulation, and although it is not being denied that the sciences provide all of these things, the limitations of laboratory practice and the effects of a high regard for precision on freedom of expression and the pursuit of sensation are fairly obvious.

In addition to the important fact that our model of style acknowledges that some individuals are endowed with apparently more than adequate access to both modes (as opposed to simply not displaying any particularly strong bias), so that they are able to employ the one to 'check out' the other, as it were, by accommodating differences in intensity as well as differences in bias within the same framework, it is also possible to acknowledge the kind of individual who displays neither obvious stylistic bias, nor any kind of particularly active environmental engagement at all. But essentially, the model emphasizes that, however strong a bias may be, the two modes are *interdependent* as well as complementary, and the one mode does not operate to the total exclusion of the other.

Even the most spontaneous and uncontrolled kind of artist discovers, confronts, and deals with incontrovertible facts sometimes, and although tuned to the phenomenological to the extent of always being alert to the value of exploiting the 'happy accident', he or she must still conduct the occasional experiment, even if not with the same dedication to objectivity as the scientist. Similarly, the scientist can be said to be exercising aesthetic sensibilities every time a 'hunch' is played: as he or she responds to a feeling rather than a fact. In much more basic terms it can be argued that the scientist is entirely dependent on a repertoire of sensory experience acquired in early childhood: on all of the concentrated sensory interaction with people, places, and things, and on the kind of exploratory sensing which artists consciously continue to do all of their lives, in order to be able to manipulate complex concepts, let alone communicate, at all.

One major point which emerges from these realizations is that it is nonsensical for arguments to rage in certain disciplines about whether they should be regarded as arts *or* sciences, when a very strong case can be presented in support of the fact that there is potentially an art *and* a science of everything. The argument applies most obviously to those subject areas most closely associated with the study of humanity: the embodiment of both modes. To regard the disciplines of psychology, sociology, or education, for example, as belonging either to the arts *or* the sciences is to disregard – or more accurately, possibly discredit or even invalidate – certain kinds of information and insights to be gained through the alternative mode. It seems more sensible to believe that it is only when we perceive a certain level of consistency between the results of employing *both* modes, which might then be called *bi-modal knowledge,* in the exploration of particular phenomena that we really 'know', as best we can.

Even in those subject areas in which there is not an obvious inherent need to employ both modes in order to gain a full understanding of obviously different 'hard' and 'soft' aspects of the subject, both speculative theory *and* data still have very important roles to play. Aims and hypotheses have to be formulated – imagined – before being tested, and general theoretical contexts are necessary in order to make sense of results. Although empirical findings may deny the initiating theory, such findings trigger new theories, just as many replications, or different kinds of testing, are required in order to establish hard data. Neither mode is infallible, which is why, one presumes, the species has evolved in such a way as to have simultaneous access to a variable mix of both.

It is in the exploratory nature of the perceptual process that the psychology of learning and the psychology of art, as well as the key differences in general styles of experience and behaviour characteristic of the arts and the sciences and of every other aspect of human psychology, become fused. But specifically, the analysis of the shared processes of learning and art offers particularly valuable insights into some of the most serious flaws in our education system, and show it to be very heavily biased towards the alternative (to the 'arts') mode. It can also be seen to be very heavily biased to the *already* well-orientated and/or those moderately low in orientation needs. In order not to embark on a long and detailed digression about how the processes of learning and art can be seen to relate to each other, the following concluding remarks will be confined mainly to the effects of the crucially important role played by the perception of the different levels and kinds of threats and promises which have been referred to above. Acknowledgement of their vital role is directly relevant to the concept of *engagement*, to which particular reference was made in Chapter 4 and which, in turn, relates to another key concept discussed elsewhere (Gear 1987) in connection with the role of affect in learning: namely, *the acquisition of 'purpose'* (see postulates 5–7, 13, 14, 15, Appendix 2).

Reference to these concepts suggests that major flaws in our attempts to educate the young and reasons for the consequent 'cooling out' of the system of most of them for life can be summarized as follows: (1) the system reflects a tacit assumption that *all* children *should* have acquired a sufficient degree of orientation to be able to 'key into' the same level of conceptual complexity as the most well-orientated children of the same age; (2) it offers rewards, chiefly, for the ability to sit still and the ability to absorb factual information – *internalizing*; (3) because standards are set (for the most part, and certainly in the public examinations which dominate the system) by the most effective internalizers, it rewards and reinforces the good fortune of those who already have a certain advantage (well-fulfilled, or relatively low, orientation needs) whilst punishing, very often quite literally, those who have difficulty in remaining still and have short attention spans. These types have also been defined as being dominated by unconscious mechanisms of mind and, ironically, are likely to be representative of the type of individual who responds more positively to rewards (see Figure 29).

It is being argued that it is not the style of the majority to engage easily with anything, let alone factual information or abstract ideas, while sitting still or being quiet, and that for sustained engagement with any kind of environmental stimulus to take place, interaction, not just activity, must occur (see pp. 29ff. on the *intercourse principle*). As it has also been argued that many individuals really interact only with people, one implication is that in order for the majority of pupils to be able to establish contact with teachers the number of teachers in schools should be doubled – despite falling rolls – and that a class of twenty, not thirty, should be considered large. Another implication is that for engagement with other people, places, and things to be facilitated, arts activities should be at the centre of the curriculum, not at the periphery, for most children.

As it is, education for the majority might more accurately be described as an experience of incremental deficit in self-esteem. It starts in primary school, where at least the value of expression and of only short periods of concentrated academic involvement, as well as the need for sensory stimulation, are fully respected – in practice as well as theory – but where the tacit assumptions about simple linear and equivalent levels of orientation are nevertheless expressed. Children are tested, sorted, and graded *regardless* of differences in *individual style* and consequent potential levels and kinds of *orientation need.*

The assumptions and the labelling grow and harden, as do the covert and overt environmental (and often verbal) insults; and as the victims express their antagonism, or sometimes less intense feelings of bewilderment, towards the system, those whose job it is to maintain it locate the problems more and more as being entirely under the conscious control of the confused individuals in question. The alternative view of why the majority of sixteen-year-olds emerge from school having been very effectively alienated, or at the very least feeling very inadequate, is that secondary education, in particular, pays either no attention to, or makes only a token gesture towards, the development of abilities which the theory outlined above indicates should be its central aims: gaining understanding of self; gaining understanding of others; and acquiring adequate means of effective communication and expression.

A concomitant of such aims would, again, mean shifting arts activities to a central place in the curriculum, in order to create opportunities for guided exercises in observation and self-discovery and to explore the 'other possibilities' these aims would demand. Ironically, the achievement of literacy and numeracy would be likely to be facilitated as pupils gained more focus. Fortunately, most adult educationists know better than to make the kinds of assumption which appear to blight secondary education. However, not surprisingly, relatively few of those who experience secondary school to negative effect ever return to the education system to find out. Neither is it surprising, therefore, that adult and continuing education can be seen to go on reinforcing early advantage despite its vigorous efforts to do otherwise. In fact, the conclusion being drawn is that it will continue to fail to attract working people in large numbers, and dramatic curricular change in secondary education will not take place until we manage to destigmatize pleasure among the general population and decision makers alike.

6.4 Education for pleasure instead of rewards for sitting still

It can be seen as a sad reflection on our education system, and could be taken to explain a great deal, that 'education for pleasure' is an unknown concept, and as such, may sound rather an outrageous idea. We have 'education for leisure', but that is a rather different concept; and teachers are extolled to make learning enjoyable, as best they can within the confines of mostly irrelevant curricula, but encouragement of the pursuit of psychological pleasure in quite uncontroversial and socially acceptable ways – where it exists at all – certainly has no priority value whatsoever. Maybe there is some insight to be gained from this into why, for so many, gaining pleasure requires resort to self-abuse, or the abuse of others, or their property, and why many schoolteachers work in fear of physical attack, and many attempts have been made by pupils to destroy their schools.

As long ago as 1967 Laing drew attention to the fact that a child born in the UK then stood ten times greater chance of being admitted to a mental hospital than to university, and that one-fifth of mental hospital patients were diagnosed as schizophrenic. He suggested that these facts could be taken to indicate that we are driving our children mad more effectively than we are educating them.

Many who would have contested Laing's view then may now, perhaps, be more easily persuaded that even if our education system does not actually drive people mad, it drives many to violence, and could be said to do more to *disorientate* than *orientate*. The present writer certainly subscribes to that view, as well as to the belief that secondary education contributes more to the loss of autonomy, through the promotion of personal disintegration in some cases and through the promotion of passivity in others, than it does to the positive development of persons or the promotion of creative purposes. In short, the conclusion being drawn is that it presents more threat than promise to the majority of participants.

An extremely cogent criticism of the secondary system and, in particular, the comprehensive school, has been made by David Hargreaves (1982). He, too, observes widespread damage to self-esteem bestowed by the system. He refers to it as 'a destruction of . . . dignity which is so massive and pervasive that few subsequently ever recover from it'. Although he provides a very different rationale it is interesting that we arrive at not dissimilar conclusions; but his radical proposals are seen to be not radical enough.

The shifts of *emphasis* he recommends are exactly similar to those which arise from the APM-A position as being necessary, but for different reasons. He identifies two crucial components of a new core curriculum. On the grounds that 'the very concept of ability becomes closely tied to the intellectual-cognitive domain' one of these components is the expressive arts; and on the grounds that it is necessary to 'prepare the young for an active role in society' the other component is an 'integrated course of community studies'. Other radical proposals he makes are the removal of examinations at sixteen-plus, and instead, for the core curriculum to cease at fifteen in order for pupils to start either a three-year A-level course or other, more vocational, courses.

While in full agreement about the need to move the expressive arts to the core, this is not because they are perceived to be an alternative to the 'intellectual-cognitive domain'. It is because of all of the 'process' reasons offered above and because they are seen to be, for most people, a necessary *basis* for that 'domain'. Again, perception of the need for social awareness at an early age is shared with Hargreaves; but community *studies* still represents a possible advantage to effective internalizers who are less likely to have difficulties fitting into social roles anyway. Why not *work* in the community, with community studies as an optional special interest subject? Hargreaves' other core components are in fact 'remedial options' and 'special interest' subjects.

Although I am in complete sympathy with Hargreaves' broad aims, I find at least three important problems with his approach. The first is the lack of substantial underlying theory. He makes a very strong case but, although he does explain some of the value of drama, his major arguments for moving other arts to the core of the curriculum are unlikely to help very much to convince the majority of adults who remain patently unconvinced of their value in education. Without a substantial supporting theory, 'evolutionary' change is unlikely to occur and revolutionary change is so unlikely as to make his arguments seem part of a philosophical debate only.

Second, the problem of removing the stigma from the non-academic child is not likely to be solved by the removal of examinations at sixteen-plus, or the other proposed changes, any more than it was solved by the comprehensive system in a culture in which paper qualifications are so highly valued. Finally, Hargreaves deals with child education only. In addition to these major problems, by centring his argument on the polymorphic concept of 'dignity', rather than on psychological process, definition of this key concept could come to dominate the much more crucial debate (Hamilton 1984).

For evolutionary change to take place, contact and eventual integration have to be established between all sectors of the education system, and particularly between providers of adult and secondary education. Only in this way can it be ensured that opportunities will exist at a later stage to study any part of the examinable or non-examinable curriculum not studied during childhood. The foundations for a way forward in this respect exist in the form of the community school, but this is not necessarily the only possibility.

For it to be likely for much larger numbers of people to want to re-enter the system at a later stage, or for the majority of young people to want to be able actually to enjoy school and leave it with self-esteem intact, a change of awareness is essential, but not a change of the kind proposed by Faber (1981) and referred to above (pp. 269–70). We have to de-stigmatize responsible pleasure, and we have to de-stigmatize modes of functioning which do not have the incidental effect of easy absorption of factual information. The drawbacks and benefits of all modes of perceiving have to become widely understood.

In an integrated system which equips the individual with, on the one hand, self-understanding, which might include the knowledge that particu-larly wide frames of reference are needed in some subject areas in order to be able to assimilate facts; and on the other, understanding of others (who might assimilate facts with no effort at all, but not perceive 'connections' or achieve general understanding very quickly, or be as creative), values could eventually change. There could eventually be no stigma attached to some young people spending *most* of their time *out* of school and even to being able to leave as early as the age of fourteen to take up an apprenticeship or pursue some other purpose.

With self-esteem still intact, with school having been a pleasurable experience, combining short periods of academic work in small friendly groups with long periods of interactive and expressive activities in between, for most pupils; and with more or less experience of honing social and practical skills by being involved in the maintenance of persons and property in the community, the likelihood of curiosity and/or ambition leading individuals back into the system on a part-time or full-time basis at a later date would be significantly higher. An allowance of a certain number of hours' paid educational leave during working life would then seem a reasonable reward for earlier unpaid efforts invested in local needs, and the spectre of unemployment would be far less threatening for young people who were already socially enmeshed and in possession of developed 'purposes'.

The same kind of programme, but including longer periods of academic work and more theory, is seen to be just as appropriate to those who might later pursue the three-year A-level course proposed by Hargreaves; so that some work in the community and involvement in one or more of the arts would play an important role in the curriculum of all children up to the age of fifteen. There would, of course, still be children who would require remedial help, and not all discipline problems would be solved. But given teachers with different expectations and equipped with knowledge of differences in levels of unconscious needs and need for externalization of neuronal tension, discipline problems could fall to the point where (1) neither teachers nor other children would be threatened by them, and (2)

283

teachers could respond with attention to orientation needs, rather than with the kind of futile and humiliating gestures, and sometimes violent punishments, to which resort is so often made at present.

One of the most specific implications of the theory for curriculum change is the inclusion for all pupils of study of the human mind as well as the human body. Topics such as emotion, motivation, and individual differences can be seen to be at least as, if not more, important than a knowledge of carpels and metacarpels, for instance, the structure of the inner ear, or the length of the human intestine. Just as importantly, once a large enough population undergoes a change in its awareness of human nature, other kinds of curriculum change and structural change could take place very quickly indeed.

The most important implication of APM-A theory for the methodology of teaching children and adults – in addition to those set out elsewhere (Gear 1987) – is the need for a much wider understanding among teachers of human adaptability and variability and, in particular, the extraordinarily dynamic nature of variability in styles of perception and behaviour, within a holistic framework. In turn, this also implies a need to develop diagnostic techniques which would offer general indications of attentional, perceptual, memory, and emotional styles of the kind suggested in Chapter 4. The theory also lays heavy emphasis on the fact that *the achievement of orientation allows effective function.* This seems simple and uncontroversial enough, and so fundamental for it to be possible for it to become a prime goal in our efforts to educate, and to affect both methodology and the curriculum at all levels. This shift of emphasis seems especially important when we realize that the achievement of orientation allows the possibility of greater conscious self-control of behaviour – by diminishing the urgency of unconscious needs – and therefore also of expressing a more caring attitude towards others, as our own needs become less demanding.

Thus an alternative to the unitary model of regression presented in Figure 26 (Chapter 4) might be termed a *reward*, rather than a punishment, model which describes what happens under the influence of perceived promise, rather than threat.

As was indicated at the beginning, this book has not been about identifying new facts or furnishing answers which can be called 'hard' data. It has been about providing alternative ways of interpreting data, about breaking down stereotypes and questioning some traditional, and some more recent, but extremely powerful, theoretical positions, and considering some of the implications of this exercise for different fields of psychology, aesthetics, and finally, education and society. It is hoped that there will be at least someone among those with whom APM-A theory finds favour (or not) sufficiently interested to subject it to tests of 'bi-modality' (see p. 278) or be stimulated to perform some new kind of research in one of the

Figure 64   An alternative to the unitary model of regression introduced in Chapter 4 (Figure 26)

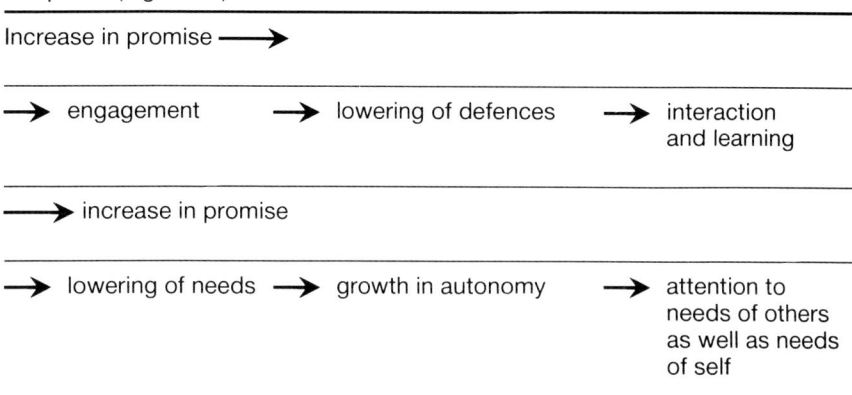

Increase in promise ⟶

⟶ engagement   ⟶ lowering of defences   ⟶ interaction and learning

⟶ increase in promise

⟶ lowering of needs ⟶ growth in autonomy   ⟶ attention to needs of others as well as needs of self

fields in question. It is also hoped that the new perspective may help promote greater understanding of the links between the disciplines which have been drawn on as well as between the broad areas of arts and science.

However, beyond APM-A theory being offered as a holistic framework and a general psychological context holding some implications for lifelong education in particular, it is also offered as a tool for sharpening some educational, as well as psychiatric concepts. For example, the importance of 'relevance' is generally acknowledged, but to pay attention to the inducement of affect seems more to the point and refers directly to processes which go on in human organisms without inviting the question 'to what?'. Similarly, we all know that 'participation' facilitates learning, but an individual cannot participate with another person, a thing, or a place – only in a *situation* created by others. On the other hand, it is possible for an individual to be encouraged to *interact* with all of these rich sources of sensory 'nourishment', to provide 'food for thought'. Above all, the position which has been adopted offers a strong theoretical underpinning for the incorporation of a fitting paradox into the education system; namely, that it should become both more integrated and more pluralistic. But in common with other apparent paradoxes to which attention has been drawn, integration and pluralism are not incompatible when both level *and* kind are taken into account. In this instance, integration refers predominantly to level, and pluralism to kind of provision. In other words, APM-A theory suggests that urgent consideration should be given to reforms which pay respect to adaptive modes and adaptive stages, rather than continuing to reflect obsessions with paper qualifications and age.

It is hardly new to suggest that lasting peaceful democracy can be achieved only through the education of the electorate. But the perspective which has been developed suggests that it is even more crucial that we examine very critically indeed what *kind* of exercises are performed under the banner of 'education' if the aim really is to equip people with the possibility of being able to choose between authentic alternatives. Education for democracy will never emerge from education for madness, education for confusion, or even education for internalizers and those relatively few externalizers who happen to be reasonably good at internalizing as well.

For all of the players of any game to be able to participate fully they must gain full access to the ground rules in order really to understand the range of potential roles and moves open to them and to the other participants. A partial and/or heavily biased view is obviously likely to obstruct effective action, but a partial view which includes first principles at least allows us to learn as we go. When we finally realize that deception, violence, many kinds of dependency, and the escalation to counter-productive effect of activities associated with 'the four F's'[4] can be attributed to increases in consciously or unconsciously perceived threat and concomitant escalation of orientation needs as defined in Figures 4 and 5, we also gain insight into a new possibility for education and a new possibility for the species.

In short, it is proposed that education which reflects a view of the species more consistent with experience, and which allows us to apply our knowledge of the human organism to the design of our social institutions, instead of attempting to match people to myth, would also offer education for caring autonomy. By subscribing to *education as orientation*, we could have education for a 'grown-up' species able to overcome emotional dependencies and stylistic prejudices, without confusing growing up with loss of capacity for play or the privilege of free expression. We would also be able to express stylistic preferences while enjoying the tolerance – and interest – of others.

The APM-A framework

The explanation offered below is a skeletal outline only of the 'mechanics' of APM-A theory and how its various models relate to one another. Just as *Homo sapiens* is actually organic, sentient, and intelligent, in addition to having a bone structure, there is very much more to the new theoretical position than this series of key points. However, they are offered rather in the spirit in which the painter of nudes is encouraged to study anatomy: in order for the reader to gain as full an understanding as possible of how to interpret whatever 'colours', 'textures', and 'tones' are perceived on the 'flesh'. The evidence for the following statements is cited mainly in Part 1, but some of the key figures are reduced and reproduced here as pointers and, in the same spirit, relevant postulates (Appendix 2) are cited alongside.

The theory concerns the evolution of relatively stable but, to varying extents, modifiable styles of processing and responding to environmental information. It also defines the styles in question as holding different (positive and negative) potentials, according to particular environmental factors.

Specifically, there follow *six fundamental APM-A concepts* from which the others arise:

two (1.1, 1.2) refer to the *dynamics of the APM-A process*, i.e. the interaction of attention, perception, memory, and arousal, and correlations which can be made between levels of arousal and kinds of awareness;

two (2.1, 2.2) refer to the underlying biochemistry of the response described by Pavlov as the 'orientation reflex' – or, more simply, the 'What is it?' response – and by Cannon as the fight/flight response, and define characteristics of SNS–PNS interaction which form the basis of the dynamic model at the core of the theory;

two more (3.1, 3.2) refer to *psychological needs* arising from the orientation reflex or, in APM-A terms, the *'need for* orientation response': sensory, cognitive and expressive needs common to the species, but *varying in intensity within and between individuals*. Because the needs in question are all defined as emanating from what is perceived to be a fundamental need for 'locating' ourselves successfully and finding 'direction' within our individual 'worlds', they are called *orientation needs*.

Some of the ways in which 1.1–3.2 interact to provide the holistic model and new ways of looking at certain facets of mind are described under 4.1–4.10.

1 Dynamics of the APM-A process

1.1 Rather than attention, perception, memory, and arousal being viewed as sequential events which take place in one order or another (according to particular theorists), they are seen as interacting dynamically with one

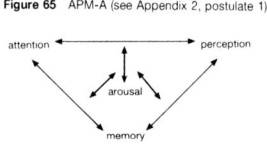

Figure 65   APM-A (see Appendix 2, postulate 1)

attention ← → perception

arousal

memory

Figure 3   A unidimensional* representation of the relationship between key concepts of mind employed within the APM-A framework (see also Figures 66 and 68 (Appendix 2))

UNCONSCIOUS SCANNING & FOCUS	CONSCIOUS SCANNING & FOCUS

Increasing tendency towards highly individual interpretations of events and/or increase in physical activity (see Chaps. 3 & 4)

Creativity – given 'purpose' (identified problem) & medium	—— IMAGINATION —— anticipation, flexibility of thought & action	creativity – given 'purpose' & medium

Increase in arousal & increase in orientation needs to include greater anticipation, more future planning (given 'purpose') & anxiety

unconscious & sub-threshold selection from alternatives	—— AWARENESS —— use of expectancy and prediction	consciousness of choice & selection from alternatives

Increase in arousal & in sub-threshold *and* conscious scanning activity

as species learning	—— REACTIVITY ——	as a result of individual learning (conditioning)

Increase in arousal & in resources for coping with *current* internal and external demands

environmental change

LOW AROUSAL

LEVELS OF 'MINDING'
relevant to phylogenetic, ontogenetic, and
phenomenological changes in arousal

Not, for instance, taking into account the inverted U shape created by correlates of efficiency and arousal, and not taking into account the different kinds of arousal identified in Chapter 3.

another: change in one is seen to affect the others, to however minor an extent. Further, changes in the APM-A process are seen to be dependent on a hierarchy of signal values as well as on internal states of the organism (see postulates 1–6 and Figs. 66/67, Appendix 2). Following from this, and as outlined in postulate 4, an interactive view is also taken of cognition and emotion.

1.2 The second fundamental concept under this heading refers to phylogenetic, ontogenetic, and phenomenological changes in APM-A, particularly in scanning and focusing functions of attention correlative with changes in levels of arousal. Evolutionary, developmental, and phenomenological changes in levels of consciousness and shifts between reactivity and creativity, as means of coping and defending, are referred to as 'levels of minding' (postulates 7 and 8 and Fig. 3).

2 Significant characteristics of SNS–PNS interaction

2.1 The theory makes use of evidence supporting the notion of individual differences in *patterning* of adrenergic–cholinergic activity, namely: (1) individual differences in the release of adrenalin and noradrenalin, and (2) correlations between adrenalin and noradrenalin levels and particular kinds of mental and physical activity respectively (postulates 18–20 and Figs. 12, 13).

2.2 In addition to the interaction of differences in patterning of the release of adrenalin and noradrenalin (i.e. different *kinds* of SNS activity) and different relative *intensities* of SNS and PNS activity, account is also taken of relative dominance of limbic arousal over cortical arousal, as a whole. The dynamic model of style which emerges, therefore, accommodates a potentially infinite variety of patterning of possible biases and levels of arousal, including the possibility of very high levels of both SNS *and* PNS activity and associated capacities for highly effective scanning and focusing functions of attention. Other key outcomes of what are viewed as underlying differences in *relative speeds (urgency) of processing* and concomitant attempts to take on different amounts of information simultaneously, include relative breadths of perceptual and conceptual boundaries and the extent to which experience and behaviour can be deemed to be 'normal' or 'abnormal'.

3 Psychological needs

3.1 A key element of individual 'style' is defined as a highly variable need to externalize neuronal excitation, according to base levels of arousal and what are defined as individual differences in *tension thresholds*. The resulting need to interact physically, socially and/or intellectually with

Figure 4 A summary of orientation needs

		Feedback from the physical environment
Sensory needs		Physical reassurance derived from both:
	(a)	optimal levels [1] of sensory stimulation (mainly tactile/visual/aural) [2]
	(b)	(implied) optimal levels of perceived environmental stability
Cognitive needs	1	Reassurance derived from optimal levels of consistency and change, with an obvious need for a very high degree of predictability.
	2	An explanatory system, including
	(a)	a need to know which may rest on (i) simplistic rationalization based on experience, (ii) folklore, myth, or legend, (iii) magico-religious beliefs, (iv) a corpus of knowledge; [3]
	(b)	a need not to know when existing belief systems, experience or knowledge prove inadequate to provide explanation.
	3	'Purpose': [4] in terms of engagement with identifiable problems – offering optimal levels of threat and promise and concomitant optimal balance of focusing and scanning functions of attention.
	4	a medium of expression. [5]
		Feedback from social, cultural and intellectual environments
Sensory needs		Reassurance of social acceptability and personal identity derived from optimal levels of contact (mainly tactile/visual/aural) with intimate and familiar social bonds as well as with unfamiliar individuals and groups.
Cognitive needs	1	Reassurance derived from optimal levels of consistency and change in the perceived behaviour of self and others.
	2	An explanatory system including a need to know and a need not to know (as above).
	3	'Purpose'.
	4	A medium of expression.
	5	Shared communication. [6]
	6	Shared values.

[1] Optimal levels dependent on species learning – of the species norm – but variable between and within individuals (species and individual adaptation levels).
[2] It is accepted that not only may there be individual differences in the dominance of any one of the senses, but that substitution and compensation also take place.
[3] Clearly, a corpus of knowledge is viewed as holding most potential as a reliable source of explanation.
[4], [5] 'Purpose', and a medium of expression, may be furnished by the physical, social, or intellectual environment, or all three.
[6] Implicit in any notion of shared communication is what Maslow would call 'belongingness', or what can be called 'enmeshment', but here it must be pointed out that in both cases the question of degree is important, i.e. that some freedom from the demands of other individuals and groups is also of key importance.

Figure 5 A revised hierarchy of needs

Weiner's classification	Reclassification	Description of needs
(Mastery and growth)	Second-order orientation needs	Heightened orientation needs as a result of intensity of affect: need for more feedback/change, greater need to know, with reference to longer term, more complex and/or more abstract issues; increased communicative and expressive needs.
(Drive reduction)	Physical survival needs	Fulfilment of physiological demands: need for shelter, warmth, avoidance of danger, food, drink, sleep, sexual expression.
(Expectancy-value)	First-order orientation needs	See Fig. 4 for a summary of orientation needs.

Note: Second-order orientation needs are not species-wide, but vary between and within individuals, as do the relative dominance of physical survival needs and kinds of orientation needs. Attention signals (see Fig. 66), on the other hand, derive from species-wide and conscious physical survival needs.

objects of attention is described in terms of a universally applicable principle labelled the *intercourse principle* (postulates 14, 15).

3.2 Emotional needs for reassurance and the security of different kinds of environmental 'feedback' (providing orientation) are defined in detail under the headings 'sensory needs' and 'cognitive needs' from our physical, social, and cultural environments. These needs are also defined as varying in intensity between individuals and are therefore described as being of 'first- or second-order' (postulates 11, 12 and Figs. 4, 5).

4 Ways in which 1.1–3.2 interact to provide a dynamic model of style

4.1 *The Structure* The model represents increases in *limbic arousal* and gradual dominance of *SNS activity* over PNS activity in *three different ways*: I_1–I_2 represents increase in adrenalin-biased arousal; I_1–E_1 noradrenalin-biased arousal; and I_1–E_2 arousal accompanied by balanced release of adrenalin and noradrenalin. It should be noted, however, that this forms the basis of a relatively simple explanatory model, representing gradual dominance of SNS over PNS activity only. In fact it is acknowledged that variability in patterning of SNS–PNS interaction could be so complex that the only really adequate way of representing it would be a figure with a very large number of transparent overlays (Figs. 12, 13).

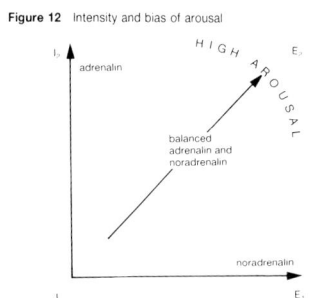

Figure 12 Intensity and bias of arousal

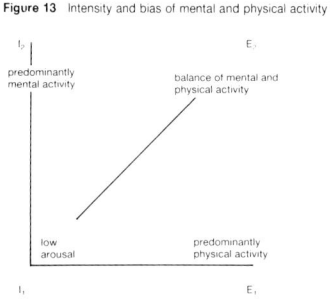

Figure 13 Intensity and bias of mental and physical activity

Note: I_1, I_2, E_1, and E_2 will eventually be defined as representing different kinds of internalizers and externalizers.

4.2 *Internalizers and externalizers* Division of the model in half vertically provides two major elements of adaptive style: internalizers on the side of the model representing adrenalin-biased arousal (correlated with fear and anxiety), and externalizers on the side representing noradrenalin-biased arousal (correlated with increase in physical activity). However, because individual styles may be represented by any point framed by the model, it allows for *kinds* of internalizers and externalizers: first- and second-order internalizers (I_1 and I_2) and first- and second-order externalizers (E_1 and E_2), according to levels and kinds of arousal (Fig. 14).

Figure 14 Externalizers (E_1 and E_2) and internalizers (I_1 and I_2) viewed in terms of intensity and bias of kinds of arousal and kinds of activity, according to Figs. 12 and 13

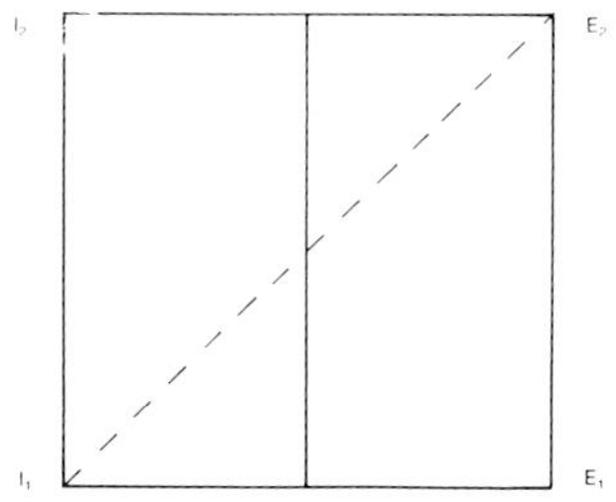

4.3 *Key differences in styles between internalizers and externalizers*
Characteristic styles of processing information are identified by relating to
one another research findings about arousal from a number of different
fields, so that human variability is viewed initially in terms of general
tendencies in *kinds of person–environment interaction* likely to be
undertaken by individuals represented by the four quarters (I_1, I_2, E_1, E_2)
of the model (Fig. 15).

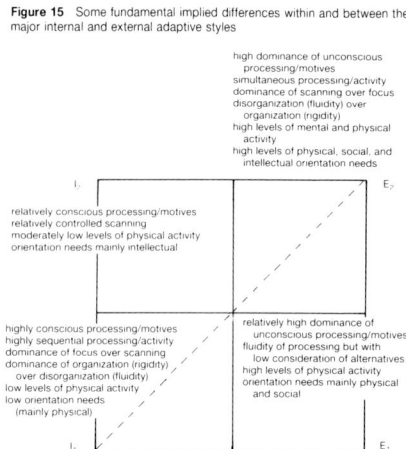

Figure 15 Some fundamental implied differences within and between the major internal and external adaptive styles

4.4 *Different aspects of the person* In the case of *levels* of needs it is
appropriate to divide the model horizontally, as levels of psychological
needs are seen to relate to levels of mental activity (represented by the
upper half of the model) rather than physical activity. Hence first- and
second-order needs are experienced by first- and second-order internalizers and externalizers.

However, key dimensions of individual style are seen to share the
polarity I_1–E_2 which, taking no account of *kinds* or arousal, provides the

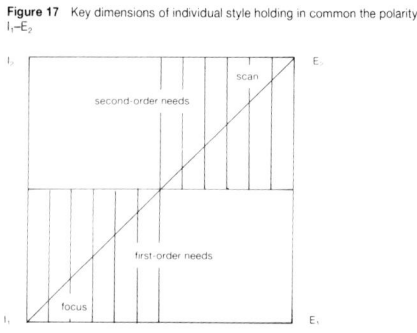

Figure 17 Key dimensions of individual style holding in common the polarity I_1–E_2

simplest possible, but potentially very misleading, conventional bipolar view of personality (Fig. 17).

4.5 *Intelligence* By reference primarily to speed and accuracy (as the conventional criteria of intelligence) as well as to other characteristics of information-processing, the model not only allows 'high' intelligence to be located in relation to other aspects of APM-A, but it also allows the identification of *kinds* of intelligence and, perhaps more significantly, kinds of *un*intelligence. These are also related to what is called 'classroom stereotypy' in terms of 'styles' of person–environment interaction (Figs. 19, 20).

Figure 19 Examples of kinds of intelligence (see also Figure 15)

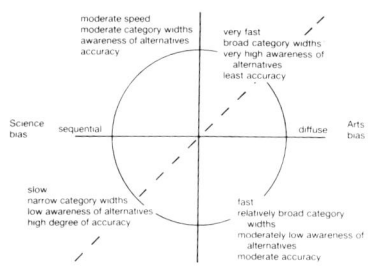

* The term 'category width' is being used to imply perceptual *and* conceptual boundaries.

Figure 20 Examples of kinds of 'unintelligence' related to classroom stereotypy

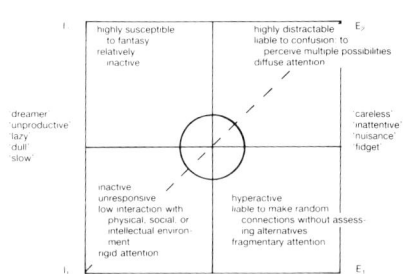

4.6 *Creativity* Whereas creativity is usually explored under the separate headings of 'person', 'process', and 'press' (environmental factors), more aspects of each can be identified by examining them within the holistic APM-A framework. For example, although the 'archetypal artist' described in the literature is identified as a second-order (E_2) externalizer (in the polar-extreme position from first-order internalizers, along the simple bipolar dimension referred to under 4.4 above), different styles of output are also attributed to second-order internalizers (I_2s) and first-order externalizers (E_1s). Links between creativity and schizophrenia are also interpreted in APM-A terms, as is the significance of different kinds of symbolism, including religious symbolism.

4.7 *'Maleness' and 'femaleness'* A finding about creativity that 'female elements' contribute to male creativity and 'male elements' to female creativity is explained as a concomitant of artists requiring both, imaginative qualities (conventionally regarded as female) *and* physical energy, to be productive. The exercise of plotting these characteristics on to the model, and relating them to other characteristics represented by the relevant locations, incidentally also allows definition of 'male' internalizers and externalizers and 'female' internalizers and externalizers in ways which cross the boundaries of physical gender (Fig. 21).

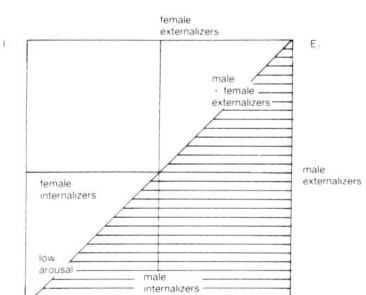

Figure 21 Adaptive style in relation to traditional views of male and female traits

4.8 *'Normal' and 'abnormal' experience and behaviour* Using evidence correlating adrenalin with fear and anxiety and noradrenalin with anger and impulsivity, 'normal' APM-A styles can be related to their more extreme and 'stressed' versions (including criminality) – usually referred to as 'abnormal'. This exercise is made easier by the fact that some correlations have also been made between particular neuroses and

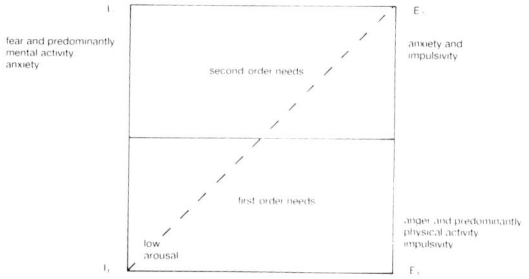

Figure 22 Different kinds of potential for 'abnormal' experience and behaviour, with so-called 'weak personalities' located in the lower left-hand side of the model (see also Figs. 15, 19, 20)

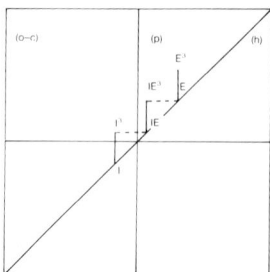

Figure 23 Examples of possible extreme differences in manifestations of more or less intense patterning of ANS activity, when I^3, IE^3, and E^3 are taken to be stressed (exaggerated) patternings of ANS activity and potential examples of obsessive–compulsive (o–c), paranoid (p) and hysterical (h) neurotic styles respectively (with I^3 remaining PNS dominant, IE^3 manifesting very intense PNS and ANS activity, and E^3 heavily SNS-dominant), while I, IE, and E represent so-called normal styles

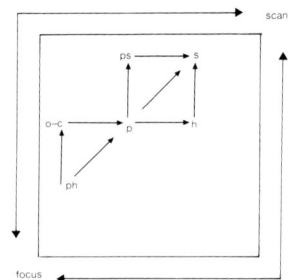

Figure 24 Relative positions of phobics (ph): obsessive–compulsive (o–c), paranoid (p), and hysterical (h) neurotic styles; paranoid schizophrenia (ps) and non-paranoid schizophrenia (s), in connection with increases in cognitive disorganization

psychoses and certain patterns of adrenergic–cholinergic interaction. The linking of 'normal' and 'abnormal' states not only offers pointers towards different levels and kinds of susceptibility to 'abnormal' experience and behaviour, it also holds potential for a means of diagnosis and classification which can indicate *intensities* and *kinds* of pathologies within a holistic framework (Figs. 22, 23, 24).

4.9 *Regression* The theory gives rise to a simplified, unitary model of regression and a model of its alternative. The model of regression relates increase in primitive styles of behaviour to increase in relative dominance of limbic arousal in response to perceived environmental (physical, social, and/or cultural) threats. The alternative model relates to yet another model – of biological alternatives (Fig. 25) – in which the 'saint–psychopath' syndrome and other legendary 'alternative behaviours' are explained as arising from shared patterning of SNS–PNS activity interacting with environmental influences which differ in specific ways (Figs. 26, 64).

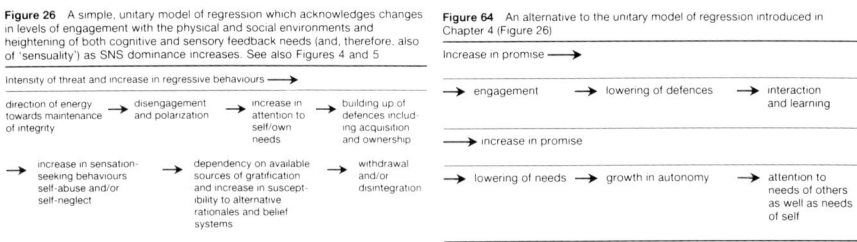

Figure 26 A simple, unitary model of regression which acknowledges changes in levels of engagement with the physical and social environments and heightening of both cognitive and sensory feedback needs (and, therefore, also of 'sensuality') as SNS dominance increases. See also Figures 4 and 5

Intensity of threat and increase in regressive behaviours ⟶

direction of energy towards maintenance of integrity → disengagement and polarization → increase in attention to self/own needs → building up of defences including acquisition and ownership

→ increase in sensation-seeking behaviours self-abuse and/or self-neglect → dependency on available sources of gratification and increase in susceptibility to alternative rationales and belief systems → withdrawal and/or disintegration

Figure 64 An alternative to the unitary model of regression introduced in Chapter 4 (Figure 26)

Increase in promise ⟶

→ engagement → lowering of defences → interaction and learning

⟶ increase in promise

→ lowering of needs → growth in autonomy → attention to needs of others as well as needs of self

4.10 *Artistic and cultural styles* Changes in, and interaction between, biochemical responses and physical, social, and cultural environmental conditions are also shown to effect the most fundamental changes in individual and group *needs and preferences*, including preferences for different kinds of symbolism. This, in turn, is also seen to affect artistic and cultural styles. Key changes in style are seen to be intimately related to the levels and kinds of stimulation we can tolerate and/or seek and the levels and kinds of 'externalization' (in accordance with the 'intercourse principle' (see postulate 4) which result.

Postulates of APM-A theory

Full explanations of postulates 1–7 appear in *Attention, Affect and Learning* (Gear 1987) which offers a unified view of attention, emotion, and learning while introducing the rationale behind the original APM-A model. However, postulates 8–25 are fully explained in the preceding text. Those before number 16 refer mainly to human adaptability, while 17–25 refer most obviously to variability.

1 that above all else the human organism strives to fulfil its need for orientation in response to long- and short-term environmental change

Because APM-A theory views change as the source of both threat and promise, and human beings as essentially vulnerable, it suggests that the definition of the ways in which attention is given and gained, and analysis of the relationship between attention, perception, memory, and arousal are of crucial importance to acquiring insights into the functioning of mind. Its conception of the so-called 'attention mechanism', however, differs in several important respects from conventional views.

Instead of postulating a particular temporal order of events between attention, perception, and memory, or that *either* attention *or* perception is responsible for the selection of information, as others have indicated,[1] it offers a dynamic model.

It dismisses the conventional view of a linear sequence of separate processes, such as attention→perception→thought→feeling→memory, and instead promotes a model which shows these reactions to environmental information as simultaneous and interactive aspects of the same process. It accommodates the possibility that, initially, the process may be activated by attention to, perception of, or memory of, sense data; or, that a physiologically initiated change in state of arousal may itself prompt changes in attention, perception, and memory.

As the APM-A position stresses our predominantly active rather than passive nature, it leads to a view of attention which differs from prevalent models in another respect. It regards the concept of the attention

Figure 65 The APM-A model: a model representing the interactive relationship between attention, perception, memory, and arousal which results in the acquisition of sensory experience which, at levels of conceptual organization and skill improvement, is recognized as learning

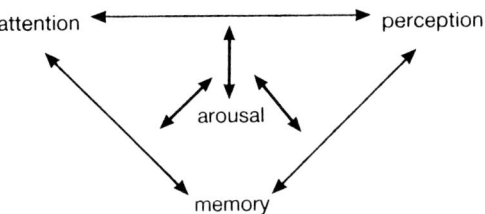

mechanism as a filter as both limited and misleading, and suggests instead that predominantly active unconscious and conscious selection of signals takes place.

Further, four other key factors, all derived from our knowledge of the limited capacity of attention (Miller 1956), suggest three important dimensions beyond the conventional internal–external dimension which must be incorporated into a definition of attention.

The factors in question are (1) that in order to enhance likelihood of survival, selection must take place according to some kind of *priority system*; (2) the likelihood of efficient and unequivocal identification of signals being effected in urgent situations is stronger if selection takes place at *sub-threshold levels of consciousness* first; (3) that in the interests of economy of attention *most signals are scanned* rather than commanding focused attention; and (4) that as, again in the interests of economy, the majority of our responses are routinized, it is necessary to take into account the fact that attention is likely to be *gained* as a result of *unconscious motivations and instinct*, as well as being *given* consciously on command. The four dimensions of attention incorporated into APM-A theory are therefore as follows: internal–external; scanning–focus; given–gained; and conscious–unconscious.

2 that the human organism is tuned (adapted) to adapt to change at all levels of biological organization – *i.e. cellular, individual, and species – and that the process of adaptation may be more or less transient or more or less permanent: to effect* phenomenological *adjustment or* short-term *or* long-term learning, *or provide instinctive responses in the form of* species learning

3 that the experience of emotion and cognition *involves the* same interactive process *and similar changes from general to specific arousal, so that in the one the dominant experience is of a bodily reaction and in the other mental*

activity; that a theory of learning may also therefore provide a theory of attention and a theory of emotion

In adopting an interactive model APM-A theory necessarily also takes into account the interaction of limbic and cortical arousal, and following Luria (1973:273–5) regards the limbic region – significantly, the oldest part of the brain – as the primary basis of attention.

The relationship between the two kinds of arousal holds special significance within the APM-A perspective: as the basis of general and specific arousal; as the underlying process of the relationship between emotion and cognition; and for the key dimension of scanning–focus: all of which are seen to hold as much significance for human variability as for human adaptability.

Schacter and Singer's (1962) supplementation of Cannon's (1927) much earlier theory of emotion with attributional concepts can be used to illustrate the APM-A position. Their definition of the sequence of events which occur in the experience and identification of emotion can be seen to apply equally well to cognition, when considered in terms of general and specific arousal.

Schacter and Singer's well-known description is as follows:

(a)   there is a bodily reaction;   general

(b)   the individual becomes *aware* of this reaction;

(c)   there is a need to seek reasons or
      explanations of the reaction;

(d)   an external cue is identified, and this internal
      reaction is labelled. This *labelling* provides
      the quality of the emotion.   specific

       (The present writer's italics and references
      to general and specific arousal)

The same stages can just as well be identified as occurring in the process of cognition:

(a)   arousal   general
          ↓
(b)   awareness
          ↓
(c)   need for explanation
          ↓
(d)   labelling   specific

Converted into the language of APM-A theory, this becomes:

arousal
↓
perception
↓
attention
↓
memory   (as recognition, registration, and
                              labelling for future recall)

However, this is conceived only as the interactive process identified in Figure 65, postulate 1. To introduce a general–specific dimension into this would demand a third dimension drawn through 'arousal', which would be labelled 'scan–focus'.

Such a model represents processing which goes on at all levels of consciousness, often taking only milliseconds to complete, so that our only conscious experience of it is as instantaneous labelling or recognition when the source of arousal is 'obvious'; but if ambiguity and a concomitant high degree of affect persist, a signal may be presented for prolonged conscious and unconscious scanning of stored information before satisfactory identification takes place. If focus is not achieved before attention is required elsewhere the problem is returned to, and an event may be given several possible identities before classification takes place.

The APM-A view of the relationship between affect and cognition is that on some occasions the *dominant* experience is the conscious attempt at orientation, classification and labelling, although arousal will be present (it having directed attention), whereas on other occasions the *dominant* experience will be the physiological changes providing what Schacter and Singer call 'a bodily reaction'. In this case the labelling is likely to be experienced as being of lesser significance, and the whole event as 'emotion'.

4 that the organism responds according to intensity of affect *as a result of* consciously or unconsciously perceived *environmental* threat or promise, *i.e. information from the physical, social, or cultural environment holding direct or indirect potential for physical or mental comfort or discomfort*

As a deeply instinctive and highly interactive mechanism involving autonomic and central nervous systems, the attention mechanism is not viewed as a neat mechanism located as an isolable piece of machinery at a specific site within the organism, but as a multi-dimensional process. It is seen as a defence mechanism (as is mind itself seen to be a grand defence mechanism *par excellence*) monitoring internal as well as external changes, to provide for food or cover, search for a mate (or simple utilization of sexual opportunity), and the assimilation of 'useful' information for other more complex or idiosyncratic purposes.

The APM-A model is quite consistent with Craik and Lockhart's (1972) depth-processing model of memory, in which strength of trace corresponds to the level of processing which the information undergoes. Their model implies that items receiving full attention and analysis, or which bear reference to existing experience and knowledge, lead to fairly permanent traces, as does the APM-A position.

The quest for the filter, which has absorbed so many researchers and theorists to date, is not regarded as a particularly fruitful area of enquiry, as firing of neuronal cells or not, and to what effect, is seen to be dependent on whether interest is sufficiently highly aroused and/or maintained. The position adopted indicates that the amount of continuous, or more or less interrupted neuro-cortical feedback (neuro-cortical activity in neuronal pathways and brain) following change in the environment, relates directly to the affective value of a signal and the degree of interest it arouses, which in turn relates to whether it is remembered or not, and if so, for how long.

It is also stressed that a model of attention must account for *continuous* neural (monitoring) activity, i.e. exteroceptor ←→ brain, interoceptor ←→ brain *feedback*. A simple one-way joining of mind to sensations (as in a filter model), *or* a simple selection model which accounts for one-way processing only, is seen to be inadequate.

5 *that attention is given and gained according to a* hierarchy of diminishing interest: *a priority system which relates primarily to the* evolutionarily oldest, *and most unitary, concept of species survival, as opposed to individual adaptation and survival*

APM-A theory postulates that absolute priority is given to, or gained by, signals bearing any consciously or unconsciously perceptible, direct, or symbolic relationship to species purposes, i.e. physical survival and propagation: in the absence of stimuli suggestive of physical threat attention is given to any which are indicative of sexual promise (which, in circumstances not too difficult to imagine, clearly hold at least slightly lower priority than those denoting physical danger).

Qualities associated with what are being called *first-priority signals* have been usefully summarized (Child 1977:68) as: intensity of stimuli; novel stimuli; variable and changing stimuli; and certain colours; the final class of stimuli likely to gain attention falls into the group referred to within our perspective as *third-priority signals,* i.e. conditioned and habitual stimuli.

In the absence of first-priority signals (related to species purposes) attention will shift to signals to do with individual 'purposes', and only in the absence of either, to stimuli associated with *un*developed interest or, in the phenomenological absence of all three kinds of environmental information or symbolism, to signals of a quite trivial nature.

Whereas Maslow's hierarchy of needs (Maslow 1970: 35–47) implies that new needs are attended to only after basic and safety needs (his order) are satisfied, and that attention then ascends to higher-order needs and eventually to self-actualization, the APM-A hierarchy implies that attention shifts to self-actualization only under certain circumstances; one requirement being the possession of what has been called the 'symbolic goods' (Brown 1973:71–112) necessary for its expression, and another is the possession of the kind of biological tuning which creates the high level of need which a need for self-actualization is seen to represent. Obviously, signals associated with needs identified by Maslow command attention, but within the new perspective it is argued that because of the phenomenological nature of attention, interaction takes place between conscious or unconscious attention given to internal needs, and sub-threshold scanning of quite unrelated (external) information.

For example, Maslow's group of ego needs could coincide with various kinds of purpose or interest, but during involvement in group activity, say, a signal associated with a career opportunity would temporarily command full attention, which in turn could be overridden if the barman shouted 'Fire'.

Figure 66 Maslow's hierarchy of needs compared with the APM-A hierarchy of *attention* as a *hierarchy of diminishing interest*, in which capacity of attention remains unchanged, and first- and second-priority signals relate directly to the survival of the individual and survival of the species respectively; and in which 'self-actualization' may occur as a concomitant of developed 'purposes' only

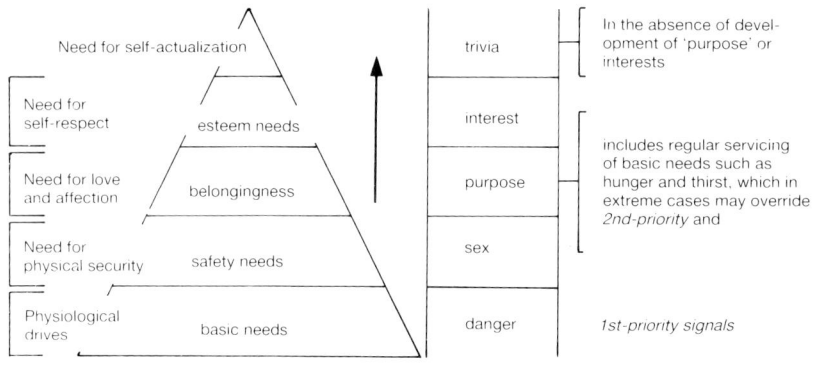

Figure 67 APM-A → *Verstand:* a model adopted to describe identifiably different, but simultaneous, kinds of information-processing as a phenomenological *and* a long-term, dynamic process. See note 2 on Norman's (1976) top-down, conceptually driven processing and bottom-up, data-driven processing

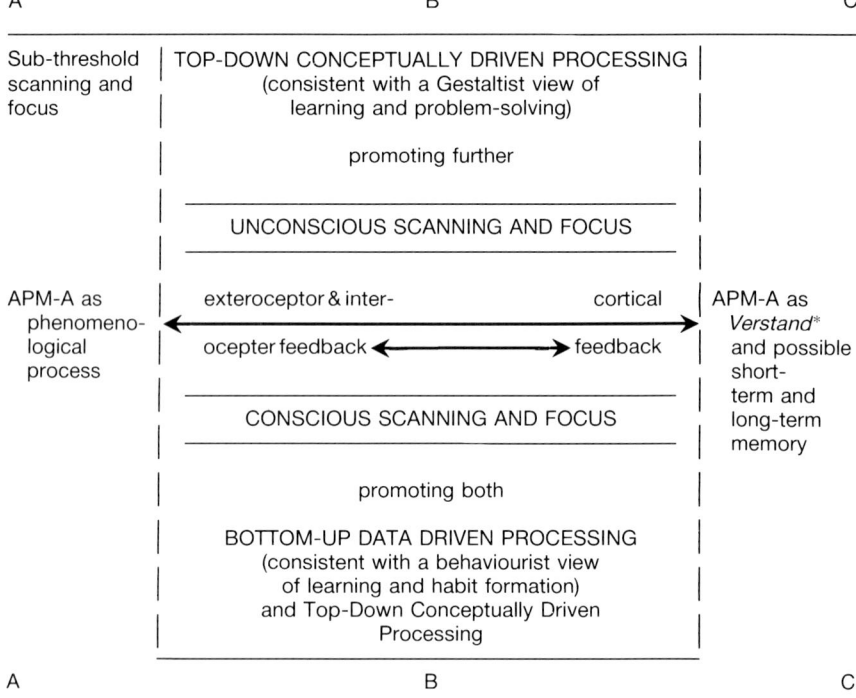

A   Attention, perception, memory, and arousal interacting as sub-threshold scanning and focus to produce possible registration of stimuli and further processing

B   Attention, perception, memory, and arousal maintained during further conscious and unconscious scanning and focus (resulting in conscious and unconscious classification), and possible addition of data to long-term store

C   Understanding and memory ranging from the readily available and consciously known to a long-term store at unconscious level, as a result of sustained conscious or unconscious effort

*   (German) 'understanding': a term used here to imply all that the term 'Gestalt' implies, but with an added long-term and mutable dimension

The APM-A position is quite consistent with Deutsch's (1963) postulate that the level of general arousal within the organism will be increased, and increased for varying lengths of time in proportion to the importance of the message; i.e. messages which would not normally be heeded will command attention if they follow in the wake of some significant information. On the other hand, more important messages than those present at an immediately preceding time will break in. Further, Deutsch notes that awareness and behavioural responsiveness to peripheral stimuli are absent without arousal, and that some degree of general arousal is necessary for selective attention to operate, and that individuals will attend to any incoming message providing that it is not concomitant with a more important one.

The view being expressed is that attention and learning both derive from the function of a deeply instinctive (species-learned) process, which is still vigilant for threat above all else, but which operates in such a way that not only is attention still gained by lower-priority environmental events if actual threat does not materialize, but, in the idiom of Marshall McLuhan (1967), it is also possible that the medium – if composed of the kind of stimuli described above – and not the message, will command full attention. Therefore, a *priority signal* may have *intrinsic affective value*, and be remembered as an event in its own right, or it may have what is being called *cue value* and, as graphic designers in particular understand, for ever be associated with something quite mundane.

6 that human orientation *is dependent on* two different but simultaneous kinds of information-processing *and that these can be directly related to Gestalt and behaviourist psychologies as well as to more recent models of attention, perception and memory (see Figure 67)*

7 that individual 'purposes' *develop incidentally to the fulfilment of species needs and adaptation, and according to a* hierarchy of developing purpose

Figure 68 A hierarchy of developing purpose as an application of the APM-A hierarchy of diminishing interest related to Razran's (1971) phylogenetic levels of learning

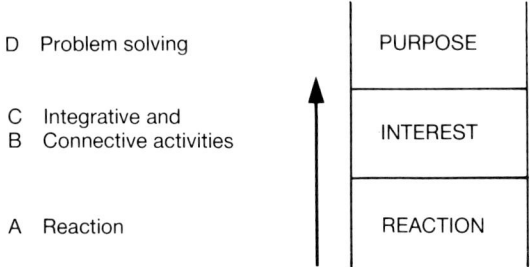

8 that changes in level of arousal *produce some predictable* changes in

attention, perception, memory, and behaviour *and that a direct relationship exists between levels and kinds of arousal and* levels and kinds of awareness *(see Figures 3, 12–20)*

9 *that* fascination *may be defined as our response to situations in which we perceive what is referred to as* manageable threat, *and that* pleasure *also derives from the* perception of optimal combinations of threat and promise: *that the same process underlies all human* learning and aesthetic experience

10 *that* all decision making *may be described as involving conscious and/ or unconscious* aesthetic choices

11 *that all psychological needs may be described as* orientation needs *(see Figures 4, 5) and all human needs as* homeostatic, *i.e. as arising from the need to adapt to change, which in turn demands some kind of compensatory activity within the organism, or by the organism within the environment, although the outcome or incidental effects of any such response may be apparently maladaptive*

12 *that* unmet orientation needs are potentially life-threatening *because maintenance of physical integrity, including and beyond the effective avoidance of danger and conscious fulfilment of physical needs, is dependent on the maintenance of psychological integrity: that there exists an intimate relationship between the level of psychological stress and the effective activity of the immune system – between psychological equilibrium and physiological equilibrium*

13 *that a* minimal degree of focus, *on which the maintenance of psychological integrity is taken to depend,* derives from short- or long-term aims, objectives, or goals and/or systems of belief: *more generally it is possible to say that focus derives from 'purpose', but where multiple purposes are experienced focus may be equated with the capacity to* identify, order, *and* select *priorities*

14 *that neuronal excitation which rises beyond* tension threshold *(susceptibility to psychological threat dependent on what is referred to as tuning or adaptation level) will be* externalized, *and manifested either as gestures associated with so-called restlessness or, if related to a particular source of threat or promise, activity according to the* intercourse principle

15 *that in addition to* manner of externalization *being dependent on the* intercourse principle *it is also dependent on* acquired means *(learning and* availability *of tools) of expression*

16 that a unifying theory of human nature must accommodate and explain apparent paradox

17 that dichotomies relating to different kinds of thinking conceived variously by researchers into cognitive style *and by researchers into* asymmetry of brain function, *and referred to in APM-A theory primarily as* sequential and diffuse styles, *can be related to each other and explained as manifestations of* different degrees of urgency of information-processing *and* individual differences in tension thresholds

18 that in addition to phenomenological changes in arousal within the organism which promote changes in the functioning of the autonomic nervous system, consistency in relative dominance of PNS (parasympathetic nervous system) or SNS (sympathetic nervous system) activity *accounts for key aspects of perceptual and behavioural styles as well as constituting* a human variable

19 that given the crucial role of the experience of pleasure and pain in the motivation of behaviour, in order to explain differences in personality and relate them to other aspects of individual style, *it is necessary to take account of (1) the key role of* limbic arousal, *(2) differences in* biases and kinds *of arousal as well as differences in* intensity *of arousal, and (3) the* interaction *of limbic and cortical arousal (see Figures 12–20)*

20 that differences in levels and kinds of SNS activity *account for fundamental individual differences in styles of perception (including aesthetic preferences) and behaviour beyond, and in addition to, those accounted for by degrees of consistency in relative dominance of PNS or SNS activity* per se *(see Figure 15)*

21 that the range of human variability is more adequately described by a dynamic model of style *which allows relationships to be shown between functional and dysfunctional states, and between 'normal' and 'abnormal' states within the same* holistic framework, *than by separate bipolar continua (see Figures 12–20, 22–24)*

22 that levels and kinds of need *are related to levels and kinds of arousal and share the same extreme polarities as extremes of personality (see Figure 17)*

23 that aspects of individual style which fall under the general headings of personality and motivation can also be related to levels and kinds of intelligence, *which, in APM-A terms, is defined quite simply as 'the ability to cope effectively with new situations' (see Figures 19, 20)*

24 that within a dynamic model of style levels and kinds of creativity *can be seen to relate to levels and kinds of intelligence as well as to other characteristics of individual style, particularly with reference to capacities for (1) making novel associations (*ideas), *and (2) levels of physical, social, and intellectual orientation needs and consequent* action

25 that a unifying theory of human nature must be based on an organic model of mind

Notes

General introduction

1 In the view of J. Z. Young (personal communication) we no longer need the concept of mind, but should refer to brain activity. On the other hand, Richard Gregory (personal communication) supports the view that both concepts are valid and useful whether a dualist point of view is adopted or not.
2 In fact, APM-A theory contains several models, but at its nub is a 'dynamic model of style' which is described in detail in Chapters 3 and 4, and a broad outline of the theory and how its models relate to one another is offered in 'The APM-A Framework', Appendix 1. The rationale for the original APM-A model – an interactive model of attention, perception, memory, and arousal, on which the theory is based – is explained under postulate 1, Appendix 2.
3 E.g. within psychoanalysis, behaviourism, or sociology.

Introduction to Part 1

1 E.g. Gestalt psychology, behaviourism, humanistic psychology, physiological psychology, psychoanalysis.
2 E.g. clinical, educational, experimental, general, industrial.
3 As distinct from Gray's (1975) two processes, or Mowrer's (1947) two factors cited by Van Toller (1979:112ff.).

Chapter 1 Maintaining the balance

1 Psychologists who, at the turn of the century, became interested in the function of mind as it is used in the adaptation of the organism to its environment.
2 While J. B. Watson is viewed as having announced the behaviourist position, which is currently most closely identified with B. F. Skinner, and Freud is generally seen to be the father of psychoanalysis, the founding of sociobiology was marked by the publication of E. O. Wilson's *Sociobiology: the New Synthesis* (1975).
3 This is not to invoke the potentially misleading 'law of recapitulation' which in its very simplest form states that, in its development an animal *necessarily* rehearses its own evolutionary history, passing through stages comparable to the adult stages of its various evolutionary forerunners (see Medawar and Medawar 1978).
4 The master gland is so called because of its control over the endocrine system.
5 Phylogenetic adaptation or 'innate information', which Lorenz speaks of as

taking 'a simple plus or minus form, of what feels good or what feels bad' (see Alsop 1969:73–4) is to be referred to as *species learning*. See postulate 2 and p. 31.

6 See Chapter 3 for a full discussion of dichotomies which relate to modes of thinking.

7 I.e. the rates and patterns of firing produced in the ANS are dependent on whether transmitters precipitate SNS or PNS dominance in response to internal or external stimuli. See Leukel (1976:71ff.).

8 Eysenck's physiological model of personality and Zuckerman's related work on sensation seeking (both of which have obvious relevance here) are referred to in detail in Chapters 3 and 4. See note below.

9 Marvin Zuckerman's identification of sensation seeking as a human variable for which he devised the Sensation Seeking Scale (SSS), includes scales of risk-taking behaviour. See Zuckerman (1979).

10 Implied by the need to alleviate the kind of 'mismatch' identified as painful by both cognitive and psychoanalytic theories and discussed by K. Oatley, 'Metaphors and the nature of consciousness', in Underwood and Stevens (1981:100).

11 For an example of how man can change his own biology, see p. 116 which refers to evolutionary changes in female form as an incidental effect of cultural changes which created a demand for the male to be lured back to a domiciliary unit. Other examples include the effects of dietary changes on teeth and internal organs.

12 I.e. the recognition of commonality in patterning of stimuli and the construction of analogues.

13 E.g. yin–yang, the negative and positive principles in Chinese Taoist philosophy which are deemed responsible for all existence, and underlie and control all things.

14 Gilbert Ryle's (1949) phrase used to describe the dualist position currently sustained by Sir John Eccles and Sir Karl Popper.

15 Although Skinner accepts genetic influences (see *Beyond Freedom and Dignity*: 1971), in evolutionary terms these are actually also environmentally induced.

16 In their book *Creative Aggression* (1976), Bach and Goldberg used the phrase 'creative aggression' to imply different kinds of energetic interaction (including self-assertion techniques) which aid communication and help to develop personal relationships.

Chapter 2 Psychological survival

1 Arousal, tension, stress, motivation, and drive are all viewed here as deriving from the attentional and physiological processes described in postulates 1–8 in particular, and in Chapter 1.

2 'Higher needs' are discussed by Maslow (1970, 2nd ed.: 72, 97–104), while APM-A first- and second-order needs are defined at the end of this chapter.

3 However sweeping the assumption may seem the thesis being developed rests on the belief that all psychological needs remain unconscious, unless they can be rationalized within a non-threatening explanatory system.

4 See postulates 7, 13, 14, 15, Appendix 2, and Gear 1987.

5 A factor most stressed by psychoanalysts (e.g. Storr 1963) and humanists (e.g. Rogers 1980).

6 A great deal of ambiguity and confusion arises in discussion of illnesses in which stress is a factor – e.g. in an article attributing allergies and feelings of

disorientation and depression to *physical* causes, in which criticism is made of diagnoses of problems as psychosomatic, a doctor apparently supporting the notion of such illnesses always being attributable to physical causes, comments on factors such as moving house or the death of a close relative as the 'point of imbalance' in a highly ambiguous manner. He says, 'The stress is not the prime cause of the subsequent illness, though it may appear so. It is merely the trigger' (the *Guardian*, 15 Sept. 1982). Presumably he does mean that in certain cases the physical problem would not have arisen had it not been so triggered.

7 Relevant to mind–body interaction, the importance of focus to the integrity of the psyche, and dominance of psychological over physical well-being, is work being done in America on patients focusing the mind on rejection of alien cells and visualizing the immune system in action. An account of successful eradication of a malignant tumour by this means appeared in the *Guardian*, 30 Sept. 1982.

8 It is interesting to note that the central tenets of Zen Buddhism appear to acknowledge key psychological principles: the need for directed thought for effective action; the value of attention to the present (being); and adjustment to change. (See Humphreys 1962:29, 46.)

9 Bryant (1974), for instance, challenges Piaget's hypothesized stages of development.

10 Pertinently, Dr Faith Spicer, Director of the London Youth Advisory Service, at a conference at the University of Hull, 25 Sept. 1982, drew attention to the need for individuation in adolescence as well as in early childhood, and to similarities in feelings of dependence and helplessness between youths and babies. She also drew attention to the fact that youths also have their oral, anal, and genital phases but that at the later stage they are manifested as greediness, dirtiness, and sexual obsessions.

11 A full discussion of questions concerning the role of emotion in attention and learning appears in *Attention, Affect and Learning* (Gear 1987).

Chapter 3 Individual differences

1 Educationally subnormal.

2 Mild brain damage, a syndrome described by Pincus and Tucker (1978:165–8).

3 E.g. field-dependence–independence, reflective–impulsive, risk-taking–cautiousness. See also p. 81.

4 Some indirect support for this position is offered by R. J. Williams in his book *Biochemical Individuality* (1977), in which he argues that there are no 'normal' people – biochemically speaking – but that there is an enormous range of variability in this respect.

5 The term 'dominance' in our context implies only relative dominance of one hemisphere over the other. It is not used to imply total dominance or used in the sense in which the left hemisphere is traditionally considered to be the 'dominant hemisphere', as will be discussed.

6 In the table reproduced in Fig. 6, Springer and Deutsch refer to 'sequential' and 'simultaneous'; in Fig. 8, Semmes, Weinstein, Ghent, and Teuber refer to 'discrete' and 'diffuse'. The preferred terms here are *sequential* and *diffuse*.

7 I.e. presently irrelevant, conflict-laden, or otherwise too threatening to be consciously acknowledged, but which may be 'significant' enough to demand unconscious processing to allow its conscious acknowledgement either in a 'managed' form, or in a less threatening context later.

8 Ruddock (1980:47) uses the terms 'ritual' and 'encounter' to describe

personality dimensions with reference to teachers and teaching. Obsessives are seen as being involved in 'ritual': concentrating habitually as a means of handling anxiety, while hysterics 'encounter' – being given to 'dramas' and 'connecting' all of the time, to the extent that consciousness may 'split' and 'fragment'.

9 The view here is that biological adaptation, and indeed human motivation, occur as dynamic reactions to multiple pressures which incidentally allow a confusing – or convenient – array of possible rationalizations, providing that more than one possible explanation of a given phenomenon is in fact recognized. Further, the concept of 'reinforcement' is seen to hold as much relevance to species learning as to the kind of learning recognized by behaviourist psychologists.

10 No assumption should be made here of any particular link with the Jungian concept of complementarity.

11 (a) Degree of suggestibility will eventually be seen to be dependent on the tuning of the organism which, alongside the resources of physical and mental energy which such tuning endows, is assumed to be one of the key aspects of human functioning to be biologically determined. Genetic influence is not necessarily assumed, as pre-natal and birth experience itself must also be taken into account.
(b) Obviously, degrees of suggestibility relate to the question of how much of human behaviour is acquired as a result of environmental influence. The answer to such a question from the new position being adopted, would be 'all of it'. This answer takes into account *species* 'development' and 'learning', whereas the question usually takes into account only individual learning. The APM-A framework indicates that a potentially much more fruitful approach to the nature–nurture debate would be to take into account interaction between the organism and *all* other biology, chemistry, and physics (i.e. total environment), and long-term (over millions of years) as well as short-term conditioning. Such an approach would allow debate to shift beyond the unresolvable innate–learned dichotomy (apparently rooted in creationism) to questions about which behaviours have been so strongly reinforced to have become fixed (in individual terms); which responses remain relatively plastic; and which, as far as can be verified, remain to be acquired as part of an individual (as opposed to part of the species) repertoire.

12 I.e. primarily sequential or diffuse (a dichotomy preferred here to the more common sequential–simultaneous). See Figures 6–10 and note 6.

13 The use of the phrase 'control by the left hemisphere' is used in acknowledgement of the fact that the same information may be held in different modes, and therefore by both hemispheres. It is not meant to imply *necessary* control by the left.

14 Springer and Deutsch (1981) discuss the slow recognition of the importance of the right hemisphere, while making reference to some of the data which indicate the complexity of its role. The need to take account of much greater complexity in the relationship between right and left hemispheres is also stressed by Gordon (1983).

15 The phrase 'most effective' is used in recognition of the fact that in most cases a whole battery of tests would be necessary in order even to be sure that a commissurotomy operation had taken place, as most patients continue to behave apparently normally.

16 Aphasia: defect or loss of the power of expression by speech, writing, or signs, or of comprehending spoken language (Ornstein 1973).

17 The hypothesis being developed suggests that much of what is perceived at the stage of sub-threshold scanning may be edited out of organized and/or verbal consciousness by the right hemisphere, especially if perceived to be threatening to existing rationales or belief systems.

18 Deikman actually attributes changes occurring in body boundaries, in muscle tension, in sensory vividness, in EEG, in imagery, in logic, and in self-awareness, all to manifestations of these two basic organismic states or modes.

19 In fact, as Hudson acknowledges, the terms 'converger' and 'diverger' were first used by Guilford (1950).

20 Hudson argues that 'it is logically possible for a converger actually to have a higher open-ended score than a diverger, either by virtue of having a quite exceptionally high I.Q. score, or by virtue of the diverger's I.Q. score being exceptionally low' (1967:56).

21 See note 8 above.

22 This dichotomy is not quite the same as Deikman's action and receptive modes, which, he points out, must not be confused with activity and passivity. See Deikman (1973:70–1).

23 The phrase 'relative bias' is used in acknowledgement of the already argued species bias toward psychological survival.

24 Within our context it will eventually be seen to be more appropriate to refer to scanners making a *different kind of* demand on memory and reasoning skills, rather than *more* demand.

25 L. W. Morris (1979) points out that the atypical spelling of the word by H. J. Eysenck became the accepted spelling in the subject index of *Psychological Abstracts* beginning in 1974. In this text where authors are quoted the original spelling is used.

26 In fact the typology owes very little to Jung, although his name is so closely linked with it; as Eysenck points out (1981:9) the terms were in use in Europe long before their use by Jung.

27 The other dimensions being neuroticism–stability and psychoticism.

28 A concept which embodies the notion of interaction of a number of different polarities, e.g. conscious–unconscious, thinking–feeling, progression–regression.

29 Claridge's own view is that on balance, and for certain purposes, the physiologically less real, but operationally more precise division into 'cortical' and 'autonomic' and other forms of arousal may have an advantage, so long as the quotation marks are kept in mind (1981:133).

30 Some of the relationships between the polarities have been indicated already in this chapter, and the explication of others is implicit in the subject matter of the rest of this and the next chapter in particular.

31 Presumably on the grounds that extraverts seek more stimulation than introverts (see Zuckerman 1979:43).

32 Various findings have suggested that extraverts indulge in more physical activity than introverts. Most obvious evidence is that which associates extraversion with sport (see Eysenck 1981:224ff.). Higher levels of *cortical inhibition* in extraverts is seen here as evidence of *greater mental* activity, not less.

33 Evidence exists to suggest that extraverts have less expressive control than introverts: observed in behaviours such as taking bigger strides, forming bigger handwriting, talking more, making more eye contact (see Eysenck 1981:215).

34 See Eysenck (1971:45ff.) on individual differences in free response speed.

35 Cortical inhibition refers to the lowering of arousal in the cortex. See p. 86.

36 See M. W. Eysenck (1977:202), on differences in short-term and long-term memory between extraverts and introverts.

37 See Beatty (1982) for support for the notion of mental energy. Strong correlations between task demands and pupillary dilation are taken to suggest correlations between limited capacity and the arousal system.

38 Reference to the *Cumulated Index Medicus* of the US Department of Human Services, under epinephrine and norepinephrine and the research papers listed there, suggest that differential responses are extremely likely. This notion is also strongly supported by Cox and Thirlaway (1983:266–7).

39 The phrase 'physical activity' is used in its broadest possible sense, implying all behavioural gestures, from finger tapping through less obvious physical pursuits such as reading and writing to gross and obvious physical activities such as tossing the caber.

40 PNS dominance can, of course, only be *relative* because, as was argued in Chapter 1, the human organism is viewed as essentially active.

41 The only findings concerning differences in personality and adrenalin and noradrenalin levels which exist so far are with reference to types known as 'type A' and 'type B' personalities. By APM-A definition, 'A types' are characteristically second-order externalizers (E_2s); and 'B types' first-order internalizers (I_1s). Cox and Thirlaway (1983:263–7) discusses 'at least three studies in this area' which are consistent with our placing of internalizers and externalizers.

42 Thus allowing for the same physiological type to be expressed as, for example, artist or criminal. This notion is developed in Chapter 4.

43 Eysenck's correlation between intellectuality and the well-ordered, quiet, and emotionally unexpressive type will later be seen to take into account only *one kind* of intelligence (see pp. 107–10 and Fig. 19) and only one kind of introvert.

44 Both of these factors relate very closely to the major sub-factors of extraversion: impulsivity and sociability.

45 E.g. the theories of Freud, Murray, Skinner, Allport, Erikson, Kelly, Rogers, Maslow.

46 Heightened arousal being labelled by Pavlov (1927) the 'orientation reflex'.

47 Different levels of need and differences in kinds of interest/orientation – mainly towards physical, social, or intellectual phenomena – have already been associated in Figs. 4 and 15, and links between personality and differences in interest in places, people and ideas are also implicit in Hudson's observations (see pp. 78–9).

48 It must be noted that this is not to adopt a similar position to that of Howard Gardner (1983), who argues that there are six quite different and separate kinds of intelligence subject to different 'information-processing operations and mechanisms'. While the APM-A view of intelligence is non-unitary, it is not of discrete processes.

49 The behavioural evidence for this is very strong, but hitherto it has been assumed that provided levels are expressed in body-weight no sex difference can be demonstrated empirically (see Karki 1956). Recently, however, findings have become much more controversial, although the number of studies is still small (see Cox and Thirlaway 1983:267).

50 The mode which Deikman describes as action mode is seen to be rather more aptly described as a 'ready for action' mode, in the light of arguments presented above about internalizers/externalizers and focusing and scanning functions of attention.

51 The term 'reinforcement' is used here not just in its strict behaviourist sense,

but to include reinforcement of behaviour which derives from the satisfaction of unconscious needs; e.g. from the satisfaction of orientation needs such as those Maslow calls 'belongingness needs'. See also note 9.
52 E.g. cellular: in the operation of the immune system; individual: the reinforcement of self-image; group: maintaining group identity; community: racism, patriotism, nationalism, etc.
53 Professor Reuven Feuerstein expresses the belief that intelligence is not fixed, but rather that cognitive skills can be taught and cultural experience enriched in order to raise 'intelligence'. See Feuerstein (1980).

Chapter 4 Individual style and psychopathology

1 A test in which the subject may project current fantasies or inclinations through, and on to, his or her own free interpretation of ink blots.
2 For a discussion of the use of life-event scales, from which these findings derive, see Dohrenwend (1979:7–9). It should also be noted that events classified as 'life events' could, alternatively, be labelled *sources of disorientation*: events so classified relate directly to our revised hierarchy of needs (pp. 60–3) representing changes in, or loss of, sources of satisfaction of orientation needs.
3 Specific items of evidence will be presented under the discussion of particular disorders.
4 See Figs. 4, 5, 15, and 16 with reference to levels and kinds of orientation needs.
5 Shapiro tells us that the most conspicuous fact about the activity of the obsessive–compulsive is its sheer quantity, besides its intensity of concentration (ibid.:31).
6 Although there is no internationally agreed definition of schizophrenia, all four of the commonly accepted major forms (paranoid, simple, hebephrenic, and catatonic) are characterized by a more or less severe loss of reality.
7 Results from follow-up studies from a 1972 survey of three-year-olds which assessed levels of autonomic nervous system activity, together with findings that hospitalized schizophrenics give either an abnormally high ANS response, or no response at all in tests involving flashing lights or sudden sounds, have led to the conclusion that it is possible to identify potential schizophrenics by these means up to fifty years before symptoms cause breakdown. See Venables 1983.
8 Body signs as iconic signs of body illness: as a means of communication between sufferers and helpers.
9 Identity based on the identification of predicates (therefore offering numerous alternative possibilities), rather than on subjects (which offer only a limited number of deductive possibilities).
10 See also note 10, Chapter 2, with reference to the stresses of childhood and other stages of life.
11 The significance of Magaro's (1980) work, for instance, to APM-A theory is explained more fully in Gear 1985:280.
12 This may best be understood in relation to the schizophrenic's lack of rigidity of set and consequent unbiased conceptual categories, and Magaro's discussion (1980:145–6) of differences in cognition between the paranoid and the schizophrenic and his postulation that

> paranoids rely on conceptual processes without adequate restraint being imposed by perceptual data. Schizophrenics rely primarily on perceptual data without adequate categorization and classification from conceptual

processes. The demands of the situation determine if the schizophrenic or
paranoid cognitive process is adaptive or maladaptive.

13 This view is consistent with both the connection perceived by Shapiro between
the perception of truth and breadth of attention and our placing of
schizophrenia on the APM-A model.

14 See previous references to simultaneous processing (pp. 68–70) and Ruddock's
concept of 'multiple and simultaneous purposes' (p. 78).

15 In the light of recent but well-established findings indicating differences in the
development of the corpus collosum between men and women (see de Lacoste-
Utamsing and Holloway 1982) and our arguments above, about maleness and
femaleness in creativity, it is tempting to hypothesize that the 'Door in the Wall'
may indeed have an almost literal structural counterpart allowing more or less
communication between the left and right hemispheres of the brain.

16 In a controversial publication by Ian Wilson, *Jesus: the Evidence* (1984:99ff.)
it is also suggested that the historical Jesus was in fact a charismatic figure whose
particular influence was rooted in his extraordinary (but probably quite
unconscious) powers as a hypnotist.

17 This is a sentiment which is, incidentally, colourfully expressed by Philip Larkin
who refers to religion as:

That vast moth-eaten musical brocade
Created to pretend we never die.
(Aubade)

18 Ed Mitchell, former astronaut, has spoken at length and made a film about his
'peak experiences' – experiences of harmony, unity, and insight as a result of
his space flights – whereas former astronaut Charlie Duke is now working and
preaching to 'bring together' psychology and religion.

19 For instance, the 'psychic side of sport' has recently been the subject of
investigation by the American Research Council.

20 Various models of depression and other findings are discussed more fully in
relation to the APM-A model in Gear 1985:289.

21 See Mitchell (1975:59) on the surprise of relatives at suicides which happen
after the depressive victim appears to be recovering.

22 Although the interpretation of altruism may be in terms of Hans Selye's notion
of altruistic egotism (1974:21, 128–9), which is consistent with the view of
altruism offered here, and an interpretation which renders the sociobiological
explanation – in terms of kin selection – redundant (see Trivers 1971:35–7).

23 Now an international movement, it was founded in 1953 by the Rev. Chad
Varah, Rector of St Stephen's, Walbrook, London, with an original team
consisting of two priests and a psychiatric social worker, and one telephone
number manned twenty-four hours a day. However, demand for the services
of the movement is not the same as evidence to suggest that it actually helps
to prevent suicide. One study, at least, exists to suggest that this is not the case.
See Jennings and Barraclough (1979:194ff.).

24 Goodwin (1974:242) actually cites an unpublished study by Maas and Colburn
showing that *either* a psychological or a biological manipulation can accomplish
the same thing. In their experiment this was the loss of the capacity in beagle
puppies to form primary social bonds with other beagle puppies: primary bond
formation which normally depends on increase in brain norepinephrine, which
does not happen if the dog is separated from its litter during a critical period

of development, or, it was found, if the dog is left with its litter, but the elevation of norepinephrine in the puppies is knocked out.

25 As no generally agreed clinical definition of depression exists, what is meant here is that not all depressed individuals become psychiatric patients.

26 Although Mitchell (1975:119), for instance, defines depression as a mood, as an experience, as an attitude and as an illness, as well as in terms of normal (potentially healing) and abnormal (potentially disordering) responses, others (see Friedman and Katz 1974:19) adopt the continuum approach – from everyday sadness to severe melancholia.

27 See Chodoff (1974:58) on depressive features of hysterical and non-hysterical patients and Janet's thesis that hysterical features protect against depression.

28 Some support for the APM-A insistence on the significance of patterning of brain activity as an underlying feature of human variability is offered by recent research into a variety of mental illnesses carried out in the University of Pennsylvania School of Medicine. It was found that whereas in the brains of normal resting volunteers scans showed harmonious and almost symmetrical patterning of brain activity, consistent differences could be found between manic depressives, for instance, who showed pronounced asymmetry of activity occurring in many parts of the brain at the same time, and schizophrenics, who showed depressed activity in the frontal lobes. This was seen to offer the possibility of being able to recognize different forms of mental illness from particular mosaics of activity.

29 Wold and Tabachnik (1974:194) refer to Pokorny's research, which showed suicide to be the only important cause of death in depression. Pokorny offers the following suicide rate per 100,000, among former patients in the psychiatric service of a Texas veteran's hospital, over a 15-year period: depression 566; schizophrenia 167; neurosis 199; personality disorder 130; alchoholism 133; and organic reasons 78. The suicide rate for the depressed patients, therefore, was 78 times the expected rate and substantially higher than that of other psychiatric patients. They also note that a number of theorists, including Sigmund Freud and Karl Menninger, have postulated that suicide is one of the usual endpoints for severe depression.

30 For instance, Beck (1974:15) points out the need to take more account of the fact that although the depressive patient shrinks from all of the more or less elementary things he feels 'ought to do', he may nevertheless become exceptionally aroused and energetic in order to *avoid* activities which he is pressed to engage in, although a stage is reached by some patients at which even avoidance becomes passive rather than an active gesture.

31 Manic-depressive depression has received by far the greatest amount of attention by both psychoanalytical and psychiatric investigators, and Kendell (1976:26) considers the distinction made by Leonhard, in 1959, between unipolar and bipolar depressive illnesses (to distinguish patients with and without a history of mania) to be 'probably the most important area of emerging agreement' in the classification of depression.

32 It is acknowledged, however, that the method used is inextricably related to other key stylistic factors, such as conscious and unconscious motivations and the actual outcome of any act of self-harm. See Farmer and Hirsch (1979).

33 For instance, within Reversal Theory (see Apter 1982:101) depression is viewed as a form of 'unpleasant low arousal'.

34 Although Crowcroft (1967:134) suggests that this aspect of the treatment no longer plays an important part, a fairly recent report (Nov. 1981) on ECT by

the Royal College of Psychiatrists includes criticism of ill-trained staff who fail to induce a seizure.

35 Reference to our hierarchy of developing purpose (postulate 7, Appendix 2) helps to make sense of the fact that gross indulgence in stereotypic behaviours is apparently more likely in children than in adults.

36 That is, conditions which are manifestations of either low levels of adrenalin combined with high levels of noradrenalin, or low levels of both adrenalin and noradrenalin.

37 Shapiro actually attributes this highly descriptive term to David Rapaport (1945).

38 Mild brain damage, known in America as minimal brain dysfunction.

39 This hypothesis is also consistent with hypotheses concerning individual differences in the organization of cortical processing which arise from Redundancy Theory (see Powell 1979:chap. 7). He makes the point that low-(information) redundancy messages are seen to be more 'risky' since they contain fewer internal cues to meaning and a greater probability of misapprehension; but most relevant to our argument is the fact that 'redundancy *reduction* is involved when *interest* and *participation* are called forth: redundancy *enhancement* helps to *focus and restrict* the organism's sensory interaction with the situation'. Moreover, Powell cites Pribram as relating these differences to differences in performances between extraverts and introverts, with 'wide sensory involvement' (characteristic of the extravert) paralleled by low redundancy processing.

40 Recent court cases in Britain have also stimulated public interest in pre-menstrual tension (PMT). Dr Katherine Dalton, a Harley Street consultant who has studied PMT for over thirty-five years and is frequently called upon to give evidence, has established connections between many cases of female aggression and violence (as well as misdemeanours associated with forgetfulness, unpunctuality, depression, and irritability) and cyclical changes affecting the secretion of adrenalin in particular. And, to the predictable dismay of feminists everywhere, she points out that the word 'hysteria' means, literally, a condition caused by the womb and that 'lunacy' refers to the monthly cycle.

41 Eysenck is not the only psychologist to hold the view that a tendency for criminal behaviour is genetic. A recent study comparing the criminal records, if any, of adopted children and their biological parents has led its authors to the same (qualified) conclusion. See Mednick and Gabrielli (1984).

42 Author of *A Sense of Freedom* (1977) and, with Tom McGrath, a play, *The Hard Man* (1977), he made these comments during a talk, 'Art and Personal Development', at a conference *Support for the Arts: Recent Evidence for the Value of the Arts in Education,* held in London in 1984.

43 Obviously, the question of which group an individual is most likely to identify with is very complex and depends on many factors, including how powerful a model exists within the family group and whether or not cognitive and emotional styles are conducive to identification and modelling. However, where conflict between groups does exist, needs for communication and 'belongingness' are seen to favour peer-group influence.

44 SS behaviours can be seen to be concerned with sensation seeking within the physical and/or social environments as well as involving changes of mental states. This suggests that individuals falling within the I_2, E_2, or E_1 area of the APM-A model may all be potentially high scorers on the SS if purposeful means of gratification are unavailable.

45 Some support for this position is offered by Landau and Beit-Hallahmi (1983)

on world aggression, in the context of which they consider the effects of a variety of social stressors and consequent group and individual reactions.

Introduction to Part 2

1 Freud and Maslow provide the most obvious examples of polar-extreme positions on questions of homeostasis and heterostasis respectively. According to Hjelle and Ziegler (1976:16) these diametrically opposed positions are irreconcilable.

Chapter 5 Nineteenth-century refuges and twentieth-century prospects

1 Wölfflin in *Principles of Art History* (first published in English in 1932) identified the following five binary criteria: linear vs. the painterly; plane vs. recession; closed form vs. open form; multiplicity vs. unity; clearness vs. unclearness.
2 The term 'aesthetic' was introduced in the eighteenth century as a neologism for the science of perceptible beauty, but soon became a generic term to include the enjoyment of both artefacts and nature. Currently there tends to be a strong line drawn between 'empirical aesthetics' (practised by psychologists) and 'speculative aesthetics' seen to be the domain of philosophers, art historians, and critics.
3 A distinction between the terms 'style' and 'preference' is made on pp. 209–16.
4 A definition of physiognomy – which is not used with its commonly understood, and more specific, meaning of the art of reading character from the features of the face – appears on p. 199.
5 In particular Berlyne (1971:chap. 3) cites the mystique which surrounds art and the consequent difficulty in 'adopting the sober dispassionate stance that scientific examination of aesthetic phenomena must require'; failure to separate normative and factual questions; an apparent need by philosophers to offer a unitary definition of art at the beginning of any enquiry; a tendency to view art in isolation; and the popular wisdom that 'there is no accounting for taste'.
6 See section 4.5 (Sensation seeking) and the model of regression (Fig. 26).
7 The idea that the basis of our aesthetic reactions to visual stimuli is founded in their relationship to survival needs is strongly supported by empirical findings by Gordon Orians (1980) with reference to his belief that human preferences for particular tree shapes evolved during the species' early life in the savanna.
8 Edmund Leach in *Culture and Communication* (1976:chap. 13) discusses reasons for the non-existence of a completely universal cross-cultural symbolic language, and the complications which arise from the fact that symbols occur in sets, i.e. their meanings are to be found in contrasts with other symbols rather than in the symbols themselves, so that *specific* meanings of colour, for instance, can differ dramatically from one culture to another.
9 The nineteenth and twentieth centuries have actually witnessed artists theorizing more and more about their own work. See Chipp (1968). This phenomenon itself will be seen to be consistent with the general argument of this chapter.
10 See Figs. 66 (hierarchy of diminishing interest) and 68 (hierarchy of developing purpose), Appendix 2.
11 In *Civilisation and its Discontents*, tr. Riviere (1930), Freud opened debate among psychoanalysts about the possibility of neuroses operating at cultural levels. This is referred to again at the end of the chapter.

12 Although Appleton's theory of landscape aesthetics is called 'prospect-refuge theory', the concept of 'hazard' also plays a part in that it is seen to give prospect and refuge meaningful roles; i.e. prospect and refuge symbolism are seen to demand hazard symbolism to make them work. See Appleton 1975:95–6.

13 In fact one of the problems prospect-refuge theory has encountered has been to do with attribution and subjectivity of response. See Appleton 1984a:98.

14 Berlyne cites evidence suggesting that the peak of pleasantness experienced in the perception of tone (intensity of lightness or darkness) is compatible with the intensity-pleasantness relationship following an inverted U-shaped curve, in common with size perception and other kinds of perception such as perception of complexity and novelty. See Berlyne 1971:177–8, 220. There is also a weight of consensual evidence about the shapes of takete and maluma referred to above, and cited by Lindauer (1983).

15 Berlyne's findings on pleasantness and unpleasantness and brightness (intensity) perception in relation to the inverted U-shaped curve offer indirect evidence of the fact that any marked change from adaptation-level holds threat to the organism; as well as it having been argued in Part 1 that the reason sudden change commands attention is because of its association with hazardous situations within the natural environment.

16 Those of the German school, most active between 1910 and 1915, whose main concerns were free means of expression and social protest.

17 Holge Höge (1983) cites findings confirming the crucial nature of the emotional state of the subject in aesthetic experience.

18 The most notable exception to this trend was the phenomenon of Super Realism, sometimes called Photo Realism, which occurred towards the end of the 1960s and had its roots in Pop Art, the style which used comic strips and other popular imagery as a source.

19 Known drug addicts quadrupled between 1976 and 1983, and in 1983 alone rose by 50%. Other manifestations of psychological stress (according to APM-A theory and without reference to figures directly related to increases in mental disorders) include escalations in violence against the person (more than doubled between 1971 and 1983); criminal damage (increased fifteenfold in the same period); suicide (established cases rose by one-fifth between 1975 and 1983). See *Social Trends*, 15 (1985 edition).

20 The concept of compensation has already been identified as important to the inner–outer (organism–environment) dimension, in addition to underlying internal homeostasis, at the end of Chapter 3.

21 According to earlier arguments (see pp. 37–8), an explanation of why inconsistency rather than consistency is traditionally associated with romanticism lies in the fact that high levels of arousal (emotion) produce motor disturbance.

22 The sculpture of ex-prisoner and convicted murderer Jimmy Boyle actually provides a current example of strikingly primitive-looking forms created by an artist who sees his sculpture, above all, as a channel of expression for his energy.

23 A group formed in 1848 led by Dante Gabriel Rossetti, William Holman Hunt, and John Everett Millais. Its underlying conceptions were 'truth to nature', acquired from John Ruskin, and conscious rebellion against the academic establishment.

24 The label seems especially appropriate as Gordon Rattray Taylor (1979:28ff.)

calls the mid-brain (the oldest part) the 'hot brain' – in contrast to the cortex, which he calls the 'cold brain'.

25 More complex and more random associations of ideas were related in Chapter 3 (3.3) to high levels of SNS activity.

26 For instance, in a recent exhibition of 'New Art' at the Tate Gallery Joseph Beuys exhibited what looked like a printing press with a keyboard covered in vomit and apparently babbling (recorded) nonsense. It was called 'Terramoto'.

27 One of a number of techniques adopted by the Surrealists in attempts to explore unconscious processes.

28 For example, Pointillism, Expressionism, Cubism, Abstract Expressionism, and Body Art.

29 For example, Robert Smithson's 'Spiral Jetty', 1970; a curl of bulldozed rock, built on the edge of the Great Salt Lake, Utah, projecting a quarter of a mile into the brine.

30 Symbolism was a collection of styles reflecting a literary form of painting rather than a particular style.

31 The central ideas of Fry and Bell are contained in Bullen (1981) and Bell (1982).

32 Mondrian's own statement about the importance of objectivity, 'Plastic art and pure plastic art', is reprinted in *Modern Artists on Art* (Herbert 1964).

33 So-called partly because they were of night and partly with reference to the musical form. See Gaunt 1945:82ff.

34 An alternative name for Abstract Expressionism: one which emphasizes a view of the importance of painting as a record of the process of its creations and used particularly of the work of de Kooning and Pollock (see Figure 43).

35 See note 39, Chapter 4, on redundancy theory.

36 A technique of juxtaposing dots and dabs of complementary colours on the canvas in order to heighten their effects. See note 40.

37 'Biomorphism' is a term used to describe the organic forms used by the Surrealists and typical of the work of, for instance, Jean Arp.

38 The term 'Constructivism' is broadly applied to art produced in the first two decades of this century which was consciously composed rather than being extemporaneous. The Soviet movement was more specific: it eschewed illusion, exploiting the actual properties of materials.

39 The hallmark of Art Nouveau is its long sinuous, flowing lines, reminiscent of plant forms. Initially a movement in the graphic arts, its influence spread through design and into the fine arts.

40 Complementary colours are combinations of colours which include one colour composed of two of the primary colours (red, blue, and yellow in pigment), and the third primary. Their juxtaposition has the effect of intensifying each other, and when of the same tone they create a vibrating effect.

41 Rates of known offending amongst females, though lower than males, has risen considerably during the last two decades. A comparison between Table 13.3, *Social Trends* 10, 1980, and Table 12.11, *Social Trends* 15, 1985 (see note 19), shows a dramatic increase.

42 The need to create resemblances.

43 The achievement of a dialectical mode is, of course, not being seen to be an inevitable outcome of increase in limbic dominance: only when accompanied by 'developed purpose' (Fig. 68 and see sections 4.2 and 4.3).

Chapter 6 Understanding and expression

1 Some of the ideas contained in the rest of this chapter are developed in more detail elsewhere (Gear 1984).

2 For instance, the relationship between memory and the cognitive styles of field-dependence and field-independence is discussed by M. W. Eysenck (1977:chap. 12).

3 This is, of course, quite consistent with the discussions in previous chapters (4.5, 5.6) about sensation-seeking behaviour and levels of arousal and the placing of arts bias on the APM-A model.

4 A phrase used by McLean (1958) to describe the functions of the oldest regions of the brain as servicing 'feeding, fighting, fleeing and undertaking mating activity'.

Appendix 2 Postulates of APM-A theory

1 *attention* as selection (Underwood 1976:268); *memory* as selection (Loftus and Loftus 1976:13); *perception* as selection (McGinnies 1974:408–17).

2 Norman (1976:41) concludes from analysis of theories of 'early' and 'late' selection of information that it is necessary to acknowlege *both* 'top-down' or 'conceptually driven' processing (associated with late selection) and 'bottom-up' or 'data-driven' processing (early selection) of environmental events, which he suggests take place simultaneously. It has been argued elsewhere (Gear 1987) that in APM-A terms 'top-down' processing can be seen to correlate with processes identified by Gestalt psychologists and 'bottom-up' with the kind of linking of information described by the early behaviourists, and that both do take place simultaneously.

Bibliography

Abel, E. L. (1974) *Drugs and Behavior*, New York: Wiley.

Abelson, R. P. (ed.) (1968) *Theories of Cognitive Consistency*, Chicago: Rand McNally.

Ades, D. (1974) *Dada and Surrealism*, London: Thames & Hudson.

Adler, N. (1972) *New Life Styles and the Antinomian Personality: the Underground Stream*, New York: Harper & Row.

Adler, N. (1983) 'Sublimation and addiction', paper delivered to the International Conference on Psychology and Art, of the British Psychological Society, held at the University of Cardiff, Sept.

Alexander, R. D. (1980) *Darwinism and Human Affairs*, London: Pitman.

Alsop, J. (1969) 'Interview with Konrad Lorenz', in J. Brener *Readings and Study Guide for Psychology*, Iowa: Kendall Hunt.

Appleton, J. (1975) *The Experience of Landscape*, Chichester: Wiley, reprinted, Hull University Press (paperback), 1986.

Appleton, J. (1984a) 'Prospects and Refuges Re-visited', *Landscape Journal* 3(2):91–103.

Appleton, J. (1984b) 'Landscape art and the symbolism of habitat', a paper delivered as a public lecture in a series, *Landscape and the Visual Arts*, Hull University, 7 Nov.

Apter, M. (1982) *The Experience of Motivation: the Theory of Psychological Reversals*, London: Academic Press.

Ardrey, R. (1977) *The Hunting Hypothesis*, London: William Collins.

Arieti, S. (1976) *Creativity: the Magic Synthesis*, New York: Basic Books.

Arieti, S. (1981) *Understanding and Helping the Schizophrenic*, Harmondsworth: Pelican Books (first pub. USA, 1979).

Arnheim, R. (1966) *Towards a Psychology of Art*, London: Faber.

Atkinson, R. C. and Shiffrin, R. M. (1968) 'A proposed system and its control processes', in K. W. Spence and J. T. Spence (eds) *The Psychology of Learning and Motivation: Advances in Research and Theory*, vol. 2, New York: Academic Press.

Ax, A. F. (1953) 'The physiological differentiation between fear and anger in humans', *Psychosomatic Medicine* 15:433–42, cited by C. Van Toller, *The Nervous Body*, Chichester: Wiley, 1979.

Bach, G. and Goldberg, H. (1976) *Creative Aggression*, London: Coventure.

Bachrach, A. J. (1970) 'Diving behaviour', in *Human Performance and Scuba Diving*. Proceedings of the Symposium on Underwater Physiology, Chicago: The Athletic Institute, 4, cited by D. A. Norman, *Memory and Attention*, New York: Wiley, 1976.

Back, K. W. (1968) 'Equilibrium as motivation: between pleasure and enjoyment' in R. P. Abelson (ed.) *Theories of Cognitive Consistency*, Chicago: Rand McNally, 1968.

Badcock, C. R. (1983) *Madness and Modernity*, Oxford: Blackwell.

Baker, R. R. (1981) *Human Navigation*, London: Hodder & Stoughton.

Barrett, J. E. (ed.) (1979) *Stress and Mental Disorder*, New York: Raven Press.

Bateson, G. (1973) *Steps to an Ecology of Mind*, St Albans: Granada.

Bean, P. (1983) 'The nature of psychiatric theory', in P. Bean (ed.) *Mental Illness: Changes and Trends*, Chichester: Wiley.

Beatty, J. (1982) 'Task-evoked pupillary responses, processing load and the structure of processing resources', *Psychological Bulletin* 91(2):276–92.

Beck, A. T. (1974) 'The development of depression: a cognitive model', in R. J. Friedman and M. M. Katz (eds) *The Psychology of Depression*, Washington, DC: V. H. Winston.

Beit-Hallahmi, B. (1983) 'Understanding religion through the psychology of art', paper delivered to the International Conference on Psychology and Art, of the British Psychological Society, held at the University of Cardiff, Sept.

Bell, C. (1982) 'The aesthetic hypothesis', in F. Frascina and C. Harrison, *Modern Art and Modernism: a Critical Anthology*, London: Harper & Row.

Berkowitz, L. (1968) 'The motivational status of cognitive dissonance theorizing', in R. P. Abelson (ed.) *Theories of Cognitive Consistency*, Chicago: Rand McNally.

Berlyne, D. E. (1960) *Conflict, Arousal and Curiosity*, New York: McGraw-Hill.

Berlyne, D. E. (1971) *Aesthetics and Psychobiology*, New York: Appleton-Century-Crofts.

Bogen, J. E. (1973) 'The other side of the brain: an appositional mind', in R. E. Ornstein (ed.) *The Nature of Human Consciousness*, San Francisco: W. H. Freeman.

Borger, R. and Seaborne, A. E. M. (1966) *The Psychology of Learning*, Harmondsworth: Penguin.

Boulton, J. T. (ed.) (1958) *Edmund Burke: a Philosophical Enquiry into the Origins of Our Ideas on the Sublime and the Beautiful*, London: Routledge & Kegan Paul.

Bowness, A. (1983) Foreword, in M. Compton *New Art at the Tate*, London: Tate Gallery.

Boyle, J. (1977) *A Sense of Freedom*, London: Pan Books.

Boyle, J. and McGrath, T. (1977) *The Hard Man*, Edinburgh: Canongate.

Brener, J. M. (1980) 'Energy, information and man', in A. J. Chapman and D. M. Jones (eds) *Models of Man*, British Psychological Society, Leicester.

Broadhurst, P. L. (1957) 'Emotionality and the Yerkes–Dodson law', *Journal of Experimental Psychology* 54:345–52, cited by B. Weiner, in *Human Motivation*, New York: Holt, Rinehart & Winston, 1980.

Brothwell, D. (ed.) (1976) *Beyond Aesthetics: Investigations into the Nature of Visual Art*, London: Thames & Hudson.

Brown, K. (ed.) (1973) *Knowledge, Education and Cultural Change*, London: Tavistock Publications.

Bruner, J. S. (1956) 'On going beyond the information given' in *Contemporary Approaches to Cognition*, Cambridge, Mass.: Harvard University Press, cited by A. J. Cropley in 'Theoretical contributions', in P. E. Vernon (ed.) *Creativity*, Harmondsworth: Penguin, 1970.

Bruner, J. S., Goodnow, J., and Austin, G. A. (1956) *A Study of Thinking*, New York: Wiley, cited by A. Floyd, *Cognitive Styles*, Milton Keynes: Open University Press, 1976.

322

Bryant, P. (1974) *Perception and Understanding in Young Children*, London: Methuen.

Buck, R., Miller, R. E., and Caul, W. F. (1974) 'Sex, personality and physiological variables in the communication of affect via facial expression', *Journal of Personality and Social Psychology* 30:587–96, cited by L. W. Morris, in *Extraversion and Introversion*, Washington: Hemisphere.

Bullen, J. B. (ed.) (1981) *Roger Fry: Vision and Design*, London: Oxford University Press.

Burke, E. (1958) *A Philosophical Enquiry into the Origins of our Ideas on the Sublime and Beautiful*, ed. J. T. Boulton, London: Routledge & Kegan Paul.

Campbell, F. and Singer, G. (1979) *Brain and Behaviour*, Pergamon Press (Australia).

Cannon, W. B. (1927) 'The James-Lange theory of emotion: a critical examination and an alternative theory', *American Journal of Psychology* 39:106–24.

Cannon, W. B. (1929) 'Organisation for physiological homeostasis', *Psychological Review* 9:339–431.

Cattell, R. B., Eber, H. W., and Tatsuoka, M. M. (1970) *Handbook of the Sixteen Personality Factor Questionnaire*, Institute for Personality and Ability Testing, Champaign, Ill.

Central Statistical Office, *Social Trends* 15, London: HMSO, 1985 edn.

Child, D. (1977) *Psychology and the Teacher*, Chichester: Holt, Rinehart & Winston (2nd edn).

Child, I. L. (1978) 'Aesthetic theories', in E. C. Carterette and M. P. Friedman *Handbook of Perception X Perceptual Ecology*, New York: Academic Press.

Chipp, H. B. (1968) *Theories of Modern Art: a Source Book for Artists and Critics*, Berkeley: University of California Press.

Chodoff, P. (1974) 'The depressive personality: a critical review', in R. J. Friedman and M. M. Katz (eds) *The Psychology of Depression*, Washington, DC: V. H. Winston.

Clare, A. W. (1983) 'Treatment and cure in mental illness', in P. Bean (ed.) *Mental Illness: Changes and Trends*, Chichester: Wiley.

Claridge, G. (1981) 'Arousal' in G. Underwood and R. Stevens (eds) *Aspects of Consciousness*, vol. 2, London: Academic Press.

Clark, A. (1980) *Psychological Models and Neural Mechanisms*, Oxford: Oxford University Press.

Clark, K. (1976) *The Romantic Rebellion: Romantic versus Classic Art*, London: Fontana.

Clark, K. (1982) *Civilisation*, Harmondsworth: Penguin (first pub. BBC and John Murray, 1969).

Coan, R. (1974) *The Optimal Personality*, London: Routledge & Kegan Paul.

Cohen, S. and Taylor, L. (1978) *Escape Attempts*, Harmondsworth: Penguin (first pub. Allen Lane, 1976).

Compton, M. (1983) *New Art at the Tate*, London: Tate Gallery.

Cooper, D. (1980) *The Language of Madness*, Harmondsworth: Penguin (first pub. Allen Lane, 1978).

Corsini, R. J. (ed.) (1973) *Current Psychotherapies*, Itasca, Ill.: F. E. Peacock.

Corsini, R. J. (ed.) (1984) *Encyclopedia of Psychology*, New York: Wiley.

Cotman, C. W. and McGaugh, J. L. (1980) *Behavioral Neuroscience*, New York: Academic Press.

Cox, T. (1978) *Stress*, London: Macmillan.

Cox, T. and Thirlaway, M. (1983) 'The psychological and physiological response to stress', in A. Gale and J. A. Edwards *Physiological Correlates of Human Behaviour*, London: Academic Press.

Craik, F. I. M. and Lockhart, R. S. (1972) 'Levels of processing in learning: a framework for research', *Journal of Verbal Learning and Verbal Behaviour* 11:671–84.

Crook, J. H. (1980) *The Evolution of Human Consciousness*, Oxford: Oxford University Press.

Cropley, A. J. (1970) 'S–R psychology and cognitive psychology', in P. E. Vernon (ed.) *Creativity*, Harmondsworth: Penguin.

Crowcroft, A. (1967) *The Psychotic: Understanding Madness*, Harmondsworth: Penguin.

Darwin, C. (1858) *On the Origin of Species*, London: Murray.

Davis, D. D. (1981) *The Unique Animal*, London: Prytaneum Press.

Davis, K. E. (1968) 'Needs, wants and consistency', in R. P. Abelson (ed.) *Theories of Cognitive Consistency*, Chicago: Rand McNally.

Day, M. D. (1979) *Autonomic Pharmacology*, Edinburgh: Churchill Livingstone.

de Bono, E. (1982) *de Bono's Thinking Course*, London: BBC Books.

Deikman, A. J. (1973) 'Bimodal Consciousness', in R. E. Ornstein (ed.) *The Nature of Human Consciousness*, San Francisco: W. H. Freeman.

de Lacoste-Utamsing, C. and Holloway, R. L. (1982) 'Sexual dimorphism in the human corpus collosum', *Science* 216:1431–2.

Deutsch, J. A. and Deutsch, D. (1963) 'Attention: some theoretical considerations', *Psychological Review* 70:80–90.

Dohrenwend, B. P. (1979) 'Stressful life events and psychopathology: some issues of theory and method', in J. E. Barrett (ed.) *Stress and Mental Disorder*, New York: Raven Press.

Ellenberger, H. F. (1970) *The Discovery of the Unconscious: the History of the Evolution of Dynamic Psychiatry*, New York: Basic Books.

Ellis, A. (1973) 'Rational emotive therapy', in R. J. Corsini (ed.) *Current Psychotherapies*, Itasca, Ill.: F. E. Peacock.

Emshoff, J. G. and Davis, D. (1981) 'Social support and aggression', in A. P. Goldstein, E. G. Carr, W. S. Davidson II, and P. Wehr *In Response to Aggression*, New York: Pergamon Press.

Eppinger, J. and Hess, L. (1915) 'Die Vagotonie', *Mental and Nervous Disease Monograph*, 20, cited by C. Van Toller in *The Nervous Body*, Chichester: Wiley.

Eysenck, H. J. (1967) *The Biological Basis of Personality*, Springfield, Ill.: Charles C. Thomas.

Eysenck, H. J. (1970) *Crime and Personality*, London: Granada (first pub. Routledge & Kegan Paul, 1964).

Eysenck, H. J. (ed.) (1971) *Readings in Extraversion–Introversion: Three Bearings on Basic Psychological Processes*, London: Staple Press.

Eysenck, H. J. (ed.) (1981) *A Model for Personality*, Berlin: Springer Verlag.

Eysenck, H. J. and Eysenck, S. B. G. (1964) *The Eysenck Personality Inventory*, San Diego: Educational Industrial Testing Service.

Eysenck, H. J. and Eysenck, S. B. G. (1976) *Psychoticism as a Dimension of Personality*, London: Hodder & Stoughton.

Eysenck, M. W. (1977) *Human Memory: Theory, Research and Individual Differences*, Oxford: Pergamon Press.

Eysenck, M. W. (1981) 'Effects of introversion and extraversion on learning and memory', in H. J. Eysenck (ed.) *A Model for Personality*, Berlin: Springer Verlag.

Faber, M. D. (1981) *Culture and Consciousness: the Social Meaning of Altered*

Awareness, New York: Human Sciences Press.

Farmer, R. D. T. (1979) 'The relationship between suicide and parasuicide', in R. D. T. Farmer and S. R. Hirsch (eds) *The Suicide Syndrome*, London: Croom Helm.

Farmer, R. D. T. and Hirsch, S. R. (eds) (1979) *The Suicide Syndrome*, London: Croom Helm.

Farr, D. (1978) *English Art 1870–1940*, Oxford: Oxford University Press.

Ferster, C. B. (1974) 'Behavioral approaches to depression', in R. J. Friedman and M. M. Katz (eds) *The Psychology of Depression*, Washington, DC: V. H. Winston.

Festinger, L. (1962) *A Theory of Cognitive Consistency*, London: Tavistock.

Feurerstein, R. (1980) *Instrumental Enrichment: an Intervention Program for Cognitive Mutability*, Baltimore, Md.: University Park Press.

Freeman, J., Butcher, H. J., and Christie, T. (1971) *Creativity: a Selective Review of Research*, London: Society for Research into Higher Education.

Freud, S. (1922) *Introductory Lectures on Psychoanalysis*, tr. J. Riviere, London: Allen & Unwin.

Freud, S. (1930) *Civilisation and its Discontents*, tr. J. Rivière, London: Hogarth Press.

Friedman, R. J. and Katz, M. M. (eds) (1974) *The Psychology of Depression: Contemporary Theory and Practice*, Washington, DC: V. H. Winston.

Fuller, P. (1980) *Seeing Berger: a Revaluation of 'Ways of Seeing'*, London: Writers and Readers.

Fuller, P. (1983) *The Naked Artist: 'Art and Biology' and Other Essays*, London: Writers and Readers.

Funkenstein, D. H. (1956) 'Norepinephrine-like and epinephrine-like substances in relation to human behaviour', *Journal of Nervous and Mental Diseases* 124:58–66, cited by C. Van Toller in *The Nervous Body*, Chichester: Wiley, 1979.

Gardner, H. (1983) *Frames of Mind: the Theory of Multiple Intelligences*, London: Heinemann.

Gaunt, W. (1945) *The Aesthetic Adventure*, London: Jonathan Cape.

Gaunt, W. (1972) *The Restless Century: Paintings in Britain 1800–1900*, London: Phaidon.

Gazzaniga, M. S. (1973) 'The split brain in man', in R. E. Ornstein (ed.) *The Nature of Human Consciousness*, San Francisco: W. H. Freeman.

Gear, J. (1984) 'Where do we come from? What are we? Where are we going?' in *Aspects: Journal of Contemporary Art* 26.

Gear, J. (1985) *Perception and the evolution of style: a unified view of human modes of learning and expression*, Ph.D. thesis, University of Hull.

Gear, J. (1986) 'A new means of discrimination or a measure of "good taste"? A critique of Eysenck's visual aesthetic sensitivity test (VAST)', and subsequent exchange with H. J. Eysenck, in M. Ross (ed.) *Curriculum Issues in Art Education*, vol. 6: *assessment in the arts*, Oxford: Pergamon Press.

Gear, J. (1987) *Attention, Affect and Learning*, Newland Paper, no. 13, School of Adult and Continuing Education, University of Hull.

Getzels, J. W. and Jackson, P. W. (1962) *Creativity and Intelligence*, New York: Wiley.

Gibson, E. J. and Walk, R. D. (1960) 'The "visual cliff"', *Scientific American* 202:64–71.

Glaser, W. and Zunin, L. M. (1973) 'Reality therapy', in R. J. Corsini (ed.) *Current Psychotherapies*, Itasca, Ill.: F. E. Peacock.

Goffman, E. (1968) *Stigma*, Harmondsworth: Penguin (first pub. USA, 1963).

Goffman, E. (1971) *The Presentation of Self in Everyday Life*, Harmondsworth: Penguin (first pub. USA, 1959).

Golding, W., quoted in the *Guardian*, 10 Dec. 1983.

Goldstein, A. P., Carr, E. G., Davidson, W. S. II, and Wehr, P. (1981) *In Response to Aggression*, New York: Pergamon Press.

Goldstein, K. M. and Blackman, S. (1978) *Cognitive Style: Five Approaches and Relevant Research*, New York: Wiley.

Gombrich, E. H. (1977) *Art and Illusion*, London: Phaidon (5th edn.).

Gombrich, E. H. (1978) *Meditations on a Hobby-Horse*, London: Phaidon (3rd edn).

Gooch, S. (1973) *Personality and Evolution: the Biology of the Divided Self*, London: Wildwood House.

Goodwin, F. (1974) 'On the biology of depression', in R. J. Friedman and M. M. Katz (eds) *The Psychology of Depression*, Washington, DC: V. H. Winston.

Gordon, H. W. (1983) 'Music and the right hemisphere', in A. W. Young *Functions of the Right Hemisphere*, London: Academic Press.

Gossop, M. (1981) *Theories of Neurosis*, Berlin: Springer Verlag.

Granger, G. W. (1979) 'Psychology of art', in K. Connolly (ed.) *Psychology Survey No. 2*, London: Allen & Unwin.

Gray, J. A. (1970) 'The psychophysiological basis of introversion–extraversion', *Behaviour Research Therapy* 8:249–66.

Gray, J. A. (1975) *Elements of a Two-Process Theory of Learning*, New York: Academic Press.

Gray, J. A. (1981) 'A critique of Eysenck's theory of personality', in H. J. Eysenck (ed.) *A Model for Personality*, Berlin: Springer Verlag.

Great Exhibition (1851) *Illustrated Catalogue [of the Great Exhibition, 1851]*, London: Virtue.

Greenhalgh, M. and Megaw, V. (eds) (1978a) *Art in Society*, London: Duckworth.

Greenhalgh, M. and Megaw, V. (1978b) 'A study of art in society', in M. Greenhalgh and V. Megaw (eds) *Art in Society*, London: Duckworth.

Greer, G. (1971) *The Female Eunuch*, St Albans: Granada (first pub. McGibbon & Kee, 1970).

Gruber, H. E. (1980) 'Darwin on man, mind and materialism', in R. W. Rieber (ed.) *Body and Mind*, New York: Academic Press.

Guilford, J. P. (1950) 'Creativity', *American Psychologist* 5:444–54.

Hamilton, T. (1984) 'Hargreaves' concept of dignity', in J. Ackland (ed.) *The Hargreaves Challenge: a Response*, Perspectives 13, School of Education, University of Exeter.

Hare, R. D. (1970) *Psychopathy: Theory and Research*, Chichester: Wiley.

Hargreaves, D. H. (1982) *The Challenge for the Comprehensive*, London: Routledge & Kegan Paul.

Harrington, A. (1974) *Psychopaths*, St Albans: Granada Publishing.

Harrison, C. (1981) *English Art and Modernism 1900–1939*, London: Allen Lane.

Hebb, D. O. (1955) 'Drives and the conceptual nervous system', *Psychological Review* 62:243–54.

Helson, H. (1964) *Adaptation-Level Theory*, New York: Harper & Row.

Herbert, R. L. (1964) *Modern Artists on Art: Ten Unabridged Essays*, Englewood Cliffs, NJ.: Prentice-Hall.

Herriot, P. (1974) *Attributes of Memory*, London: Methuen.

Hilgard, E. R. and Bower, G. H. (1975) *Theories of Learning*, Englewood Cliffs, NJ: Prentice-Hall (4th edn).

Hillier, B. (1983) *The Style of the Century*, London: The Herbert Press.

Hinde, R. A. (1982) *Ethology*, Glasgow: William Collins.

Hjelle, R. A. and Ziegler, D. J. (1976) *Personality*, Tokyo: McGraw-Hill (International Student Edn).

Hochberg, J. (1972) 'The representation of things and people', in E. H. Gombrich, J. Hochberg, and M. Hochberg, *Art, Perception and Reality*, Baltimore, Md.: Johns Hopkins University Press.

Hoebel, B. G. and Teitelbaum, P. (1962) 'Hypothalamic control of feeding and self-stimulation', *Science* 135:375–77.

Höge, H. (1983) 'The emotional impact on aesthetic judgements: an experimental investigation of a time-honoured hypothesis', a paper delivered at the International Conference on Psychology and Art, of the British Psychological Society, held at the University of Cardiff, Sept.

Hudson, L. (1967) *Contrary Imaginations*, Harmondsworth: Penguin (first pub. Methuen 1966).

Hull, C. L. (1943) *Principles of Behavior*, New York: Appleton-Century-Crofts.

Humberside Education Committee, *Disaffected Pupils: Notes for Guidance for Use in Schools and Special Units*, Humberside County Council, 1982.

Humphreys, C. (1962) *Zen, a Way of Life*, London: Hodder & Stoughton.

Huxley, A. (1977) *The Doors of Perception* and *Heaven and Hell*, St Albans: Triad/Panther (*The Doors of Perception* first pub. Chatto & Windus, 1954; *Heaven and Hell* first pub. Chatto & Windus, 1956).

Ineichen, B. (1979) *Mental Illness*, London: Longman.

Janowsky, D. S., Davis, M., and Sekerke, H. J. (1972) 'A cholinergic–adrenergic hypothesis of mania and depression', *Lancet* 2:632–3, cited by F. Whitlock (1982), *Symptomatic Affective Disorders*, Sydney: Academic Press.

Januszczak, W. (1985) 'The kiss of art and commerce', *Guardian*, 19 Jan.

Jenkyns, R. (1980) *The Victorians and Ancient Greece*, Oxford: Blackwell.

Jennings, C. and Barraclough, B. M. (1979) 'The effectiveness of the Samaritans in the prevention of suicide', in R. D. T. Farmer and S. R. Hirsch (eds) *The Suicide Syndrome*, London: Croom Helm.

John, E. R. (1978) 'A model of consciousness', in G. E. Schwartz and D. Shapiro (eds) *Consciousness and Self-Regulation*, vol. 1, New York: Wiley.

Jullian, P. (1973) *The Symbolists*, Oxford: Phaidon.

Kalina, K. *et al.*, 'On the pathology of family dwelling', an unpublished paper by staff of the Psychiatric Clinic, Charles University, Prague.

Kaplan, S. and Kaplan, R. (1982) *Cognition and Environment: Functioning in an Uncertain World*, New York: Praeger.

Karki, N. T. (1956) 'The urinary excretion of noradrenalin and adrenalin in different age groups, its diurnal variation, and the effect of muscular work on it', *Acta Physiol. Scand.* 39, Suppl. 132.

Katschning, H., Sint, P., and Fuchs-Robetin, G. (1979) 'Suicide and parasuicide: identification of high and low risk groups by cluster analysis with a 5-year follow-up', in R. D. T. Farmer and S. R. Hirsch (eds) *The Suicide Syndrome*, London: Croom Helm.

Kaufman, G. (1979) *Visual Imagery and its Relation to Problem Solving*, Oslo: Universitetsforlagt.

Kemplar, W. (1973) 'Gestalt therapy', in R. J. Corsini (ed.) *Current Psychotherapies*, Itasca, Ill.: F. E. Peacock.

Kendell, R. E. (1976) 'The classification of depression: a review of contemporary confusion', *British Journal of Psychiatry* 129:15–28.

Kendell, R. E. and Gourlay, J. (1970) 'The clinical distinction between psychotic and neurotic depression', *British Journal of Psychiatry* 117:257–60.

Kinsbourne, M. (1980) 'Brain-based limitations on mind', in R. W. Rieber (ed.) *Body and Mind*, New York: Academic Press.

Kinsey, A. C., Pomeroy, W. B., and Martin, C. E. (1948) *Sexual Behavior in the Human Male*, Philadelphia: Saunders.

Kinsey, A. C. and Staff of the Institute of Sex Research, Indiana University (1953) *Sexual Behavior in the Human Female*, Philadelphia: Saunders.

Klerman, G. L. (1979a) 'Stress adaptation and affective disorder', in J. E. Barrett (ed.) *Stress and Mental Disorder*, New York: Raven Press.

Klerman, G. L. (1979b) 'Discussion Part 11', in J. E. Barrett (ed.) *Stress and Mental Disorder*, New York: Raven Press.

Klingender, F. D. (1972) *Art and the Industrial Revolution*, St Albans: Granada.

Köhler, W. (1947) *Gestalt Psychology: an Introduction to New Concepts in Modern Psychology*, New York: Liveright.

Kreitler, H. and Kreitler, S. (1972) *Psychology of the Arts*, Durham, NC: Duke University Press.

Kuhn, T. S. (1970) *The Structure of Scientific Revolutions*, Chicago: University of Chicago Press.

Lacey, J. I. (1950) 'Individual differences in somatic response patterns', *Journal of Comparative Physiological Psychology* 43:338–50, cited by C. Van Toller, *The Nervous Body*, Chichester: Wiley.

Laing, R. D. (1967) *The Politics of Experience and the Bird of Paradise*, Harmondsworth: Penguin.

Lancaster, J. B. (1975) *Primate Behavior and the Emergence of Human Culture*, New York: Holt, Rinehart & Winston.

Landau, S. R. and Beit-Hallahmi, B. (1983) 'Israel: aggression in psychohistorical perspective', in A. P. Goldstein and M. H. Segall (eds) *Aggression in Global Perspective*, New York: Pergamon.

Leach, E. (1976) *Culture and Communication: the Logic by which Symbols are Connected*, London: Cambridge University Press.

Leukel, F. (1976) *Introduction to Physiological Psychology*, St Louis, Mo.: The C. V. Mosby Co. (3rd edn).

Lief, A. (ed.) (1948) *The Commonsense Psychology of Adolf Meyer*, New York: McGraw-Hill.

Lindauer, M. S. (1983) 'Physiognomy and art: approaches from above, below and sideways', a paper delivered at the International Conference on Psychology and Art, of the British Psychological Society, held at the University of Cardiff, Sept.

Lindauer, M. S. (1984) 'Physiognomy', in R. J. Corsini (ed.) *Encyclopedia of Psychology*, New York: Wiley.

Loftus, R. L. and Loftus, E. F. (1976) *Human Memory*, Hillsdale, NJ: Lawrence Erlbaum Associates.

Lorenz, K. (1967) *On Aggression*, London: Methuen (first pub. Vienna, 1963).

Lorenz, K. (1974) *Civilised Man's Eight Deadly Sins*, London: Methuen (first pub. Munich, 1973).

Lucie-Smith, E. (1980) *Art in the Seventies*, Oxford: Phaidon.

Lundholm, H. (1921) 'The affective tone of lines: experimental researches', *Psychological Review* 28:43–60.

Luria, A. R. (1973) *The Working Brain*, Harmondsworth: Penguin.

Luria, A. R. (1976) *The Nature of Human Conflicts*, New York: Liveright (first pub. Liveright, 1932).

McGaugh, J. H. (1980) 'Adrenalin, a secret agent of memory', *Psychology Today* 14(7):132.

McGinnies, E. (1974) 'Emotionality in perceptual defence', in P. A. Fried

Readings in Perception, Lexington, Mass.: D. C. Heath.

McLean, P. D. (1958) 'Contrasting functions of limbic and neocortical systems of the brain and their relevance to psychophysiological aspects of medicine', *American Journal of Medicine* 25:611–26.

McLuhan, M. (1967) *The Medium is the Message*, London: Allen Lane.

Magaro, P. A. (1980) *Cognition in Schizophrenia and Paranoia: the integration of cognitive processes*, Hillsdale, NJ: Lawrence Erlbaum.

Maher, B. (1980) 'Experimental psychopathology', in P. C. Dodwell (ed.) *New Horizons in Psychology* 2, Harmondsworth: Penguin (2nd edn).

Malmo, R. B. (1966) 'Studies of anxiety: some clinical origins of the activation concept', in C. D. Spielberger (ed.) *Anxiety and Behavior*, New York: Academic Press, cited by B. Weiner *Human Motivation*, New York: Holt, Rinehart & Winston, 1980.

Mannheim, H. (1965) *Comparative Criminology*, vols. 1 and 2, London: Routledge & Kegan Paul.

Maslow, A. H. (1970) *Motivation and Personality*, New York: Harper & Row (2nd edn).

Masters, W. H. and Johnson, V. E. (1966) *Human Sexual Response*, London: Churchill.

Medawar, P. B. and Medawar, J. S. (1978) *The Life Science: Current Ideas in Biology*, St Albans: Granada, p. 80, 1st edn, Wildwood House, 1977.

Mednick, S. A. and Gabrielli, W. F. (1984) 'Genetic influences in criminal convictions: evidence from an adoption cohort', *Science* 22:891–3.

Melville, J. (1979) *Phobias*, London: Allen & Unwin (first pub. 1977).

Menninger, K. *et al.* (1963) *The Vital Balance*, New York: Viking Press.

Messick, S. *et al.* (1976) *Individuality and Learning*, San Francisco: Jossey-Bass.

Milburn, T. W. and Watman, K. H. (1981) *On the Nature of Threat*, New York: Praeger.

Milgram, S. (1974) *Obedience to Authority: an Experimental View*, London: Tavistock.

Miller, G. A. (1956) 'The magical number seven plus or minus two: some limits on our capacity for processing information', *Psychological Review* 63:81–7.

Miller, W. R., Rosellini, R. A., and Seligman, E. P. (1977) 'Learned helplessness and depression', in J. D. Maser, and M. E. P. Seligman (eds) *Psychopathology: experimental models*, San Francisco: W. H. Freeman.

Milner, P. M. (1970) *Physiological Psychology*, New York: Holt, Rinehart & Winston.

Mitchell, R. (1975) *Depression*, Harmondsworth: Penguin.

Mondrian, P. (1964) 'Plastic art and pure plastic art', in R. L. Herbert *Modern Artists on Art: Ten Unabridged Essays*, Englewood Cliffs, NJ: Prentice-Hall.

Morris, L. W. (1979) *Extraversion and Introversion: an Interactional Perspective*, Washington, DC: Hemisphere Publishing.

Mosak, H. H. and Dreikurs, R. (1973) 'Adlerian psychotherapy', in R. J. Corsini (ed.) *Current Psychotherapies*, Itasca, Ill.: F. E. Peacock.

Mowrer, O. H. (1947) 'Preparatory set (expectancy) – a determinant in motivation and learning', *Psychological Review* 45:62–91.

Murray, H. (1938) *Explorations in Personality: a Clinical and Experimental Study of Fifty Men of College Age*, New York: Oxford University Press.

Nias, D. K. (1976) 'Varieties of abnormal behaviour', in H. J. Eysenck and G. D. Wilson *A Textbook of Human Psychology*, Lancaster: MTP Press.

Norman, D. A. (1976) *Memory and Attention*, New York: Wiley (2nd edn).

Oatley, K. (1978) *Perceptions and Representations*, London: Methuen.

Oatley, K. (1981) 'Metaphors and the nature of consciousness', in G. Underwood and R. Stevens (eds) *Aspects of Consciousness*, London: Academic Press.

Olds, J. and Milner, P. M. (1954) 'Positive reinforcement produced by electrical stimulation of the septal area and other regions of the brain', *Journal of Comparative and Physiological Psychology* 47:419–37.

Orians, G. H. (1980) 'Habitat Selection: general theory and application to human behavior', in J. S. Lockard (ed.) *Human Social Behavior*, New York: Elsevier.

Orians, G. H. (1986) 'An ecological and evolutionary approach to landscape aesthetics', in E. Penning-Rowsell and D. Lowenthal *Landscape Meaning and Values*, London: Allen & Unwin.

Ornstein, R. E. (ed.) (1973) *The Nature of Human Consciousness*, San Francisco: W. H. Freeman.

Osborne, H. (1981) *Oxford Companion to Twentieth Century Art*, Oxford: Oxford University Press.

Ousby, W. J. (1967) *The Theory and Practice of Hypnotism*, Wellingborough: Thorsons.

Pavlov, I. P. (1927) *Conditioned Reflexes*, Oxford: Clarendon Press.

Peckham, M. (1962) *Beyond the Tragic Vision: the Quest for Identity in the Nineteenth Century*, Cambridge: Cambridge University Press.

Peckham, M. (1967) *Man's Rage for Chaos: Biology, Behavior and the Arts*, New York: Schocken Books (first pub. USA, 1965).

Peters, G. A. and Merrifield, P. R. (1958) 'Graphic representation of emotional feelings', *Journal of Clinical Psychology* 14:375–8.

Piaget, J. (1971) *Biology of Knowledge: an Essay on the Relations between Organic Regulations and Cognitive Processes*, Edinburgh: Edinburgh University Press.

Pilgrim, D. (1983) *Psychology and Psychotherapy*, London: Routledge & Kegan Paul.

Pincus, J. H. and Tucker, G. J. (1978) *Behavioral Neurology*, New York: Oxford University Press (2nd edn).

Poffenberger, A. T. and Barrows, B. E. (1924) 'The feeling value of lines', *Journal of Applied Psychology* 8:187–205.

Pointon, M. (1980) *History of Art: a Student's Handbook*, London: Allen & Unwin.

Postle, D. (1980) *Catastrophe Theory*, Glasgow: William Collins.

Powell, G. (1979) *Brain and Personality*, Farnborough: Saxon House.

Prentky, R. A. (1980) *Creativity and Psychopathology*, New York: Praeger.

Price, U. (1794) *An Essay on the Picturesque as compared to the Sublime and Beautiful: and on the Use of Studying Pictures for the Purpose of Improving Real Landscape*, London: Robson, cited by F. D. Klingender *Art and the Industrial Revolution*, St Albans: Granada, 1972.

Pugin, A. W. N. (1969) *Contrasts*, Leicester: Leicester University Press; based on the 2nd edn of 1841, pub. London: Dolman.

Pyle, D. W. (1979) *Intelligence*, London: Routledge & Kegan Paul.

Rapaport, D. *et al.* (1945) *Diagnostic Psychological Testing*, vol. 11, Chicago: Yearbook Publishers, cited by Shapiro (1965).

Razran, G. (1971) *Mind in Evolution: an East–West Synthesis of Learned Behavior and Cognition*, Boston: Houghton Mifflin.

Reiser, D. (1972) *Art and Science*, London: Studio Vista.

Rieber, R. W. (ed.) (1980) *Body and Mind: Past, Present and Future*, New York: Academic Press.

Riedl, R. (1984) *Biology and Knowledge: the Evolutionary Basis of Reason*, Chichester: Wiley (first pub. Berlin, 1980).

Roethlisberger, F. J. and Dickson, W. S. (1939) *Management and the Worker*, Cambridge, Mass.: Harvard University Press.

Rogers, C. R. (1980) *A Way of Being*, Boston: Houghton Mifflin.

Rookmaaker, H. R. (1970) *Modern Art and the Death of a Culture*, Leicester: Inter-Varsity Press.

Ruddock, R. (1980) *Perspectives in Adult Education*, Manchester: University of Manchester.

Russell, J. (1981) *The Meanings of Modern Art*, London: Thames & Hudson.

Ryle, G. (1949) *Concept of Mind*, London: Hutchinson.

Sackeim, H. A. and Gur, R. C. (1978) 'Self-deception, self-confrontation and consciousness', in G. E. Schwartz and D. Shaprio (eds) *Consciousness and Self-Regulation*, vol. 2, New York: Wiley.

Samuel, I. (1959) 'Reticular mechanisms and behaviour', *Psycholological Bulletin* 56:1–25.

Schacter, S. and Singer, J. E. (1962) 'Cognitive, social, and physiological determinants of emotional state', *Psychological Review* 69:379–99.

Schneider, W. and Shiffrin, R. M. (1977) 'Controlled and automatic human information processing: I detection, search and attention', *Psychological Review* 84(2):1–66.

Schrag, P. and Divoky, D. (1981) *The Myth of the Hyperactive Child: and Other Means of Child Control*, Harmondsworth: Penguin (first pub. in the USA, 1975).

Schutz, W. C. (1973) 'Encounter', in R. J. Corsini (ed.) *Current Psychotherapies*, Itasca, Ill.: F. E. Peacock.

Sedgwick, P. (1982) *Psycho Politics*, London: Pluto Press.

Selye, H. (1974) *Stress Without Distress*, London: Hodder & Stoughton.

Shapiro, D. (1965) *Neurotic Styles*, New York: Basic Books.

Shapiro, F. J. and Alexander, J. E. (1975) *The Experience of Introversion*, Chapel Hill, NC: Duke University Press.

Shiffrin, R. M. and Schneider, W. (1977) 'Controlled and automatic human information processing: II perceptual learning, automatic attending and a general theory', *Psychological Review*, 84(2):127–90.

Shouksmith, G. (1970) *Intelligence, Creativity and Cognitive Style*, London: Batsford.

Skemp, R. R. (1979) *Intelligence, Learning and Action*, Chichester: Wiley.

Skinner, B. F. (1971) *Beyond Freedom and Dignity*, New York: Alfred A. Knopf.

Spilsbury, R. (1974) *Providence Lost: a Critique of Darwinism*, London: Oxford University Press.

Springer, S. P. and Deutsch, D. (1981) *Left Brain, Right Brain*, San Francisco: W. H. Freeman.

Squires, G. (1981) *Cognitive Styles and Adult Learning*, Nottingham: University of Nottingham.

Stein, M. I. (1974) *Stimulating Creativity*, vol. 1, New York: Academic Press.

Stenhouse, D. (1974) *The Evolution of Intelligence*, London: Allen & Unwin.

Storr, A. (1963) *The Integrity of Personality*, Harmondsworth: Penguin (first pub. Heinemann, 1960).

Storr, A. (1970) *Human Aggression*, Harmondsworth: Penguin (first pub. Allen Lane, 1968).

Szasz, T. (1972) *The Myth of Mental Illness*, St Albans: Paladin (first pub. Secker & Warburg, 1962).

Taylor, G. R. (1979) *The Natural History of the Mind*, London: Secker & Warburg.

Thorne, F. C. (1973) 'Eclectic psychotherapy', in R. J. Corsini (ed.) *Current Psychotherapies*, Itasca, Ill.: F. E. Peacock.

Titchener, E. B. (1908) 'Lectures on the elementary psychology of feeling and attention', delivered during tenure of a non-resident lectureship in psychology at Columbia University (Feb.) and published under the title of *The Psychology of Feeling and Attention*, New York: Macmillan, 1924.

Trivers, R. L. (1971) 'The evolution of reciprocal altruism', *Quarterly Review of Biology* 46:35–7.

Tsuang, M. T. (1982) *Schizophrenia: the Facts*, New York: Oxford University Press.

Underwood, G. (1976) *Attention and Memory*, Oxford: Pergamon Press.

Underwood, G. and Stevens, R. (eds) (1981) *Aspects of Consciousness*, vol. 2, London: Academic Press.

US Department of Human Sciences, *Cumulated Index Medicus*, National Library of Medicine, Maryland.

Uznadze, D. N. (tr. B. Haigh (1966)) *The Psychology of Set*, New York: Consultants Bureau (first pub. Georgia SSR, 1961).

Vaizey, M. (1983) 'Following the signs at New Art's crossroads', *Guardian*, 16 Sept.

Van Toller, C. (1979) *The Nervous Body*, Chichester: Wiley.

Venables, P. H. (1983) 'Outcome at age nine of psychophysiological selection at age three for risk of schizophrenia: a Mauritian study', *British Journal of Developmental Psychology* 1:21–30.

Vernon, P. E. (ed.) (1970) *Creativity*, Harmondsworth: Penguin.

Wallace, R. K. and Benson, H. (1973) 'The physiology of meditation', in R. E. Ornstein (ed.) *The Nature of Human Consciousness*, San Francisco: W. H. Freeman.

Wallach, M. A. and Kogan, N. (1965) *Modes of Thinking in Young Children*, New York: Holt, Rinehart & Winston, cited by A. J. Cropley in 'S–R psychology and cognitive psychology', in P. E. Vernon (ed.) *Creativity*, Harmondsworth: Penguin, 1970.

Ward, C. H., Beck, A. T., Mendelson, M., Mock, J. E., and Erbaugh, J. K. (1978) 'The psychiatric nomenclature', in J. M. Neale, G. C. Davison, and K. P. Price *Contemporary Readings in Psychopathology*, New York: Wiley.

Watson, J. B. (1919) *Psychology from the Standpoint of a Behaviorist*, Philadelphia: J. B. Lippincott.

Wees, W. C. (1972) *Vorticism and the English Avant-Garde*, Manchester: Manchester University Press.

Weiner, B. (1980) *Human Motivation*, New York: Holt, Rinehart & Winston.

Weir, D. (1977) *Immunology*, Edinburgh: Churchill & Livingstone (4th edn).

Welford, A. T. (1973) 'Stress and performance', *Ergonomics* 16:567, cited by T. Cox (1978) *Stress*, London: Macmillan.

Werner, H. and Wapner, S. (1952) 'Toward a general theory of perception', *Psychological Review* 59:324–38, cited by M. S. Lindauer, 'Physiognomy and art', a paper delivered at the International Conference on Psychology and Art, of the British Psychological Society, Cardiff, Sept. 1983.

West, D. J. (1982) *Delinquency: its Roots, Careers and Prospects*, London: Heinemann.

Westland, G. (1978) *Current Crises in Psychology*, London: Heinemann.

Whitlock, F. A. (1982) *Symptomatic Affective Disorders: a Study of Depression and Mania associated with Physical Disease and Medication*, Sydney: Academic Press.

Wiedmann, A. (1979) *Romantic Roots in Modern Art*, Old Woking, Surrey: Gresham Books.

Williams, R. J. (1977) *Biochemical Individuality*, Chichester: Wiley (first pub. Univ. of Texas 1956).

Wilson, C. (1980) *Frankenstein's Castle*, Sevenoaks, Kent: Ashgrove Press.

Wilson, E. O. (1975) *Sociobiology: the New Synthesis*, Cambridge, Mass.: Harvard University Press.

Wilson, I. (1984) *Jesus: the Evidence*, London: Weidenfeld & Nicolson.

Wold, C. I. and Tabachnik, N. (1974) 'Depression as an indicator of lethality in suicidal patients', in R. J. Friedman and M. M. Katz (eds) *The Psychology of Depression*, Washington, DC: V. H. Winston.

Wölfflin, H. (1950) *Principles of Art History: the Problem of the Development of Style in Later Art*, London: Bell & Hyman in association with Dover Publications, 7th edn (first pub. in English, 1932).

Wollheim, R. (1978) 'Aesthetics, anthropology and style: some programmatic remarks', in M. Greenhalgh and V. Megaw (eds) *Art in Society*, London: Duckworth.

Wood, C. (1976) *Victorian Panorama: Paintings of Victorian Life*, London: Faber.

Woodman, D. D. (1980) 'What makes a psychopath?', *New Society*, 4 Sept.:447–9.

Yerkes, R. M. and Dodson, J. D. (1908) 'The relation of strength of stimulus to rapidity of habit formations', *Journal of Comparative Neurology and Psychology* 18:459–82, cited by G. Claridge, in 'Arousal' in G. Underwood and R. Stevens (eds) *Aspects of Consciousness*, vol. 2, London: Academic Press, 1980.

Young, J. Z. (1978) *Programs of the Brain*, Oxford: Oxford University Press.

Zubek, J. P. (1969) *Sensory Deprivation: Fifteen Years of Research*, New York: Appleton-Century-Crofts.

Zubin, J. 'Discussion Part IV and overview', in J. E. Barrett (ed.) *Stress and Mental Disorder*, New York: Raven Press, 1979.

Zuckerman, M. (1979) *Sensation Seeking: Beyond the Optimal Level of Arousal*, Hillsdale, NJ.: Lawrence Erlbaum.

Zurcher, L. (1977) *The Mutable Self: a Self-Concept for Social Change*, Beverly Hills: Sage Publications.

Author index

General index